World Population Profile: 1996

With a Special Chapter Focusing on Adolescent Fertility in the Developing World

by Thomas M. McDevitt

Issued July 1996

U.S. Agency for International Development

Bureau for Global Programs, Field Support, and Research
Sally Shelton, Assistant Administrator

Office of Population
Elizabeth S. Maguire, Director

U.S. Department of Commerce
Michael Kantor, Secretary

Economics and Statistics Administration
Everett M. Ehrlich, Under Secretary for Economic Affairs

BUREAU OF THE CENSUS
Martha Farnsworth Riche, Director

Economics and Statistics Administration
Everett M. Ehrlich, Under Secretary
for Economic Affairs

BUREAU OF THE CENSUS
Martha Farnsworth Riche, Director

Bryant Benton, Deputy Director

Paula J. Schneider, Principal Associate Director
for Programs

Nancy M. Gordon, Associate Director
for Demographic Programs

Nampeo R. McKenney, Acting Chief
Population Division

INTERNATIONAL PROGRAMS CENTER
Judith Banister, Chief

SUGGESTED CITATION

U.S. Bureau of the Census, Report WP/96,
World Population Profile: 1996
by Thomas M. McDevitt

U.S. Government Printing Office, Washington, DC, 1996.

Contents

Figures

Population Size and Growth

Population Composition

Components of Change

Focus on Adolescent Fertility in the Developing World—Continued

Appendix A. **Detailed Tables**

Appendix B. **Population Projections and Availability of Data**

Highlights

In 1994, the governments of 180 nations came together at the International Conference on Population and Development (ICPD) in Cairo, Egypt, to seek agreement on how to cope with the task of integrating population and development issues and programs. One of the most difficult elements of the task is that of stabilizing world population growth.

- The latest projections of the Bureau of the Census indicate that world population will increase from its present level of 5.8 billion persons to pass the 6 billion milestone by the year 2000. These projections also show world population reaching a level of 7.6 billion persons over the next quarter century, an *increase* over 1996 roughly equivalent to adding three more Sub-Saharan Africas to the present world total.

- In 1996, 95 out of every 100 persons added to world population live in less developed countries (LDC's).

- Between now and the year 2000, population increase will be concentrated in Asia because its present population is so much larger than that of any other region. Also, interregional differences in growth rates — the second key determinant of shifting population distribution — have a relatively limited effect in the short term. Developing countries of Asia will contribute 176 million persons to world population increase during the next 4 years, with a fourth of this increase, or 44 million persons, to be added in China. The Asian increment to world population is about 25 percent greater than the net addition attributable to all other countries combined. Other developing countries will contribute about 126 million persons; the United States and other more developed countries, about 18 million persons.

- Sub-Saharan Africa's growth rates will be the highest of all major world regions for the next 25 years. In spite of rising mortality in some countries due to the HIV/AIDS pandemic, total population for the Sub-Saharan Africa region as a whole will double within 32 years if present trends continue.

- India and Nigeria are emerging as two countries making disproportionate contributions to world population growth during the 1996-2020 period because of their continued high fertility and already massive populations. India presently contributes about 19 percent of total world population increase, more than any other country. If Nigeria's rapid growth continues, its population will nearly double during the coming quarter century, boosting Nigeria past Bangladesh, Japan, Pakistan, Russia, and Brazil among the world's most populous nations.

- The elderly population is the fastest growing age group worldwide. Persons ages 65 and over will increase more than twice as fast as total population between 1996 and 2020. The growth rate of this age group in less developed countries will be double that in more developed countries. By 2020, two-thirds of the world's elderly will live in LDC's.

- Even with the rapid growth of the elderly, however, most of the dependent population (ages 0 to 14 and 65 and over) in developing countries is, and will remain, children. Nearly 9 in every 10 persons making up the combined dependent age groups in less developed countries are under age 15 in 1996. This fraction declines, but is still 8 children in 10 dependents, in 2020.

- At least 132 million births will occur every year for the next 25 years despite falling fertility. The continued high level of births in the face of declining birth rates largely reflects the still increasing numbers of women of reproductive age (the result of past high fertility) in less developed countries.

- About 8 million infant deaths will occur in 1996. More than 90 percent of these will be in the developing countries of Africa, Asia, and Latin America. If present trends continue, however, the total number of infant deaths worldwide will drop by nearly half, to 4.5 million, by year 2020 as a result of a leveling off in number of births (and, hence, number of infants at risk) and decreases in infant mortality rates.

- Of 100 babies born this year in Sub-Saharan Africa, 9 will die within 1 year. In the world's more developed countries, it will take about 60 years for these 9 deaths to occur. The difference reflects a continuing gap in mortality levels faced by the populations of the world's more and less developed countries.

A child born this year in Sub-Saharan Africa can expect to live only about 50 years, while a child born in one of the more developed countries of the world may expect to survive to age 74, or about 50 percent longer. Over the course of the coming 25 years, life expectancy at birth in more developed countries is projected to increase by 5 years; that of less developed countries, including Sub-Saharan Africa, by about 6 years; only slightly reducing the gap in life expectancy between more developed and less developed countries.

The world community adopted an agenda for action at the ICPD and the regional preparatory conferences which emphasizes demographic goals, economic growth within the context of sustainable development, improved access to reproductive health care, and the empowerment of women.

- Projections of the Bureau of the Census indicate that only 50 to 60 percent of the developing nations are likely to achieve the ICPD mortality reduction goals set for the year 2015 in spite of ongoing improvements in child survivorship in the developing world. Few countries, whether developing or more developed, will meet the goals adopted for the year 2000.

  Fewer than half of the developing countries of Asia are likely to achieve the regional goal of replacement level fertility by year 2010. China already has. India probably will not.

  The African regional goal of an annual natural growth rate of 2.5 percent by the year 2000 appears attainable; however, the follow-on goal of 2.0 percent by the year 2010 will be difficult to achieve if present trends continue.

- Access to reproductive health care, including family planning, is a key goal adopted in Cairo. Women are, in fact, using family planning in increasing numbers in every world region. In developing countries today, five times as many couples are using contraception as in the 1960's. Nevertheless, the full range of modern methods is unavailable to as many as 350 million couples worldwide.

  Improved availability of family planning services would carry important maternal and child health benefits, particularly in less developed countries. In addition, more widespread use of contraception could reduce unwanted fertility, which may be as high as 15 to 20 percent of all fertility in Asia and Sub-Saharan Africa, and as high as 30 percent in Latin America and North Africa.

- Fifteen million high-risk births occur each year to adolescent mothers, and 8 of every 10 of these take place in the developing nations of Asia, Africa, and Latin America. A substantial proportion of these births are unwanted, yet the young women involved are not using any means of contraception to delay or prevent them.

Introduction

In 1994, representatives of 180 nations met in Cairo to debate and adopt a new global agenda geared toward achieving population stabilization, reproductive health, and a balance between population and resources. In Cairo, the international community agreed to redefine the population issue in terms of a broad set of linkages involving human development and economic growth within the context of what is referred to throughout the conference document as "sustainable development."

This redefinition reflects a new international consensus that "population, poverty, patterns of production and consumption and the environment are so closely interconnected that none of them can be considered in isolation" (United Nations 1995:6). The Cairo Program of Action argues that investments in health and education, and greater effort to ensure that such investments benefit girls and women over time, are critical to the achievement of national and regional demographic objectives and to making progress toward a balance of population and resources, during the first half of the 21st century.

Two of the principal matters discussed at the ICPD — international demographic change and reproductive health (including adolescent reproductive health) — are the subject of this report. *World Population Profile: 1996* presents updates of the Census Bureau's population estimates and projections for all the countries and regions of the world. It includes information on population composition, population growth, fertility, mortality, and use of contraception. A special section focuses on adolescent fertility in the developing world.

The Program of Action and the documents of the regional preparatory meetings leading up to Cairo together indicate much of what needs to happen if the larger goals agreed upon by the world community are to be met. The demographic goals — particularly in the areas of infant, child, and maternal morbidity and mortality, and the lowering of fertility in those countries where it remains so high that development is compromised by rapid population growth — are specified well enough that progress toward their achievement can be quantified. This edition of the Census Bureau's *World Population Profile* series provides a comprehensive assessment of world demographic prospects at the beginning of the post-Cairo process. It also provides an initial assessment of whether countries are likely to attain the demographic goals agreed upon in Cairo and in the regional meetings leading up to Cairo.

Data in the report include summary demographic information for the world, major regions, and all countries and territories with a population of at least 5,000 in 1996. For the most part, estimates and projections are based on the evaluation of national data available as of September 1995. Detailed tables supporting most charts and text are presented in appendix A. The recency of available information and the methodology and assumptions used for making the population estimates and projections are described in appendix B. Additional sources of information are cited in appendix C, and technical terms and acronyms are defined in appendix D.

This year's report covers 227 countries and territories. In most of the text and figures, they are grouped into 7 regions: Sub-Saharan Africa, the Near East and North Africa, China (Mainland and Taiwan), Other Asia (excluding Japan), Latin America and the Caribbean, Eastern Europe and the New Independent States (NIS), and the Rest of the World (North America, Western Europe, Japan, and Oceania).

In the detailed tables (appendix A and the data diskette for this report), countries are listed, and regional subtotals are provided, according to a more traditional geographic perspective: Africa (Sub-Saharan and North Africa), the Near East, Asia (including Mainland China, Taiwan, and Japan), Europe (Western, Eastern, and NIS), Latin America and the Caribbean, North America, and Oceania.

Countries and territories are classified by development status according to categories used by the United Nations: The "less developed" countries include all of Africa, all of Asia except Japan, the Transcaucasian and Central Asian republics of the NIS, all of Latin America and the Caribbean, and all of Oceania except Australia and New Zealand. The "more developed" countries and areas include all of North America, Europe, and the rest of the NIS, as well as Japan, Australia, and New Zealand. Although some countries or regions may move from "less developed" to "more developed" status by the year 2020, the categorization in this report does not reflect such changes.

This report replaces those previously issued in this publication series, and it should not be used in conjunction with earlier reports to derive time series of vital rates or other measures presented. Detailed notes are maintained by the International Programs Center to document the base data used and the procedures followed in deriving the numbers for each country. Questions about the estimates and projections underlying the report, or the methodology employed in making them, should be addressed to: Chief, Population Studies Branch, International Programs Center, Population Division, Bureau of the Census, Washington, DC 20233-8860. Comments on the report are invited.

Most of the data presented in this report, including the data found in the detailed tables of appendix A, are available to users in computer-readable format through one of two means:

- Appendix A tables and some additional detail are contained on a data diskette, in Lotus 1-2-3 *.wk1 format. The disk is available on request, by contacting:

  International Programs Center
  Population Division
  Bureau of the Census
  Washington, DC 20233-8860
  Telephone: 301-457-1358
  Fax: 301-457-1539
  Internet e-mail: ipc@census.gov

- The International Data Base of the Bureau of the Census (IDB) contains statistical tables of demographic and socioeconomic data for all countries of the world. Information from censuses and surveys (for example, population by age and sex, labor force, and contraceptive use) and administrative records (for example, registered births and deaths) are available from 1950 to the present and, where possible, by urban/rural residence. The IDB contains the International Programs Center's current estimates and projections of fertility, mortality, migration, and population on a single-year basis to the year 2050. IDB estimates and projections may be more recent than those presented in this report.

  Direct access and further information about the IDB are available through the Internet at:

  http://www.census.gov/ipc/www

  Requests for specific data items from, or questions about, the IDB should be directed to:

  Chief, Information Resources Branch
  International Programs Center
  Population Division
  Bureau of the Census
  Washington, DC 20233-8860
  Telephone: 301-457-1403
  Fax: 301-457-1539
  Internet e-mail: ipc@census.gov

Population Size and Growth

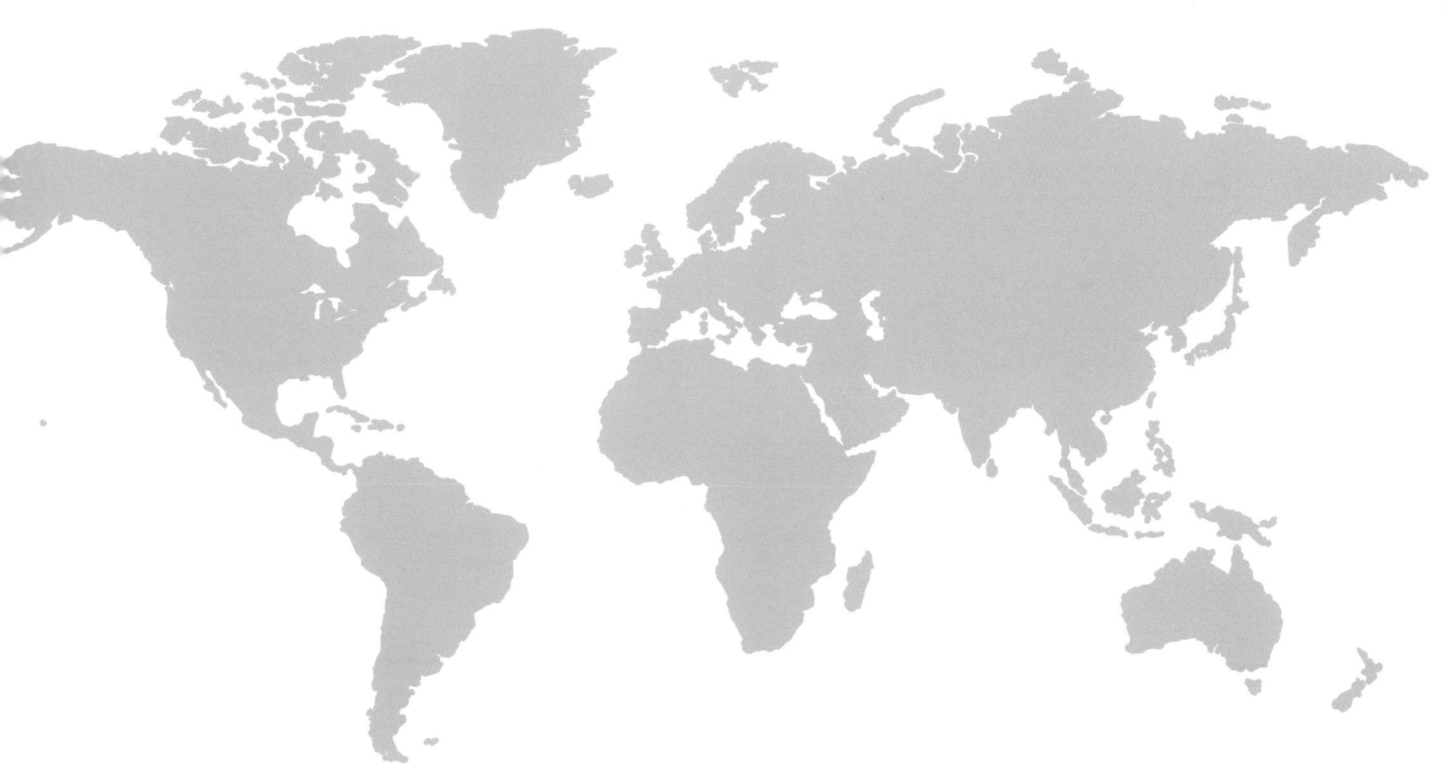

Population Size and Growth

World Population Approaches 6 Billion as Nations Seek Population-Development Balance

The 1994 International Conference on Population and Development (ICPD) in Cairo focused the world's attention on the challenge facing all nations as they seek to integrate population and development policies and programs.

For the past 25 years, the gap between birth rates and death rates worldwide — the world's rate of natural increase — has been continually, albeit slowly, shrinking. Reaching an historical peak of about 2.2 percent per year from 1962 to 1964, global population growth fell to about 1.5 percent during the first half of the present decade and is expected to drop below 1 percent per annum during the first quarter of the next century (figure 1 and table A-2). This slowing of the pace of world population increase should facilitate the achievement of many of the objectives set out in the Cairo Program of Action.

However, while the ***rate*** of world population increase continues to fall, the numbers of men, women and children are expected to continue to grow well into the next century. According to the latest projections of the Bureau of the Census, world population will increase from its present level of about 5.8 billion persons to almost 6.1 billion by the year 2000. These projections, summarized in table A-1, indicate that world population will grow by an additional 1.5 billion persons during the first two decades of the next century, reaching a level of 7.6 billion persons by the year 2020.

From the ICPD Program of Action:

"The growth of the world population is at an all-time high in absolute numbers, with current increments approaching 90 million persons annually ...

"While it had taken 123 years for world population to increase from 1 billion to 2 billion, succeeding increments of 1 billion took 33 years, 14 years and 13 years. The transition from the fifth to the sixth billion, currently under way, is expected to take only 11 years and to be completed by 1998." (section 6.1)

Figure 1.
World Population and Average Annual Rates of Growth, by Development Category: 1950 to 2020

Population *(left scale)*

Growth rate *(right scale)*

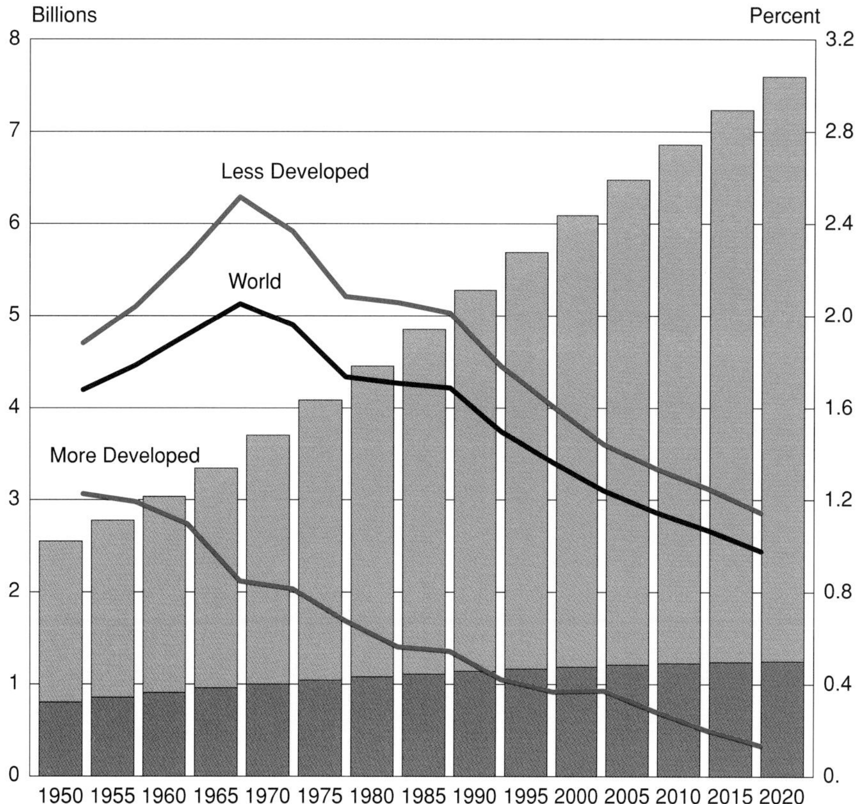

Note: Rates of growth are average rates for 5-year periods, 1950-55 through 2015-2020.
Source: Table A-1 and U.S. Bureau of the Census, International Data Base.

Average Annual Increase in World Population
(Millions)

Years	World	Less Developed Countries	More Developed Countries
1985-1990	85.4	79.3	6.1
1990-1996	81.8	77.0	4.8
1996-2000	79.8	75.4	4.4
2000-2005	77.8	73.3	4.5
2005-2020	74.6	72.1	2.5

Note: Data for this table and all subsequent text tables are from U.S. Bureau of the Census, International Data Base, unless otherwise indicated.

Developing Regions Generate Nearly All of Population Growth

Most of world population growth takes place in the developing countries of Africa, Asia, and Latin America. The combined population of less developed countries grew from 1.7 billion persons in 1950 to 4.6 billion in 1996. This figure is expected to reach 6.4 billion by the year 2020. In contrast, the combined population of the more developed countries of the world increased from 800 million persons in 1950 to 1.17 billion in 1996 and is expected to increase only modestly, to 1.25 billion, by the year 2020.

In 1996, 95 out of every 100 persons added to world population live in less developed countries.

Declining population growth rates in both groups of countries reflect declining annual increments in population size. The decreases are less pronounced in the developing countries, however, because moderately declining rates are applied to still rapidly growing base populations.

Future Population Increases Will Be Concentrated in Asia, but Sub-Saharan Africa's Share Is Growing

The pace of population growth varies from region to region, determined in part by current regional population totals and in part by differentials in regional growth rates. Asia continues to dominate other world regions in terms of the absolute number of persons added each year, because its 1996 population, even without China, is much larger than that of any other region (figure 2). Other Asia will

Figure 2.
Population of World Regions: 1970, 1996, and 2020

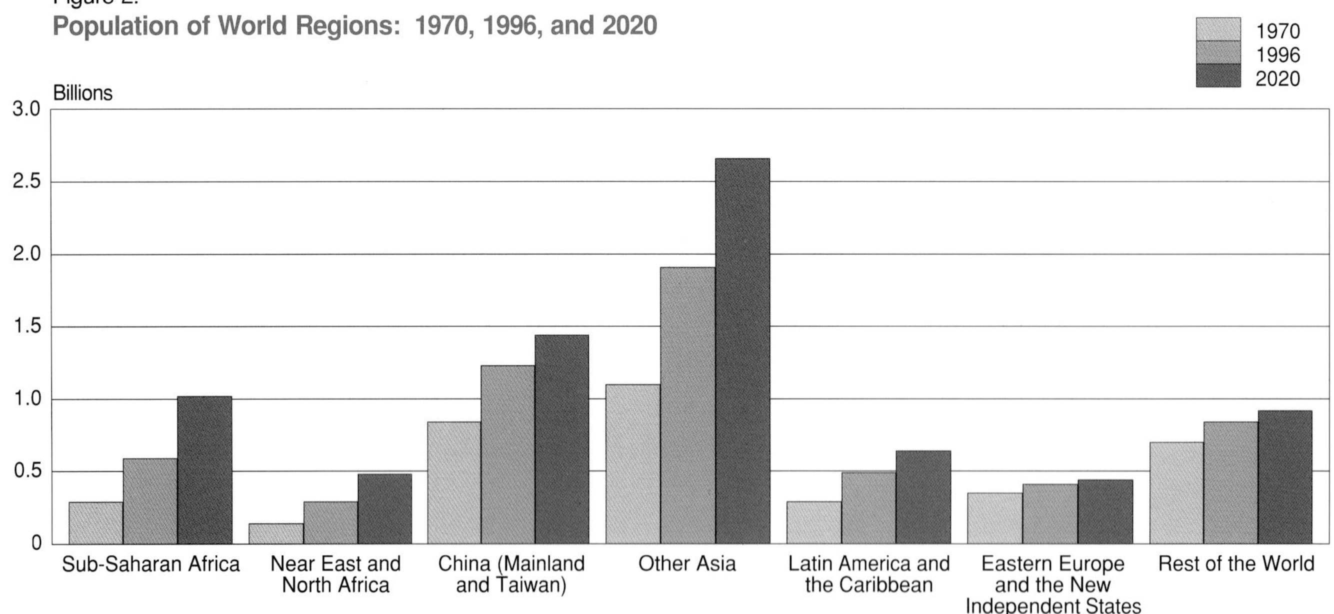

Source: Table A-1 and U.S. Bureau of the Census, International Data Base.

contribute 132 million persons to world population increase between now and the year 2000; China, another 44 million persons. The rest of the developing world will, together, add another 126 million persons during the next 4 years, and more developed countries will contribute about 18 million persons.

Among world regions, the largest proportionate increases in share of world population will continue to be in Sub-Saharan Africa, which is expected to grow from fewer than 600 million persons in 1996 to just over 1 billion in the year 2020. Between 1996 and 2020, China and the rest of Asia will remain the two largest regions, although China's share will fall.

The share represented by more developed countries has declined from 27 percent of the world total in 1970 to 20 percent in 1996. If present trends continue, more developed countries will comprise only 16 percent of world population 25 years from now.

Share of World Population

(Percent)

Region	1970	1996	2020
Less Developed Countries	72.9	79.7	83.6
More Developed Countries	27.1	20.3	16.4
Sub-Saharan Africa	7.8	10.3	13.5
Near East and North Africa	3.9	5.1	6.4
China (Mainland and Taiwan)	22.5	21.3	18.9
Other Asia	29.7	33.2	35.0
Latin America and the Caribbean	7.7	8.5	8.5
Eastern Europe and New Independent States	9.5	7.2	5.8
Rest of the World	18.9	14.5	12.0

Note: Other Asia excludes China and Japan. Rest of the World includes Western Europe, North America, Japan, and Oceania.

Africa's Growth Rates Will Remain Highest Among World Regions for the Next 25 Years

Declines in population growth rates are projected for 5 of 6 major world regions during the remainder of the 1990's, and for all major regions from the turn of the century onward. However, future trends, like past trends, vary markedly from region to region (figure 3). Sub-Saharan Africa has emerged as the region with the highest projected population growth rates during the coming 25-year period. Growth rates, just over 2.5 percent per annum since the mid-80's, are expected to remain above 2 percent through 2020 in spite of rising mortality in some countries due to the HIV/AIDS epidemic.

The developing regions of Sub-Saharan Africa, Latin America and the Caribbean, the Near East and North Africa, and Asia (excluding China and Japan) show post-World War II trends in population growth consistent with the demographic transition from high birth and death rates to relatively low vital rates. In each of these major regions, growth rates first rose as mortality fell in response to initiatives in public health, infectious disease control, and the introduction of new drugs. After a lag varying in length from region to region, crude birth rates began to fall in response to delayed marriage, changing family size preferences and greater availability of family planning services in many countries.

Growth rates for Latin America and the Caribbean were the highest among the different regions in the 1950's and 1960's but were also the first to decline to their present regional level of around 1.5 percent per annum. During the late 1960's and early 1970's, rates for Africa, Other Asia, and Latin America were clustered relatively closely together, around 2.5 percent per year, but this historical juxtaposition was temporary. Birth rates, and population growth rates, for Latin America and the Caribbean fell steadily throughout the decades of the 1960's, 70's, 80's, and 90's, and remain lower, on average, than those of other developing regions.

The average growth rate for all Asia turned downward next, peaking during the 1960's before declining to a level of about 1.5 percent in the early 1990's.

Growth rates for Sub-Saharan Africa and for the Near East and North Africa continued to rise throughout the 1960's and 1970's, largely because birth rates remained relatively high in many countries in these regions while death rates declined. Sub-Saharan Africa's history of population growth during the 1980's differs from that of North Africa and the Near East, however, not only in the fact that birth rates, and hence growth rates, have

Figure 3.
Average Annual Rates of Population Growth of World Regions: 1950 to 2020

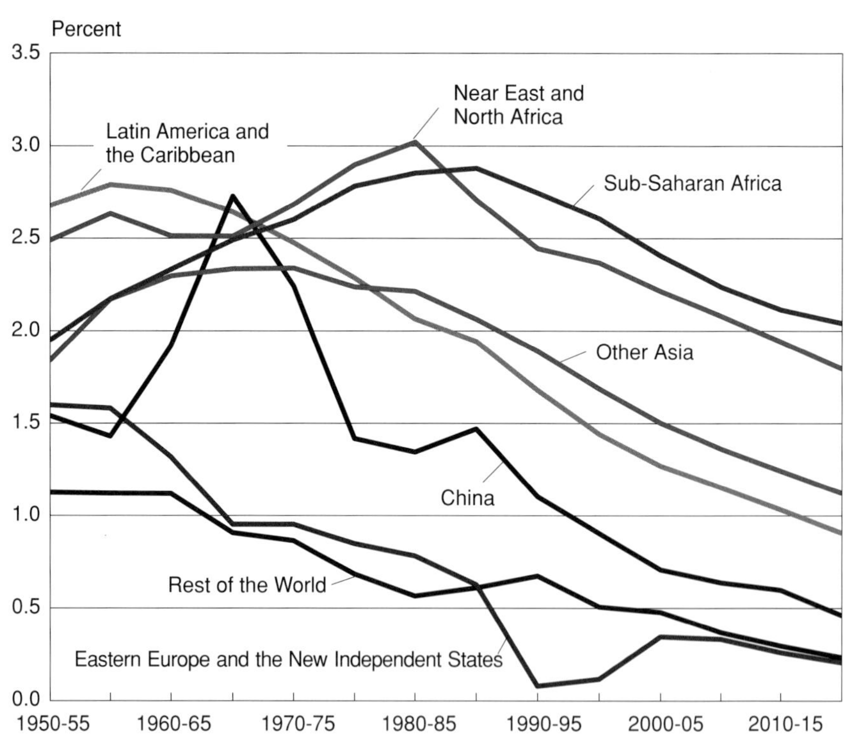

Note: Rates of growth are average rates for 5-year periods, 1950-55 through 2015-20. China includes Mainland China and Taiwan.
Source: U.S. Bureau of the Census, International Data Base.

been higher than other regions since the mid-1980's, but also by an interruption in mortality decline in a number of countries beginning in the early 1980's. Crude death rates remained relatively unchanged in 1 in 5 Sub-Saharan African countries during the mid- to late 1980's, and mortality is actually rising, rather than falling, in some Sub-Saharan African countries affected by HIV/AIDS. This reduces population growth in these countries and acts as a brake on natural increase at the regional level through the early part of the next century. Population growth rates are expected to fall in both regions, at least through the year 2020, as a result of ongoing and projected declines in birth rates and the evolving trends in mortality in these regions.

Population growth in the Rest of the World has also slowed since 1950, but the decline has been from initial levels markedly lower than those of Asia, Africa, and Latin America to a composite regional value well below 1 percent per annum today.

The continuing disparity in growth rates between Africa, Asia, and Latin America on the one hand, and Europe, North America, Japan, and Oceania on the other, accounts for the evolving regional distribution of world population during the last decade of this century and the first two decades of the next. Twenty-two of every 100 persons alive in 1950 lived in Western Europe, North America, Japan, or Oceania. By 1996 this fraction has fallen to 14 in 100; by the year 2020 only 12 in 100 persons will be living in these areas.

The trends in growth in two regions shown in figure 3 — China and the region comprising Eastern Europe and the New Independent States — are distinctly different from all the others. China's trend is a product of the country's unique post-war history of social change, population-food supply balance, and official restrictions on marriage and childbearing. The relatively low growth rate during the early 1950's reflects the relatively high mortality prevalent in China in the immediate post-war period. The dip in growth during the late 1950's and the rise in growth during the early 1960's show the impact of, and recovery from, the "Great Leap Forward" famine of 1958-61. Continued decline in death rates during the Cultural Revolution and, more importantly, resumed childbearing following the famine years account for China's peak growth rate of 2.7 percent per annum during the late 1960's. Finally, declines in growth during the 1970's and since 1987 reflect enforcement of government policies encouraging higher age at first marriage and strict limits on childbearing.

Growth rates in Eastern Europe and the New Independent States have declined rapidly in the post-war period, finishing with a precipitous drop in the late 1980's and early 1990's (figure 3). This is partly the result of pronounced declines in fertility from levels already below replacement coupled with rising mortality in the recent past in the majority of countries in this region. The trends in fertility and mortality observed in the early 1990's reflect the social uncertainties and related economic hardships of the period. In addition, the age structures of Russia and her neighbors currently feature a trough in the size of cohorts in the reproductive ages, which also suppresses the numbers of births and makes present growth rates unusually low. Fertility is expected to recover from its current levels, however, and larger reproductive age cohorts will replace today's smaller cohorts, leading to some resurgence in population growth rates in this region during the next decade (U.S. Bureau of the Census 1996a).

Between Now and the Year 2000, World Population Will Increase by Over 300 Million Persons

In spite of the fact that population growth is slowing in every world region, the number of people living in the world continues to increase, and will do so as long as the world's growth rate is greater than zero. During the next 4 years, 319 million persons will be added to world population. As figure 4 shows, 61 million persons, or 19 percent of this increase will occur in India; about 14 percent, in China; and 20 percent in Sub-Saharan Africa. More developed countries, including the United States, will account for only 6 percent of world population increase from midyear 1996 to midyear 2000.

Fifty-one Percent of World Population Lives in Six Countries...

Of the 5.8 billion people alive in 1996, almost 3 billion live in China, India, the United States, Indonesia, Brazil, and Russia (figure 5). The other 2.8 billion live in one of the remaining 221 countries. The United States, with just over 266 million people, accounts for less than 5 percent of world population.

Figure 4.
Population Added From 1996 to 2000

Total added: 319 million

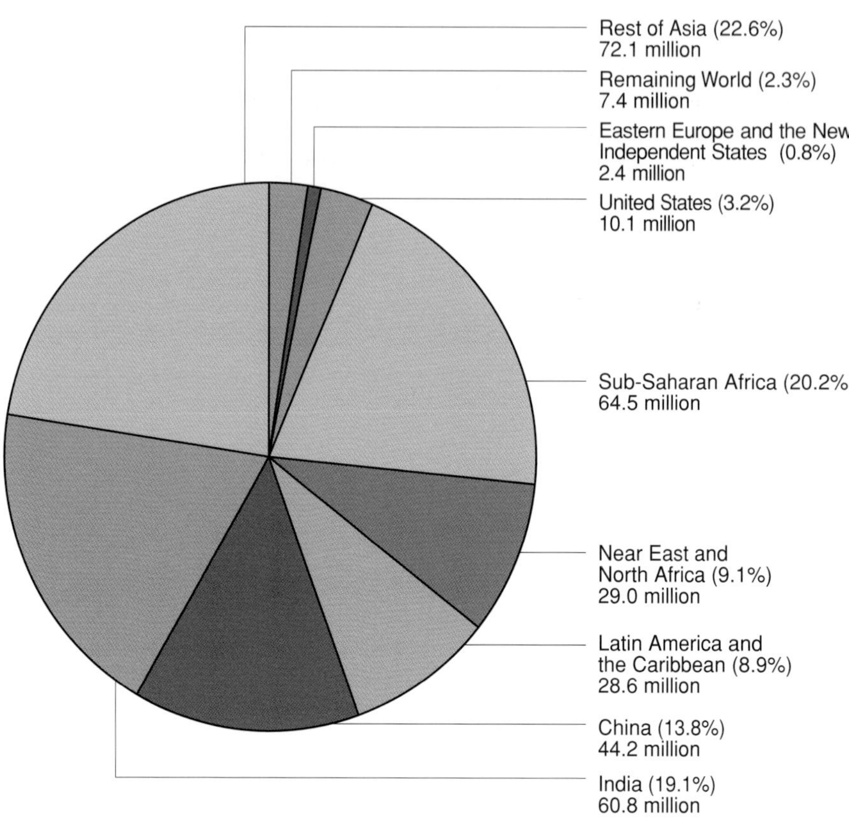

Note: Percentages are of population added from 1996 to 2000. China includes Mainland China and Taiwan.
Source: Table A-4.

Figure 5.
Distribution of World Population: 1996 and 2020

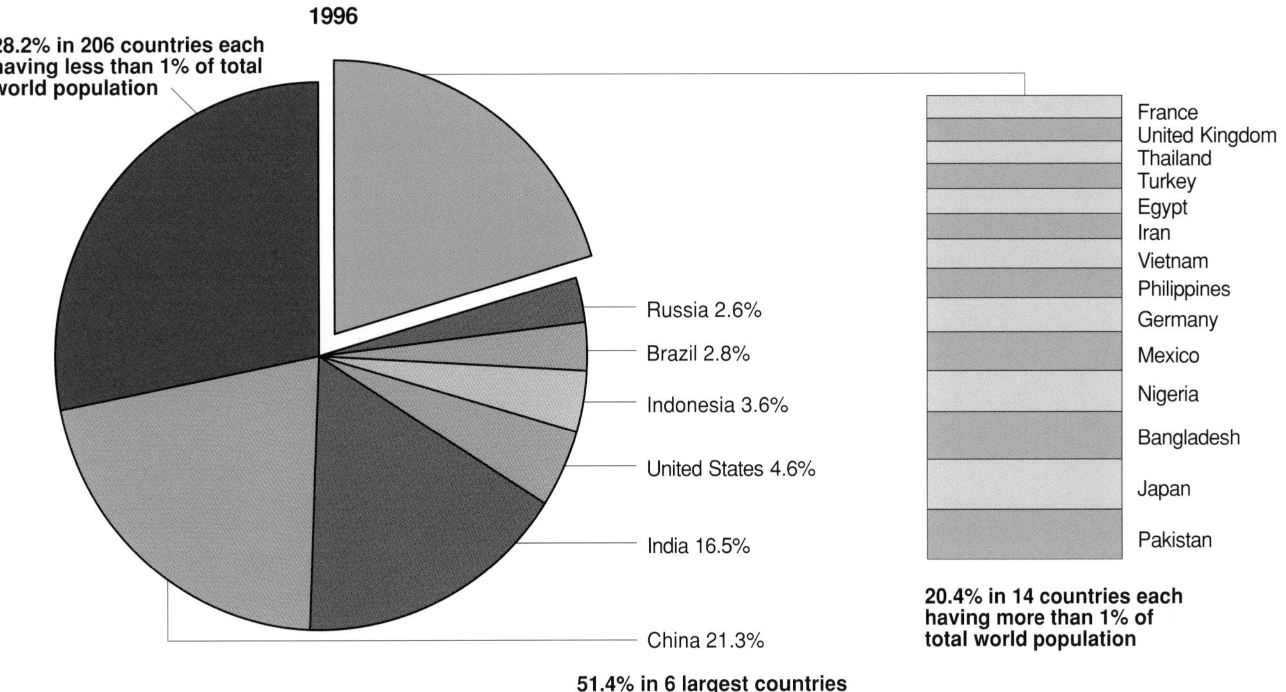

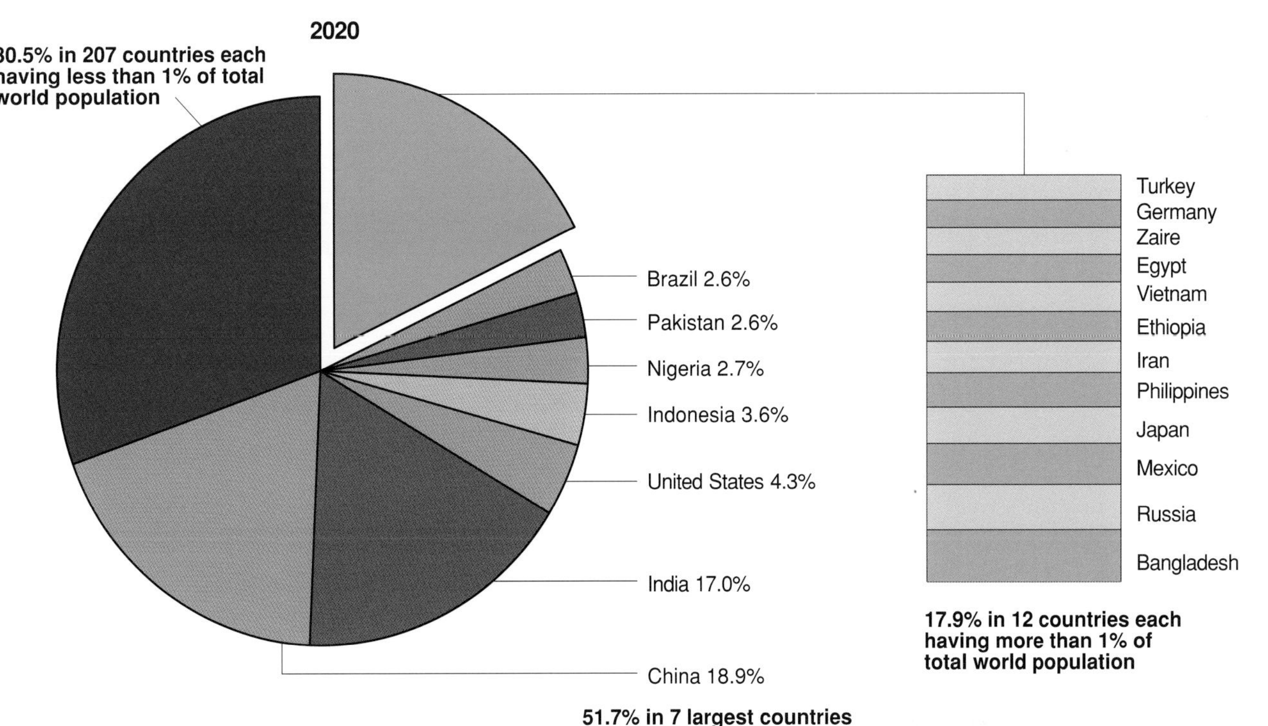

Note: China includes Mainland China and Taiwan. Percentages do not add to 100 because of rounding.
Source: Table A-4.

...but Shares and Ranks Will Change in the Next 25 Years

By the year 2020, the shares of total world population living in the countries having the largest populations will shift. For example, during the next 25 years more people will be added to India's population than to China's — about 337 million and 207 million, respectively. If present trends continue, India's population will approach China's by year 2020 and will surpass China's by the year 2040.

During the coming 25 years, country rankings among the most populous nations will change as high-fertility, high-growth countries overtake presently larger, but more slowly growing nations. Perhaps the most dramatic example of this is Nigeria, which is expected to bypass Bangladesh, Japan, Pakistan, Russia, and Brazil in size by the year 2020 (figure 5). Other notable shifts include Pakistan and Bangladesh. By 2020, Pakistan will have a larger population than Brazil or Russia, and Bangladesh's population will exceed that of Russia.

Figure 6 shows trends in growth rates and population size for countries that will play a dominant role in world or regional population change during the coming quarter century. In addition, it illustrates the effects of temporary changes in national policy or natural disaster that sometimes interrupt demographic trends. China's unique post-World War II demographic history has already been mentioned. Another example: The 1983 deportation of illegal aliens from Nigeria is responsible for the sharp discontinuity in growth rates for this country evident in figure 6.

Figure 6.
Population and Average Annual Rate of Growth, for Most Populous Countries: 1950 to 2020

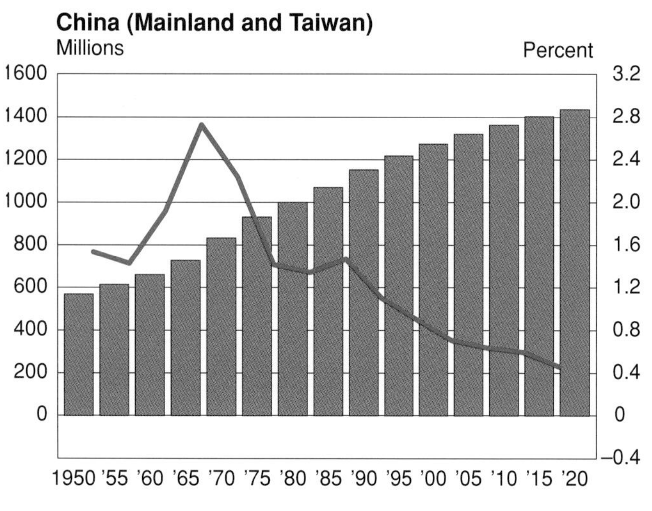

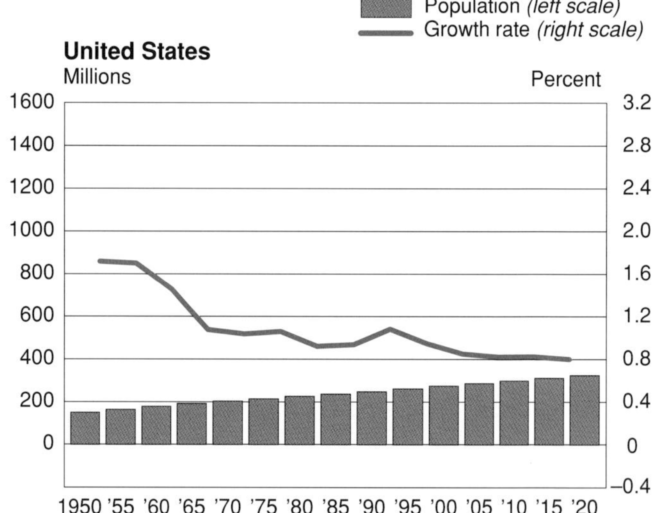

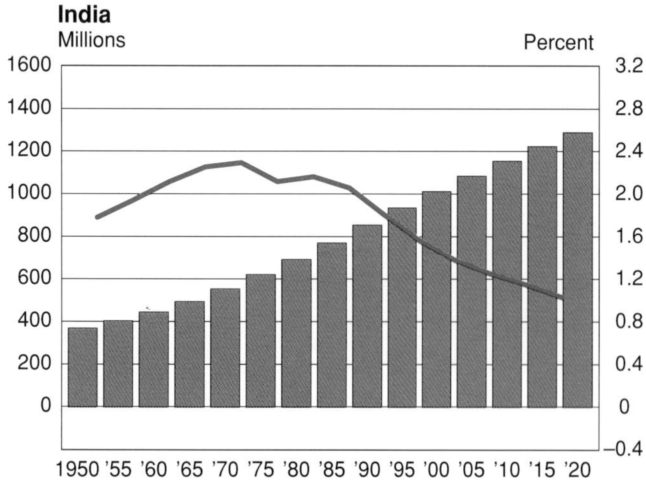

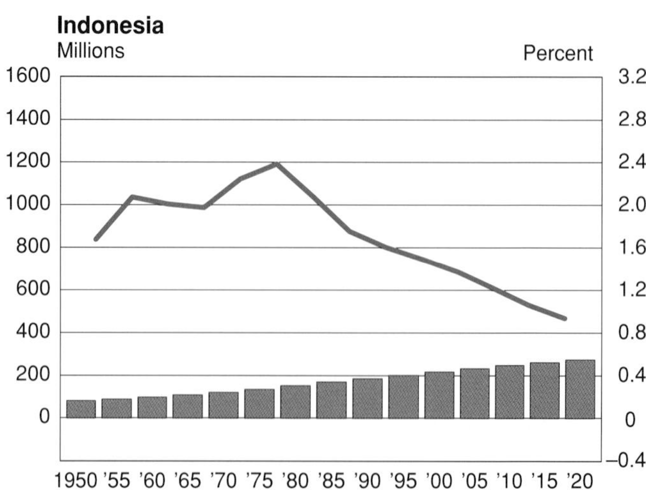

Figure 6.
Population and Average Annual Rate of Growth, for Most Populous Countries: 1950 to 2020—Continued

Population (*left scale*)
Growth rate (*right scale*)

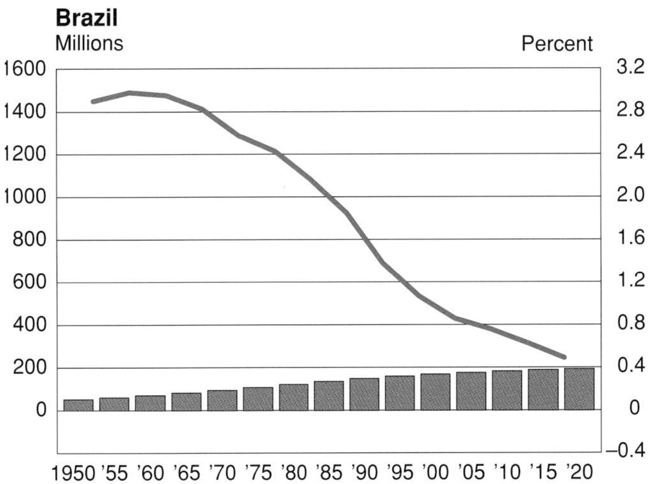

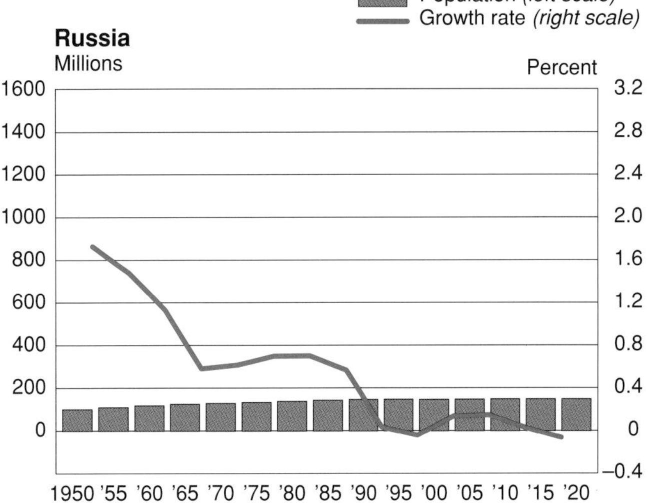

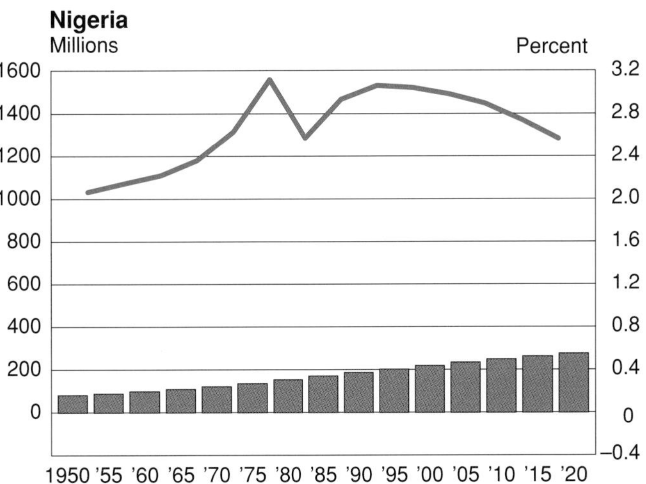

Note: Rates of growth are average rates for 5-year periods, 1950-55 through 2015-2020.
Source: Table A-4 and U.S. Bureau of the Census, International Data Base.

Population Composition

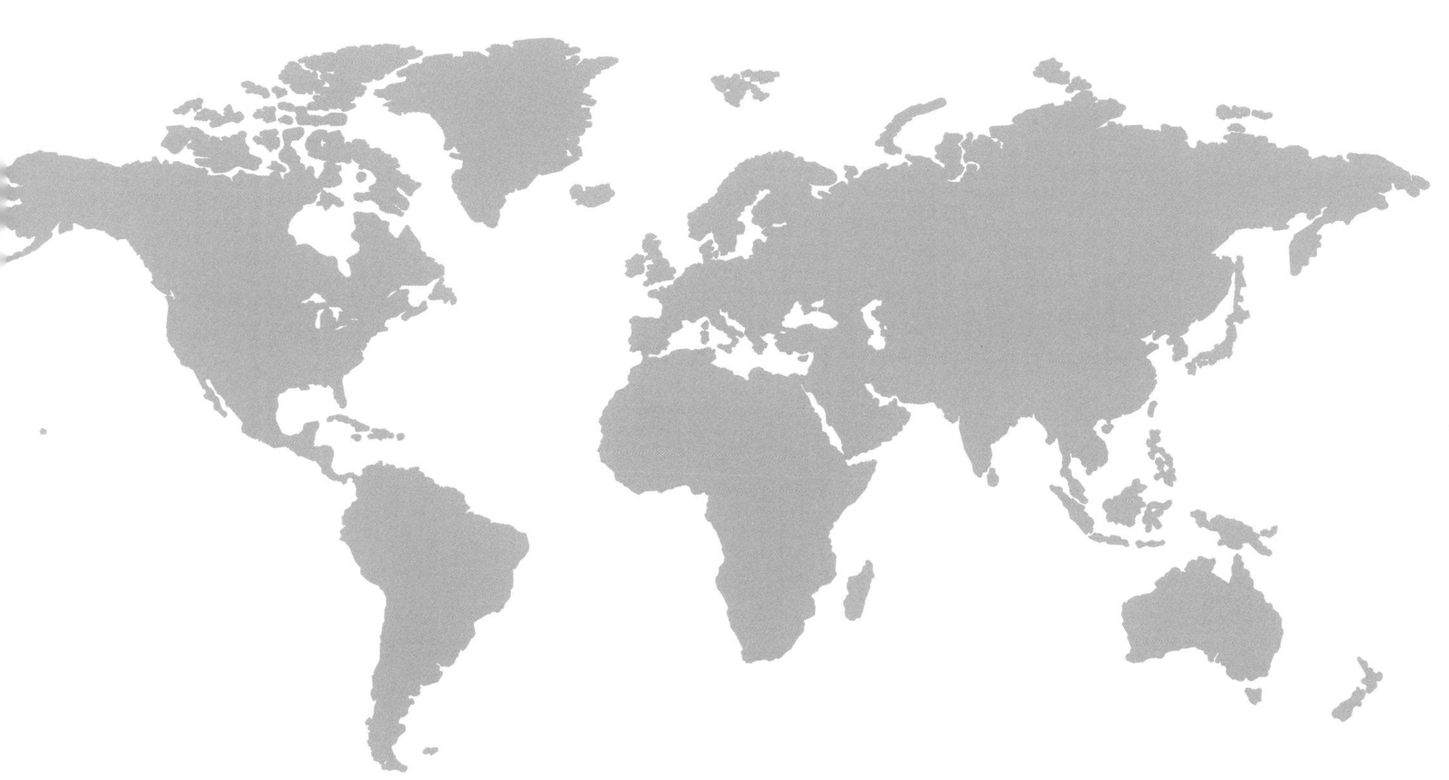

Population Composition

An important outcome of the Cairo conference was a new consensus within the international community that investments in people, including steps taken to strengthen education and health care, are essential if the goals of sustainable development and sustained economic growth are to be achieved (United Nations 1995a:5-11).

Changes in population composition over time, along with population growth, help define the magnitude and the nature of the challenges associated with making such investments for individual nations. Specific population subgroups — children, the school-age population, adolescents, women of reproductive age, men and women of labor force age, and the elderly — generate demands for particular types of services that require differing social and economic policy and programmatic responses.

Developing Nations' Age Structures Slowly Approaching Those of More Developed Countries

Less developed countries have relatively young populations as a result of high fertility and of mortality reductions over the past 40 years that have favored younger age groups. Even though fertility has been declining in most developing countries over the past 10 to 30 years, the age-sex pyramid for LDC's continues to show a large base, because the number of each successive year's births is larger than those born in earlier years (figure 7).

From the ICPD Program of Action:

"The decline in fertility levels, reinforced by continued declines in mortality levels, is producing fundamental changes in the age structure of the population of most societies ...

"The steady increase of older age groups in national populations, both in absolute numbers and in relation to the working-age population, has significant implications for a majority of countries, particularly with regard to ... modalities for assistance to elderly people." (section 6.16)

Figure 7.
Population by Age, Sex, and Development Category: 1996 and 2020

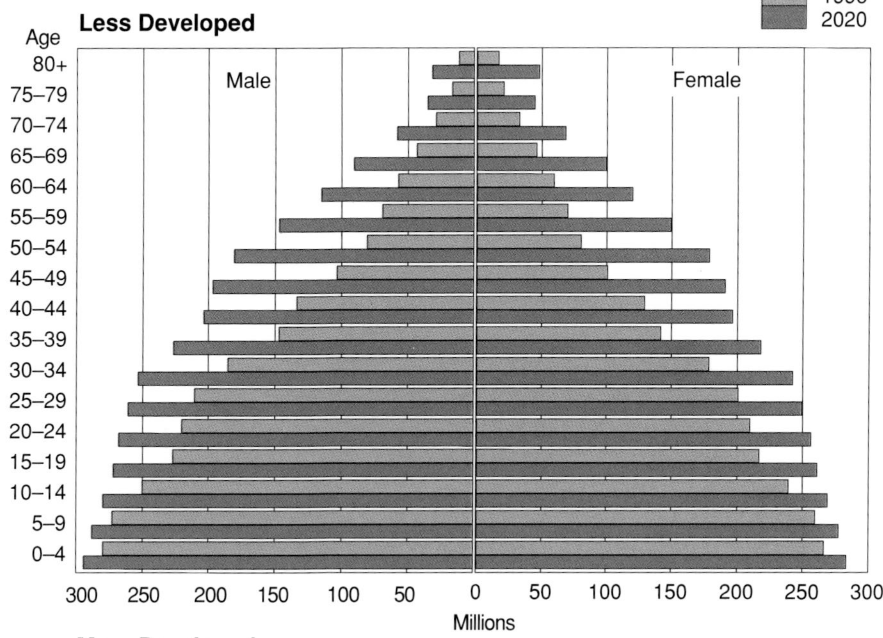

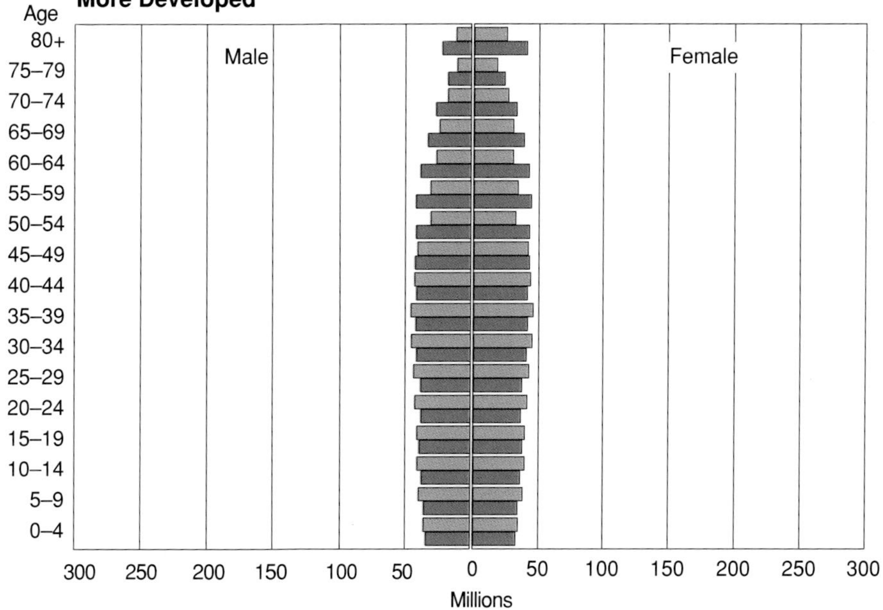

Source: U.S. Bureau of the Census, International Data Base.

Despite this, the age silhouette of today's developing nations is expected to approach that of more developed countries during the next several decades as fertility in Africa, Asia and Latin America continues to fall (figure 7). The typically broadly-based pyramid for LDC's gets noticeably less triangular (especially at younger ages) between 1996 and 2020.

In contrast, the relatively rectangular age-sex structure of more developed countries, which reflects stable levels of low fertility over several generations, is not expected to change much during the next 20 to 30 years.

Populations in Every World Region Are Growing Older

As children become a smaller proportion of the total population and older age groups become more dominant, the median age — the midpoint age that separates the younger half from the older half of the population — rises. Figure 8 shows the rising median age of the populations of both more developed and less developed countries over the period 1996 to 2020. Half the population in LDC's is under age 23 today; in 2020 the median will have risen to 29 years. During the same period the median age of population in more developed countries will rise from 36 to 42 years.

Median ages of the populations of every major world region will rise over the next quarter century, with the greatest increases taking place in the developing regions further along in their demographic transitions. The rise in median age is particularly dramatic in China, where it climbs from about 28 to about 38 between 1996 and 2020.

Figure 8.
Median Age by Development Category: 1996 and 2020

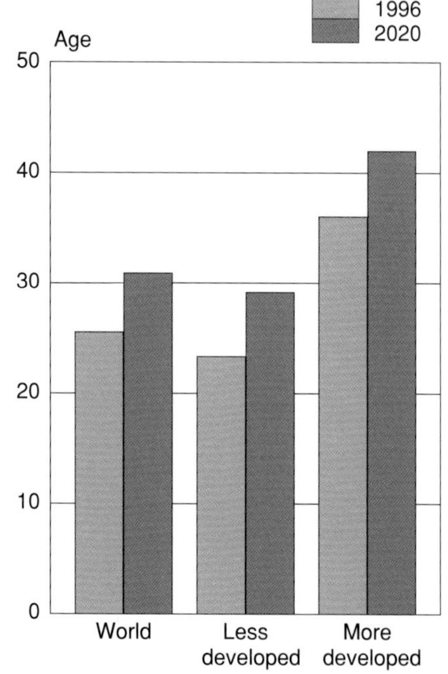

Source: U.S. Bureau of the Census, International Data Base.

Median Ages

	1996	2020
World	26	31
Less Developed Countries	23	29
More Developed Countries	36	42
Sub-Saharan Africa	17	19
Near East and North Africa	21	26
China (Mainland and Taiwan)	28	38
Other Asia	23	29
Latin America and the Caribbean	23	31
Eastern Europe and the New Independent States	33	37
Rest of the World	36	43

Figure 9.
Distribution of World Population in Selected Age Groups by Development Category: 1996 and 2020

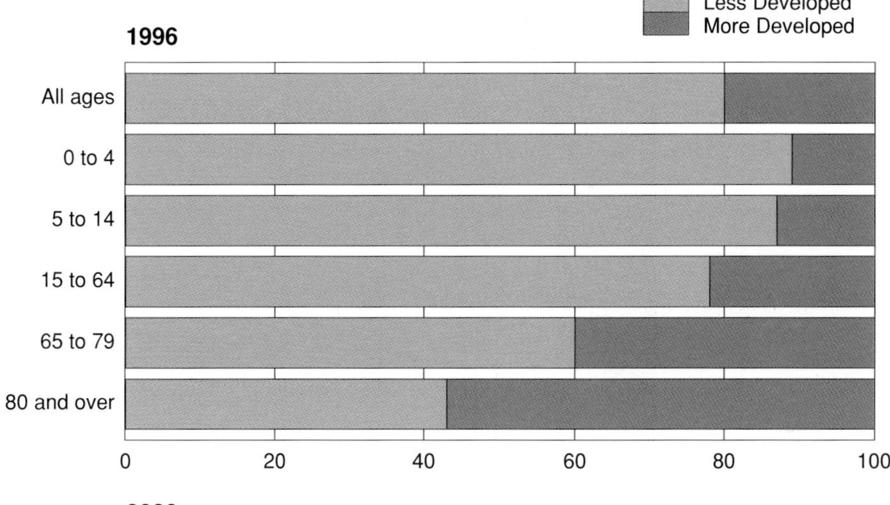

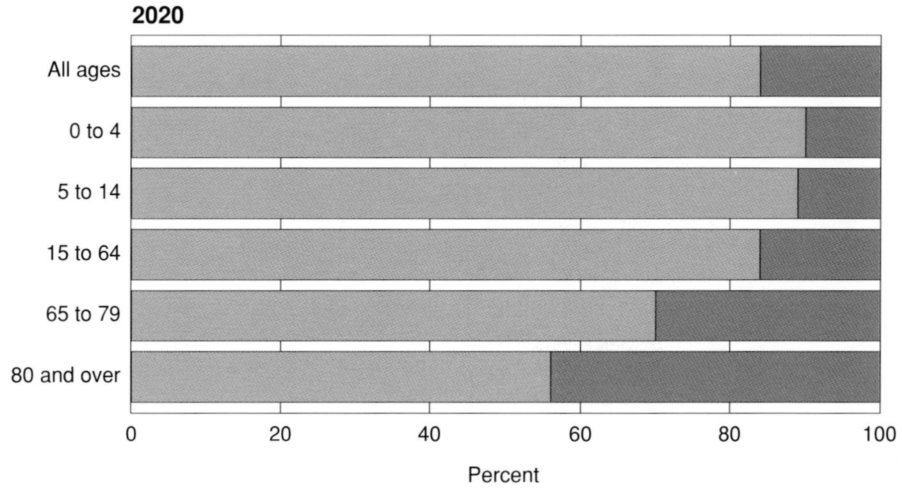

Source: Table A-7.

As developing country populations grow older, they will represent increasing proportions of the world's adult and elderly populations (figure 9). During the coming 25 years, the share of the world's population ages 80 and over living in less developed countries will grow from 43 percent to 56 percent.

In contrast, the proportion of the world's children (ages 0 to 14) living in the LDC's will continue to rise only slightly, from 87 to 89 percent.

Figure 10 illustrates the shifting age pattern within each region, highlighting the common trend among regions: falling proportions of young populations and rising shares of elderly.

The Numbers of Children Will Continue to Increase, but Less Rapidly

Over the course of the next 25 years, children will come to comprise a smaller part of the total population in all regions of the world (figure 10) as a result of lower fertility and higher life expectancy. Inasmuch as children make significant demands on a country's social infrastructure (especially for health and education), the declining shares of youngest and school age children may enable developing countries to better afford ongoing child survival and related health care programs.

However, the absolute number of children worldwide will continue to grow — 6 percent ***more*** children ages 0 to 14 will be living in the year 2020 compared with 1996 — and the age groups 0 to 4 and 5 to 14 will continue to dwarf the elderly in the developing world. Nearly 9 in every 10 persons making up the combined dependent age groups 0 to 14 and 65 and over in less developed countries are under age 15 in 1996. This fraction declines, but is still 8 children in 10 dependents, by the year 2020.

Working Age Populations Are Growing at a Moderate Pace

The population ages 15 to 64, often referred to as the working age population, will increase by 48 percent in the developing world over the next 25 years, to 4.2 billion. At the same time, the working age population in the more developed countries will increase only 3 percent, to about 800 million.

Figure 10.
Percent of Regional Populations in Selected Age Groups: 1996 and 2020

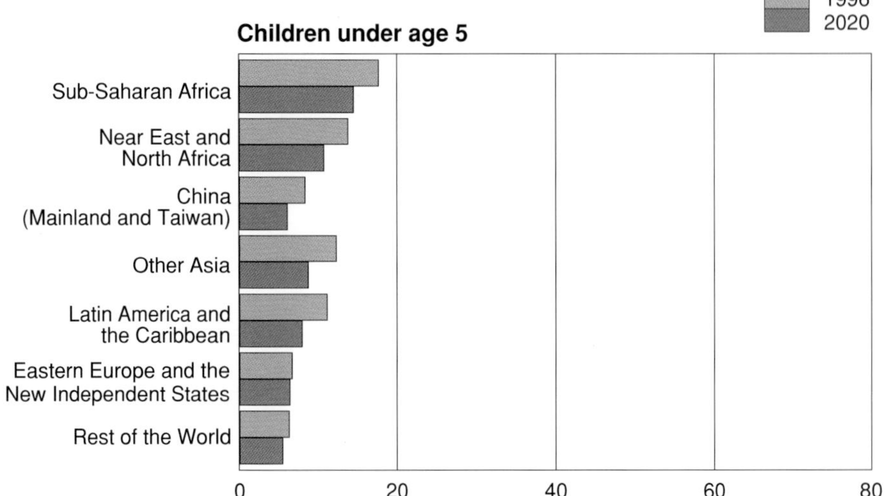

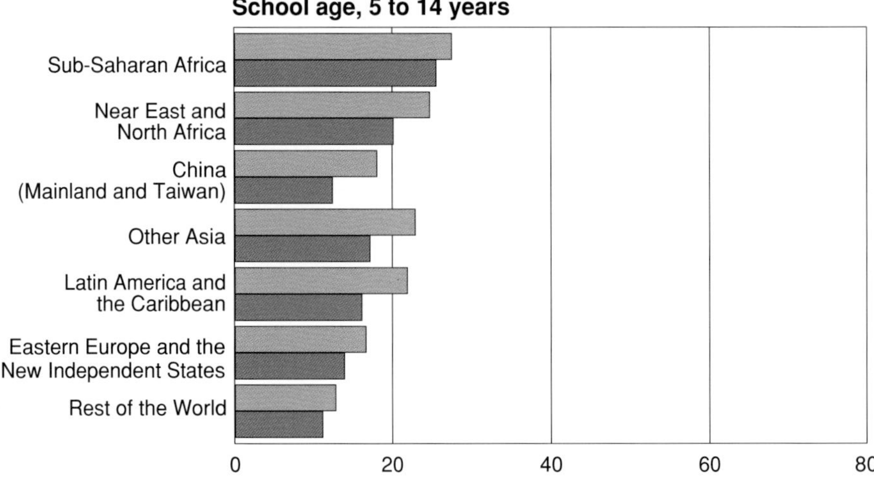

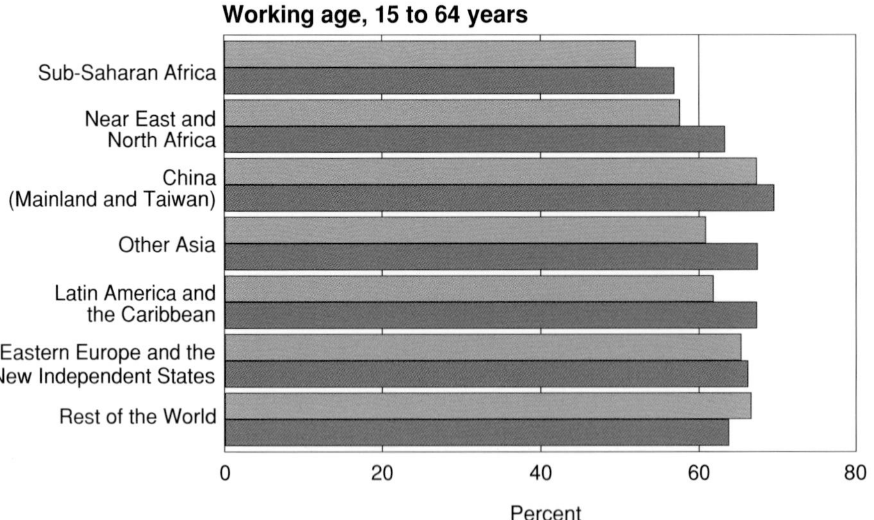

Figure 10.
Percent of Regional Populations in Selected Age Groups: 1996 and 2020—Continued

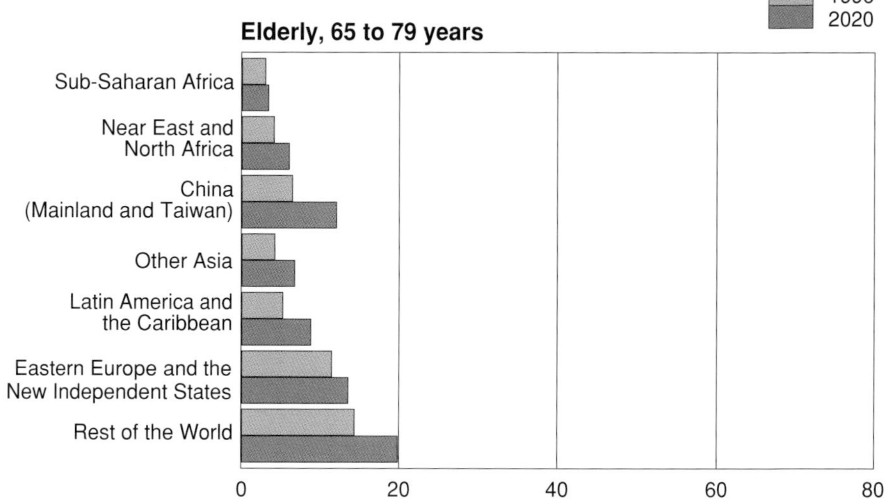

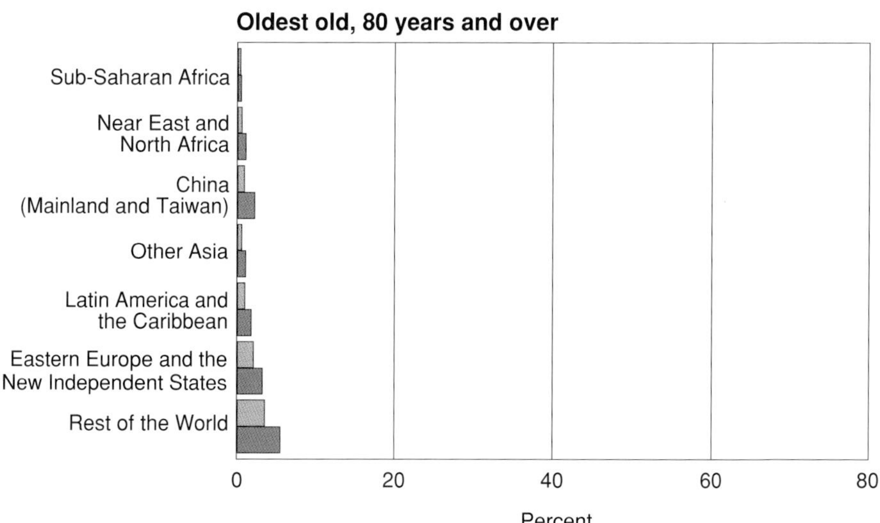

Source: Table A-7.

Average Annual Rate of Population Growth: 1996 to 2020
(Percent)

	Total	School age (5-14)	Working age (15-64)	Elderly (65 and over)
World	1.1	0.3	1.4	2.6
Sub-Saharan Africa	2.3	1.9	2.6	2.8
Near East and North Africa	2.1	1.2	2.5	3.7
China (Mainland and Taiwan)	0.6	-0.9	0.8	3.4
Other Asia	1.4	0.2	1.8	3.4
Latin America and the Caribbean	1.1	-0.1	1.5	3.3
Eastern Europe and the New Independent States	0.3	-0.5	0.3	1.0
Rest of the World	0.4	-0.2	0.2	1.7

By 2020, the working age population will become a larger proportion of total population in most regions of the world. Only in the most developed countries (Rest of the World) will the proportion fall. Accordingly, the proportion of the world's working age population living in more developed countries will fall from 22 percent today to 16 percent in 2020.

The age group 15 to 64 is the source of most economic capacity in every nation. Dependency ratios — the ratio of children or elderly to the working age population — suggest a country's ability to support the young and old.

Currently, the youth dependency ratio (the ratio of persons under age 15 to the working age population) in the developing world is 56 per 100 persons in the age range 15 to 64. This will fall to 40 by 2020 — still well above the current level of 29 in the more developed world.

In contrast, the old age dependency ratio (the ratio of persons 65 and over to persons 15 to 64) in the more developed countries is almost 3 times as great as in the LDC's (20.7 compared to 7.6). Both of these ratios will increase substantially by 2020, to 29 and 11, respectively.

The Elderly Population in Less Developed Countries Will More Than Double by 2020

By far the fastest growing part of the world's population is the elderly. And in contrast to the growth of other age groups, the rate of growth of the elderly population is expected to increase in the coming decades in all regions.

The proportion of the population ages 65 and over is increasing in all regions of the world but the average annual rate of growth for this group from now until 2020 will be twice as great in the developing countries (3.3 percent) as in more developed nations (1.5 percent). As a result, the elderly population in less developed countries will increase 121 percent over the next 25 years; 44 percent, in the more developed countries. By 2020, nearly two-thirds of the world's elderly will live in LDC's — including more than half of the oldest old (ages 80 and over) (figure 9).

The oldest old will increase by 70 percent in more developed nations between now and the year 2020. However, in less developed countries the growth of this age group will be ***relatively*** much greater: the population ages 80 and over living in the developing world will grow to nearly three times its present size during the coming 25 years. Until now, it has been primarily the demographically older societies of Europe, Japan, and North America that have had to provide for the health care, housing, and other special needs of relatively large numbers of persons over the age of 80. In the coming years, Eastern Europe and a number of countries in the developing regions of Asia and Latin America will need to support larger elderly populations.

Figure 11.
Women of Childbearing Age by Region: Percent Change From 1996 to 2020

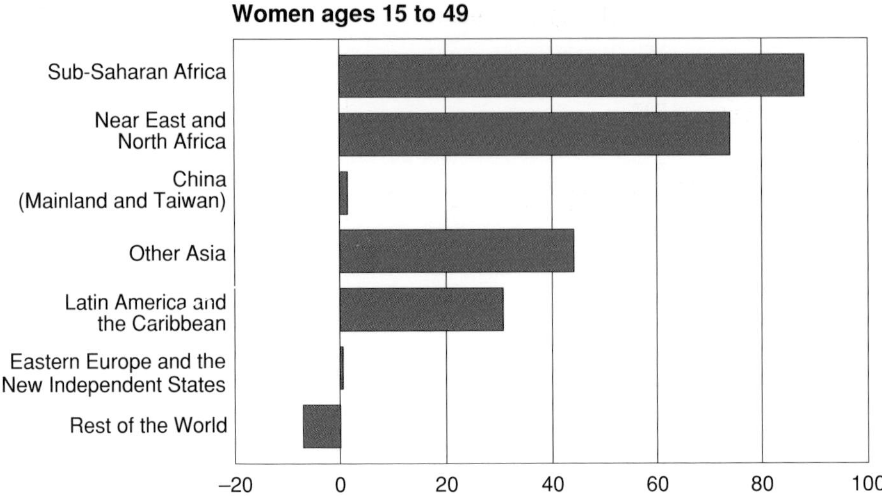

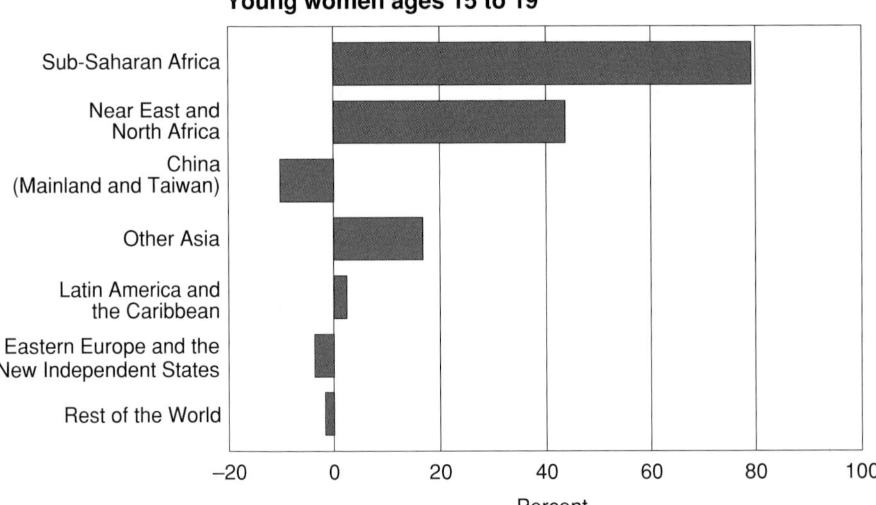

Source: U.S. Bureau of the Census, International Data Base.

Numbers of Women in Need of Reproductive Health Care to Grow Rapidly in Africa and the Near East

The number of women of childbearing age (15 to 49 years) will increase in all but the most developed countries between now and the year 2020 (figure 11), driving up the need for reproductive and maternal health care services worldwide, but especially in Sub-Saharan Africa and in North Africa and the Near East. In these regions, the number of women of reproductive age will increase by 88 and 74 percent, respectively. Just the ***increase*** (119 million) in Sub-Saharan Africa is almost as large as the total cohort of women ages 15 to 49 in the Near East and North Africa in 2020 (123 million).

More Adolescents, Greater Challenges

Currently, about 8 million more young men and women ages 15 to 19 are added to the populations of the developing regions of the world each year. Adolescents represent well-defined claims against public education and health care systems. They also present a major challenge to nations already having difficulty creating employment.

Adolescent women represent a special challenge to reproductive health care and family planning systems. These young women account for about 20 to 25 percent of all women of reproductive age in most of the developing regions of the world, and their numbers will grow in every developing region except China during the coming two decades. Worldwide, the number of women ages 15 to 19 will increase by 42 million between 1996 and 2020, rising to almost 300 million. However, the global increment hides the magnitude of the increase in the developing world, where virtually all of the increase will occur. The number of adolescent women will fall in the more developed world and in China over the period. The Focus Section of this report (Adolescent Fertility in the Developing World) describes the fertility and some of the reproductive health issues associated with this group.

Figure 12.
Urban Population by Region: 1996 and 2020

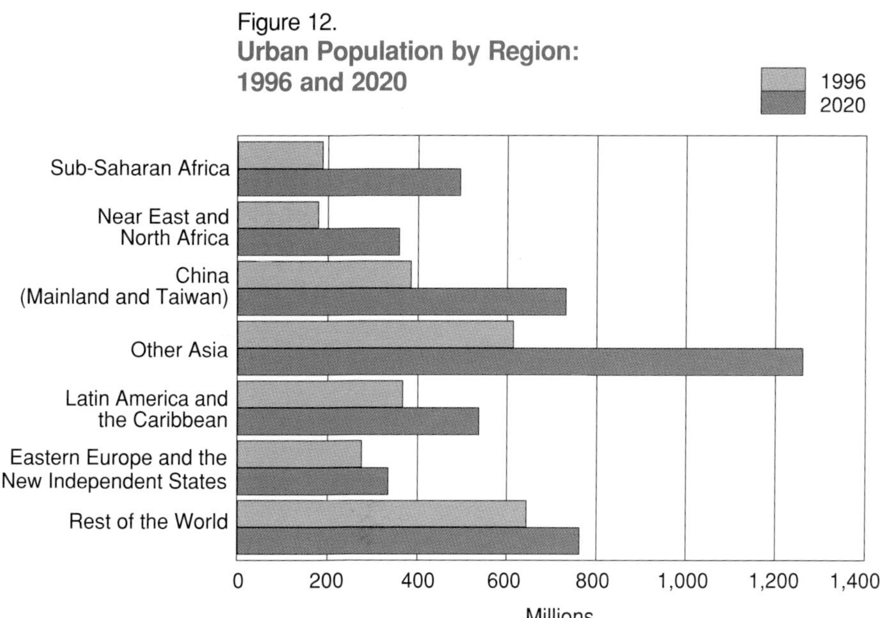

Source: United Nations (1995c) and U.S. Bureau of the Census, International Data Base.

Average Annual Rate of Growth of Urban Population: 1990 to 2020

	1990-1996	1996-2020
Sub-Saharan Africa	4.8	4.0
Near East and North Africa	3.7	2.9
China (Mainland and Taiwan)	4.0	2.7
Other Asia	3.4	3.0
Latin America and the Caribbean	2.4	1.6
Eastern Europe and the New Independent States	0.7	0.8
Rest of the World	0.9	0.7

Source: United Nations (1995c) and U.S. Bureau of the Census, International Data Base.

Urbanization Continues and Accelerates

The character of world, regional, and national populations is changing not only as a result of trends in fertility and mortality, but also through population redistribution within nations. Cities, towns, and urban agglomerations are expanding faster in every region of the world than the overall growth of population (figure 12).

From the ICPD Program of Action:

"The alarming consequences of urbanization visible in many countries are related to its rapid pace, to which Governments have been unable to respond with their current management capacities and practices." (section 9.1)

Consequently, people living in urban areas comprise a larger share of world population today than in the past, and they are projected to comprise an even larger share in the year 2020. Worldwide, urban population is expected to pass the 50 percent mark, rising from 46 to 58 percent of total population between 1996 and 2020. The most urbanized area in the developing world is Latin America and the Caribbean (already 75 percent and rising to 83 percent), while Sub-Saharan Africa will increase at the most rapid rate, growing from 31 percent urban today to 48 percent urban by the year 2020 (figure 13).

Urbanization represents a challenge to societies worldwide to provide for the needs of populations that are not only growing, not only changing markedly in composition, but also adopting significantly different, significantly broader consumption patterns over time.

Figure 13.
Shares of Regional Populations Living in Urban Areas: 1996 and 2020

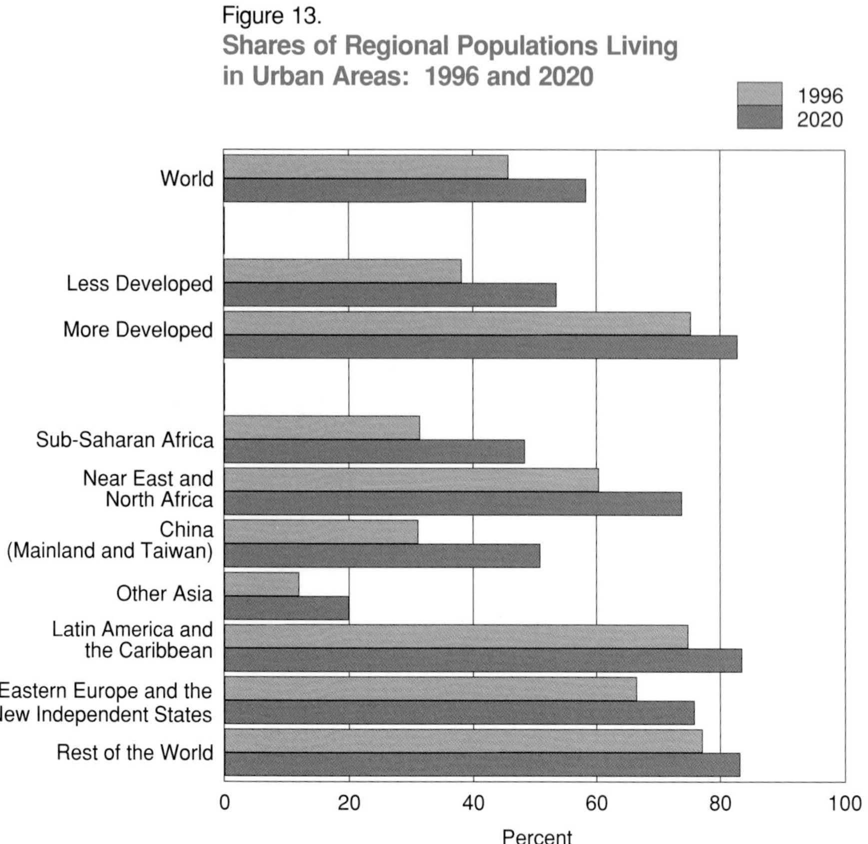

Sources: United Nations (1995c) and U.S. Bureau of the Census, International Data Base.

Components of Change

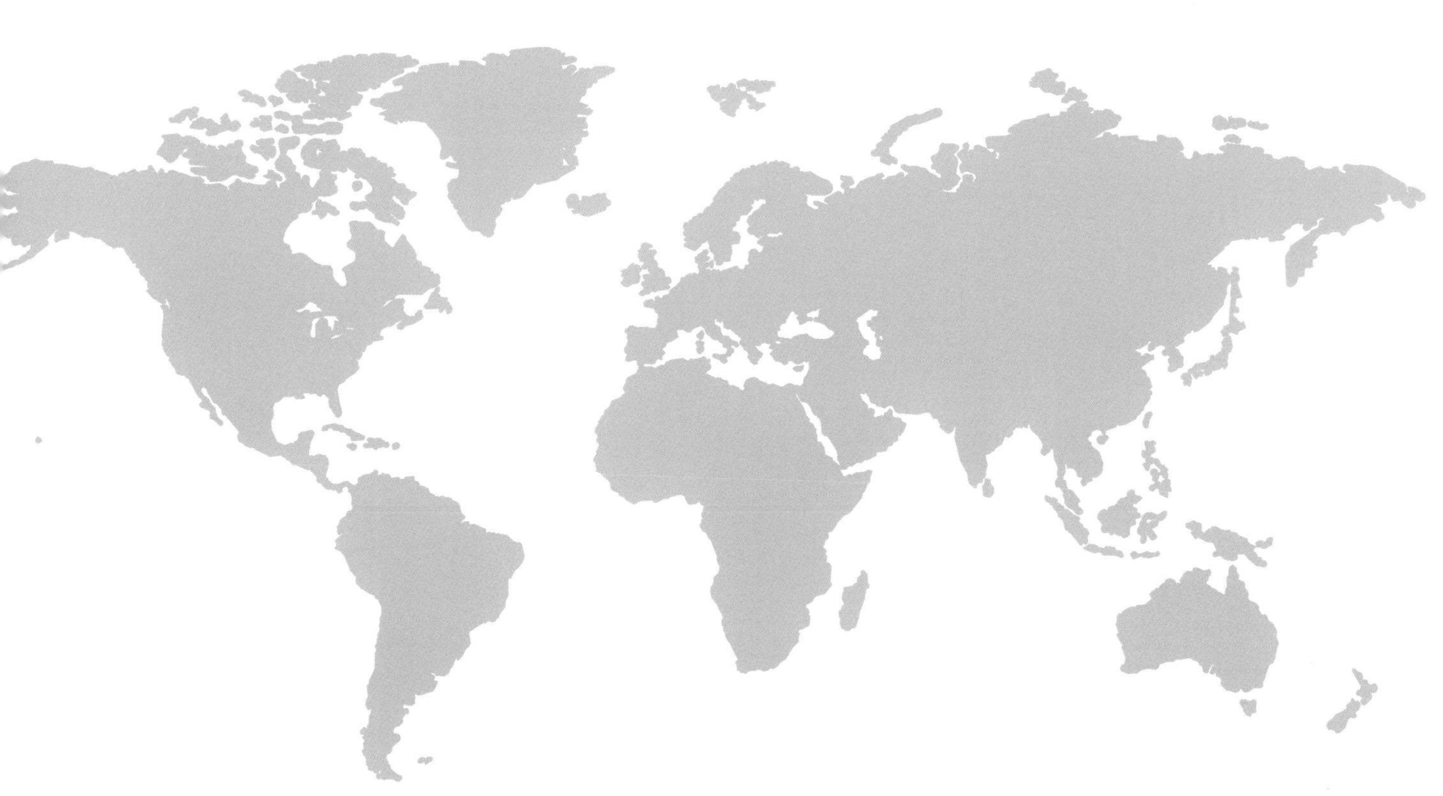

Components of Change

The demographic equation of births minus deaths plus or minus international migration determines whether populations grow or decline, and how much change occurs each year. In the developing countries of Africa, Asia, and Latin America, births typically exceed deaths by a substantial margin, and variation in fertility tends to explain most of country-to-country differences in growth. Where fertility levels are lower (as in less developed countries further along with their demographic transitions and in more developed countries), mortality has historically played a more important role in determining population growth. However, during the past decade, mortality has taken on new importance as a factor underlying population dynamics in a growing number of countries affected by the worldwide HIV/AIDS pandemic.

International migration also plays a part in determining the rate and direction of population change. International migration is particularly important to population growth in countries affected by mass movements of refugees (e.g., Afghanistan throughout the 1990's, Rwanda and her neighbors from 1994 to 1996, and the component parts of the former Yugoslavia). It is also important to countries serving as major destinations of economic migrants and asylum-seekers (e.g., Germany, for parts of Eastern Europe and the former Soviet Union; the United States, for migrants from Mexico, in particular).

At the global level, of course, population change is simply the difference between numbers of births and deaths.

From the ICPD Program of Action:

"... during the period 1985-1990, fertility ranged from an estimated 8.5 children per woman in Rwanda to 1.3 children per woman in Italy, while expectation of life at birth, an indicator of mortality conditions, ranged from an estimated 41 years in Sierra Leone to 78.3 years in Japan...[and] 44 percent of the world population were living in the 114 countries that had growth rates of more than 2 per cent per annum...

"These disparate levels and differentials have implications for the ultimate size and regional distribution of the world population and for the prospects for sustainable development." (section 6.2)

Figure 14.
World Births, Deaths, and Natural Increase, by Development Category: 1996 and 2020

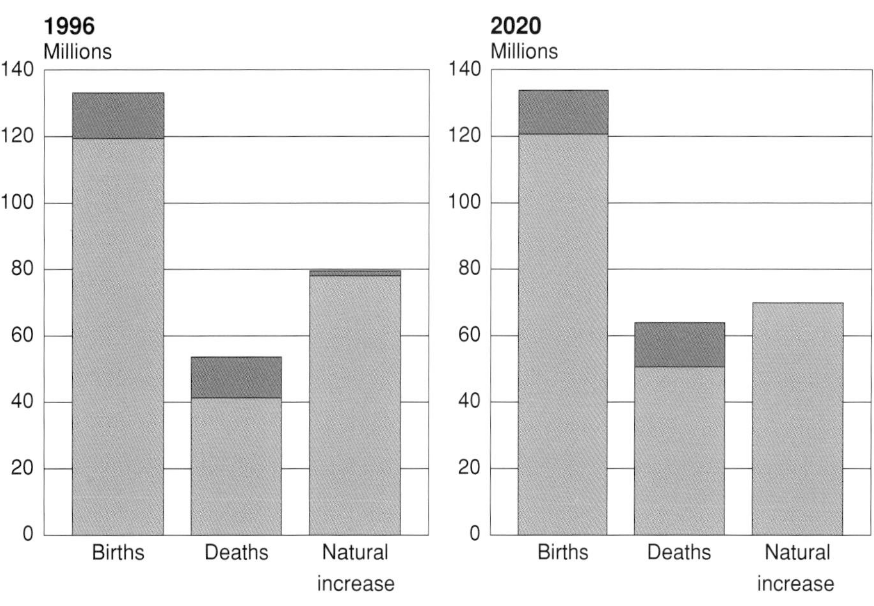

Source: Table A-3 and U.S. Bureau of the Census, International Data Base.

80 Million More People Added to World Population in 1996

Over 130 million babies will be born worldwide in 1996. Over 50 million people will die in 1996. The difference, amounting to 80 million persons, represents current world population increase (figure 14 and table A-3). The developing countries account for 98 percent of this increase, or some 78 million persons.

Most of World Growth Occurring in Developing Countries

The developing countries as a group account for about 80 percent of world population today, but about 90 percent of babies born (figure 15) because developing country birth rates are well above those typical of more developed countries. Developing countries have fewer deaths than might be expected given their higher mortality levels, because their age structures are relatively young. Indeed, the developing world's share of annual deaths worldwide is about the same as its share of world population in 1996. The difference between less developed countries' disproportionate share of births and these deaths account for the preponderance of net additions to world population in developing countries.

Twenty-five years from now, today's less developed nations are expected to have progressed further in their demographic transitions, and their fertility is expected to be markedly lower. However, the number of women of reproductive age will be much larger than today so that the less developed countries will continue to account for more than their proportionate share of births. In 2020, they will still account for about 90 percent of all births (and about 84 percent of total population).

Figure 15.
Share of World Population, Births, and Deaths, by Development Category: 1996 and 2020

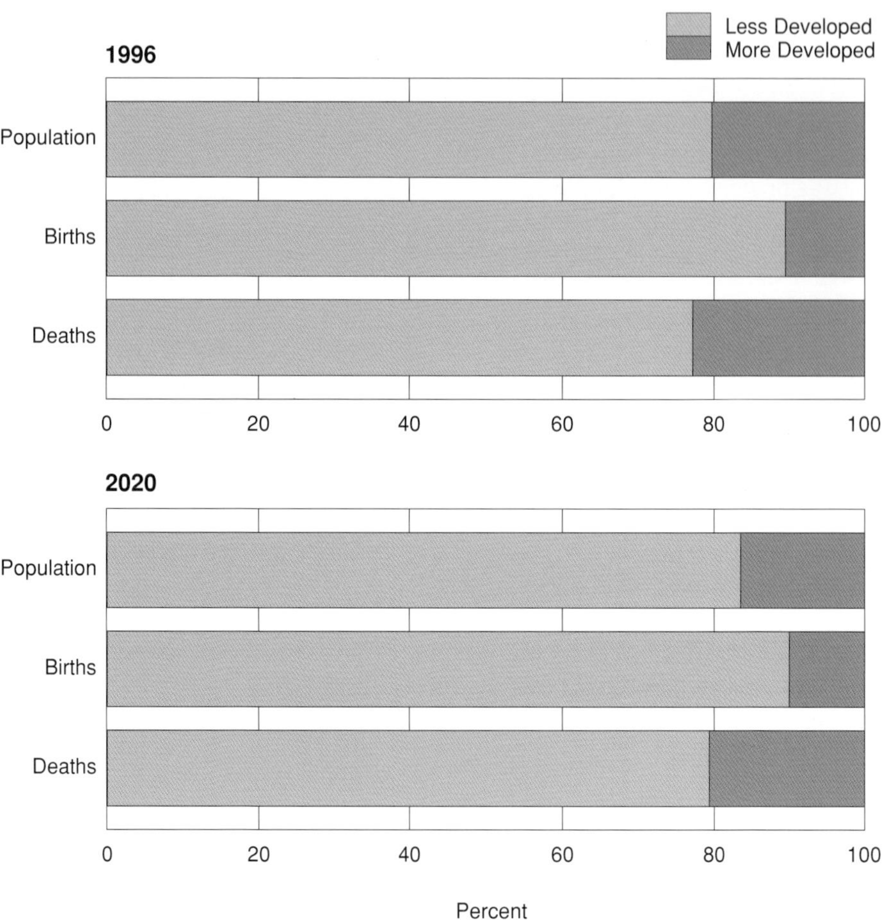

Source: Table A-3 and U.S. Bureau of the Census, International Data Base.

Figure 16.
Vital Rates by Region: 1996

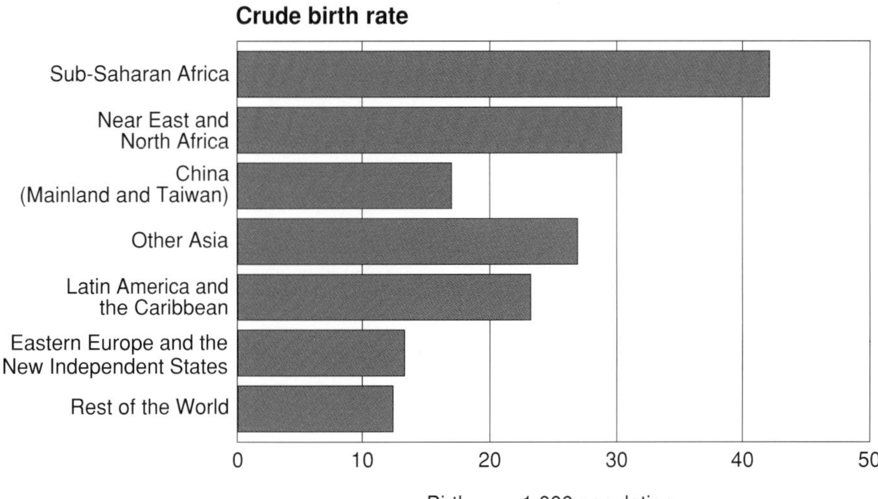

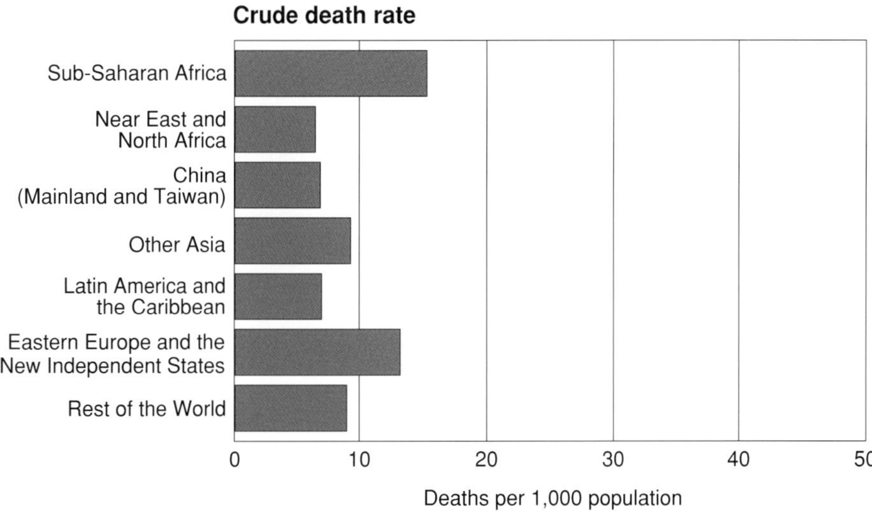

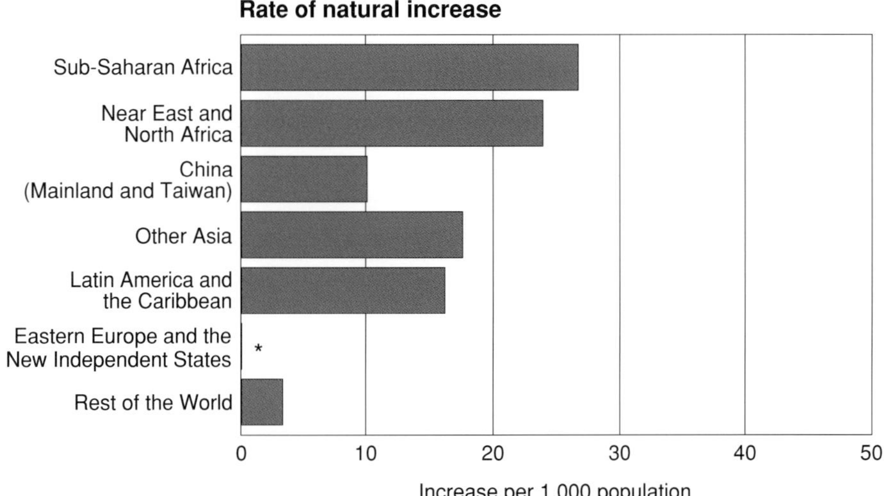

* Rate of natural increase for Eastern Europe and the New Independent States is -0.02
Source: Table A-3.

Global Crude Birth Rate of 23 per Thousand Population Is an Average of Widely Varying Rates

Worldwide there are about 23 births for each 1,000 inhabitants, but this average masks wide regional differences in fertility (table A-5 and figure 16). Sub-Saharan Africa's birth rate is by far the highest, with an average of 42 births per 1,000 population. China has the lowest rate among developing regions. However, the lowest crude birth rate worldwide is found in Western Europe, which, at about 10 births per 1,000, is one-fourth that of Sub-Saharan Africa. Over the next quarter century, crude birth rates are projected to fall by about 27 percent in the developing world; by less (10 percent), in the more developed world.

Global Crude Death Rate of 9 per Thousand Reflects Narrower Range of Rates Across Regions

While significant disparities exist in mortality among regions, the range in crude death rates is narrower among regions than is the range in birth rates (figure 16). Sub-Saharan Africa has the highest crude death rate of the major world regions today: 15 per 1,000 population. The crude death rate of Eastern Europe and the New Independent States is as high at 13 per 1,000. Crude death rates for the other regions cluster in the 7 to 9 per 1,000 range. Though its underlying mortality level is relatively low, the crude death rate for the more developed countries is comparable to that of other regions because there are relatively more older people. The effect of older population is also seen in the projected crude death rates, which will fall in most countries, but will increase in the more developed regions, and also in China.

Natural Increase Accounts for Most Population Growth in Developing World...

Regional crude rates of natural increase are the differences between regional birth rates and death rates. Because regional death rates vary less than birth rates, natural increase tends to reflect regional birth rates (table A-3 and figure 16).

Sub-Saharan Africa's rate of natural increase, at roughly 27 per thousand per year, exceeds that of all other regions. The other developing regions have crude rates of increase ranging from 16 for Latin America and the Caribbean to 24 for the Near East and North Africa; i.e., population is growing faster where the crude birth rate is higher. In contrast, the rest of the world (which includes many of the more developed countries) has a crude rate of natural increase of only 3 per thousand.

...While International Migration Boosts Growth of More Developed Countries

Additions to African, Asian, Near Eastern, and Latin American populations are determined mostly by natural increase. Net international migration accounts for only a small part of the growth in most countries of those regions. However, emigration tempers regional population growth in Latin America and the Caribbean.

Net international migration accounts for a larger share of regional population growth in Eastern Europe and the New Independent States, and in Western Europe, North America, Japan and Oceania taken together. Over 40 percent of the growth of the Rest of the World and virtually all of the growth of Eastern Europe and the NIS in 1996 is through international migration.

Components of Change: 1996
(Per 1,000 population)

	Natural increase	Net migration
Sub-Saharan Africa	+26.7	−0.1
Near East and North Africa	+23.9	+0.5
China (Mainland and Taiwan)	+10.1	−0.3
Other Asia	+17.6	−0.1
Latin America and the Caribbean	+16.2	−1.1
Eastern Europe and the New Independent States	−0.02	+0.2
Rest of the World	+3.3	+2.5

Figure 17.
Distribution of World Births by Country: 1996 and 2020

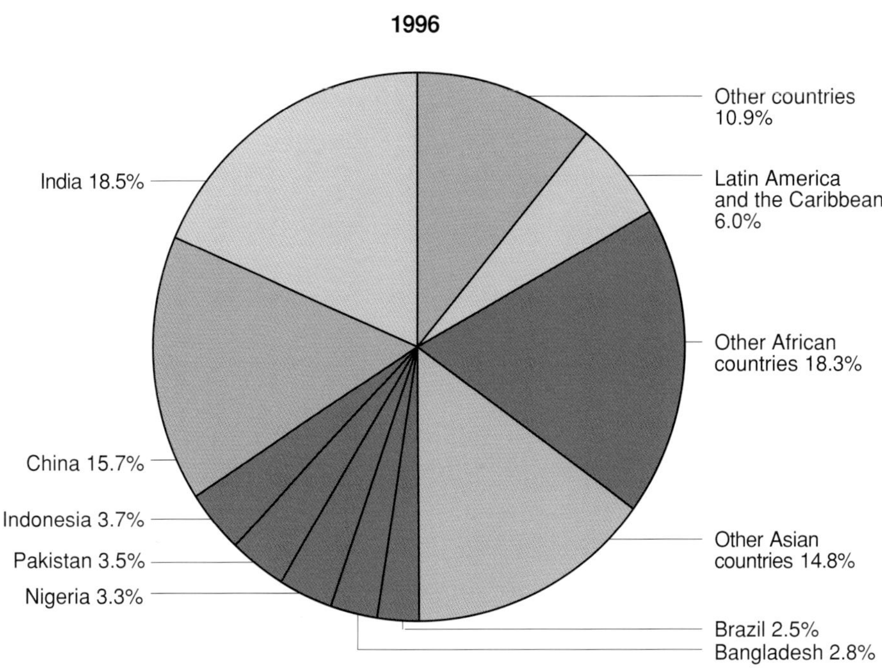

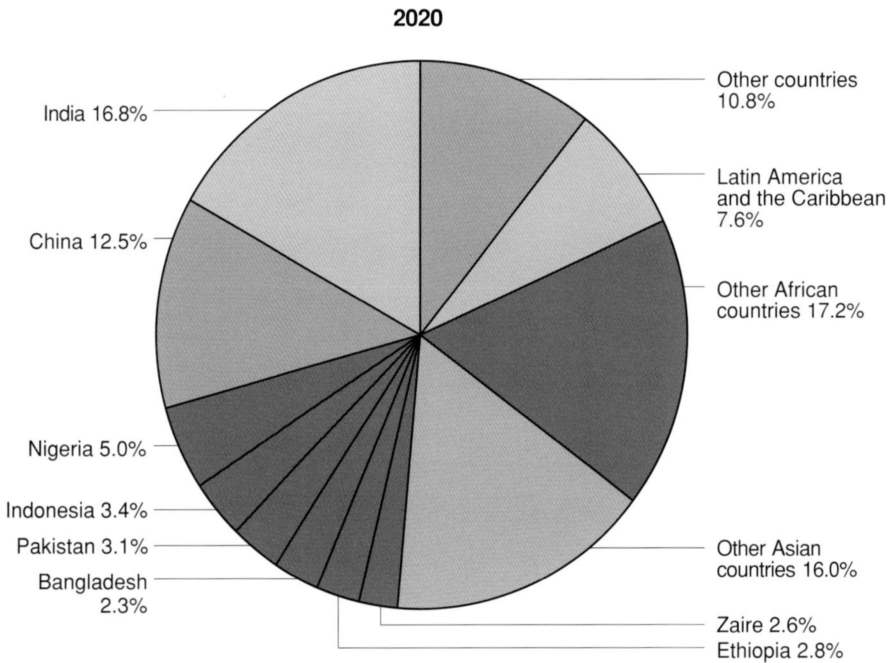

Note: China includes Mainland China and Taiwan.
Source: U.S. Bureau of the Census, International Data Base.

Fertility

One Out of Every Three Babies Is Born in India or China

Nearly 25 million babies will be born in India in 1996, more than in any other country in the world (table A-5). China has a larger population, and far more women of reproductive age (table A-6), but only 21 million babies will be born in China this year. India's much higher birth rate and its growing population (which is smaller than China's but nonetheless approaching one billion persons) together account for its distinction as the nation with the largest number of babies born in 1996. India and China together account for over a third of all babies born this year (figure 17).

Five other developing countries with large populations and relatively high fertility together account for another 15 percent of babies born in 1996. The other 220 nations of the world account for the other half of all births taking place this year.

During the coming 25 years, births will become somewhat less concentrated, largely because proportionately few children will be born in China, where the total fertility rate (TFR)[1] has already fallen below the level of 2 children per woman, and in India, where fertility is projected to fall to 2.2 children per woman by the year 2020.

[1] The total fertility rate is normally defined as the average number of children a woman would have over her reproductive lifetime if current age-specific fertility rates were to remain constant. While current rates seldom remain fixed, particularly in transitional countries, TFR provides a useful summary measure of the general level of fertility in a population, unaffected by age-composition effects.

At Least 132 Million Births Occur Every Year Despite Falling Fertility

For at least the next quarter century some 132 to 135 million births will occur annually — even though fertility rates are expected to fall during this period (figure 18). The plateau in births while fertility falls reflects the still increasing numbers of women of reproductive age, particularly in much of the developing world.

The leveling-off in births also hides significant variation among world regions. Large declines in the numbers of births in some regions (notably China and Other Asia) are being offset by increases in Sub-Saharan Africa and the Near East. The annual number of births in Sub-Saharan Africa will increase by about 8 million to 32.8 million in 2020.

Figure 18.
World Births and Total Fertility Rates: 1996 to 2020

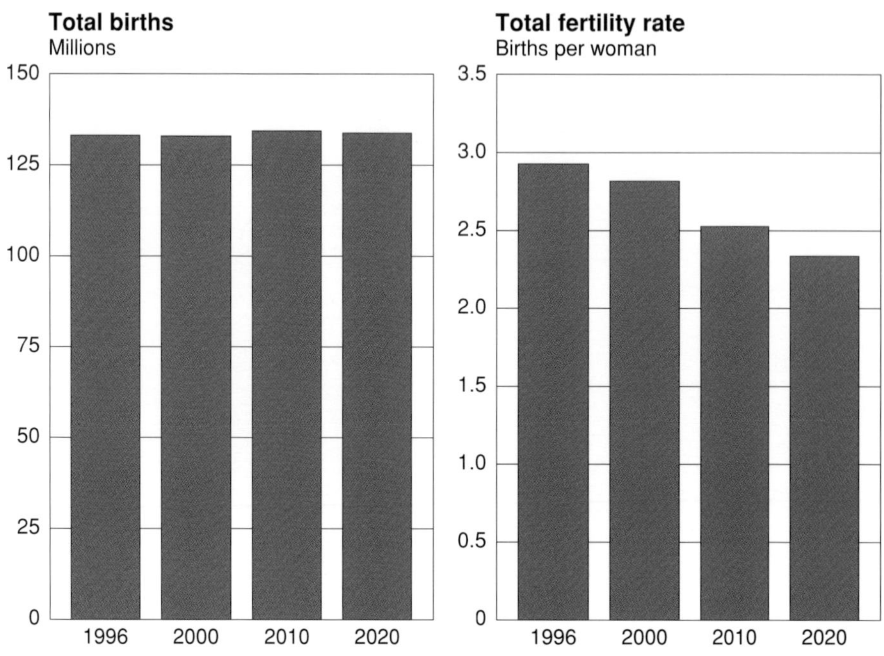

Source: Tables A-5 and A-8 and U.S. Bureau of the Census, International Data Base.

Average Family Size Ranges From 6 in Sub-Saharan Africa to 1.5 in Europe

Sub-Saharan Africa has the highest total fertility rate in 1996, and is expected to retain that distinction through the year 2020, even as its TFR falls from about 6 children per woman to around 4 children per woman (figure 19).

Though total fertility rates are lower in Latin America and the Caribbean, Asia, and the Near East and North Africa than in Sub-Saharan Africa, all currently less developed regions except China still have total fertility rates consistent with moderate to rapid population growth. Fertility is expected to decline in the rest of Asia, the Near East and North Africa, and Latin America, to levels in the 2- to 3-child family range by year 2020.

Figure 19.
Total Fertility Rates by Region: 1996 and 2020

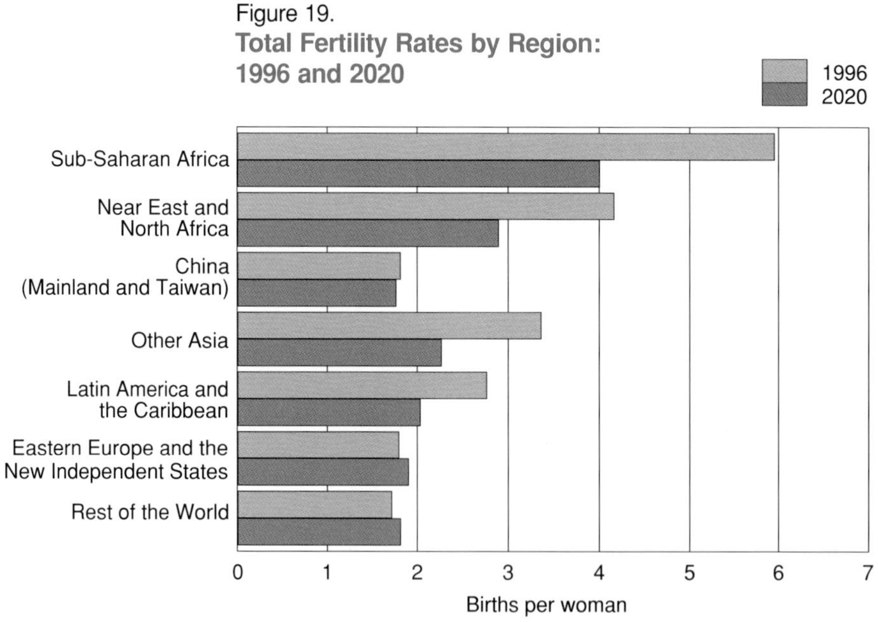

Source: Table A-8.

Countries With Largest Projected Fertility Declines

	Total fertility rate	
1990 to 2000	1990	2000
Iran	6.0	3.9
Mongolia	4.5	2.5
Kenya	5.7	3.7
Zimbabwe	5.3	3.5
Qatar	4.6	2.9
Ghana	5.7	4.0
Pakistan	6.2	4.6
Jordan	6.1	4.5
Malawi	6.9	5.3
Solomon Islands	6.3	4.8
2000 to 2010	2000	2010
Syria	5.2	3.6
Gaza Strip	7.3	5.9
Solomon Islands	4.8	3.4
Pakistan	4.6	3.2
Malawi	5.3	3.9
Mozambique	5.8	4.5
Iran	3.9	2.6
Yemen	6.9	5.6
Haiti	5.2	3.9
Laos	5.4	4.2

Nearly all of the more developed countries have fertility rates of 2.1 or fewer children per woman, roughly the level of fertility needed for population replacement through natural increase.

Twenty-eight developing countries also have achieved low TFR's of 2.1 or fewer children per woman (figure 20). Together, these nations have a quarter of the world's population.

The others, comprising primarily less developed, higher fertility countries, include most African, Asian, Latin American, North Africa and Near East countries. Six of the ten highest fertility countries are in Sub-Saharan Africa. Two dozen Sub-Saharan African countries have fertility in excess of six children per woman.

Transition to Lower Fertility Is Occurring in All Developing Regions

Based on current trends, 29 countries are likely to reduce their total fertility rates by at least one child per woman during the current decade (table A-8). An extension of these trends beyond the turn of the century indicates that 22 countries are likely to see declines of this size in TFR during the next decade.

Among the 10 countries with the largest TFR declines during the 1990 to 2000 period, 4 are in Sub-Saharan Africa, 2 are in North Africa or the Near East, 3 are in Asia, and 1 is in Oceania. Five of the ten are large countries, with populations in 1996 of at least 10 million. The countries with the largest projected declines in fertility during the 2000 to 2010 period are also all developing countries.

Figure 20.
Total Fertility Rates: 1996

Births per Women

Rank in parentheses: 1 = Country with highest rate.

6.0 or above

Afghanistan (31)
Angola (23)
Benin (13)
Burkina Faso (10)
Burundi (17)
Cape Verde (32)
Comoros (12)
Côte d'Ivoire (30)
Djibouti (34)
Eritrea (19)
Ethiopia (6)
Gambia, The (29)
Gaza Strip (1)
Iraq (21)
Liberia (28)
Libya (25)
Maldives (35)
Mali (4)
Marshall Islands (9)
Mauritania (8)
Mayotte (15)
Mozambique (27)
Niger (2)
Nigeria (26)
Oman (33)
Saudi Arabia (20)
Senegal (24)
Sierra Leone (22)
Somalia (5)
Swaziland (36)
Togo (11)
Uganda (16)
Western Sahara (7)
Yemen (3)
Zaire (14)
Zambia (18)

From 4 to 5.9

American Samoa (73)
Belize (75)
Bhutan (52)
Bolivia (72)
Botswana (71)
Cambodia (45)
Cameroon (37)
Central African Republic (50)
Chad (44)
Congo (55)
Equatorial Guinea (54)
Ghana (61)
Guatemala (62)
Guinea (46)
Guinea-Bissau (51)
Haiti (47)
Honduras (66)
Iran (59)
Jordan (57)
Kenya (65)
Laos (43)
Lesotho (69)
Madagascar (42)
Malawi (39)
Namibia (56)
Nepal (58)
Nicaragua (77)
Pakistan (53)
Papua New Guinea (64)
Paraguay (74)
Qatar (70)
Rwanda (38)
Sao Tome and Principe (68)
Solomon Islands (49)
Sudan (41)
Syria (40)
Tajikistan (67)
Tanzania (48)
United Arab Emirates (63)
Vanuatu (78)
West Bank (60)
Zimbabwe (76)

From 3 to 3.9

Algeria (88)
Anguilla (107)
Bahrain (104)
Bangladesh (91)
Brunei (95)
Burma (82)
Cook Islands (98)
Egypt (89)
El Salvador (101)
Federated States of Micronesia (79)
French Guiana (94)
French Polynesia (97)
Gabon (81)
Grenada (83)
India (102)
Kiribati (86)
Kyrgyzstan (100)
Lebanon (99)
Malaysia (96)
Mexico (108)
Mongolia (106)
Morocco (90)
Peru (105)
Philippines (84)
South Africa (93)
Tonga (92)
Turkmenistan (87)
Tuvalu (103)
Uzbekistan (85)
Western Samoa (80)

Source: Table A-8.

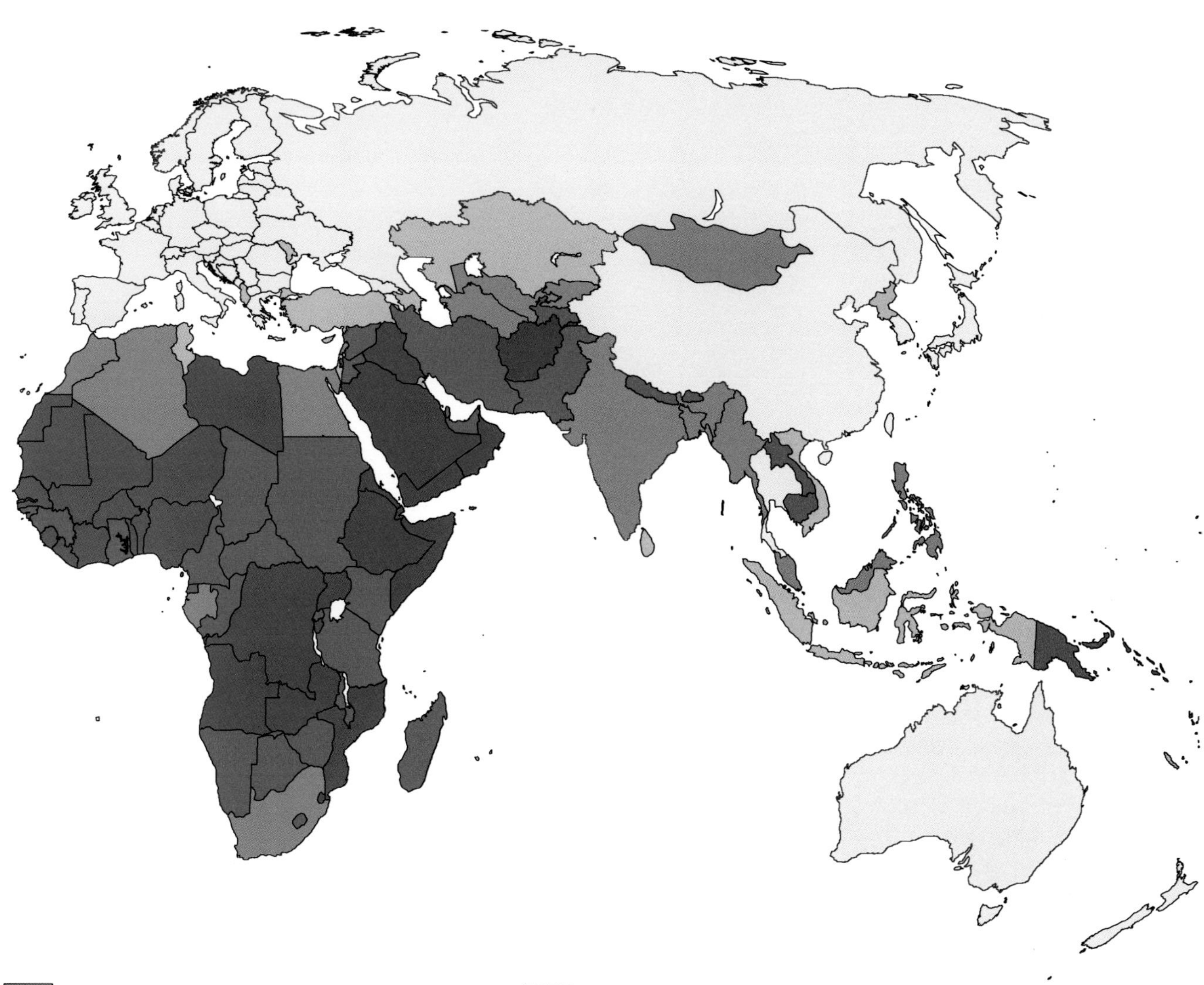

From 2.1 to 2.9

Albania (125)
Argentina (127)
Azerbaijan (126)
Brazil (135)
British Virgin Islands (140)
Chile (143)
Colombia (134)
Costa Rica (111)
Cyprus (146)
Dominican Republic (124)
Ecuador (112)
Faroe Islands (131)
Fiji (114)
Gibraltar (141)
Greenland (144)
Guam (142)
Guyana (145)
Indonesia (120)
Israel (117)
Jamaica (132)
Kazakstan (133)
Kuwait (115)
Mauritius (147)
Moldova (148)
New Caledonia (129)
North Korea (137)
Northern Mariana Is. (122)
Palau (116)
Panama (119)
Reunion (118)
Saint Kitts and Nevis (130)
Saint Lucia (138)
Suriname (123)
Tunisia (110)
Turkey (128)
Uruguay (136)
Venezuela (113)
Vietnam (121)
Virgin Islands (139)
Wallis and Futuna (109)

Under 2.1

Andorra (185)
Antigua and Barbuda (192)
Armenia (152)
Aruba (174)
Australia (170)
Austria (209)
Bahamas, The (159)
Barbados (180)
Belarus (191)
Belgium (199)
Bermuda (178)
Bosnia and Herzegovina (227)
Bulgaria (224)
Canada (175)
Cayman Islands (215)
China, Mainland (173)
China, Taiwan (183)
Croatia (216)
Cuba (193)
Czech Republic (217)
Denmark (190)
Dominica (163)
Estonia (202)
Finland (179)
France (208)
Georgia (188)
Germany (219)
Greece (211)
Guadeloupe (165)
Guernsey (184)
Hong Kong (220)
Hungary (206)
Iceland (156)
Ireland (164)
Isle of Man (177)
Italy (221)
Japan (212)
Jersey (213)
Latvia (198)
Liechtenstein (210)
Lithuania (181)
Luxembourg (194)
Macau (207)
Macedonia, The Former Yugoslav Rep. of (171)
Malta (166)
Martinique (176)
Monaco (187)
Montenegro (204)
Montserrat (161)
Nauru (151)
Netherlands (203)
Netherlands Antilles (168)
New Zealand (155)
Norway (186)
Poland (189)
Portugal (218)
Puerto Rico (160)
Romania (223)
Russia (214)
Saint Helena (226)
Saint Pierre and Miquelon (197)
Saint Vincent and the Grenadines (154)
San Marino (205)
Serbia (157)
Seychelles (149)
Singapore (195)
Slovakia (196)
Slovenia (225)
South Korea (182)
Spain (222)
Sri Lanka (153)
Sweden (162)
Switzerland (200)
Thailand (167)
Trinidad and Tobago (158)
Turks and Caicos Is. (169)
Ukraine (201)
United Kingdom (172)
United States (150)

Mortality

Gap in Life Expectancy Among World Regions Exceeds 20 Years...

Of 100 babies born this year in Sub-Saharan Africa, 9 will die before reaching age 1. In the world's more developed countries, it will take about 60 years for these 9 deaths to occur. The difference reflects a continuing gap in mortality levels faced by the populations of the world's more and less developed countries, and by the populations of the various regions of the developing world.

A child born in Sub-Saharan Africa can expect to live, on average, only about 50 years, while a child born in one of the more developed countries of the world can expect to live to age 74, or nearly 50 percent longer. Life expectancy at birth, or the average number of years a person can expect to live during his or her lifetime, is increasing in most, but not all, countries of the world. Mean levels are now over 60 years in all major regions of the world except Sub-Saharan Africa; life expectancy is 70 years in China, 68 years in Latin America and the Caribbean, and 67 years in the Near East and North Africa (table A-10). In all regions, women live longer than men (figure 21).

Countries with the lowest life expectancies are found predominantly in Sub-Saharan Africa: the 10 countries with the lowest life expectancies are in this region and 7 of these 10 countries are in HIV/AIDS-affected countries.[2] Their higher mortality is attributable in large part to excess deaths due to HIV/AIDS.

...and Is Only Slowly Narrowing

Over the course of the coming 25 years, the gap between mean life expectancy at birth for more developed countries and less developed regions will close only a little. Regional mean life expectancy at birth for less developed countries is projected to increase by about 6 years between now and the year 2020; that for more developed countries, by about 5 years. Gains in life expectancy made in some developing countries are likely to be offset by a rise in mortality (and a corresponding fall in life expectancy) in HIV/AIDS-affected countries of the region (figure 27, see below).

[2] To be more precise, the countries are among the 23 HIV/AIDS-affected countries considered by the Bureau of the Census to have AIDS-related mortality high enough to affect projections significantly. This is not to say the other 3 countries have no AIDS-related mortality.

Figure 21.
Life Expectancy at Birth by Sex and Region: 1996 and 2020

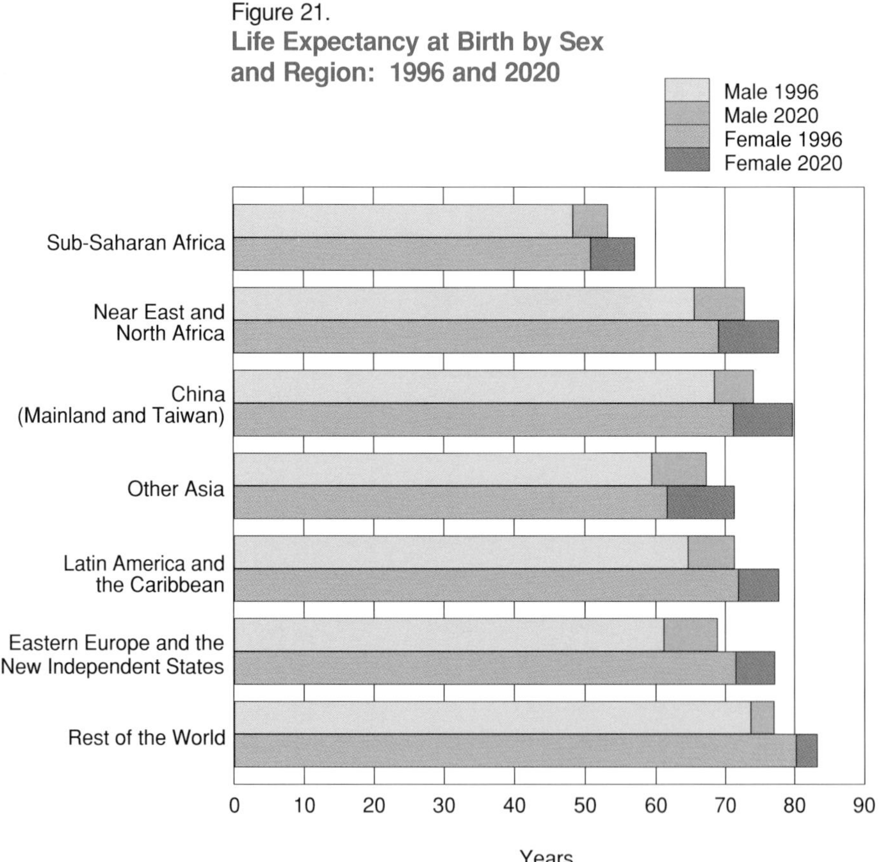

Source: Table A-10.

Figure 22.
Infant Mortality Rates by Sex and Region: 1996 and 2020

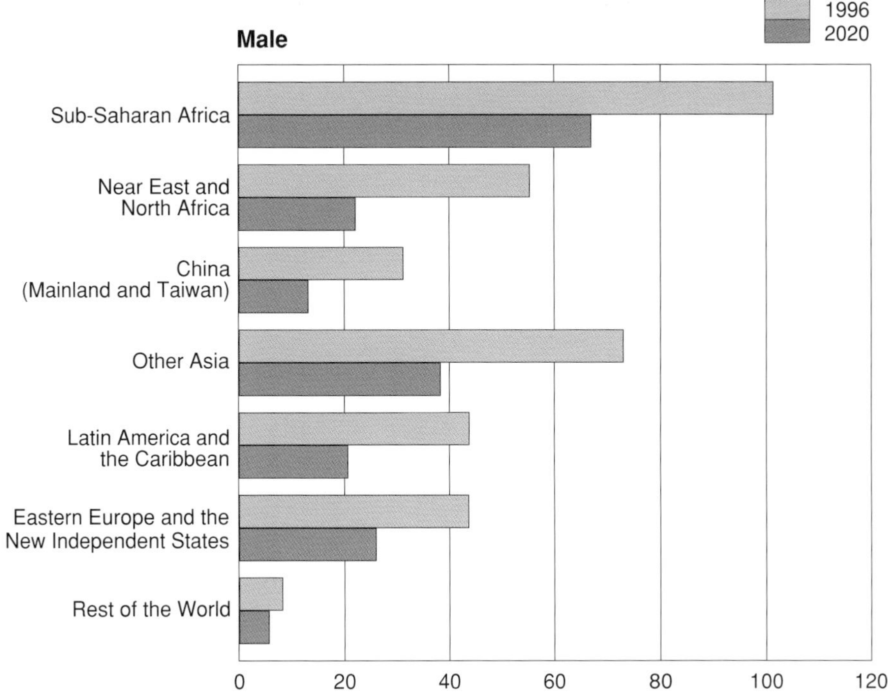

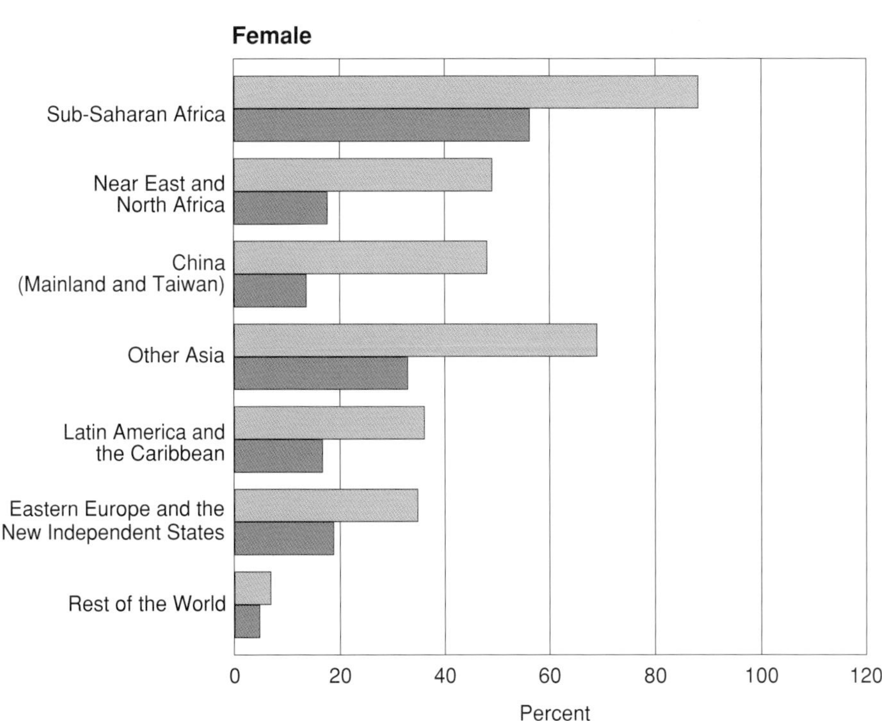

Source: Table A-9 and U.S. Bureau of the Census, International Data Base.

Sub-Saharan Africa Has the Highest Infant Mortality Rates

Sub-Saharan Africa, which has the lowest mean life expectancy of any world region, also has the highest infant mortality (95 infant deaths per 1,000 live births for both sexes combined (table A-9)). Figure 22 shows that infant mortality for both males and females is higher in Sub-Saharan Africa than in other world regions.

As overall health conditions improve, reductions in infant (and child) mortality can be precipitous. In the Near East and North Africa, infant mortality rates (IMR's) have declined by a third during the past 10 years (from 78 per 1,000 births in 1986 to 52 in 1996). In Asia (excluding China and Japan), infant mortality was cut by 25 percent (falling from 95 per 1,000 to 71 per 1,000 live births during the same period). In the other major developing regions, the decline has been less steep but substantial nonetheless. Between 1996 and the year 2020, the largest reductions in infant mortality are expected in Asia (where IMR is projected to decrease from 71 to 36 infant deaths per 1,000 live births), Sub-Saharan Africa, and the Near East and North Africa (both projected to decline by more than 30 per 1,000).

Of Every 1,000 Infants Born in 30 Countries, 100 Die Before First Birthday

Regional averages mask country-to-country variations in infant mortality rates (figure 23). While there are more high infant mortality countries in Sub-Saharan Africa than in any other world region, 23 countries in that region are joined by 7 countries from other regions in having at least 1 in every 10 infants dying before its first birthday.

Figure 23.
Infant Mortality Rates: 1996

Infant Deaths per 1,000 Live Births
Rank in parentheses: 1 = Country with highest rate.

Over 100

Afghanistan (1)
Angola (4)
Bangladesh (29)
Benin (26)
Bhutan (16)
Burkina Faso (14)
Burundi (30)
Cambodia (23)
Central African Republic (19)
Chad (10)
Congo (21)
Djibouti (24)
Eritrea (11)
Ethiopia (8)
Gambia, The (13)
Guinea (6)
Guinea-Bissau (17)
Haiti (27)
Liberia (20)
Malawi (3)
Mali (28)
Mozambique (7)
Niger (15)
Rwanda (12)
Sierra Leone (5)
Somalia (9)
Tajikistan (18)
Tanzania (25)
Western Sahara (2)
Zaire (22)

From 50 to 99

Azerbaijan (54)
Bolivia (61)
Botswana (73)
Brazil (70)
Burma (45)
Cameroon (49)
Cape Verde (72)
Comoros (52)
Côte d'Ivoire (41)
Egypt (55)
Equatorial Guinea (33)
Gabon (38)
Ghana (46)
Guatemala (77)
Guyana (76)
India (59)
Indonesia (65)
Iran (74)
Iraq (68)
Kazakstan (64)
Kenya (71)
Kiribati (32)
Kyrgyzstan (50)
Laos (35)
Lesotho (43)
Libya (69)
Madagascar (37)
Mauritania (42)
Mayotte (53)
Mongolia (60)
Nepal (48)
Nigeria (57)
Pakistan (34)
Papua New Guinea (67)
Peru (75)
Sao Tome and Principe (66)
Senegal (63)
Sudan (51)
Swaziland (39)
Togo (40)
Turkmenistan (44)
Uganda (31)
Uzbekistan (47)
Vanuatu (62)
Yemen (58)
Zambia (36)
Zimbabwe (56)

From 30 to 49

Albania (78)
Algeria (80)
Armenia (95)
Belize (105)
Bosnia and
 Herzegovina (89)
China, Mainland (94)
Dominican Republic (81)
Ecuador (103)
El Salvador (107)
Federated States of
 Micronesia (100)
Honduras (91)
Jordan (108)
Lebanon (98)
Maldives (84)
Marshall Islands (85)
Moldova (82)
Morocco (90)
Namibia (83)
Nauru (92)
Nicaragua (87)
Northern Mariana Island (97)
Philippines (99)
Saint Helena (101)
Saudi Arabia (86)
South Africa (79)
Syria (93)
Thailand (106)
Tunisia (102)
Turkey (88)
Vietnam (96)
Western Samoa (104)

Source: Table A-9.

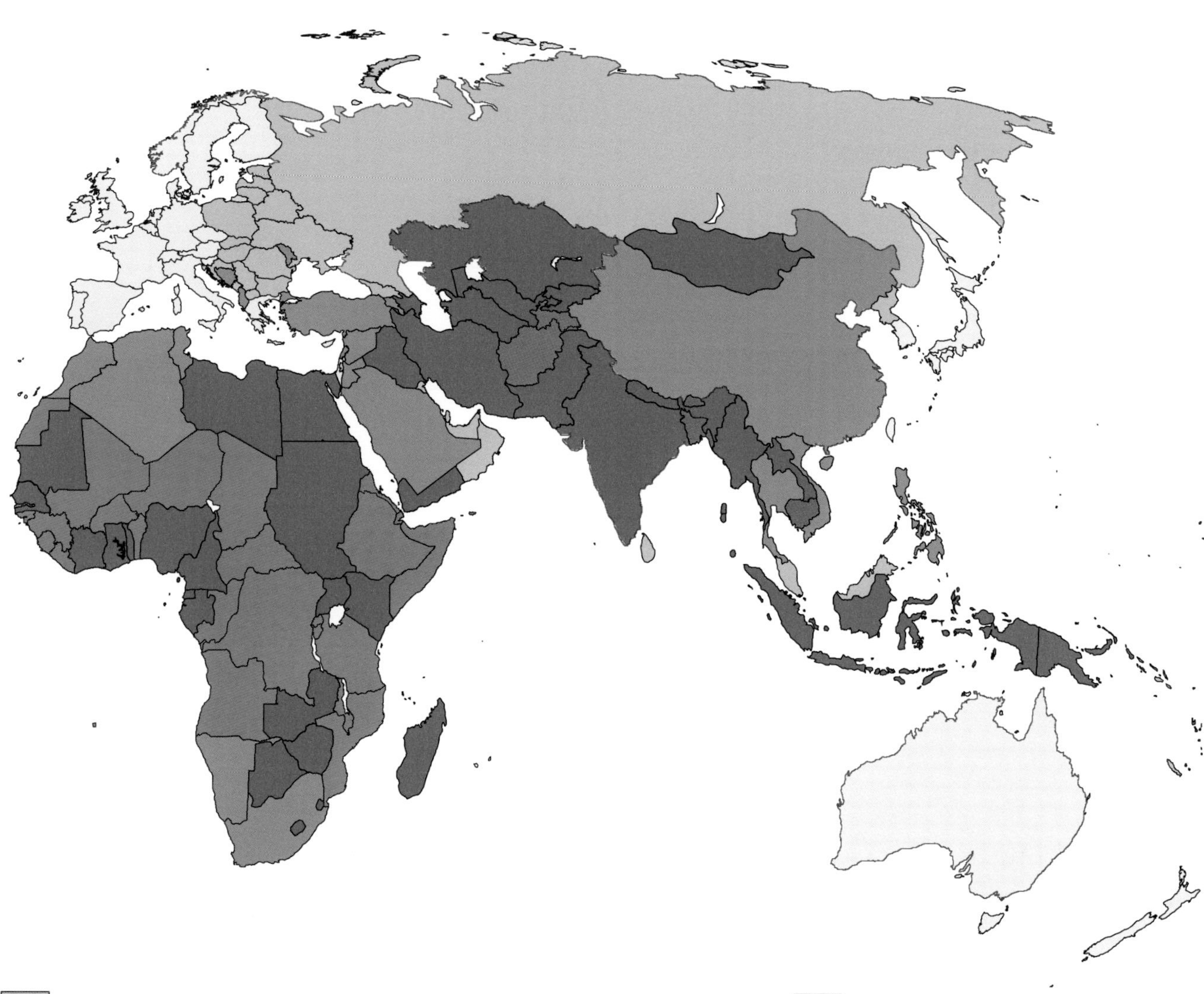

From 10 to 29

American Samoa (144)
Anguilla (151)
Antigua and Barbuda (150)
Argentina (113)
Bahamas, The (130)
Bahrain (152)
Barbados (145)
Belarus (164)
Bermuda (165)
British Virgin Islands (142)
Brunei (126)
Bulgaria (155)
Chile (162)
Colombia (121)
Cook Islands (124)
Costa Rica (163)
Croatia (176)
Estonia (148)
Fiji (147)
French Guiana (159)
French Polynesia (160)
Gaza Strip (114)
Georgia (135)
Greenland (128)
Grenada (172)
Guam (158)
Hungary (171)
Jamaica (156)
Kuwait (174)
Latvia (136)
Lithuania (153)
Macedonia, The Former
Yugoslav Rep. of (109)
Malaysia (127)
Mauritius (149)
Mexico (123)
Montenegro (116)
Montserrat (173)
New Caledonia (161)
North Korea (119)
Oman (117)
Palau (122)
Panama (110)
Paraguay (131)
Poland (170)
Puerto Rico (169)
Qatar (141)
Romania (132)
Russia (125)
Saint Kitts and Nevis (143)
Saint Lucia (139)
Saint Pierre and Miquelon (177)
Saint Vincent and the
Grenadines (154)
Serbia (133)
Seychelles (168)
Slovakia (175)
Solomon Islands (120)
Sri Lanka (137)
Suriname (112)
Tonga (140)
Trinidad and Tobago (146)
Turks and Caicos Is. (166)
Tuvalu (115)
Ukraine (134)
United Arab Emirates (138)
Uruguay (157)
Venezuela (111)
Virgin Islands (167)
Wallis and Futuna (129)
West Bank (118)

Under 10

Andorra (194)
Aruba (185)
Australia (217)
Austria (205)
Belgium (204)
Canada (212)
Cayman Islands (180)
China, Taiwan (199)
Cuba (188)
Cyprus (181)
Czech Republic (182)
Denmark (207)
Dominica (178)
Faroe Islands (191)
Finland (222)
France (219)
Germany (214)
Gibraltar (190)
Greece (187)
Guadeloupe (183)
Guernsey (210)
Hong Kong (223)
Iceland (227)
Ireland (200)
Isle of Man (189)
Israel (186)
Italy (201)
Japan (226)
Jersey (225)
Liechtenstein (220)
Luxembourg (208)
Macau (221)
Malta (195)
Martinique (198)
Monaco (202)
Netherlands (215)
Netherlands Antilles (179)
New Zealand (206)
Norway (213)
Portugal (192)
Reunion (196)
San Marino (216)
Singapore (224)
Slovenia (197)
South Korea (184)
Spain (203)
Sweden (218)
Switzerland (211)
United Kingdom (209)
United States (193)

Afghanistan, Western Sahara, Malawi, Angola, and Sierra Leone — all with infant deaths over 135 per 1,000 live births — have the highest infant mortality rates in 1996.

Greatest Reductions in Infant Mortality Taking Place in the Near East and North Africa

All nations are working to reduce infant mortality, and mortality overall, in keeping with goals set out in Cairo. During the decade of the 1990's the greatest gains are being made in the Near East and North Africa, where the IMR is expected to decline from a regional average of about 66 infant deaths per 1,000 live births in 1990 to 44 infant deaths per 1,000 births in the year 2000. Five of the ten countries with the largest IMR declines during the 1990 to 2000 period are from this region.

In general, the less developed regions of the world are expected to make substantial gains in reducing infant mortality over the next 25 years (figure 22).

In addition to the Near East and North Africa, major gains during the 1990's are underway in China (a projected decrease by year 2000 of 20 infant deaths per 1,000 live births from 51.6 in 1990) and the rest of Asia (a decrease of 17 from the 1990 regional mean of 81 per 1,000). Infant mortality actually appears to be rising in one region — Eastern Europe and the New Independent States — during the 1990's.

The Census Bureau's projections show infant mortality declining in all major world regions during the next decade (years 2000 to 2010). The largest absolute reductions in IMR after the turn of the century are likely to occur in the less developed countries of Asia (excluding China),

Countries With Largest Projected Infant Mortality Declines

Male

	Infant mortality rate	
1990 to 2000	1990	2000
Yemen	99	61
Maldives	68	35
Morocco	70	37
Angola	171	138
Sierra Leone	171	139
Afghanistan	173	142
Western Sahara	171	139
Mozambique	152	123
Turkey	66	37
Laos	124	95
2000 to 2010	2000	2010
Angola	138	106
Sierra Leone	139	107
Afghanistan	142	111
Mozambique	123	93
Guinea	135	109
Yemen	61	35
Gambia, The	119	93
Laos	95	69
Somalia	120	96
Tajikistan	124	100

Female

	Infant mortality rate	
1990 to 2000	1990	2000
Yemen	89	55
Maldives	70	35
Western Sahara	159	127
Angola	145	114
Sierra Leone	138	107
Morocco	59	29
Iran	73	44
Afghanistan	162	133
Saudi Arabia	63	34
Turkey	57	30
2000 to 2010	2000	2010
Angola	114	84
Afghanistan	133	103
Sierra Leone	107	78
Guinea	112	87
Yemen	55	30
Gambia, The	96	71
Mozambique	107	83
Benin	86	64
Liberia	90	68
Bhutan	110	88

Figure 24.
Distribution of World Infant Deaths by Country: 1996 and 2020

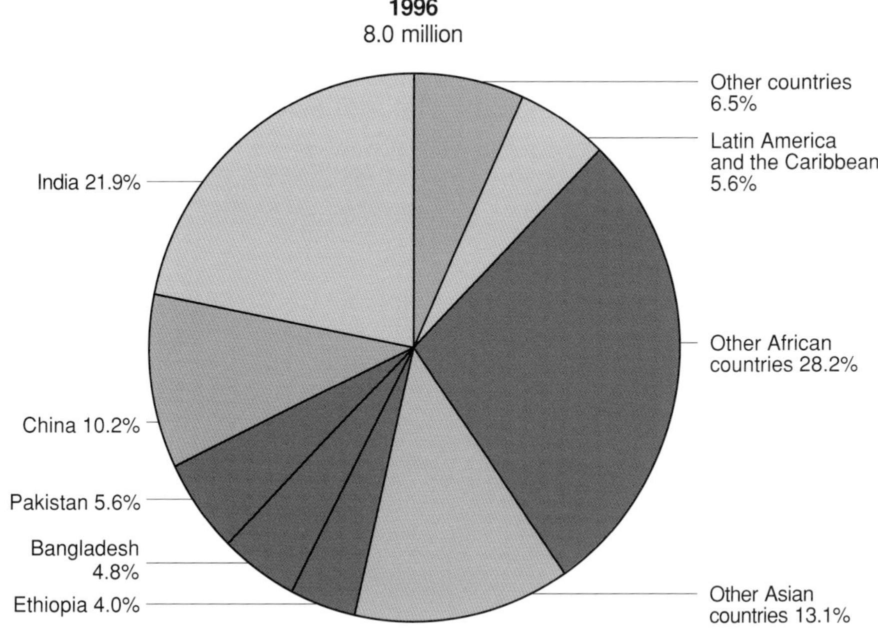

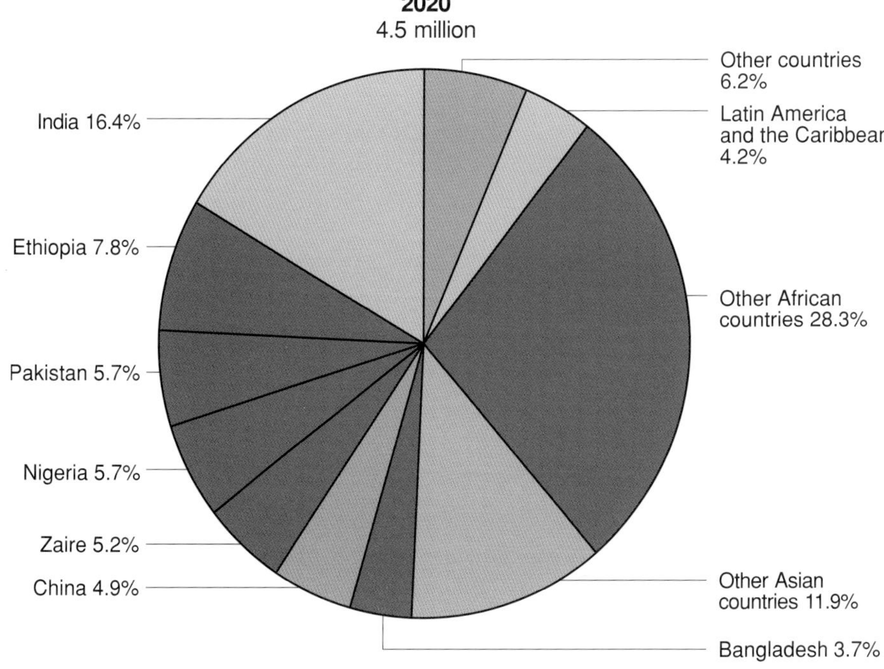

Note: China includes Mainland China and Taiwan.
Source: U.S. Bureau of the Census, International Data Base.

Sub-Saharan Africa, and the Near East and North Africa, where IMR's are now the highest and the potential for reduction is greatest.

Eight Million Infants to Die This Year...

About 8 million infant deaths will occur in 1996, and more than 90 percent of these will be in the developing countries of Africa, Asia, and Latin America. One out of every three of these deaths will occur in China or India (figure 24).

...but Number Likely to Be Cut in Half in Coming 25 Years

If present trends continue, however, the total number of infant deaths worldwide will drop by about half, to 4.5 million, by the year 2020. The drop reflects decreases in infant mortality rates as well as a leveling off in the number of births (and hence the number of infants at risk).

As Many As One of Every Four Who Die Is an Infant

About 15 percent of all deaths worldwide are infant deaths. Where overall mortality levels are still relatively high, infant deaths typically constitute a high proportion of all deaths. The highest proportions are in Sub-Saharan Africa and the Near East and North Africa, where about a fourth of all deaths occur to children under 1 year of age, followed by the developing nations of Asia (excluding China), where about 1 in 5 deaths is that of an infant (figure 25). In Europe and North America, where deaths tend to be concentrated in the older ages, only 1 of every 100 persons dying is under 1 year of age.

As infant mortality rates fall, the proportions of all deaths that occur under the age of one will also fall, to 17 percent in Sub-Saharan Africa, and to less than 10 percent of all deaths in other world regions by the year 2020.

Child Mortality in Sub-Saharan Africa Is More Than Double That in Other Regions

The proportion of children who die before their fifth birthday is a frequently used indicator of the prevailing childhood health risks in a population. Under-5 mortality may be considered an index for the overall climate governing healthy child development and, together with infant mortality rates, provides evidence of the impact of child health services over time.

Regional values of under-5 mortality range from nearly 160 per 1,000 live births in Sub-Saharan Africa to 9 per 1,000 for Western Europe, North America, Japan and Oceania (Rest of World). Sub-Saharan Africa's under-5 mortality rate is more than double that of the rest of the world combined and at least 40 percent higher than that of any other major world region in 1996 (figure 26 and table A-9). The disparity between Sub-Saharan Africa and the other world regions in under-5 mortality exceeds that for infant mortality, suggesting major differences in environmental and infectious disease risks faced by children in the 1 to 4 age group, health services availability, or both. The Sub-Saharan African under-5 mortality rate is more than ten times higher than that of the world's more developed countries in 1996.

Under-5 mortality is projected to decline in all world regions during the coming 25 years, and the absolute gap in child mortality between

Figure 25.
Infant Deaths as a Percent of All Deaths by Region: 1996 and 2020

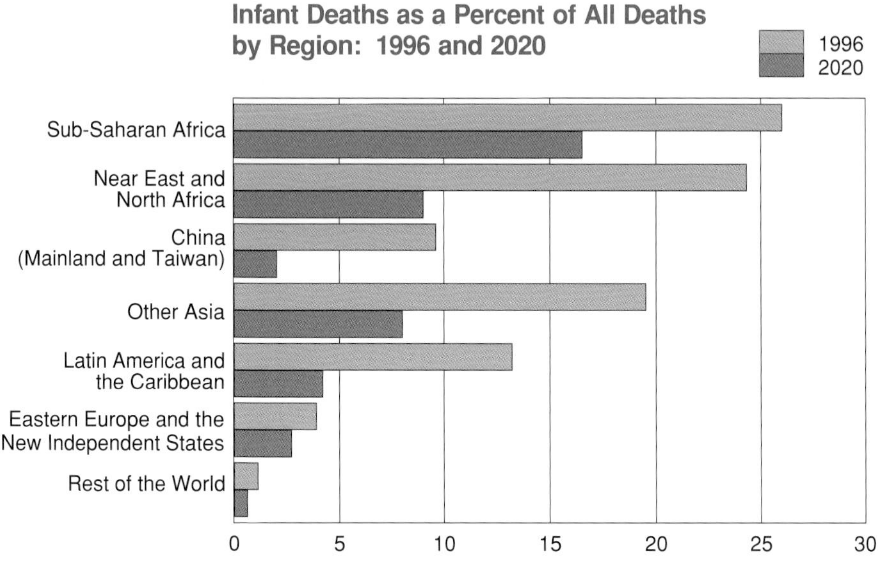

Source: U.S. Bureau of the Census, International Data Base.

Figure 26.
Child Mortality by Region: 1996 and 2020

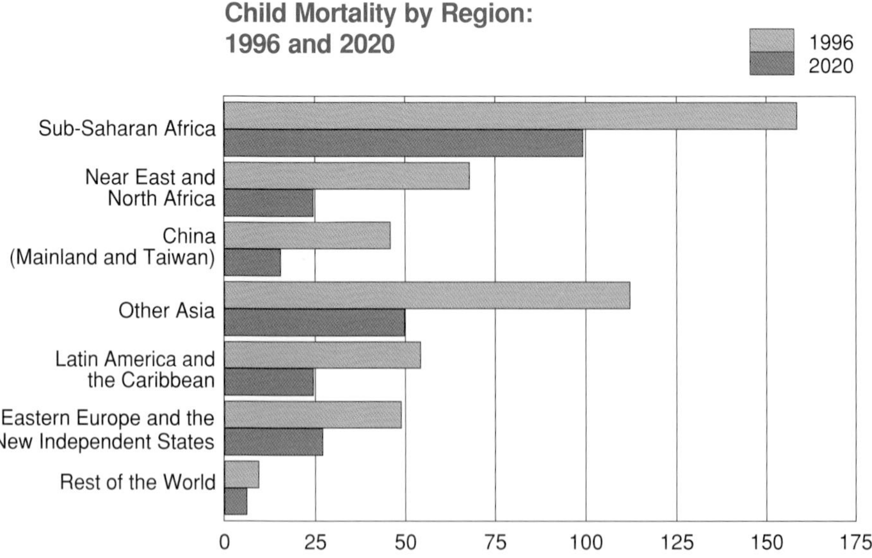

Source: Table A-9 and U.S. Bureau of the Census, International Data Base.

Sub-Saharan Africa and other regions should shrink during this period.

However, the ratio of Sub-Saharan African under-5 mortality to that of MDC's will remain about the same through the year 2020, and the ratio of Sub-Saharan African under-5 mortality to that of other LDC's will increase substantially. By the year 2020, Sub-Saharan Africa's average under-5 mortality, which is currently 60 percent higher than all developing countries taken together, will be 80 percent higher than the composite LDC level if present trends continue.

AIDS Mortality Projected to Cause 50 Million Excess Deaths by 2010

Since the outbreak of the AIDS pandemic in the early 1980's, the age-specific mortality schedules of at least some countries in every world region have been adversely affected. Age-specific death rates, particularly young adult (ages 15 to 44) death rates, have been shifted upward, in some nations many times over. The projections of the Bureau of the Census incorporate estimates of the mortality impact of the current and future AIDS epidemics in developing countries particularly hard hit by the pandemic. The projections assume that the epidemic will peak in 2010 and that AIDS mortality will decline from the level reached in that year to a negligible level in 2050 (methodology is described in more detail in appendix B).

The impact of HIV/AIDS in the 23 countries with substantial AIDS-related mortality currently being tracked by the Bureau of the Census is dramatic: nearly 2 million additional deaths attributable to AIDS in 1996, rising to 2.8 million in the year 2000 and to about 4.5 million in the year 2010. AIDS-related deaths account for about 22 percent of all deaths in these countries in 1996; about 38 percent in 2010. Altogether, nearly 50 million excess deaths attributable to AIDS are projected for the 1996-2010 period.

Figure 27 illustrates variability in the effect of AIDS-related mortality on life expectancy at birth for males and females in 6 of the 23 countries being followed by the Bureau of the Census. These data suggest that the impact of the epidemic will be severe in Botswana, moderately severe in Tanzania, and somewhat less severe in Nigeria, Thailand, Brazil, and Haiti. Life expectancy at birth in Botswana is now projected to be about 33 years in the year 2010, or just half of what it would be in the absence of AIDS. The average loss in life expectancy is approximately 20 percent in the year 2010 for the group of 23 countries taken together. Years of life expectancy lost are about the same for males and females.

Figure 27.
Effect of AIDS Mortality on Life Expectancy at Birth, Selected Countries: 1985 to 2030

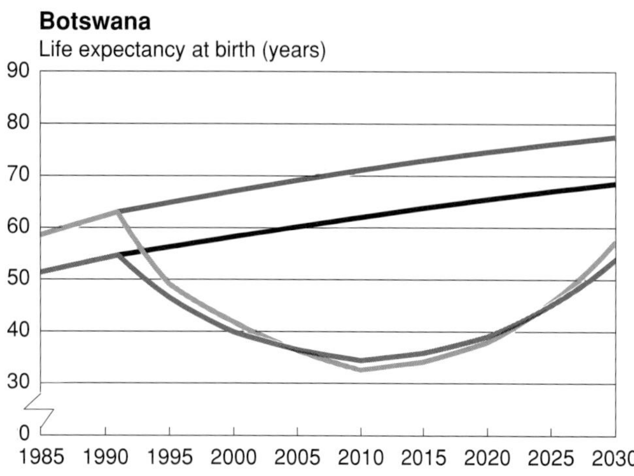

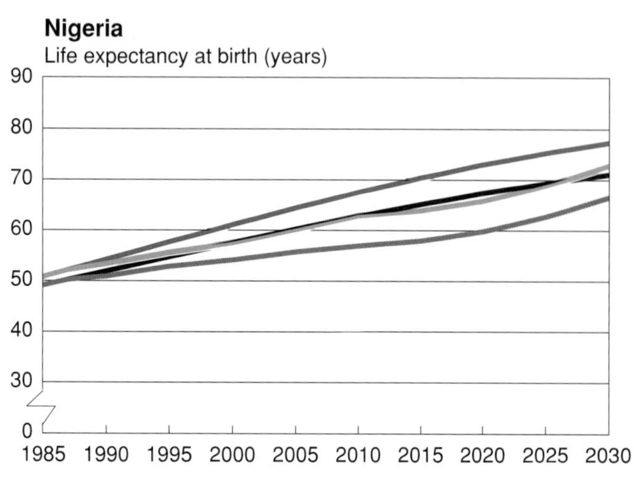

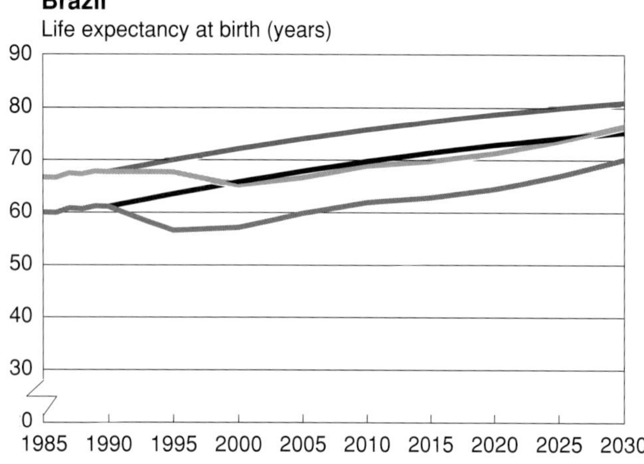

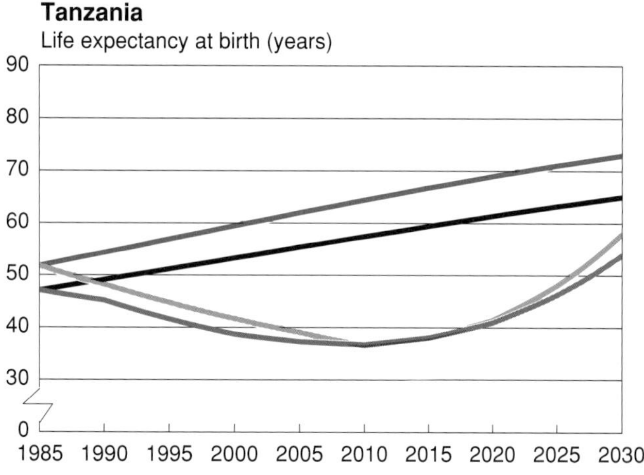

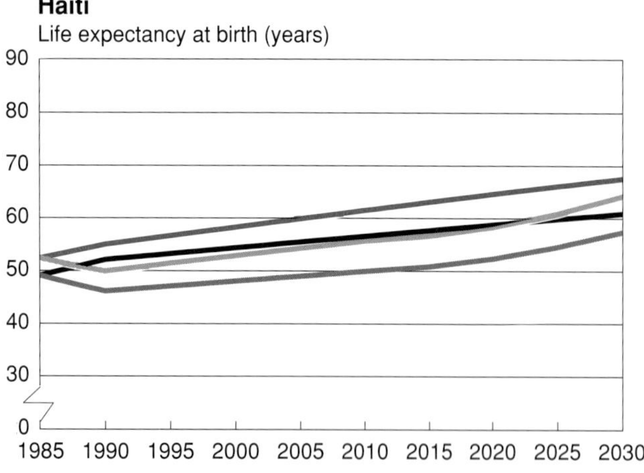

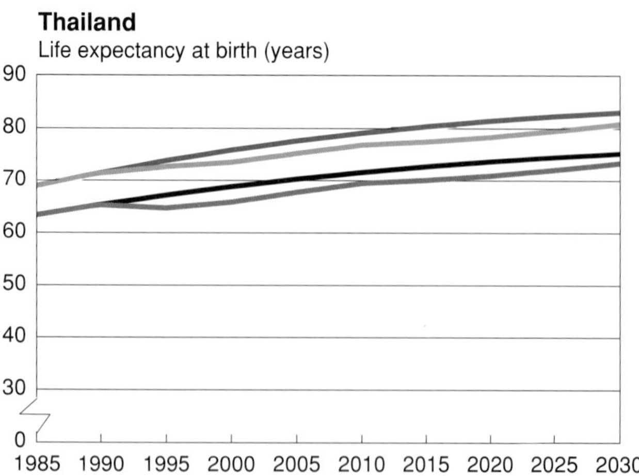

Source: U.S. Bureau of the Census, International Programs Center.

Figure 28.
Vital Rates, With and Without AIDS, for 23 Countries: 1990 to 2030

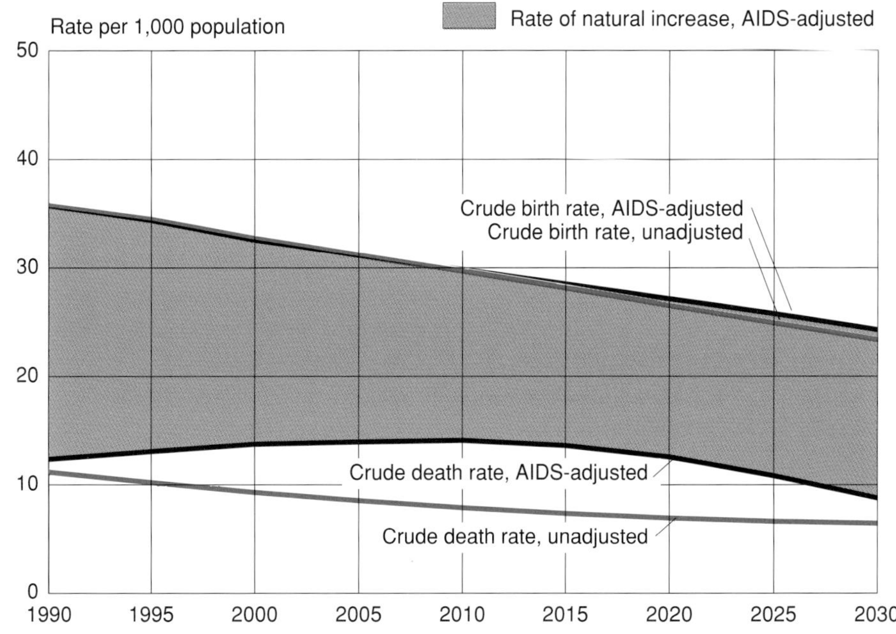

Source: U.S. Bureau of the Census, International Programs Center.

AIDS Will Slow, but Not Halt, Population Growth in Affected Countries

Because HIV/AIDS affects the numbers of births in a population less than it affects the number of deaths — most AIDS mortality occurs ***after*** the average age of childbearing — the crude birth rate in AIDS-affected populations is altered little by the disease. As a result, natural increase remains positive but is significantly smaller than it would be in the absence of AIDS (figure 28). The net difference in population size between the AIDS-adjusted and non-adjusted projections for the 23 countries is about 3 percent in the year 2000, and about 8 percent in the year 2010.

International Migration

Migration Is Key to Understanding Population Change in a Select Group of Countries

For most countries, ongoing trends in fertility and mortality will determine the future size, growth, and composition of population. When there is movement of people across international boundaries, however, a country's population growth rate may differ significantly from the rate of natural increase. While the net impact of international migration is negligible for most countries, international migration strongly influences overall population change in some (figure 29).

Whether the movement of persons across international boundaries is driven by economic and social disparities, by political conditions, by civil unrest, or by natural disaster, net international migration ***can*** have major impacts on the growth rates of both sending and receiving nations.

In some countries (Italy and Germany, for instance), more persons are added to the population through net international migration than through natural increase each year. In other countries, net emigration may exceed natural increase and the composite growth rate still may be negative (as in Georgia and Guyana), or emigration may even augment negative natural increase (as in Romania). Elsewhere, moderately high net emigration rates may have a dampening effect on what otherwise would be relatively high population growth rates (as in Tajikistan). Of course, for most countries migration is negligible compared with natural increase (e.g., India).

In general, more developed countries have been net recipients of international migrants for the past two decades while less developed countries have lost population to international movement. This pattern is expected to continue into the new millennium.

In the 1990's, in addition to well-established movements of people from the less developed countries of the "South" to the more developed nations of the "North," there are substantial movements of workers and asylum-seekers from "East" to "West;" i.e., from Central and Eastern Europe, as well as from the New Independent States of the former Soviet Union, to Germany and other destinations in Western Europe (and to some destinations in Southern and Eastern Europe (United Nations 1995b)).

Some of the largest movements of people across country borders during the 1990's have involved refugees returning to Afghanistan, Eritrea, and Mozambique, and Rwandan refugee movements from Rwanda to Zaire and back to Rwanda. However, largely economically motivated migrants have added substantially to the populations of several of the more industrialized nations during the 1990-96 period. The United States remains the most popular migrant destination. Approximately 6 million more persons entered the United States since 1990 than left the country, more net immigration than any other country. Germany and Russia are also major migrant destinations. Approximately 5.6 million more migrants entered Germany than left it

Figure 29.
Rate of Natural Increase and Net Migration Rate for Selected Countries: 1996

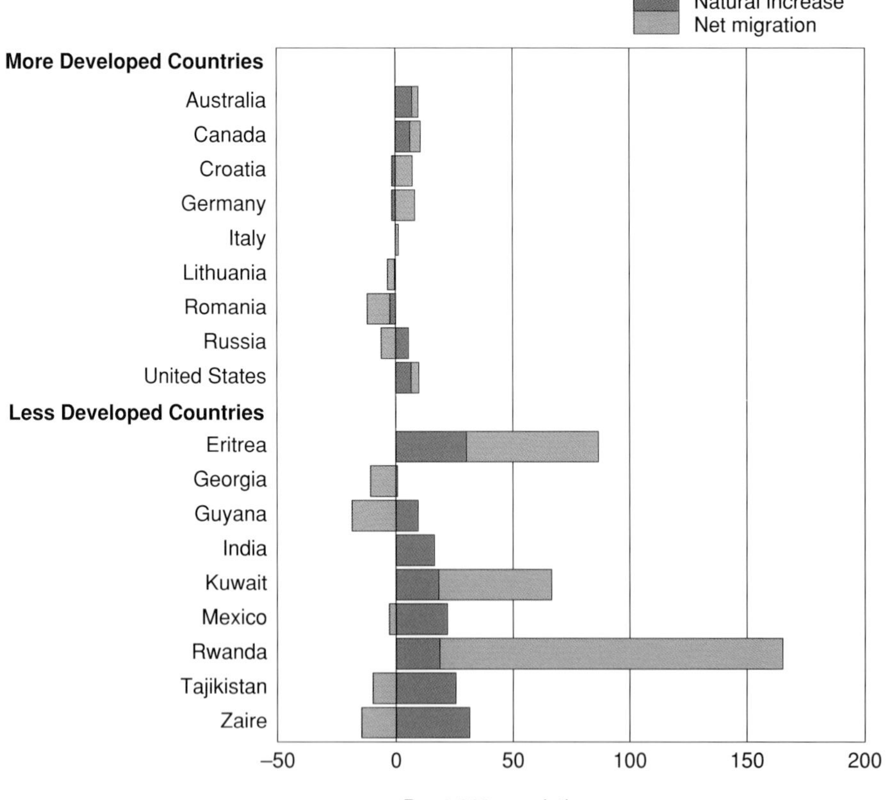

Source: U.S. Bureau of the Census, International Data Base.

from 1990 to 1996. The comparable figure for Russia is 3.3 million persons. These include both economic migrants and ethnic Russians relocating from other parts of the former Soviet Union.

Demographic Goals and Demographic Realities

Demographic change at the national, regional, and global levels during the coming quarter century will be determined by the interplay of (1) ongoing, country-specific processes of social change; (2) national demographic goals and the efforts of individual nations and the international community to achieve these goals; and (3) the present demography of nations, which sets the limits of demographic change within any specific time frame. The ICPD Program of Action, endorsed by some 180 governments in 1994, establishes a broad agenda for change very much in keeping with the overriding theme of the conference, which emphasized interpretation of population processes within the broader context of the process of sustainable development. This agenda encompasses a series of objectives in the areas of access to reproductive health care; women's rights and improved educational and employment opportunities for women; environmental protection and sustainable production and consumption patterns; the eradication of poverty; as well as specific goals in the area of mortality reduction. In addition, regional preparatory conferences held in Dakar, Amman, Bali, Mexico City, and Geneva set some regional goals that augment those of the International Conference on Population and Development.

Monitoring progress toward the achievement of the ICPD and regional goals is one part of the larger task of goal attainment. The demographic estimates and projections of the Bureau of the Census for the countries of the world provide a baseline against which to measure progress during the coming years. This section compares Bureau projections with ICPD and regional targets to suggest which countries and regions are most likely to attain specific goals in infant and child mortality reduction, improvement in life expectancy, and lowering of rates of natural increase and fertility levels.

Infant and Child Mortality Reduction

The ICPD Program of Action calls for specific reductions in infant and under-5 mortality (the probability of a child dying prior to its first or fifth birthday, respectively) by the turn of the century, with additional reductions by the year 2015. In a restatement of targets adopted at the 1990 World Summit for Children (United Nations 1995a:41-42; UNICEF 1990, 1994:56), infant mortality is to be lowered by one-third the 1990 level or to a level of 50 per 1,000 live births (whichever is less), by the year 2000. In addition, the international community has adopted a goal of 35 infant deaths per 1,000 live births by the year 2015 (United Nations 1995a: section 8.16).

Comparisons of infant mortality levels currently being projected for the year 2000 for the developing regions of the world with the two targets (two-thirds of the 1990 level and 50 per 1,000

Can the ICPD Infant Mortality Goal for the Year 2000 Be Met in Less Developed Countries?

Region	Regional median infant mortality in 2000	Total number of countries*	Number of countries meeting 50/1,000 goal	Number of countries meeting 33 percent reduction goal	Number of countries meeting lower of the two goal
Sub-Saharan Africa	89	51	7	0	0
Near East and North Africa	31	22	17	8	7
China**	–	1	1	1	1
Other Asia	40	24	13	4	4
Latin American and the Caribbean	17	45	42	9	9
New Independent States***	73	8	2	0	0
Oceania****	26	15	13	1	1

* Only developing counties for which the Bureau of the Census makes cohort component projections are represented in this table.
** Mainland China will meet the 33 percent reductions goal; Taiwan, whose infant mortality was about a sixth as large as Mainland China's in 1990, has already met the ICPD goal of 50 per 1,000 but probably will not meet the goal of an additional 33 percent reduction by the year 2000. Mainland China and Taiwan are counted as one country here.
*** Seven of the fifteen NIS are classified as more developed countries and are excluded from the table.
**** Australia and New Zealand are classified as more developed countries and are excluded from the table.

live births) highlight the variation among regions in terms of attaining the more immediate goal. Only 7 of 51 Sub-Saharan African countries are likely to attain the target of 50 or fewer infant deaths per 1,000 live births by the year 2000, and no country in this region is expected to reduce its infant mortality rate below two-thirds its 1990 level by that year. If the ICPD goal is defined as "50 per 1,000 or a reduction by one-third the 1990 level, ***whichever is less***," then every Sub-Saharan African country is projected to fail to meet the infant mortality goal for the year 2000.

If current trends in infant mortality rates continue, about three-quarters of the remaining developing countries of the world are expected to reach the 50 per 1,000 goal, though only 1 in 5 countries is also likely to reach the more difficult goal of reducing infant mortality by one-third as quickly as the year 2000. Most of the countries in the Near East and North Africa, Latin America and the Caribbean, and Oceania will have IMR's below 50 per 1,000 by the turn of the century (indeed, most of these countries have already attained IMR's at or below this level), as will half of Asia's less developed countries and 2 of 8 Asian New Independent States.[3]

The ICPD infant mortality goal for the year 2015 is 35 or fewer infant deaths per 1,000 live births. Sub-Saharan Africa, the Asian New Independent States, and parts of the rest of Asia are also unlikely to be able to reduce infant mortality to this level in the next 20 years (figure 30). Most of the countries of the Near East and North Africa, Latin America and the Caribbean, and Oceania, in contrast,

Figure 30.
Infant Mortality for Developing Countries and the ICPD Goal for Year 2015

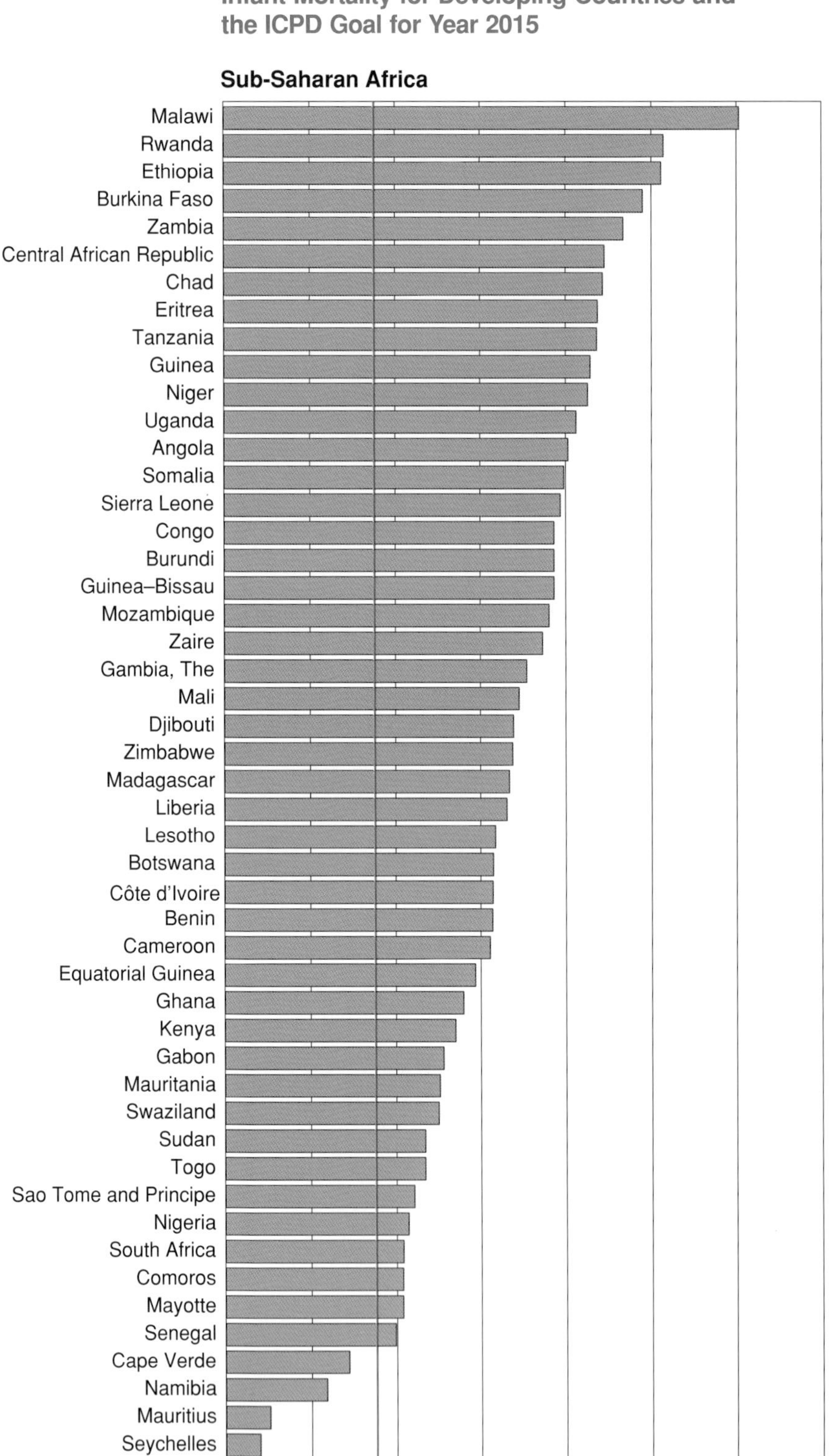

3 Eight of the newly independent states of the former Soviet Union are geographically part of Asia, are referred to here as Asian, and are classified as developing countries. However, they are not grouped with Other Asian countries in the figures of this report.

Figure 30.
Infant Mortality for Developing Countries and the ICPD Goal for Year 2015—Continued

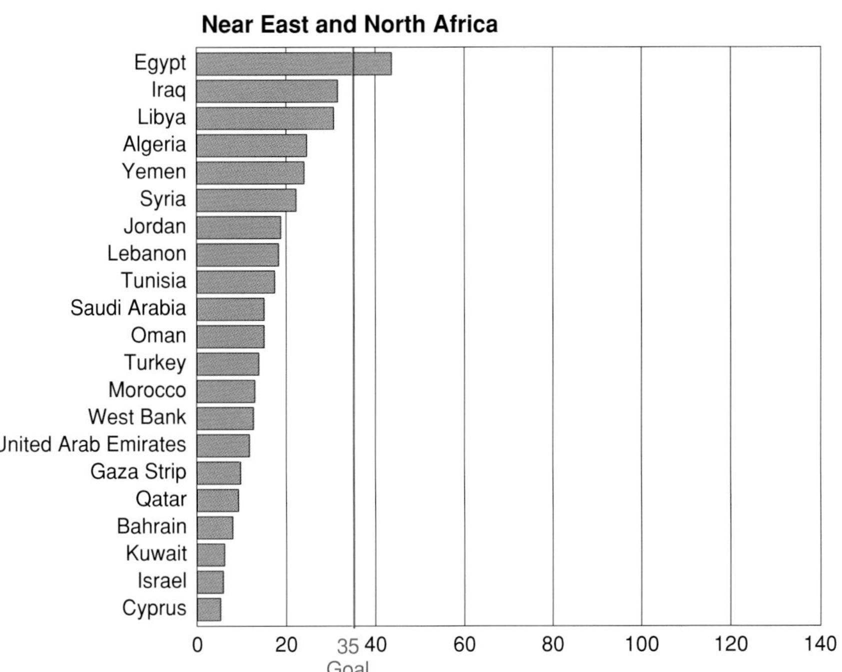

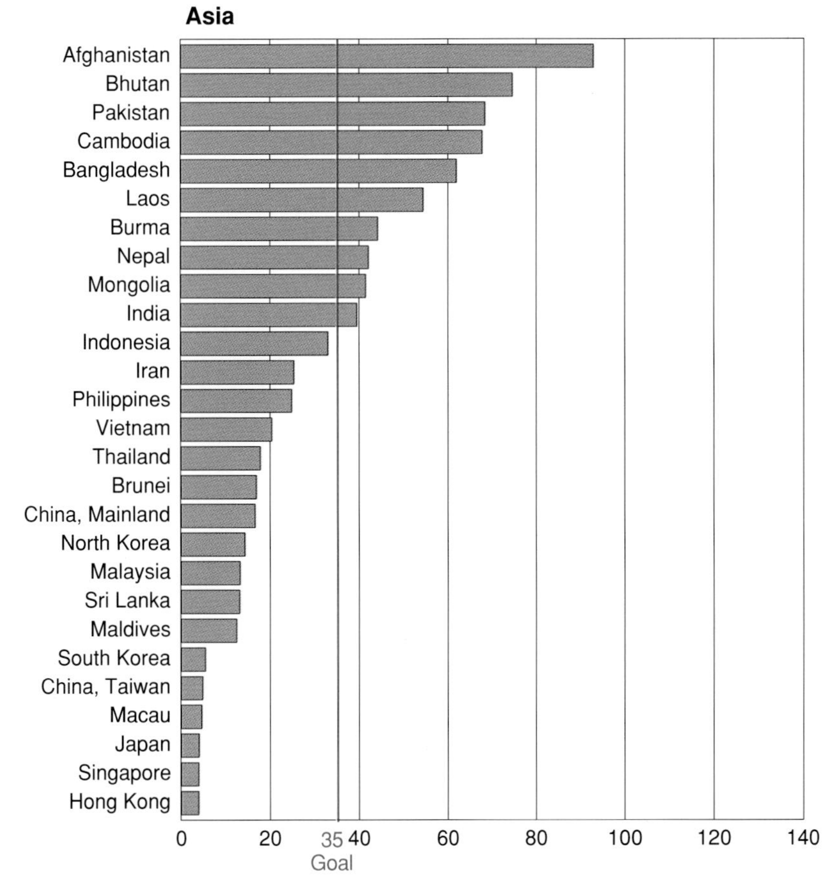

Figure 30.
Infant Mortality for Developing Countries and the ICPD Goal for Year 2015—Continued

Latin America and the Caribbean

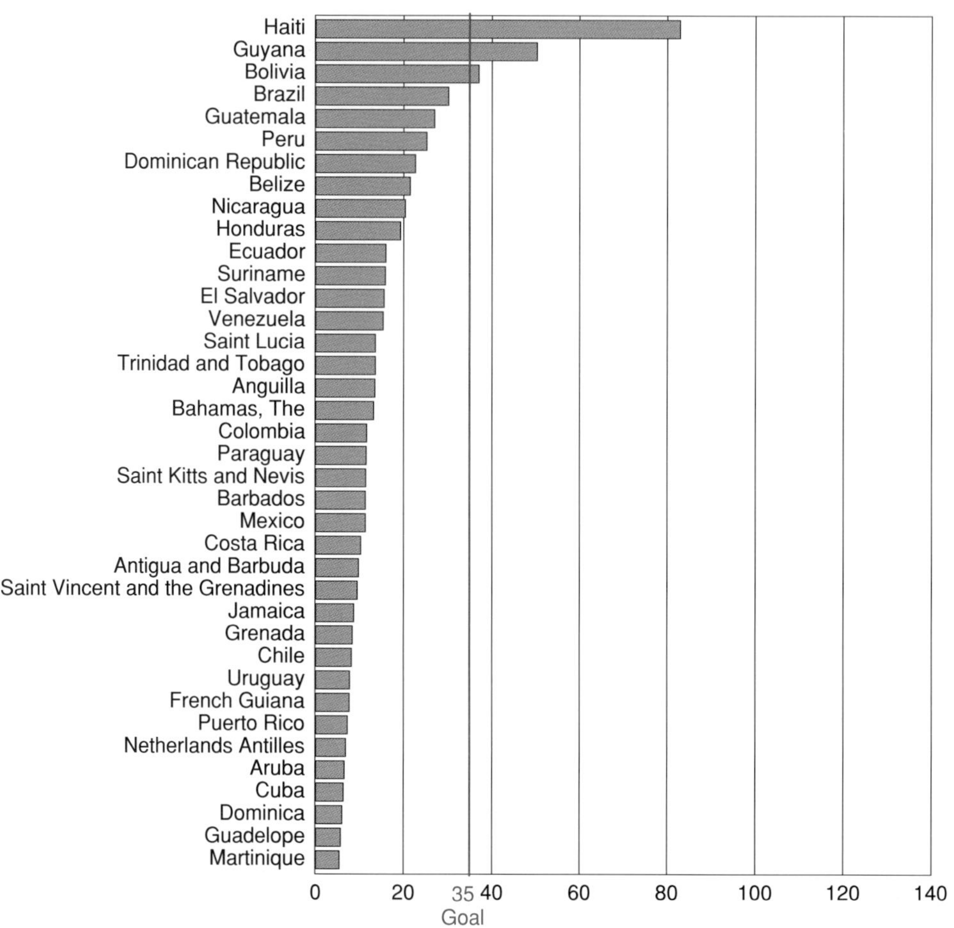

New Independent States and Oceania

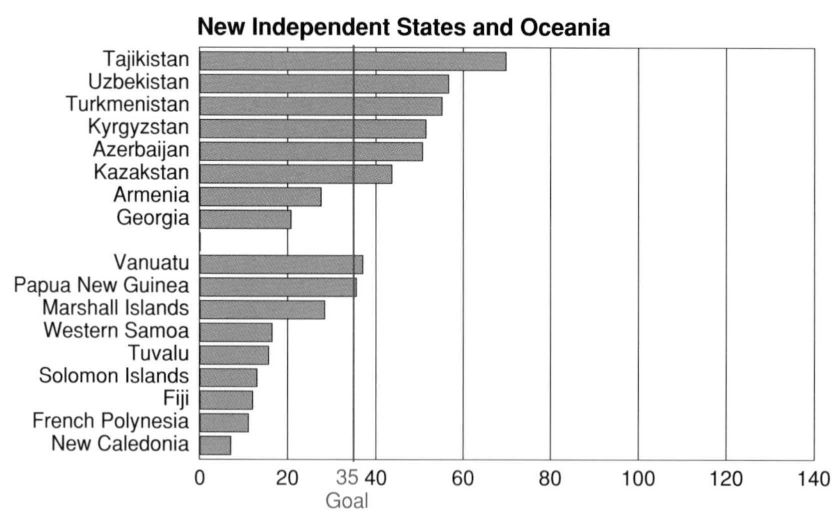

Infant deaths per 1,000 live births

Note: Argentina and Panama meet the goal. Projected IMR's for these countries are under revision.
Source: U.S. Bureau of the Census, International Data Base.

are expected to reach this longer term goal.

Mortality Under Age 5

The child mortality reduction goals specified in the Cairo document call for all nations to lower the probability of a child's failing to survive the first 5 years of life to 70 per 1,000 live births, or to two-thirds the 1990 level, whichever is less, by the year 2000. The year 2015 target is fewer than 45 deaths per 1,000.

Like the ICPD goal for infant mortality reduction, the year 2000 child mortality goal is very ambitious. Fewer than 1 in 5 developing countries, will be able to cut under-5 mortality by a third by the end of the decade.

Regional patterns in likelihood of meeting the more attainable, numerical goals for child mortality reduction mirror those for infant mortality: Only 4 of the 50 Sub-Saharan African countries are likely to meet the goal of 70 child deaths per 1,000 live births by the year 2000; about half the Asian countries and 3 of 8 Asian NIS countries will. Most other developing countries, either already have or will.

However, fewer than half the countries of the Near East and North Africa, and only 30 percent of Latin American countries should be able to meet the lower of the two under-5 mortality goals for the year 2000. No Sub-Saharan African country and none of the eight Asian NIS are likely to meet the more difficult year 2000 goal.

Just over half of all countries are expected to meet the year 2015 ICPD goal of 45 child deaths per 1,000 births. However, while most countries in the Near East and North Africa, Latin America and the Caribbean, and Oceania should be able to reach this target if ongoing infant and child mortality reductions continue, Sub-Saharan Africa and the Asian NIS will again have more difficulty than other regions in meeting this goal. Only 2 of the 8 Asian NIS and only 5 of the 50 Sub-Saharan African countries are likely to meet the year 2015 ICPD childhood mortality goal.

The ICPD Life Expectancy Goals

The International Conference on Population and Development also reaffirmed the goal, earlier stated in the Alma Ata declaration, of raising life expectancy at birth to 65 years by the year 2005 and to 70 years by the year 2015 (United Nations 1995a: section 8.5). Projected life expectancy at birth (for both sexes combined) for 2015, follows the same regional patterns described with respect to the infant and child mortality goals. Much of the Near East and North Africa, Latin America and the Caribbean, Oceania, and more than half the countries of Asia should reach this goal; the majority of Sub-Saharan African and Asian New Independent States will not, if present rates of mortality improvement continue.

Can the ICPD Under-5 Mortality Goals Be Met in Less Developed Countries?

			Year 2000 Goals			Year 2015 Goals
Region	Regional median under-5 mortality in 2000	Total number of countries*	Number of countries meeting 70/1,000 goal	Number of countries meeting 33 percent reduction goal	Number of countries meeting lower of the two goals	Number of countries meeting 45/1,000 goal
Sub-Saharan Africa	136	50	4	0	0	5
Near East and North Africa	38	21	18	9	8	20
China**	–	1	1	1	1	1
Other Asia	58	24	13	3	3	14
Latin American and the Caribbean	24	40	37	11	11	36
New Independent States***	89	8	3	0	0	2
Oceania****	37	9	7	3	3	7

* Only developing counties for which the Bureau of the Census makes cohort component projections are represented in this table.
** Mainland China will meet the 33 percent reduction goal; Taiwan, whose under-5 mortality was just under 11/1,000 in 1990, has already met the ICPD goal of 70 per 1,000 but probably will not meet the goal of an additional 33 percent reduction by year 2000. Mainland China and Taiwan are counted as one country here.
*** Seven of the fifteen NIS are classified as more developed countries and are excluded from the table.
**** Australia and New Zealand are classified as more developed countries and are excluded from the table.

The Fertility Goal Set Out in the Bali Declaration

In preparation for the ICPD, the nations of Asia and the Pacific recognized the difficulties posed for sustainable development by high rates of population growth and agreed that the countries of the region should seek to attain replacement level fertility, which they defined as approximately 2.2 children per woman, by the year 2010 or sooner (Fourth Asian and Pacific Population Conference 1992:770). Figure 31 presents projected total fertility rates for 37 Asian and Pacific Island nations and areas for the year 2010. These data suggest that the majority of these areas (22 of 37) will fail to reach that goal if present trends continue. India, Indonesia, the Philippines, Bangladesh, and Pakistan are among the countries likely to have total fertility rates above 2.2 in the year 2010.

Figure 31.
Total Fertility Rate and the Asian and Pacific Regional Fertility Goal for Year 2010

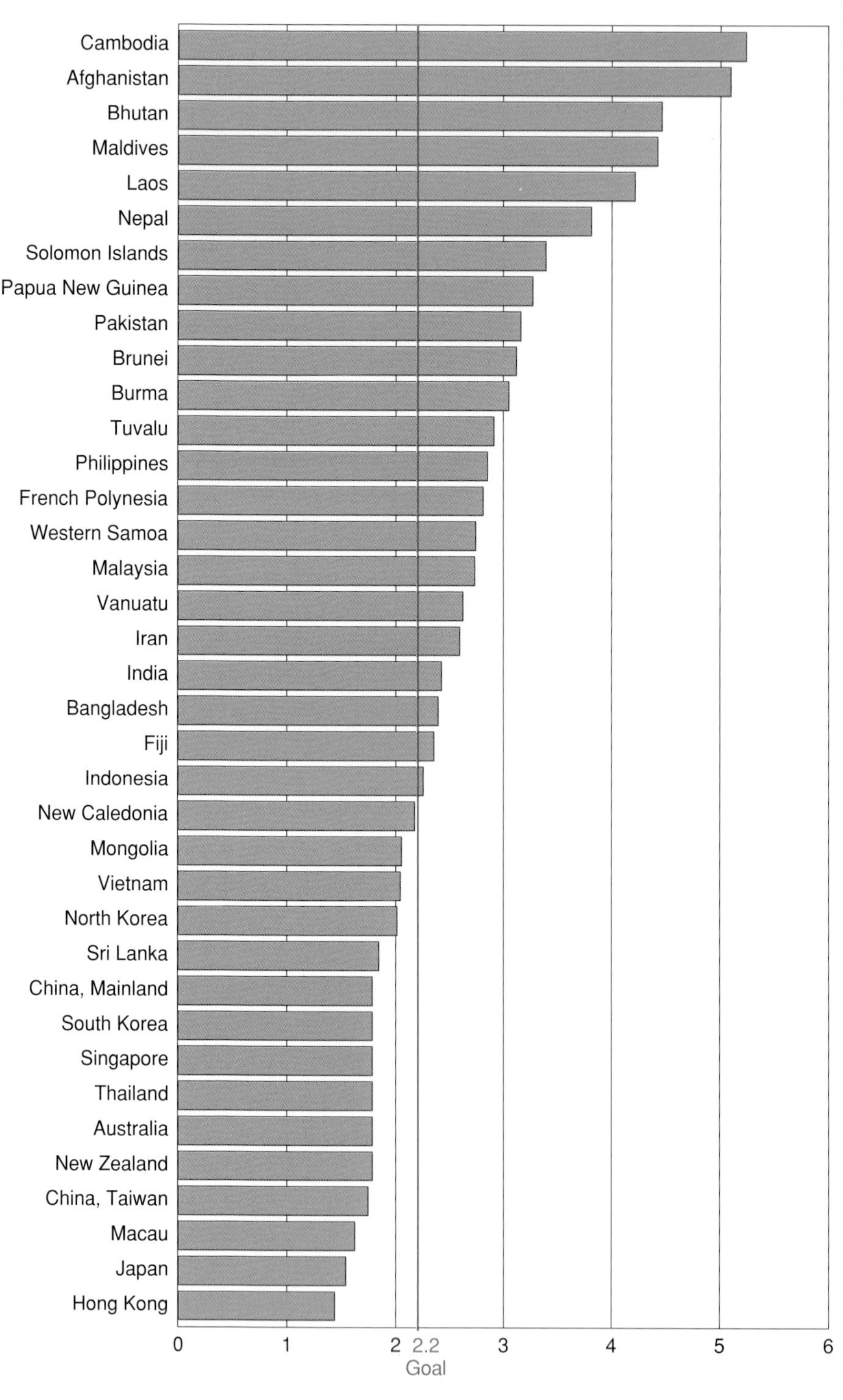

Source: U.S. Bureau of the Census, International Data Base.

Figure 32.
Natural Increase and the African Regional Natural Increase Goal for Year 2000

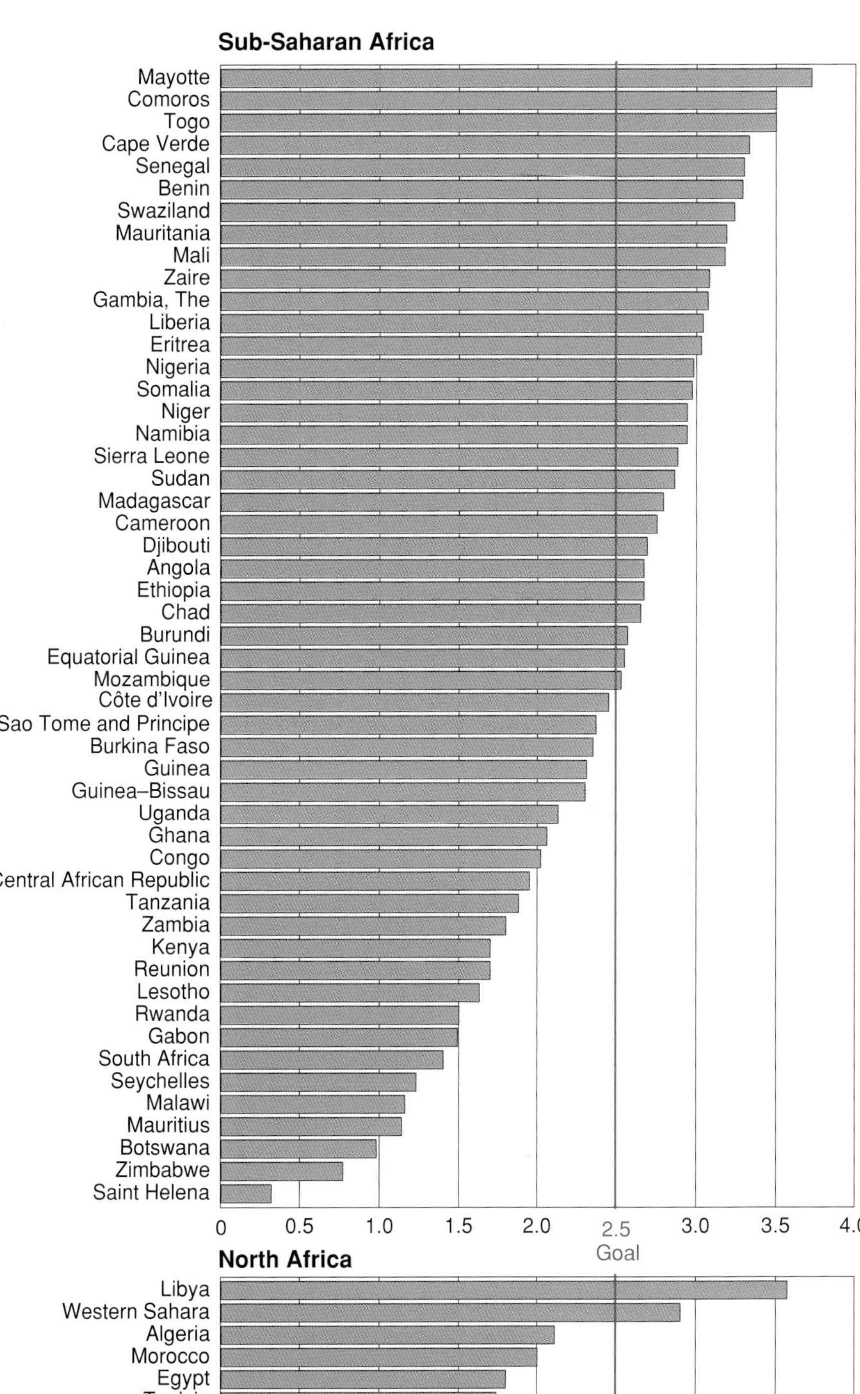

Note: The goal of a regional rate of natural increase of 2.5 percent per annum was adopted at the Third African Population Conference held in 1993.
Source: U.S. Bureau of the Census, International Data Base.

The Natural Increase Goal Set Out in the Dakar/Ngor Declaration

African governments meeting in Dakar in December of 1992 adopted a comprehensive set of principles and objectives focusing on population within the context of sustainable development and emphasizing recognition of family concerns in all development policies (Third African Population Conference 1993:209). Among the demographic goals set out in the Dakar/Ngor Declaration on Population, Family and Sustainable Development is one which calls for a reduction in the ***regional*** rate of natural increase from around 3.0 to 2.5 percent by the year 2000, and to 2.0 percent by the year 2010.

The projections of the Bureau of the Census indicate that Africa's rate of natural increase (RNI) is likely to decline to about 2.4 percent by the year 2000, meeting the first part of this goal. However, if current trends continue, the year 2010 goal of an RNI as low as 2.0 percent may not be achieved. The projected regional rate for all of Africa for the year 2010 is 2.1 percent.

Sub-Saharan Africa's rate, which was about 2.7 percent at the time of the 1994 Cairo conference, should decrease to just under 2.5 percent by the year 2000, but the projected rate for the year 2010 — 2.2 percent — is even further from the natural increase goal set in Dakar than is the all-Africa rate.

As figures 32 and 33 indicate, more than half the countries in Sub-Saharan Africa are unlikely to meet the goals for 2000 and 2010. Were it not for the fact that a number of the countries most affected by AIDS epidemics are projected to have very low rates of natural increase, the regional growth rate would be even higher.

Figure 33.
Natural Increase and the African Regional Natural Increase Goal for Year 2010

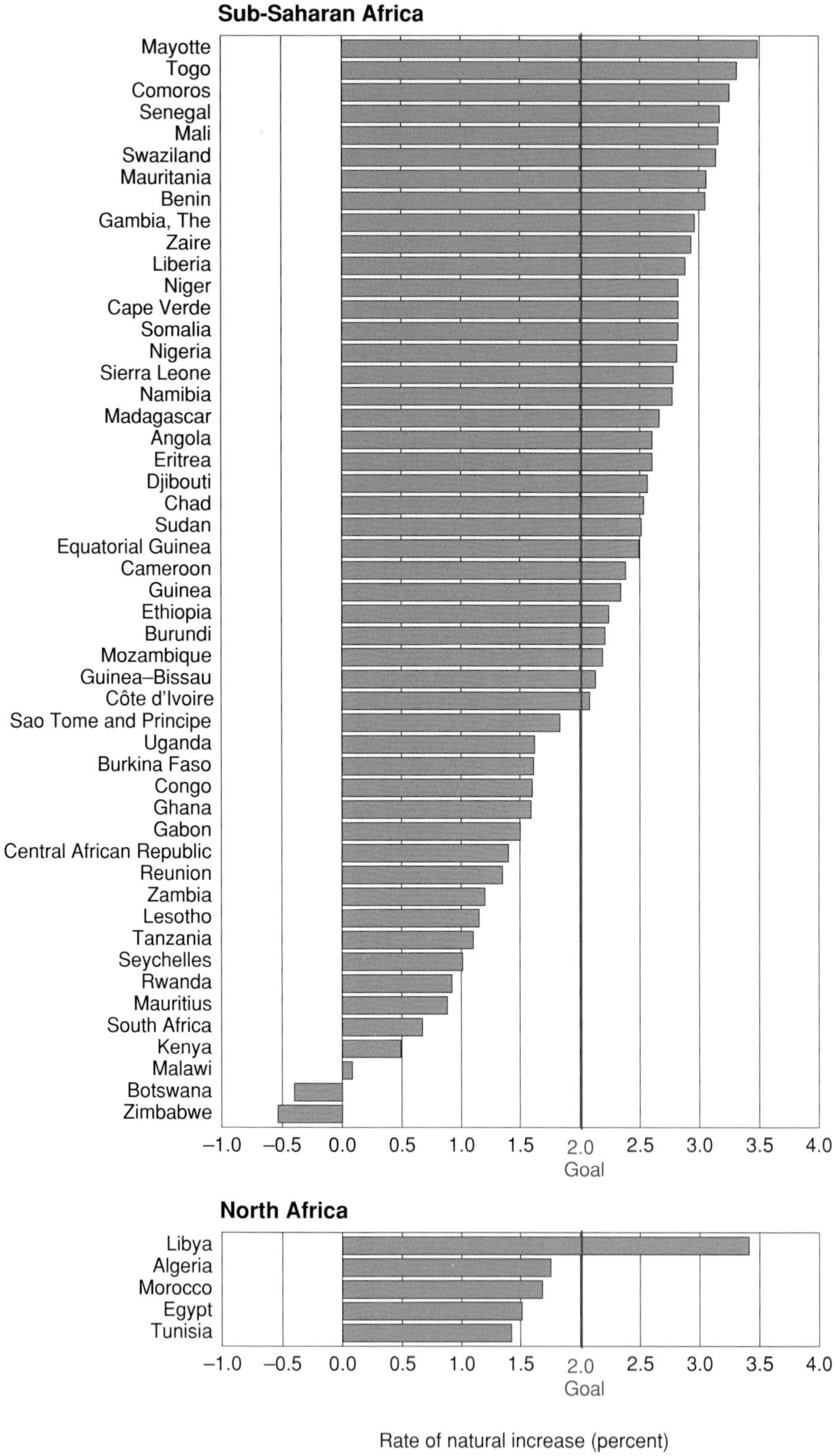

Sub-Saharan Africa

North Africa

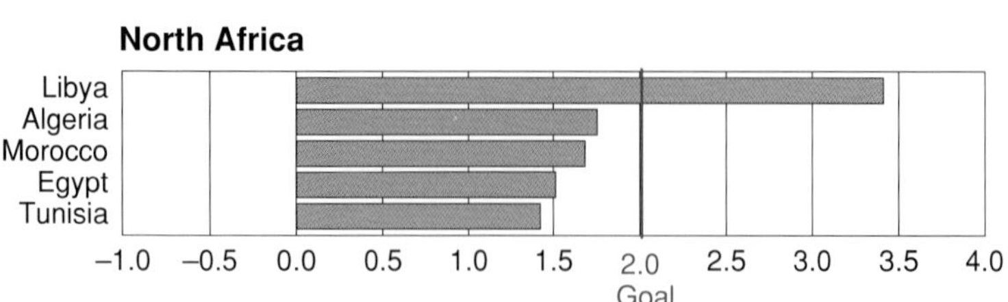

Rate of natural increase (percent)

Note: The African regional natural increase goal for 2010 is 2 percent.
Source: U.S. Bureau of the Census, International Data Base.

Contraceptive Prevalence

Contraceptive Prevalence

Only About Half of Married Women Practice Contraception in World's Largest Countries

Women in more developed countries have historically used, and continue to use, family planning to control their fertility more often than women in less developed countries. For example, about 71 percent of married women of reproductive age (MWRA) in the United States used contraception in 1990, compared to an average of 47 percent of women in the largest less developed countries in the late 1980's or early 1990's (figure 34 and table A-11). While this kind of disparity underscores the continuing disadvantage of women in the developing world in terms of reproductive health, it is also true that contraceptive use is widespread in a number of less developed countries. Among the largest countries, over three-quarters of married women in China (Mainland) and two-thirds of married women in Brazil use some method of contraception.

From the ICPD Program of Action:

"Reproductive health ... [implies that people] have the capability to reproduce and the freedom to decide if, when and how often to do so. Implicit in this last condition are the right of men and women to be informed and to have access to safe, effective, affordable and acceptable methods of family-planning of their choice ..." (section 7.2)

Figure 34.
Contraceptive Prevalence Rate for Large Countries: Late 1980's or Later

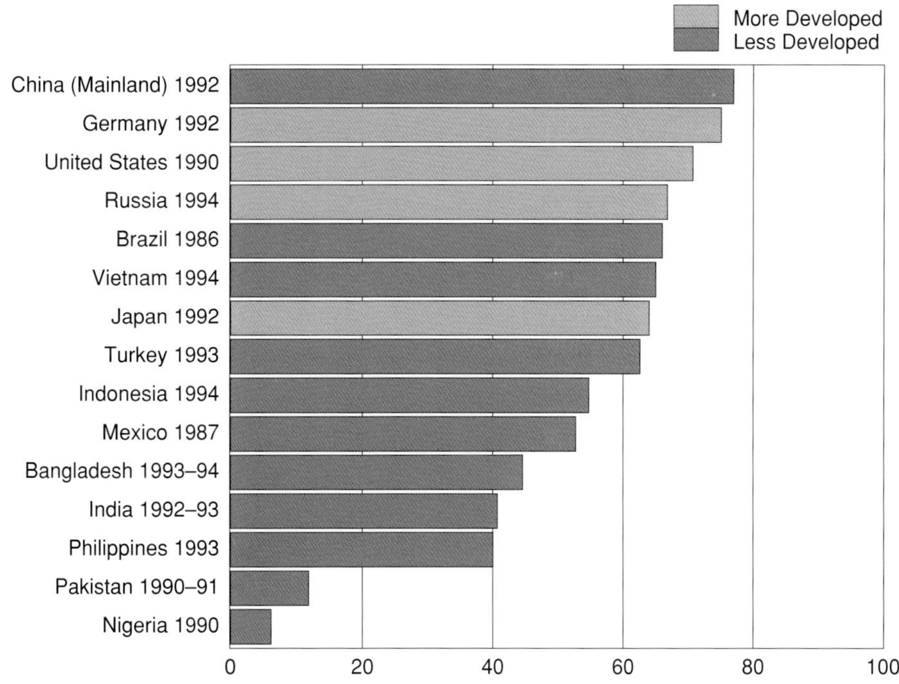

* Here and in all subsequent figures, contraceptive prevalence refers to percent of currently married women of reproductive age using contraception. In most cases, these women are ages 15-49.
Source: Table A-11.

Contraceptive Prevalence Rates Are Highest in Asia and Latin America, Lowest in Sub-Saharan Africa, Among Developing Regions

Within the developing world, use of contraception by married women of reproductive age varies substantially from region to region, as well as from country to country (table A-11).

In most of the larger countries of Sub-Saharan Africa, contraceptive prevalence is under 30 percent. The highest rates shown in figure 35 are 50 percent of MWRA in South Africa and 33 percent in Kenya. The median prevalence level for the region, based on the latest data for all countries in the region having data (table A-11), is 15 percent; that is, contraceptive prevalence levels are below 15 percent in half of the countries.

With the exception of Turkey, contraceptive use is also less common in the Near East and North Africa than in other parts of the developing world. The most recent estimates range from 7 percent for Yemen to 63 percent for Turkey.[4] The median value for the Near East and North Africa is 41 percent.

In Asia, a majority of countries now have prevalence rates for MWRA above 50 percent. In China (both Mainland and Taiwan), as well as in South Korea and Hong Kong, recent information indicates that over three-quarters of MWRA use some means of contraception to control their fertility, prevalence rates that are equal to those in many developed countries.

[4] Nearly half of Turkey's overall prevalence rate reflects use of less effective, traditional methods. Modern method prevalence in the region ranges from around 6 percent in Yemen to about 45 percent in Egypt. For purposes of international comparison, both total and modern method prevalence have advantages. Method-specific prevalence rates for currently-married women are shown in table A-11.

Figure 35.
Contraceptive Prevalence and Total Fertility Rates for Largest Countries, by Region: 1985 or Later

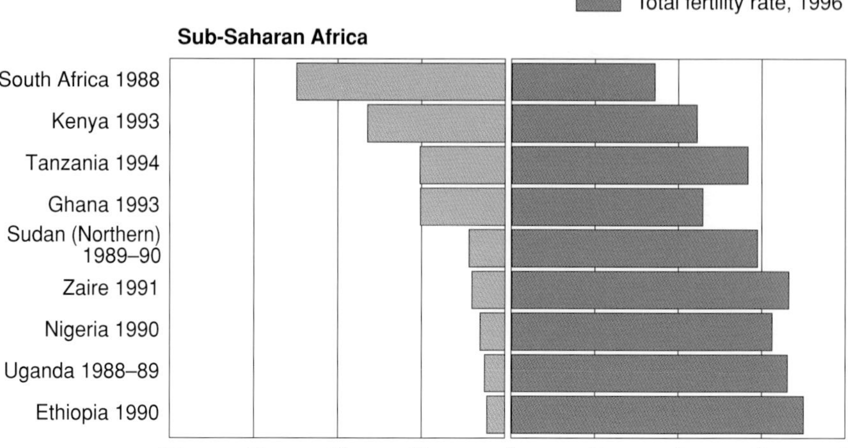

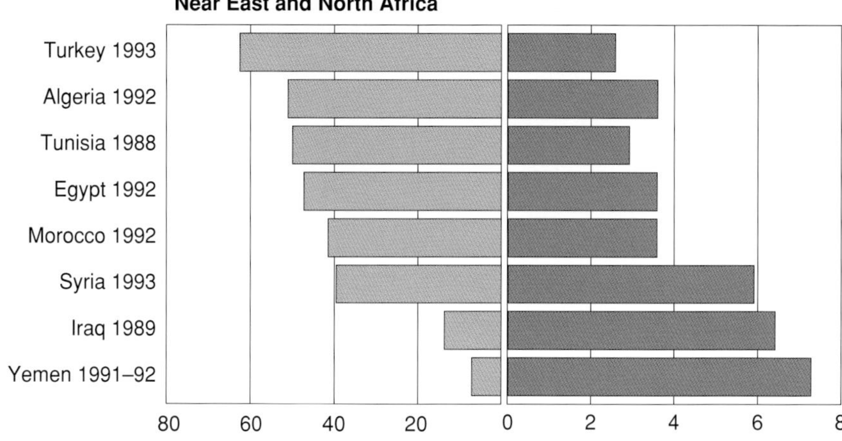

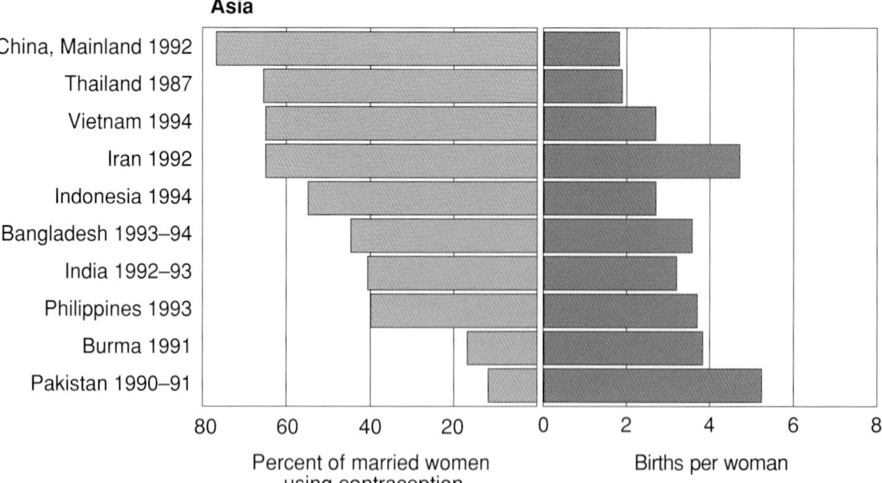

Figure 35.
Contraceptive Prevalence and Total Fertility Rates for Largest Countries, by Region: 1985 or Later—Continued

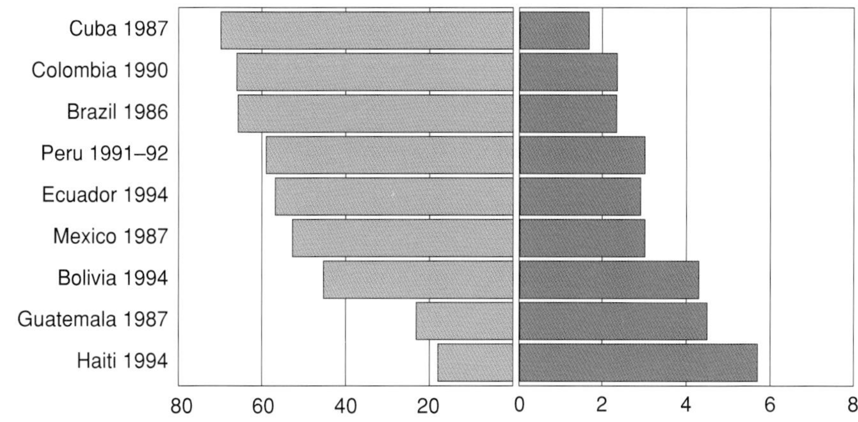

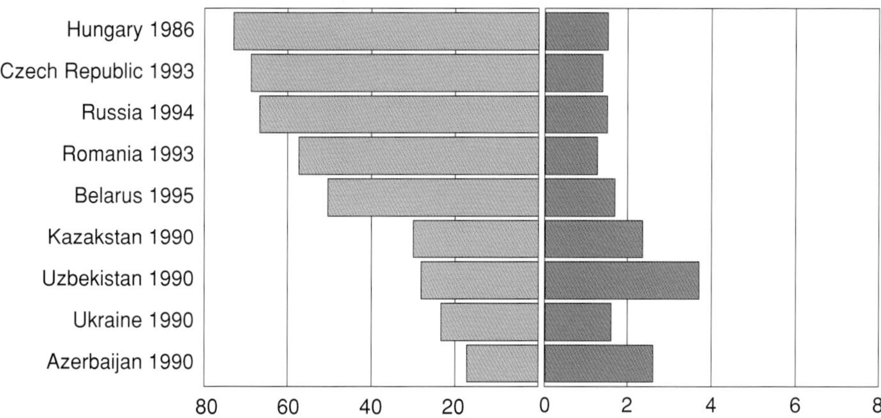

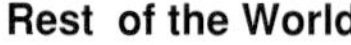

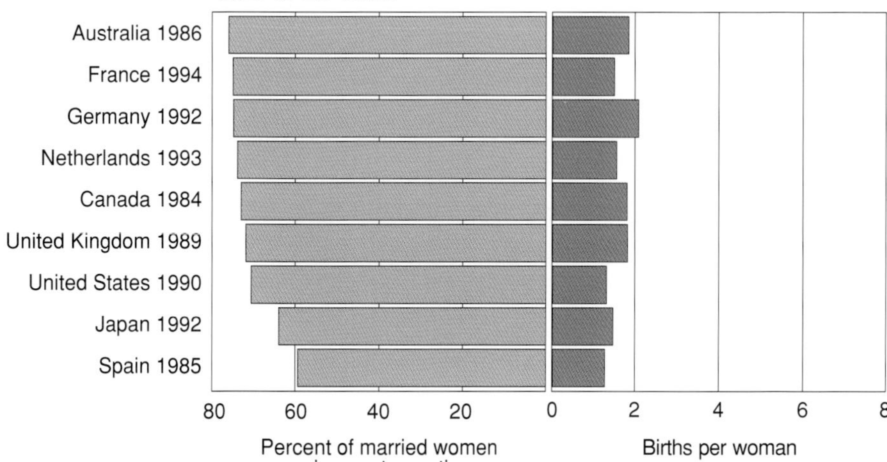

Source: Tables A-8 and A-11.

The median level for Asian countries with data, including China but excluding Japan, is 58 percent.

In Latin America and the Caribbean, the most recent data from surveys indicate that use of family planning among MWRA in the most populous countries varies from 18 percent in Haiti to 70 percent in Cuba. Cuba, Colombia, and Brazil have the highest prevalence rates in the region (well over 60 percent); Guatemala and Haiti, the lowest (under 30 percent). The regional median prevalence rate for Latin America and the Caribbean is 53 percent.

Contraceptive prevalence rates among the largest countries of Eastern Europe and the former Soviet Union range from 17 percent to 73 percent. Eastern European rates are generally comparable to, or higher than, those for Western Europe. The corresponding values for the New Independent States tend to be lower, though in Russia, about two-thirds of MWRA report that they use contraception. Prevalence is much lower in Azerbaijan and Georgia, where the latest available data suggest the rate is on the order of 17 percent.

The regions of the developing world and the New Independent States contrast sharply with the remaining world (Western Europe, Japan, and Oceania) in terms of percentages of women using family planning. Contraceptive prevalence in the United States and the largest countries in the rest of the world ranges from 59 to 76 percent.

The contribution of family planning to reducing fertility (and national population growth) is underscored in figure 35. Fertility (as measured by TFR) and contraceptive prevalence are inversely related for the largest countries of each major world region except the Rest of the World. Though family planning is used to delay or space wanted births as well as to limit childbearing once desired family size is reached, countries with higher proportions of MWRA making use of family planning tend also to be countries with lower fertility.

Family Planning Use Is Typically Higher in Urban Areas...

In developing countries, use of contraception is virtually always higher in urban areas than in the countryside, although the difference is sometimes minimal. In Indonesia, Bangladesh, and Turkey, for example, married women of reproductive age in rural areas are 80 to 90 percent as likely as their urban counterparts to plan their families (figure 36), but in other countries, as in Côte d'Ivoire, rural women are only about a third as likely as urban women to use contraception.

These kinds of differences are partially attributable to educational differentials between urban and rural populations, partially to higher costs of living and smaller family norms prevailing in urban areas, and partially to the greater availability of family planning services and products in urban settings.

...and Among More Educated Women

Female educational attainment has repeatedly been found to be closely linked to fertility regulation and to use of more effective methods of contraception. Women with some primary schooling are consistently more likely to be using contraception than women with no education, and women with more than a primary education have even higher prevalence rates in the countries shown in figure 37.

Figure 36.
Contraceptive Prevalence Rate for Selected Countries by Rural/Urban Residence: Early 1990's

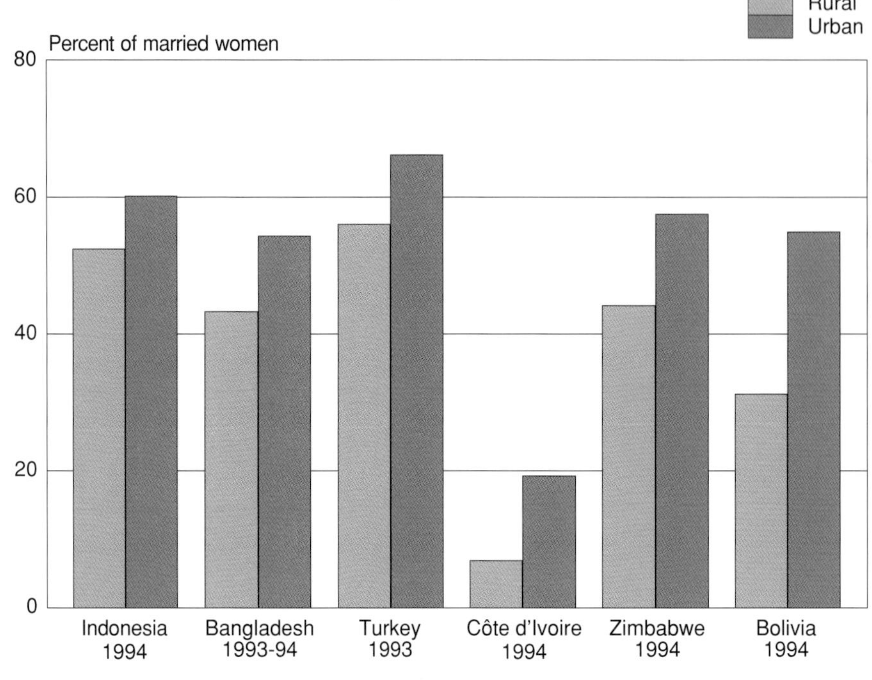

Source: Demographic and Health Surveys.

Figure 37.
Contraceptive Prevalence Rate for Selected Countries by Level of Education: Early 1990's

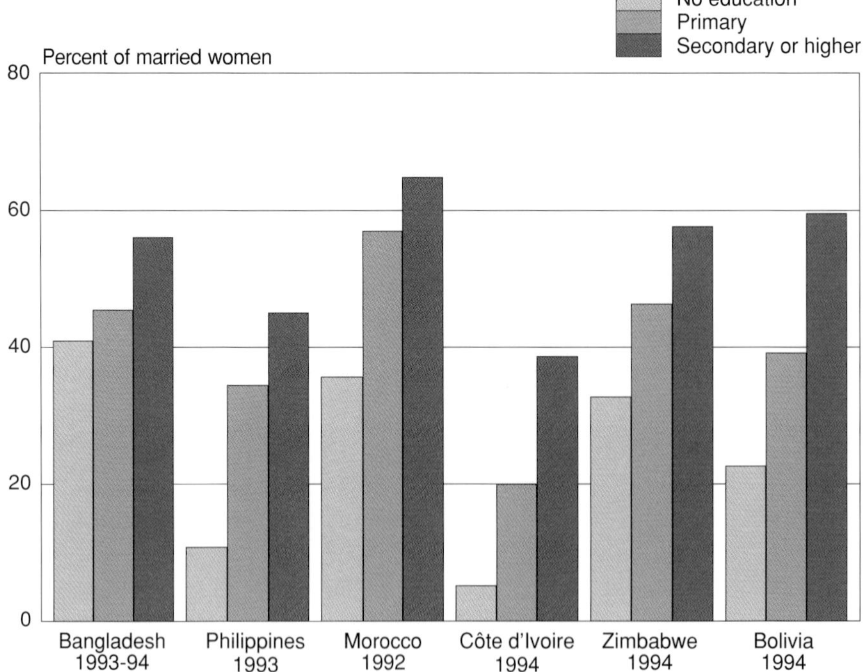

Source: Demographic and Health Surveys.

Figure 38.
Trends in Contraceptive Prevalence for Selected Countries: 1965 to 1994

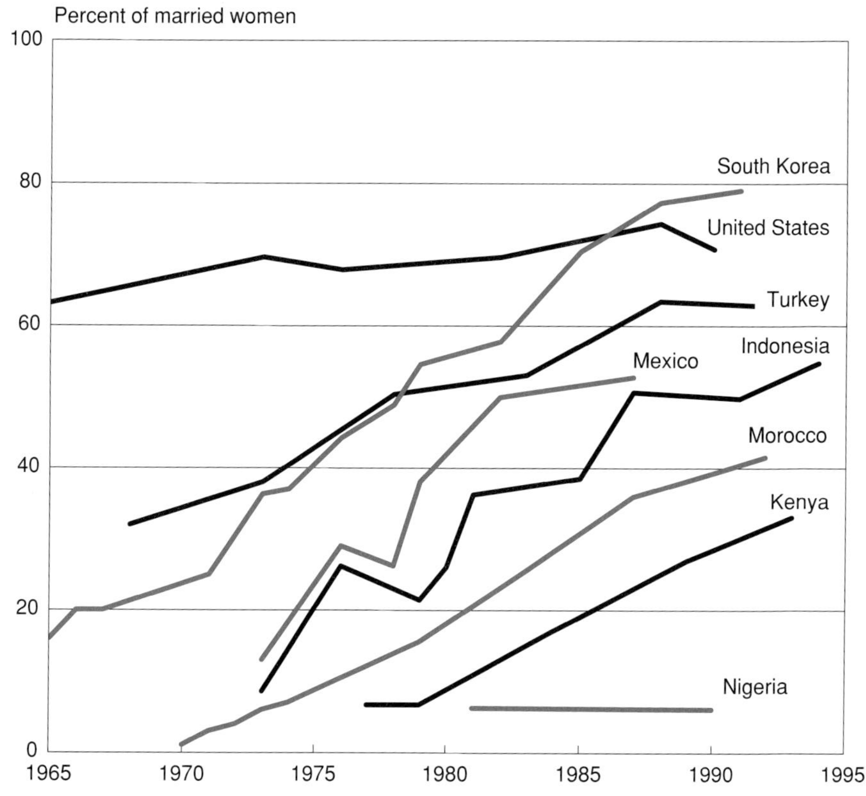

Source: Table A-11.

Women Are Adopting Family Planning in Increasing Numbers in Every World Region

In countries with multiple surveys the trend in contraceptive prevalence is upward virtually everywhere. As a result of the rapid growth in contraceptive prevalence in countries previously having lower levels of use, the gap between high- and low-prevalence countries (and between more- and less-developed regions) has continued to narrow.

Country-specific trends vary considerably within and between the world's regions, however. In Nigeria and Kenya, for example, only 6 to 7 percent of MWRA were using contraception when first measured in the late 1970's or early 1980's (figure 38). The latest surveys show the prevalence rate to have increased to 33 percent in Kenya (1993), while remaining unchanged in Nigeria (1991). In some other countries, where family planning was introduced much earlier, prevalence rates have grown more. For example, in South Korea, the rate increased from 16 percent of married women in 1965 to 79 percent in 1991; in Morocco, it increased from an estimated 1 percent in 1970 to 42 percent in 1992.

Contraceptive Method Mix Varies Among Countries...

Methods of contraception used in both less developed and more developed world regions vary considerably from country to country. Specific method mixes depend on the availability and relative cost of public and private sector-supplied contraceptive services, community norms and personal preferences. Large proportions of couples in the developing world, as well as in more developed countries, are using more effective, modern methods of family planning (table A-11 and figure 39).

Where overall use of contraception is low, it is not unusual for a third or more of users to rely on traditional methods, which tend not to require the use of contraceptive devices. Such methods include periodic abstinence, withdrawal and douche, as well as various folk methods (herbs, amulets, etc.). In Sub-Saharan Africa, where contraceptive use is generally the lowest among world regions, married women who do plan their families have relied heavily on traditional methods, but this is changing.

Where overall use of contraception is relatively high, modern methods dominate, though again, method mix varies from country to country. Among modern methods used worldwide, sterilization is becoming increasingly widespread. About half of users in the United States and Mainland China, and about three-quarters of users in India rely on sterilization to limit family size.

Figure 39.
Contraceptive Method Mix for Selected Countries: 1990 or Later

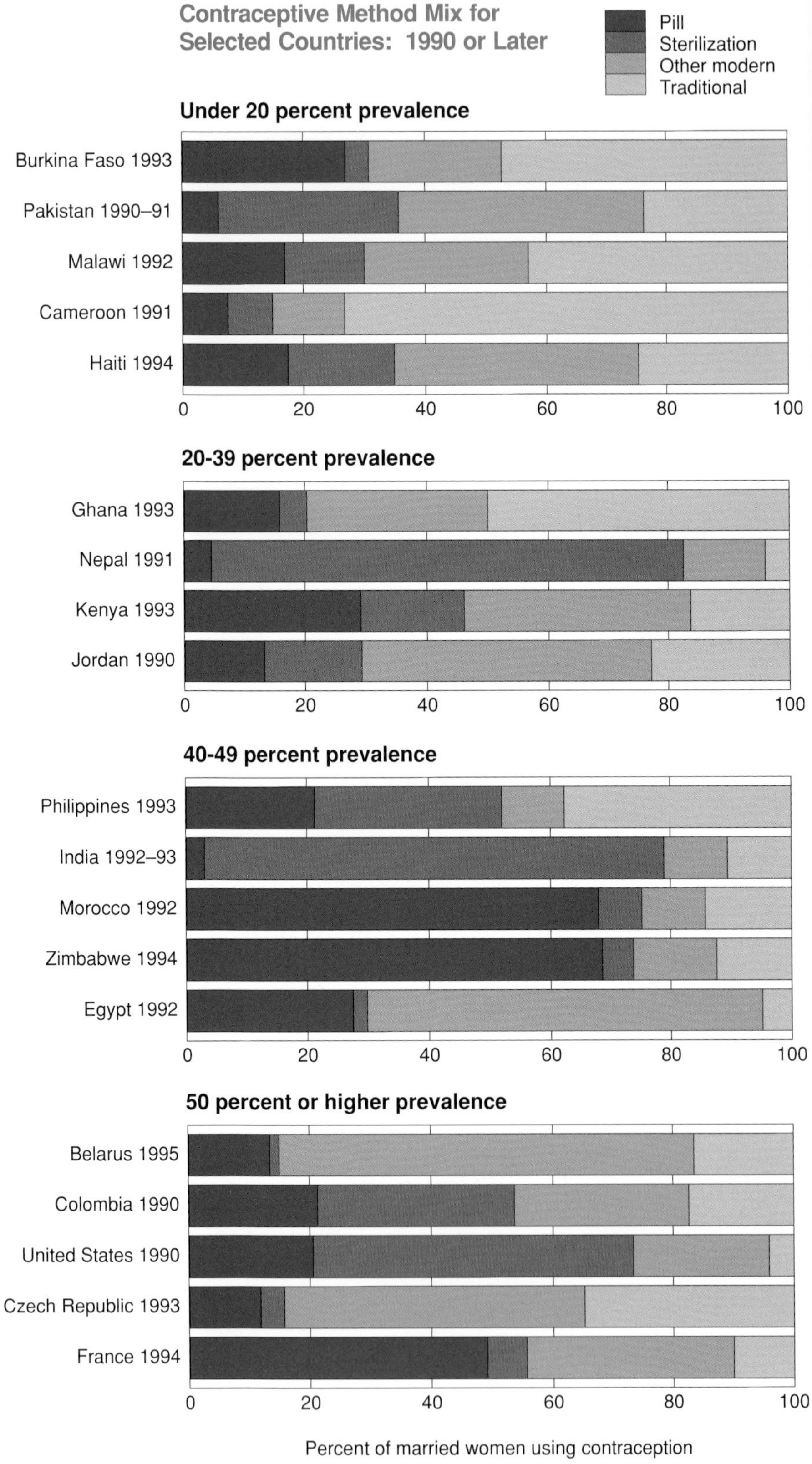

Note: Refers to method of contraception reported by currently married women ages 15 to 49. For Ghana, Morocco, Egypt, Japan, and the Czech Republic, male sterilization is not reported.
Source: Table A-11.

Figure 40.
Trends in Use of Modern and Traditional Methods of Contraception: Selected Countries

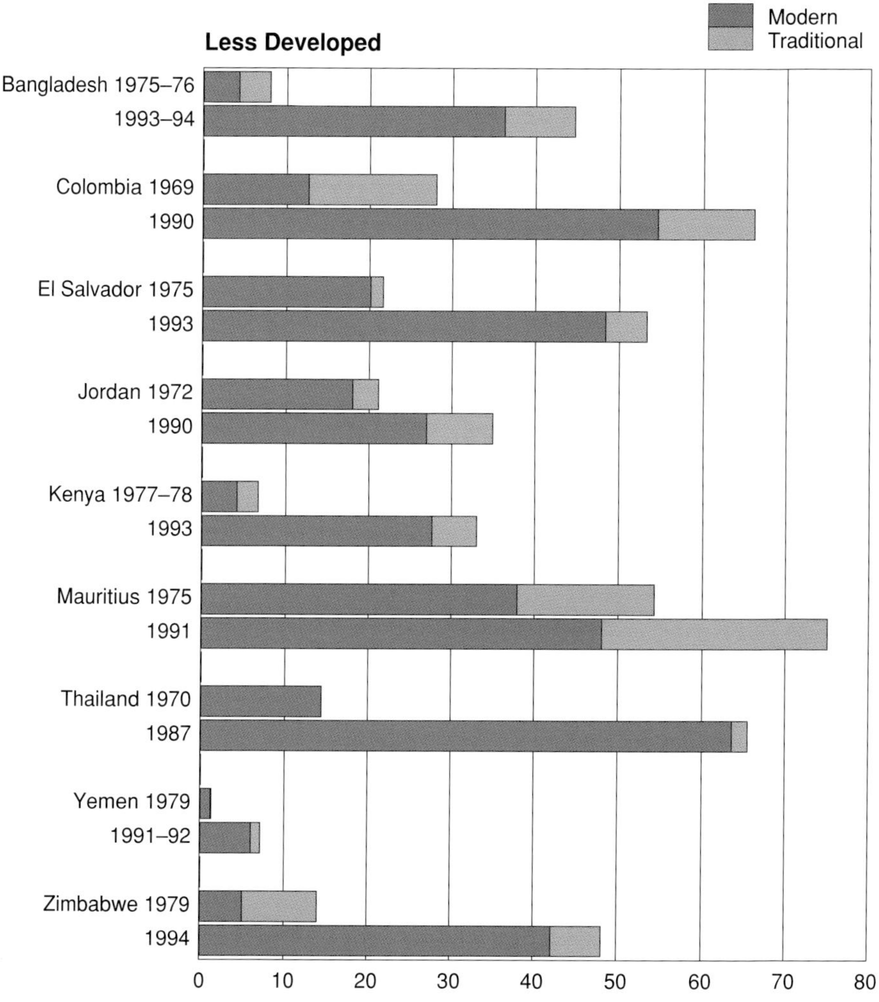

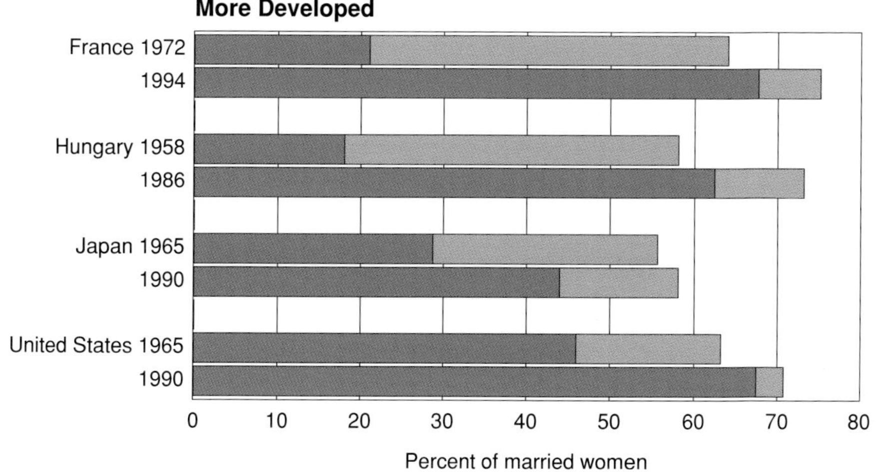

Source: Table A-11.

...and the Trend Is Towards Use of More Effective Modern Methods

Though not a universal pattern, increases in overall use over time are more often than not accompanied by increases in the percentage of users opting for more effective, modern methods of family planning (figure 40).

One of the best examples is Zimbabwe, where about two-thirds of users chose a traditional method, such as rhythm, in 1979. By 1984, however, only about 3 in 10 users relied on traditional methods, and in 1994 only 12 percent of married women using contraception chose traditional methods.

In Kenya the contraceptive prevalence rate increased from 7 percent to 33 percent of married women ages 15 to 49 between 1978 and 1993. During the same period, the proportion of these users selecting modern methods increased from 63 percent to 84 percent. In Hungary, as overall prevalence increased from 58 percent of MWRA in 1958 to 73 percent in 1986, the proportion of users relying on modern methods rose from 31 to 85 percent. Recent surveys show similar trends in Colombia, Thailand, and other countries.

There are also exceptions to the rule: In Mauritius, Jordan, Yemen, and El Salvador, for example, the proportion of traditional methods has actually risen slightly since the 1970's, while the overall prevalence rate has increased substantially.

In two-thirds of the less developed countries with multiple data points included in table A-11, the proportion of users relying on modern methods has risen between the earliest and latest surveys.

Contraceptive Use Is Typically Highest Among Women in Their Late Thirties...

Married women in their thirties, usually their late thirties, are the most likely to use contraception to plan their families (table A-12). As illustrated by a sample of countries from all developing regions, this is true regardless of the level of overall use, although differences among age groups are largest when overall use is high (figure 41). In Mainland China and Peru, for example, where overall rates are relatively high, contraceptive use follows a pattern of low rates at ages 15 to 19 years, climbing to a high at ages 35 to 39 years, and declining again for the older reproductive ages. In Namibia, which has one of the lowest overall rates among the countries shown (29 percent), prevalence is roughly constant for age groups 20 to 24 through 35 to 39.

In Haiti, which has the lowest overall prevalence of the countries shown, the spread in age-specific prevalence rates is only 11 percentage points. In Mainland China, in contrast, age group 35 to 39 has a prevalence rate 80 percentage points higher than age group 15 to 19.

Figure 41.
Contraceptive Prevalence Rate by Age for Selected Countries: 1988 or Later

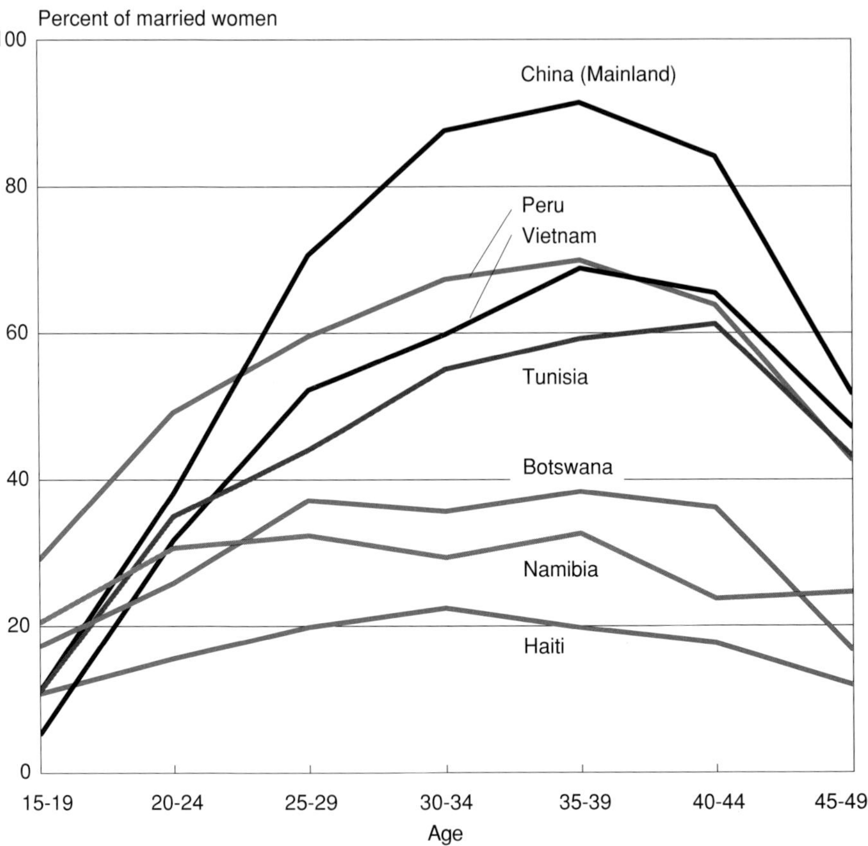

Source: Table A-12.

Figure 42.
Trends in Contraceptive Prevalence Rate by Age for Selected Countries: 1976 to 1994

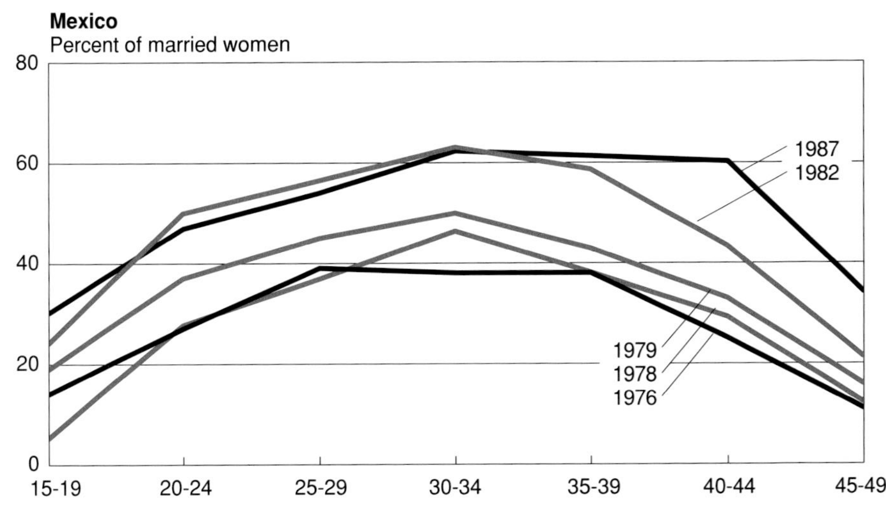

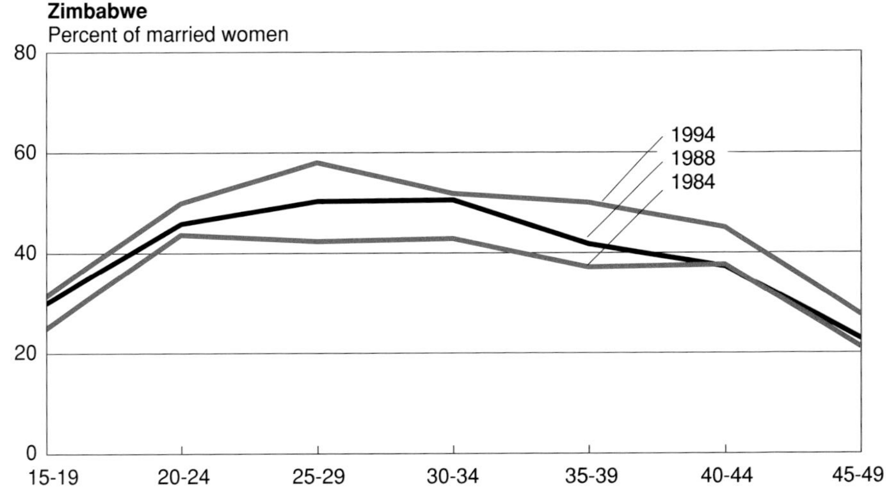

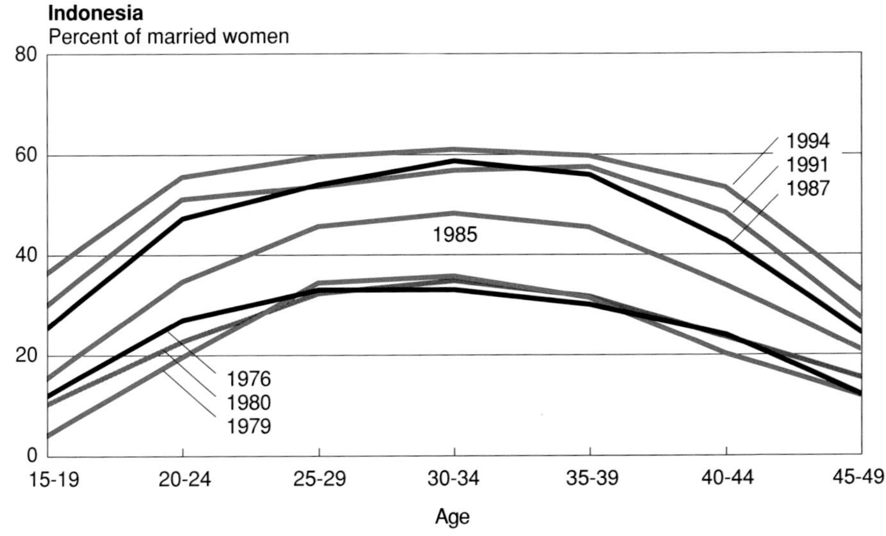

Source: Table A-12.

...but Patterns of Increase in Age-Specific Prevalence Depend on Reasons for Use

Over time, increases in contraceptive use within populations that use family planning to limit, rather than space, childbearing tend to be smallest among younger women, who have yet to attain their desired family size; largest, among women in their thirties and early forties, who ***have*** attained desired family size but are not yet subject to the decreased fecundity characteristic of the 45 to 49 age group (figure 42). In Mexico, for example, while the overall contraceptive prevalence rate was increasing from 29 percent to 53 percent between 1976 and 1987, the rate for women ages 25 to 29 years increased by 15 percentage points; and that for women ages 40 to 44 years, by 35 percentage points, the largest increase in any age group.

Where contraception is used more to space births or where family planning and educational attainment are highly correlated, increases in age-specific prevalence may be concentrated in the 20's and 30's, as in Zimbabwe (Zimbabwe, Central Statistical Office and Macro International 1989:50).

In Indonesia, where some 55 percent of married women of reproductive age were using family planning in 1994, increases in prevalence rates since 1976 have been about equal for every age group other than the very youngest (15 to 19) and oldest (45 to 49). These increases, averaging 27 percentage points, reflect widespread use of contraception for both child spacing and family size limitation (Indonesia, Central Bureau of Statistics, et al. 1995:70).

Continued Expansion in Contraceptive Prevalence Is Partially a Matter of Access

If family planning is to continue to play an important role in improving reproductive health around the world, and in the developing world in particular, couples must know about contraceptive methods, including the demonstrated benefits of lower-risk pregnancies to maternal and child health; couples must be motivated to use family planning; and family planning services must be readily available to them. Evidence from surveys conducted in the late 1980's and early 1990's shows that modern method prevalence is associated with proximity of a source of supply (figure 43).

Moreover, the general pattern is that women have fewer children (TFR) where modern methods are more readily available, again as measured by proximity (figure 44).

Figure 43.
Modern Method Contraceptive Use by Proximity to Supply Source
(23 countries)

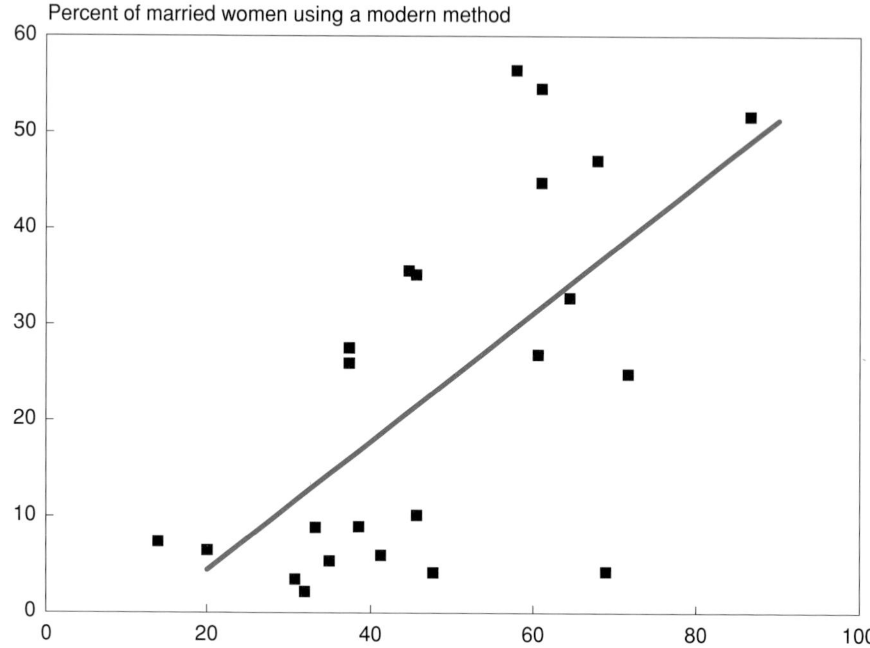

Source: Demographic and Health Surveys.

Figure 44.
Total Fertility Rate by Proximity to Supply Source
(23 countries)

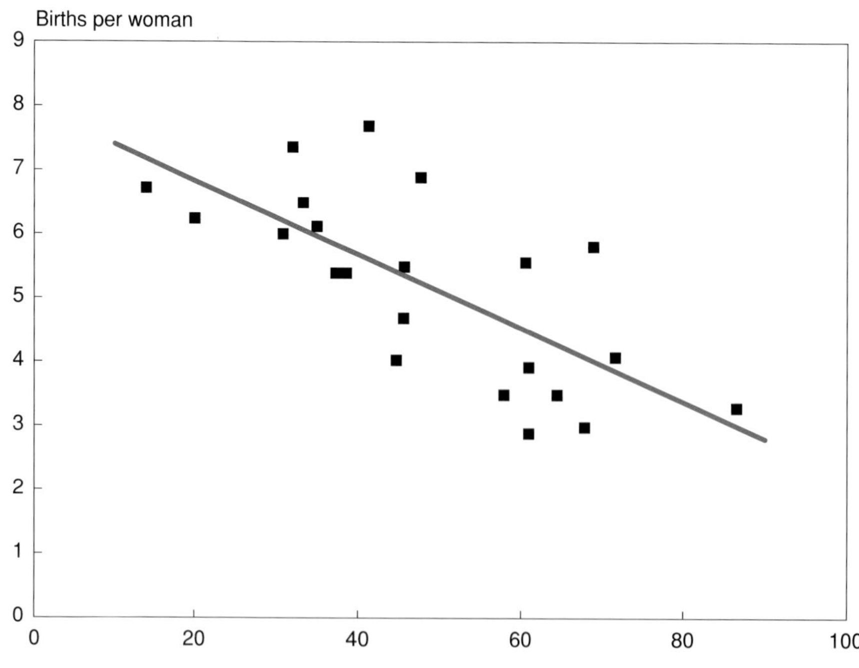

Source: Demographic and Health Surveys.

Figure 45.
Unmet Need for Family Planning Among Currently Married Women for Selected Countries by Region: 1985 or Later

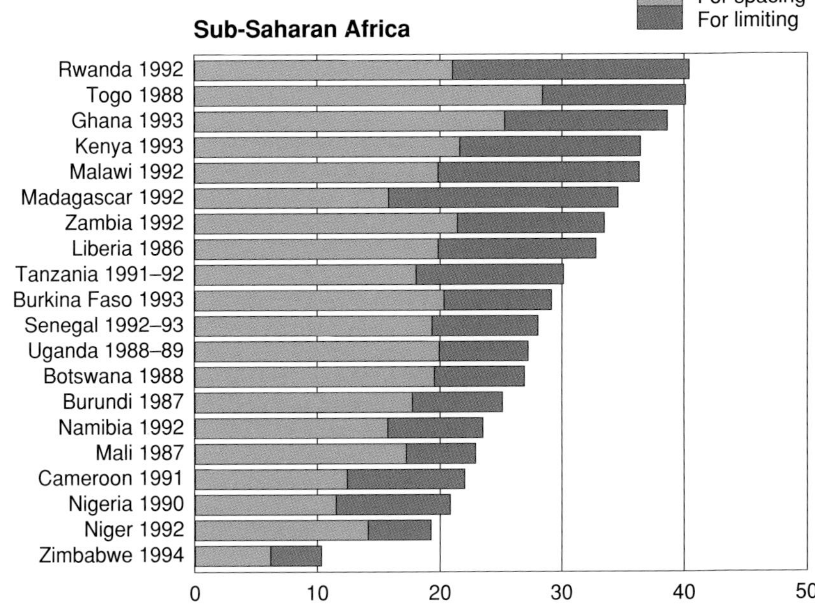

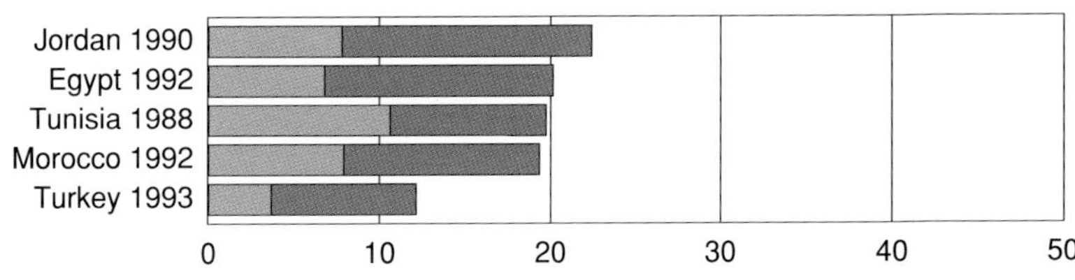

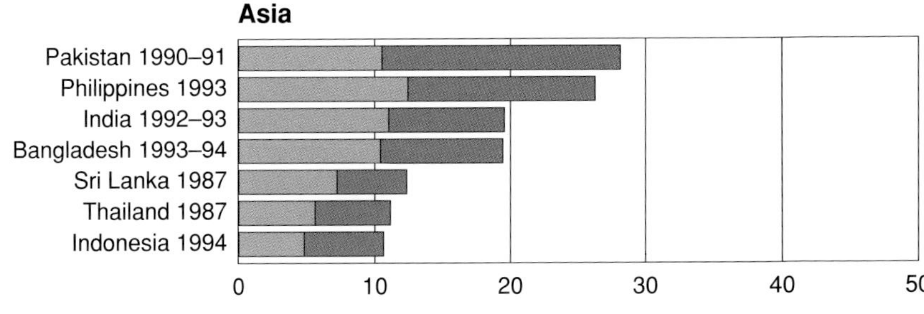

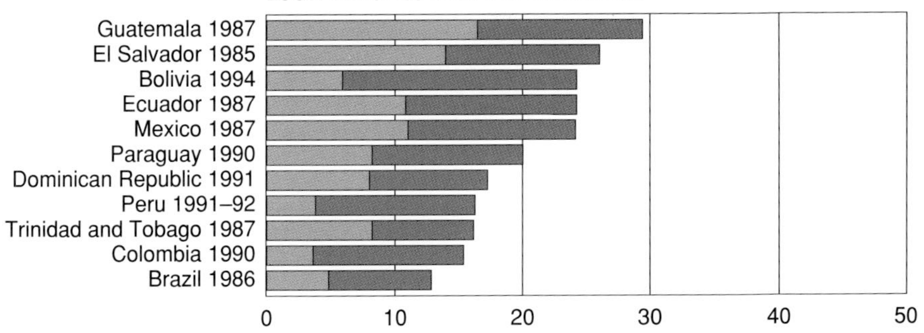

Source: Most recent Demographic and Health Surveys.

Growing Body of Evidence Indicates Unmet Need for Family Planning Is Widespread

Many women at risk of childbearing say they would like to delay the onset of childbearing, postpone their next pregnancy, or have no additional births, but are not using contraception. Since the publication of data about this unmet need for 25 countries in 1991 (Westoff and Ochoa 1991, reproduced in *World Population Profile: 1994*), information on unmet need has become available for an additional 18 countries. These data and the earlier data together portray each major region of the developing world as having substantial unmet need for family planning (figure 45).

Unmet need is generally highest in Sub-Saharan Africa, where the primary component is the need for methods for spacing births. Unmet need is particularly high in Rwanda, Togo, Kenya, and Ghana where roughly 2 in every 5 currently married women of reproductive age are not using contraception but desire to control their fertility.

Unmet need is high in some Latin American, Near East and North Africa, and Asian countries as well. Pakistan (28 percent), the Philippines (26 percent), El Salvador (26 percent), and Guatemala (29 percent) have particularly high levels of unmet need. In Latin America and the Caribbean, and in the Near East and North Africa, the primary component of unmet need is often a need to limit rather than a need to space births.

In the seven Asian countries with information on unmet need, evidence suggests overall unmet need is moderate, with a balance between unsatisfied demand for family planning for spacing and limitation.

The ICPD Program of Action (United Nations 1995a: section 7.13) notes that, while five times as many couples are using some method of family planning today in developing countries, compared with the situation prevailing in the 1960's, the full range of modern methods is unavailable to as many as 350 million couples worldwide. In recognition of this unmet need, much of it in the developing countries of Africa, Asia and Latin America, the International Conference on Population and Development adopted universal access to family planning methods and related reproductive health services as a key goal to be pursued over the course of the next two decades.

Improved availability of family planning services, leading to more widespread use of family planning, would carry widely recognized maternal and child health benefits, particularly in less developed countries (United Nations 1995d, Maine 1981, Omran 1984). The ICPD Program of Action draws attention to survey evidence indicating that some 120 million additional women worldwide would use a modern method of contraception if services were more accessible and if their partners, families, and communities were more supportive of family planning.

Giving couples more control over the number and spacing of their children could have substantial demographic effects apart from expected impacts on infant, child, and maternal mortality. Specifically, greater use of family planning could reduce unwanted fertility, which may be as high as 15 to 20 percent of all fertility in Asia and Sub-Saharan Africa, and as high as 30 percent in Latin America and North Africa.[5]

[5] Unweighted region-specific means of percentage differences between total fertility rates and desired total fertility rates taken from Westoff (1991: table 5.1). Westoff's data are from 26 DHS surveys conducted in the late 1980's.

From the ICPD Program of Action:

"All countries should, over the next several years, assess the extent of national unmet need for good-quality family-planning services and its integration in the reproductive health context, paying particular attention to the most vulnerable and underserved groups in the population. All countries should take steps to meet the family-planning needs of their populations as soon as possible and should, in all cases by the year 2015, seek to provide universal access to a full range of safe and reliable family-planning methods and to related reproductive health services ..." (section 7.16).

"... approximately 120 million additional women worldwide would be currently using a modern family-planning method if more accurate information and affordable services were easily available, and if partners, extended families and the community were more supportive. These numbers do not include the substantial and growing numbers of sexually active unmarried individuals wanting and in need of information and services." (section 7.13)

Focus on

Adolescent Fertility in the Developing World

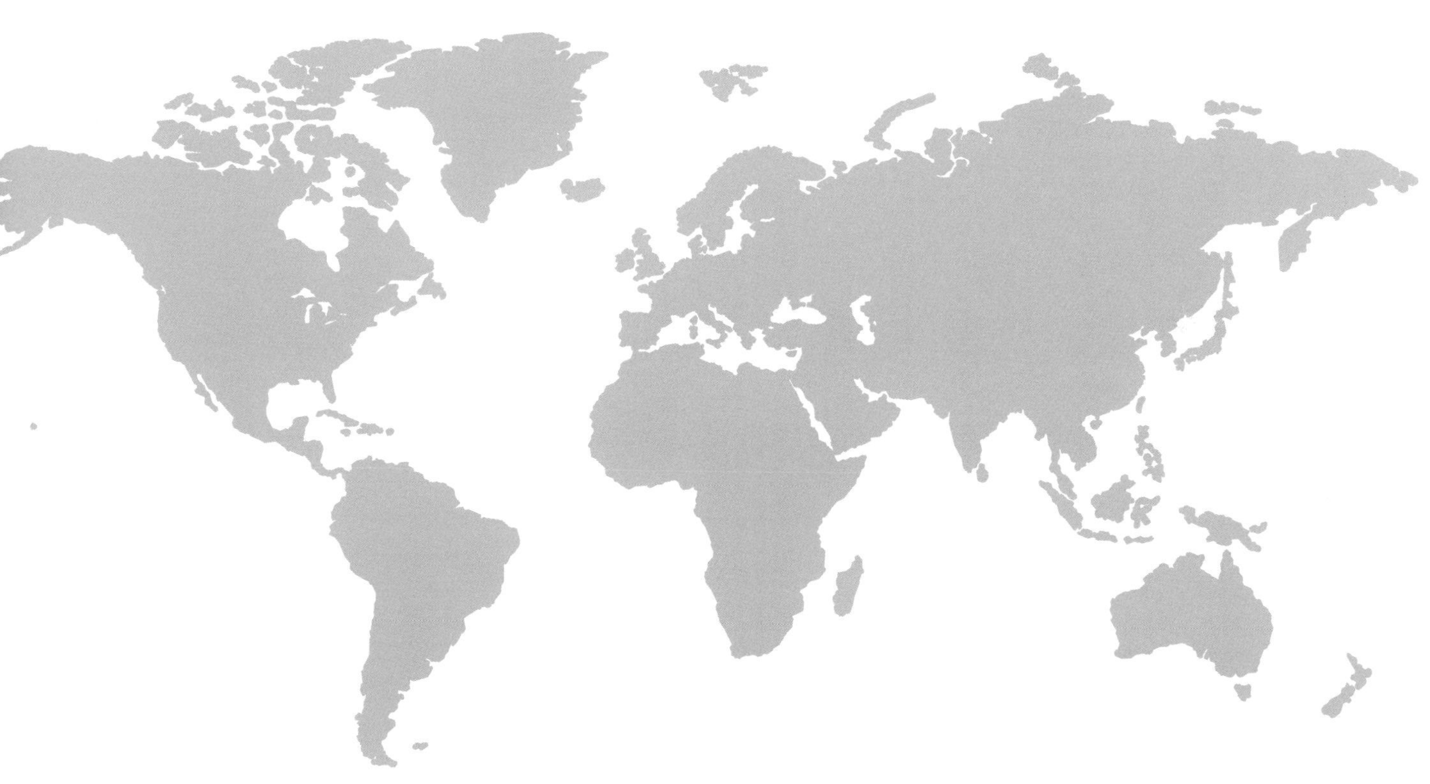

Focus on

Adolescent Fertility in the Developing World[6]

Reproductive health was a key theme of the 1994 International Conference on Population and Development. The Cairo Program of Action's chapter on reproductive rights goes beyond the earlier World Population Plan of Action in specifically underscoring the need to contend with the adolescent reproductive health issues of unplanned pregnancies, sexually transmitted disease, and unsafe abortion. The Program of Action acknowledges the need to urgently address the well-documented maternal and infant health problems of high risk pregnancies including, by definition, the pregnancies of adolescent women.

[6] "Developing countries" in this section of *World Population Profile: 1996* refers to Sub-Saharan Africa, Asia (excluding Japan and China [Mainland and Taiwan], but including the central Asian republics of the former Soviet Union), the Near East and North Africa, Latin America and the Caribbean, and Oceania (excluding Australia and New Zealand). The difference between this grouping and that used elsewhere in the report is the exclusion of China. The term "Asia" refers to Asia except for China, Japan, and the central Asian republics of the former Soviet Union, because none of the survey data reported were collected from China or any of the NIS. Thus, "Asia" in this section corresponds to "Other Asia" as used elsewhere in the report. "Remaining World" includes North America and Europe, the New Independent States, Japan, Oceania and China.

This part of *World Population Profile: 1996* brings together internationally comparable survey data collected over the past 25 years to show how adolescent reproductive behavior has changed, and to quantify current levels and regional variation in teenage fertility. It also suggests the magnitude of the challenge to improve adolescent reproductive health, insofar as it is linked to adolescent childbearing, that faces the nations of the developing world during the coming 25 years.

300 Million High-Risk Births Expected in Developing Countries During Next 25 Years

About 15 million babies are born to young women ages 15 to 19 (hereafter, "adolescents" or "teenagers") each year. These are high-risk births from the perspective of the health of both mother and child. They are also high-cost births when the associated negative effects on the quality of life and role of women in society are considered. About 8 in every 10 of these babies, or 13 million, are born in the developing countries of Asia, Africa, and Latin America. Thirteen percent of all children born in these countries are born to teenage mothers.

This section of *World Population Profile: 1996* highlights the principal findings of a report recently issued by the Bureau of the Census, entitled *Trends in Adolescent Fertility and Contraceptive Use in the Developing World.* This excerpt and the report on which it is based draw upon information from the Demographic and Health Surveys (DHS) program carried out by Macro International, Inc. from 1984 to the present; the World Fertility Surveys (WFS) program overseen by the International Statistical Institute during the 1970's and early 1980's; the family health and contraceptive prevalence surveys carried out by the Centers for Disease Control (CDC) since 1985; as well as a number of other data sources, including the Census Bureau's International Data Base. The survey data are available for 56 countries representing about three-quarters of the developing world's population (excluding China).

Population size and fertility data in this section have been updated to be consistent with the data in the current report. However, the definitions of less developed countries and "Rest of the World" used in this section of *World Population Profile: 1996* differ from those employed elsewhere in the report. They reflect the geographic classification employed in *Trends.* Population size and fertility data underlying statements about regional populations have been updated for 1996 so that such statements may differ from those found in *Trends.*

Adolescent Fertility Raises Health, Women's Status, and Population Growth Concerns

The health risks associated with adolescent pregnancy and childbearing include higher risks of maternal and infant morbidity and mortality. Reproductive health problems are a particular concern in the case of early adolescent pregnancy and childbearing; i.e., where the mother is age 17 or younger, rather than age 18 or 19.

Young women are more likely than more mature women to suffer pregnancy-related complications that endanger their lives or lead to infertility. Maternal mortality ratios for women ages 15 to 19 may be more than double those of women in their 20's and early 30's (figure 46).

Younger, unmarried women also are more likely than older married women to consider late, unsafe abortions as an alternative to carrying a pregnancy to term (Senderowitz 1995:16-17; cf. WHO 1989:7).

Figure 46.
Maternal Mortality Ratio by Age of Mother

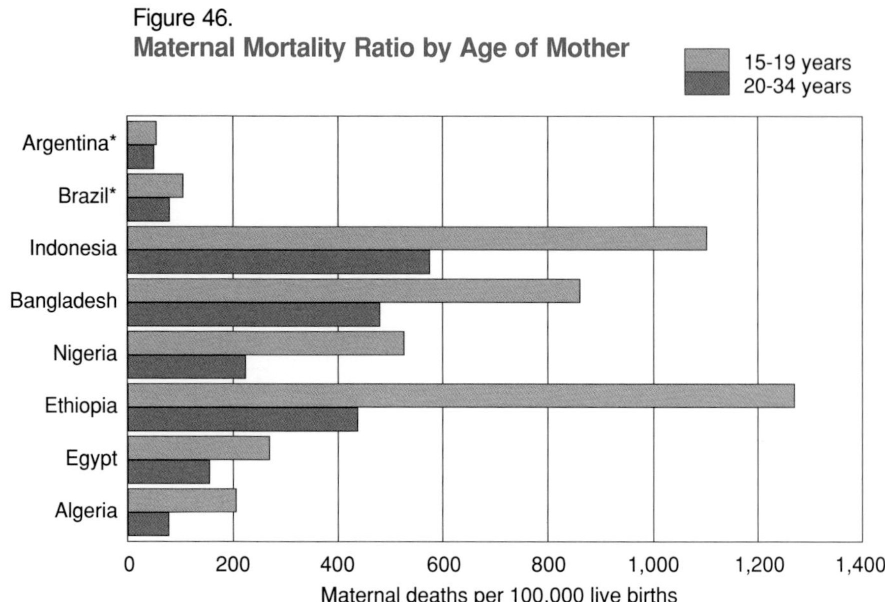

* For Argentina and Brazil, older women are 20 to 29 years.
Source: World Health Organization (1989).

Figure 47.
Infant Mortality Rate by Age of Mother: 1987 or Later

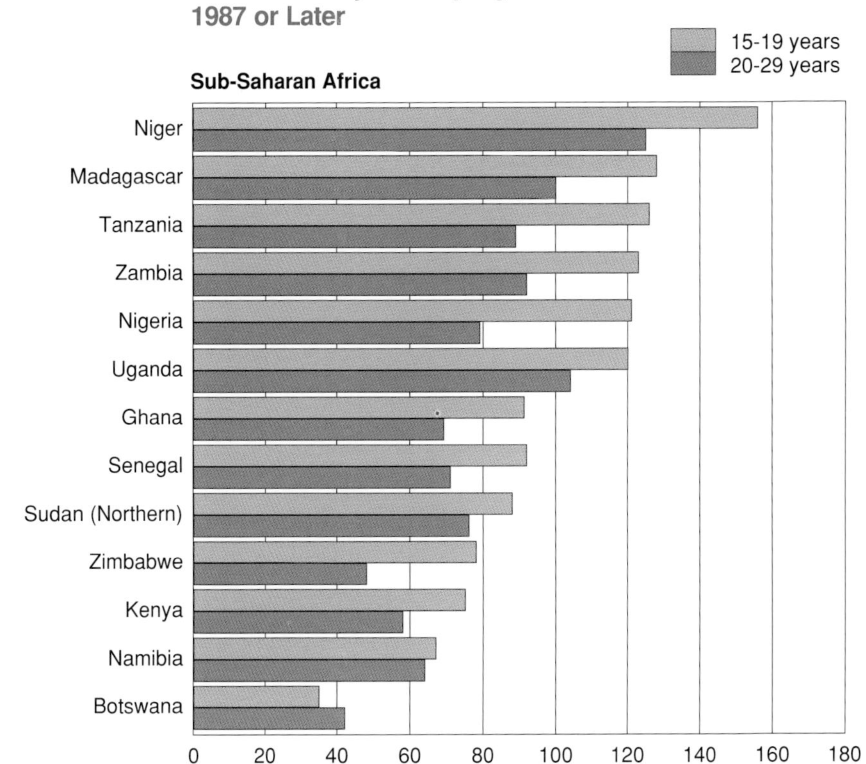

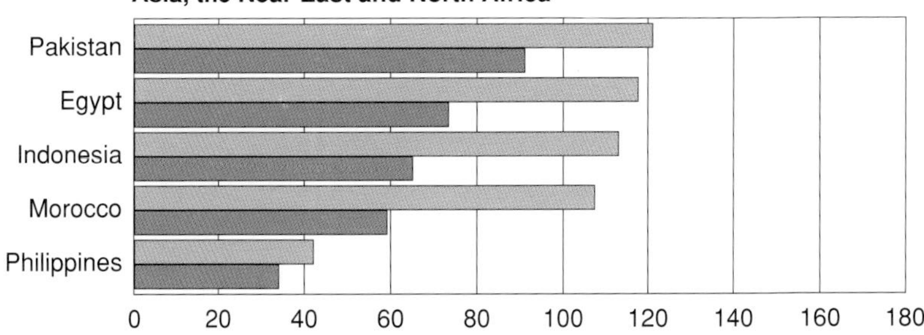

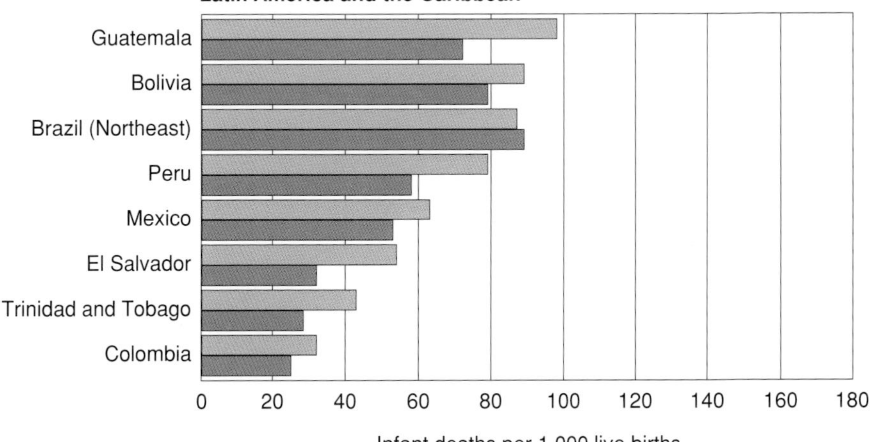

Source: U.S. Bureau of the Census (1996b).

Infants born to adolescent mothers face greater risks of low birth weight, prematurity, birth injuries, stillbirth, and mortality than do babies born to older women (Bledsoe and Cohen 1993:6; WHO 1989:5). Infant mortality rates for teenage births are as much as 80 percent higher than those for women in the age group 20 to 29 (figure 47).

Infant mortality among babies born to adolescent mothers is highest in those countries with the largest proportions of early teenage births (figure 48, cf. United Nations 1995d).

Apart from the health risks, adolescent childbearing and the conditions associated with it are fundamental factors determining the quality of life and role of women in a society. Untimely pregnancy can force young women to discontinue their education, reducing their employment options later in life.

In addition, national efforts to achieve the kinds of demographic goals referred to in the third section of this report may suffer because childbearing at early ages tends to be associated with higher fertility over women's reproductive lives. Rapid population growth continues to represent a challenge to many nations in terms of providing education, health services and employment for their people now and in the future.

Figure 48.
Infant Mortality by Percentage of Women With One or More Births by Age 17
(24 countries)

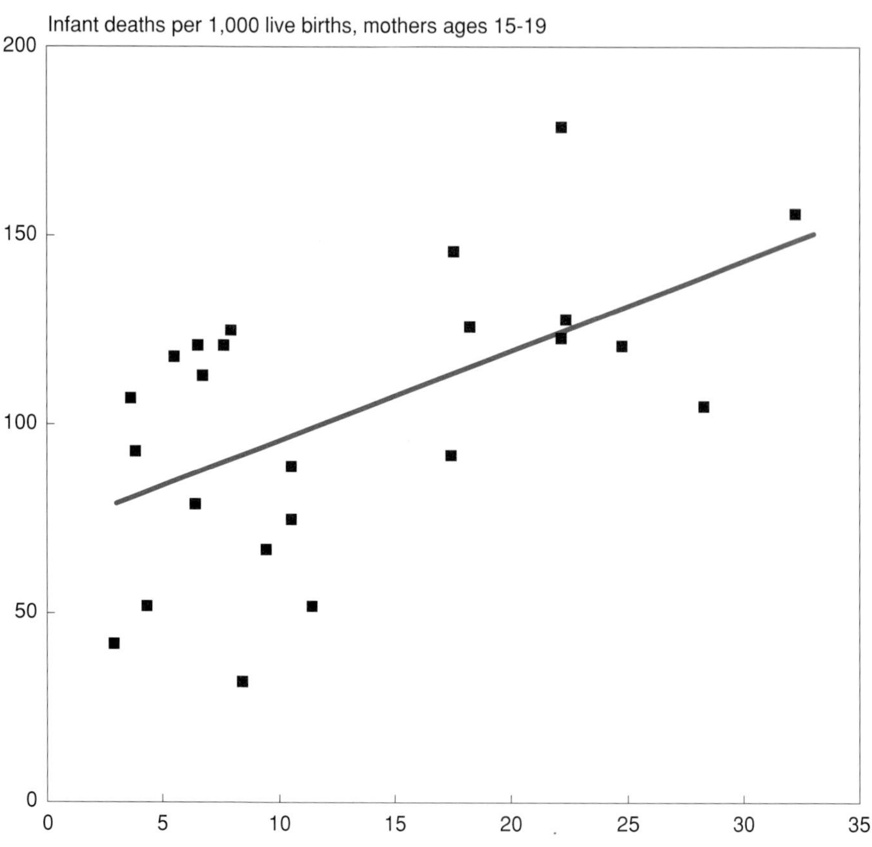

Source: U.S. Bureau of the Census (1996b).

Figure 49.
Trends in Number of Women Ages 15 to 19 by Region: 1996 to 2020

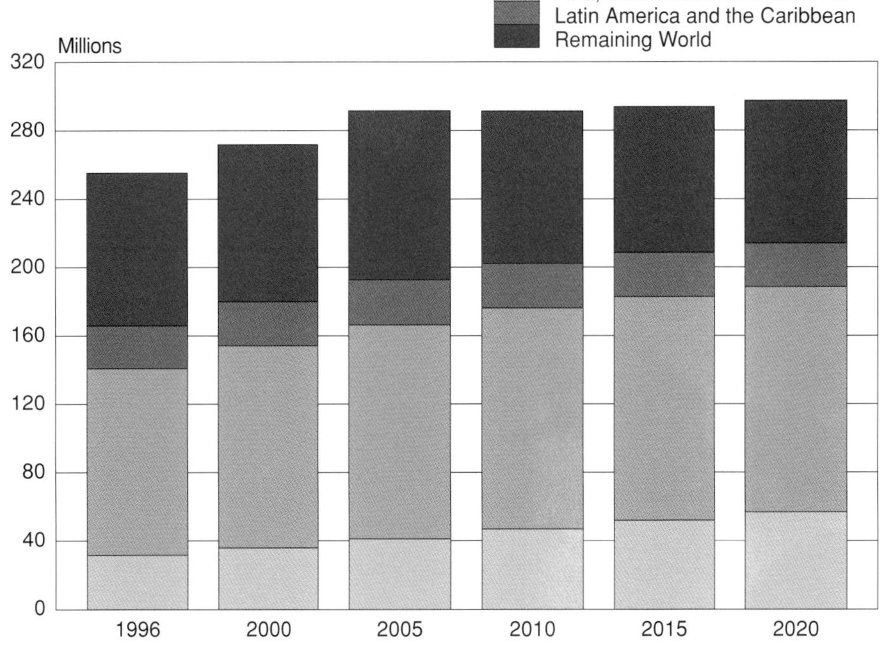

Note: Asia, the Near East and North Africa excludes China and Japan.
The Remaining World includes North America, Europe, Japan, Oceania, and China.
Source: U.S. Bureau of the Census, International Data Base.

Figure 50.
Trends in Adolescent Births by Region: 1996 to 2020

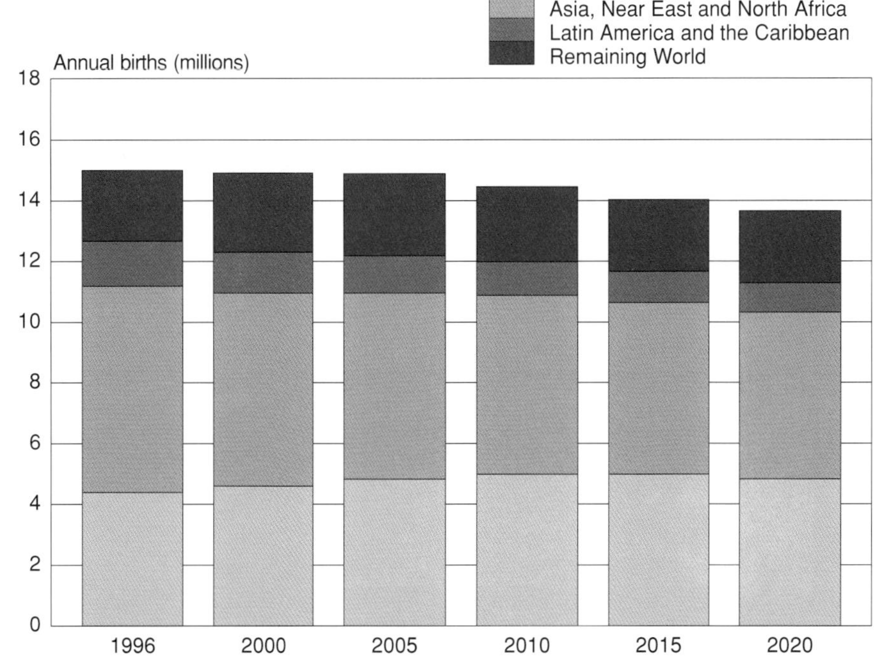

Note: Asia, the Near East and North Africa excludes China and Japan.
The Remaining World includes North America, Europe, Japan, Oceania, and China.
Source: U.S. Bureau of the Census, International Data Base.

Growing Teen Population Spurs Adolescent Births and Determines Their Geographic Distribution

If present trends continue, over 300 million babies will be born to adolescent women living in Africa, Asia, and Latin America over the next quarter of a century. The number of births to teenage mothers will decrease slowly, from nearly 15 million in 1996 to 13.7 million in the year 2020, as a result of significant declines in fertility that have occurred in many developing countries during the past 10 to 20 years and that are continuing today (both among adolescents and among all women of reproductive age). The decline would be more rapid were it not for the fact that numbers of adolescent women will continue to grow during the coming quarter century as the result of past high fertility, and this is particularly true for Sub-Saharan Africa, where fertility levels have fallen less than in other regions of the world.

There are some 256 million women ages 15 to 19 alive in 1996, and about 2 in every 3, or 166 million, live in Africa, Asia, the Near East, or Latin America and the Caribbean (table A-13). These numbers are projected to increase during the next quarter century. The size of the adolescent cohort will grow by about 40 million, to 298 million young women by the year 2020, and nearly all of this growth will occur in these regions (figure 49). By the end of the next 25 years, the number of adolescent women living in the Remaining World will actually have declined by about 6 million persons. Nearly 3 in every 4 adolescent women will then be living in Asia, Africa, the Near East, and Latin America.

As a result of the interplay of trends in the size of the adolescent cohort and adolescent fertility, projected births to teenage mothers will decline by about 9 percent of the number occurring in 1996 over the course of the next 25 years. This overall decrease

Figure 51.
Adolescent Fertility Rates: 1996

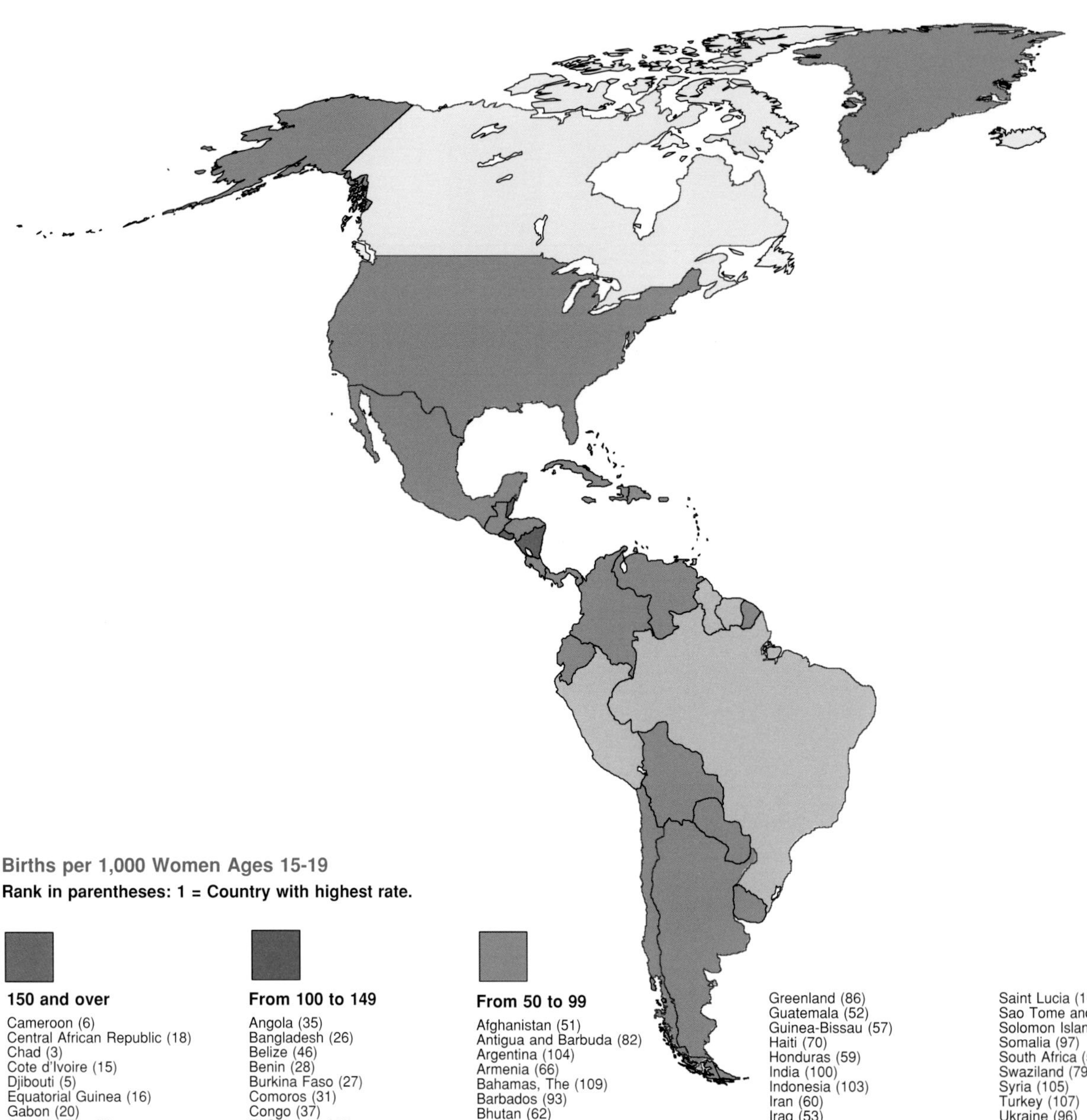

Births per 1,000 Women Ages 15-19

Rank in parentheses: 1 = Country with highest rate.

150 and over

Cameroon (6)
Central African Republic (18)
Chad (3)
Cote d'Ivoire (15)
Djibouti (5)
Equatorial Guinea (16)
Gabon (20)
Gambia, The (7)
Gaza Strip (8)
Guinea (19)
Liberia (11)
Mali (2)
Marshall Islands (21)
Mauritania (14)
Mayotte (1)
Niger (4)
Nigeria (9)
Senegal (22)
Sierra Leone (12)
Uganda (13)
Zaire (10)
Zambia (17)

From 100 to 149

Angola (35)
Bangladesh (26)
Belize (46)
Benin (28)
Burkina Faso (27)
Comoros (31)
Congo (37)
El Salvador (43)
Eritrea (39)
Ethiopia (36)
Grenada (47)
Laos (44)
Libya (29)
Madagascar (25)
Malawi (30)
Maldives (34)
Mozambique (33)
Namibia (45)
Nicaragua (24)
Oman (40)
Saudi Arabia (42)
Sudan (48)
Tanzania (32)
Togo (23)
West Bank (41)
Zimbabwe (38)

From 50 to 99

Afghanistan (51)
Antigua and Barbuda (82)
Argentina (104)
Armenia (66)
Bahamas, The (109)
Barbados (93)
Bhutan (62)
Bolivia (64)
Botswana (68)
Bulgaria (106)
Burma (108)
Burundi (98)
Cambodia (77)
Cape Verde (89)
Chile (92)
Colombia (111)
Costa Rica (71)
Cuba (65)
Dominica (117)
Dominican Republic (76)
Ecuador (91)
Egypt (99)
Fiji (90)
French Guiana (50)
French Polynesia (74)
Ghana (56)
Greenland (86)
Guatemala (52)
Guinea-Bissau (57)
Haiti (70)
Honduras (59)
India (100)
Indonesia (103)
Iran (60)
Iraq (53)
Jamaica (85)
Jordan (114)
Kenya (61)
Kyrgyzstan (95)
Lesotho (83)
Mexico (80)
Moldova (87)
Nepal (49)
Pakistan (81)
Panama (75)
Papua New Guinea (73)
Paraguay (67)
Puerto Rico (110)
Qatar (112)
Reunion (113)
Russia (115)
Rwanda (94)
Saint Kitts and Nevis (78)
Saint Lucia (101)
Sao Tome and Principe (63)
Solomon Islands (58)
Somalia (97)
South Africa (55)
Swaziland (79)
Syria (105)
Turkey (107)
Ukraine (96)
United Arab Emirates (69)
United States (88)
Uruguay (116)
Vanuatu (84)
Venezuela (72)
Western Samoa (102)
Yemen (54)

Source: Table A-13.

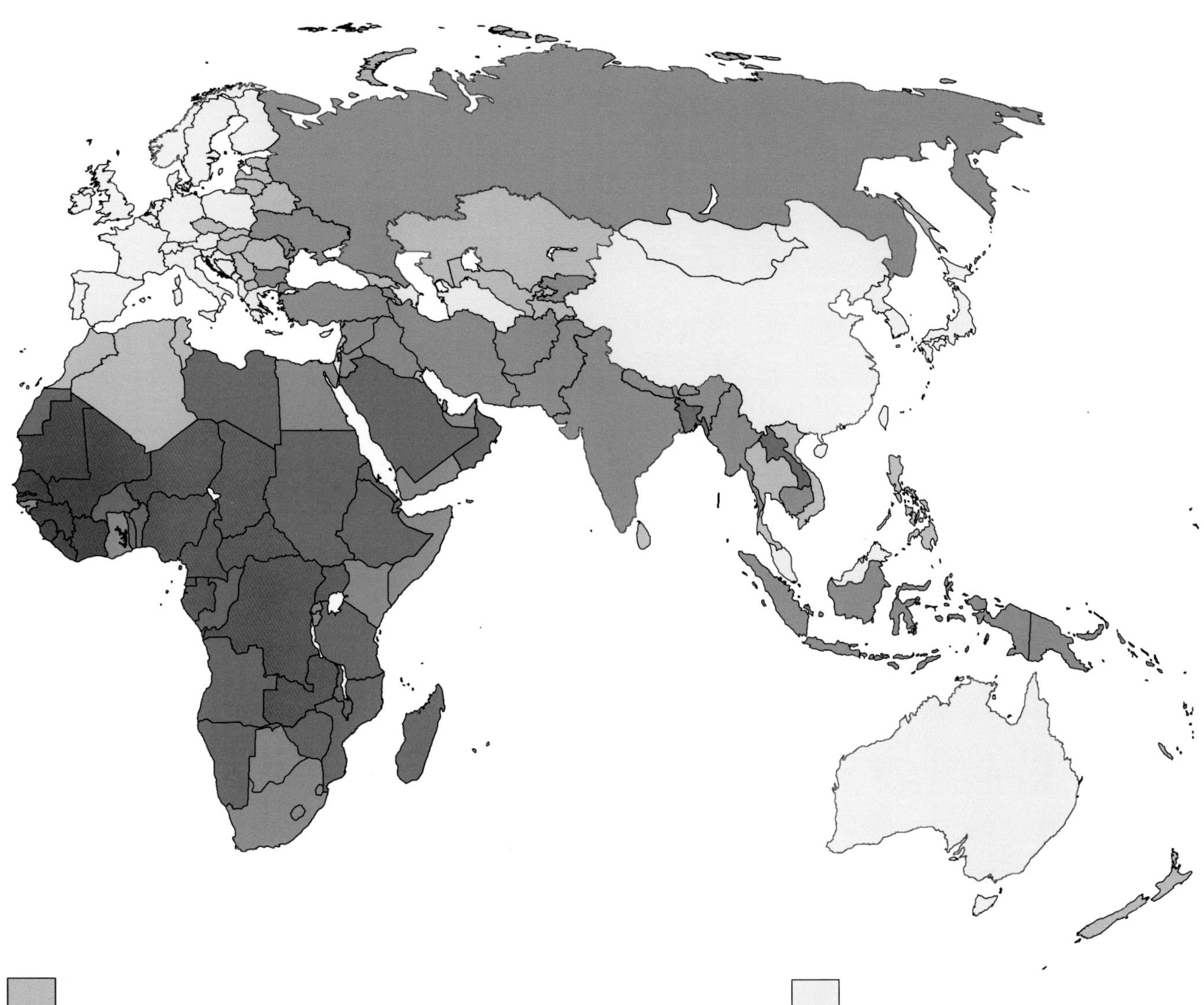

From 30 to 49

Algeria (129)
Aruba (137)
Belarus (126)
Brazil (132)
Brunei (142)
Czech Republic (147)
Estonia (125)
Georgia (124)
Guadeloupe (153)
Guyana (141)
Hungary (154)
Isle of Man (151)
Kazakhstan (119)
Kuwait (149)
Latvia (127)
Lebanon (133)
Lithuania (128)
Macedonia, The Former Yugoslav Rep. of (144)
Mauritius (122)
Morocco (135)
Netherlands Antilles (136)
New Caledonia (134)
New Zealand (155)
Peru (121)
Philippines (120)
Romania (138)
Saint Vincent and the Grenadines (118)
Serbia (139)
Seychelles (143)
Slovakia (146)
Sri Lanka (152)
Suriname (123)
Tajikistan (130)
Thailand (131)
Trinidad and Tobago (145)
Tunisia (150)
Uzbekistan (140)
Vietnam (148)

Under 30

Albania (186)
Andorra (178)
Anguilla (183)
Australia (170)
Austria (173)
Azerbaijan (157)
Bahrain (165)
Belgium (194)
Bosnia and Herzegovina (172)
Canada (161)
China, Mainland (179)
China, Taiwan (180)
Croatia (166)
Cyprus (162)
Denmark (197)
Faroe Islands (168)
Finland (190)
France (188)
Germany (192)
Gibraltar (189)
Greece (164)
Guernsey (175)
Hong Kong (204)
Iceland (160)
Ireland (184)
Israel (177)
Italy (201)
Japan (207)
Jersey (191)
Liechtenstein (206)
Luxembourg (193)
Macau (202)
Malaysia (171)
Malta (195)
Martinique (185)
Monaco (200)
Mongolia (159)
Montenegro (174)
Netherlands (205)
North Korea (198)
Norway (182)
Poland (163)
Portugal (176)
San Marino (196)
Singapore (199)
Slovenia (181)
South Korea (208)
Spain (156)
Sweden (187)
Switzerland (203)
Turkmenistan (169)
Tuvalu (158)
United Kingdom (167)

reflects a drop in adolescent births in several regions offset by an increase in Sub-Saharan Africa. Adolescent births are expected to fall by about 20 percent of the 1996 level in Asia, the Near East and North Africa; by 35 percent in the relatively more developed countries of Latin America and the Caribbean (figure 50). However, over 400,000 more births to teenage mothers — a 10 percent increase over the 1996 level — will occur in Sub-Saharan Africa by the end of the 1996-2020 period.

Sub-Saharan African adolescent fertility rates (births per 1,000 women ages 15 to 19) are generally higher than those for countries in other regions of the world (figure 51). The regional level is over twice that of the other developing regions, and the fertility of young women in Africa is expected to remain well above that of adolescent women in other parts of the developing world through 2020 (table A-13).

Declines in Adolescent Fertility Exceed Those of Older Women

Data from the World Fertility Survey studies of the late 1970's and early 1980's, and from surveys undertaken by the DHS program and Centers for Disease Control in the late 1980's and early 1990's show that the fall in adolescent fertility has tended to exceed changes for women in the prime reproductive years (ages 20 to 34) during the past 10 to 15 years (table A-14 and figure 52).

Differences in fertility decline for adolescent women vis-a-vis older women reflect trends toward later marriage in many developing countries, which affect the younger group more than the older group. The differences may also reflect ongoing urbanization and the progress being made by many nations toward providing greater educational opportunities for girls and women, commensurate with those available to boys and men.

Figure 52.
Percent Change in Fertility by Age of Mother: Mid-1970's to Early 1980's Versus Mid-1980's to Early 1990's

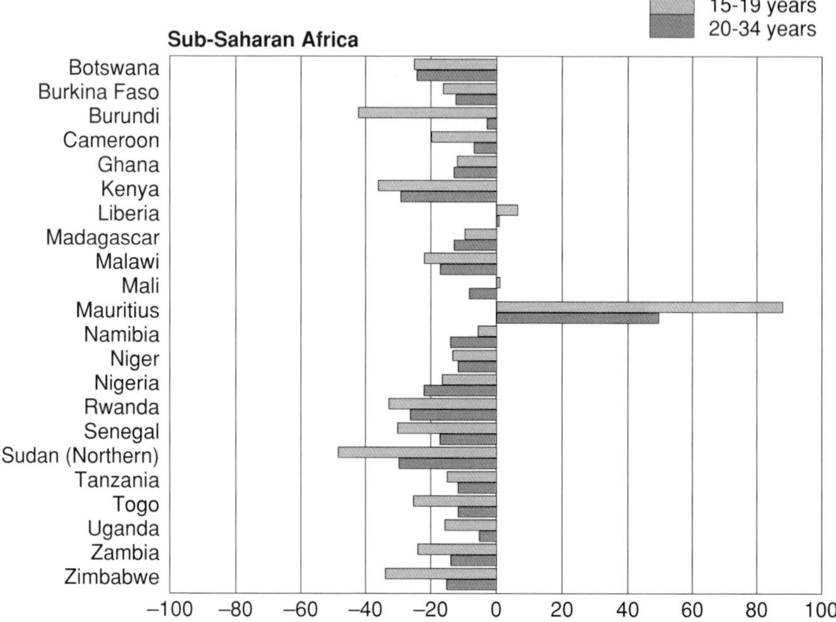

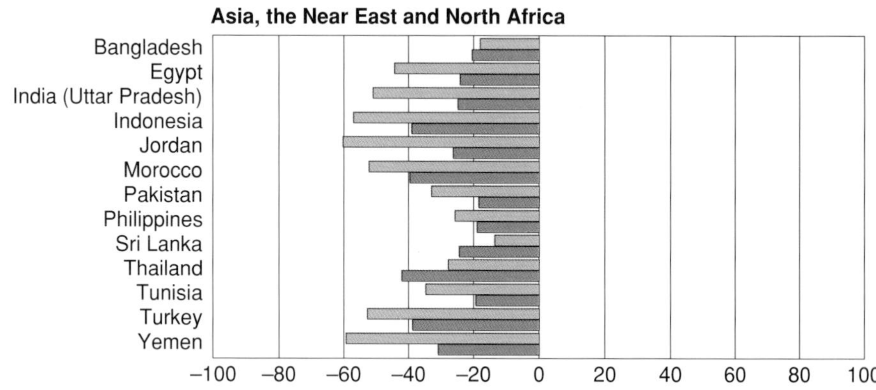

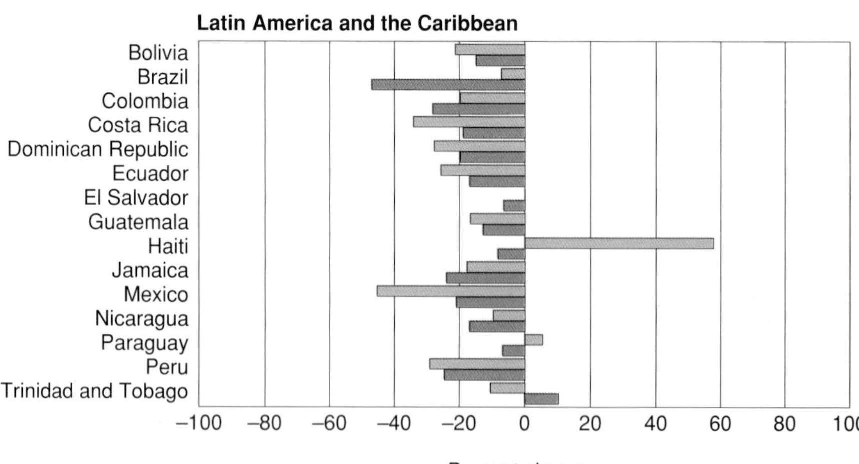

Note: Percent change in fertility shown is standardized for a 10-year period.
Source: Table A-14.

Figure 53.
Adolescent Women Who Have Begun Childbearing by Rural/Urban Residence

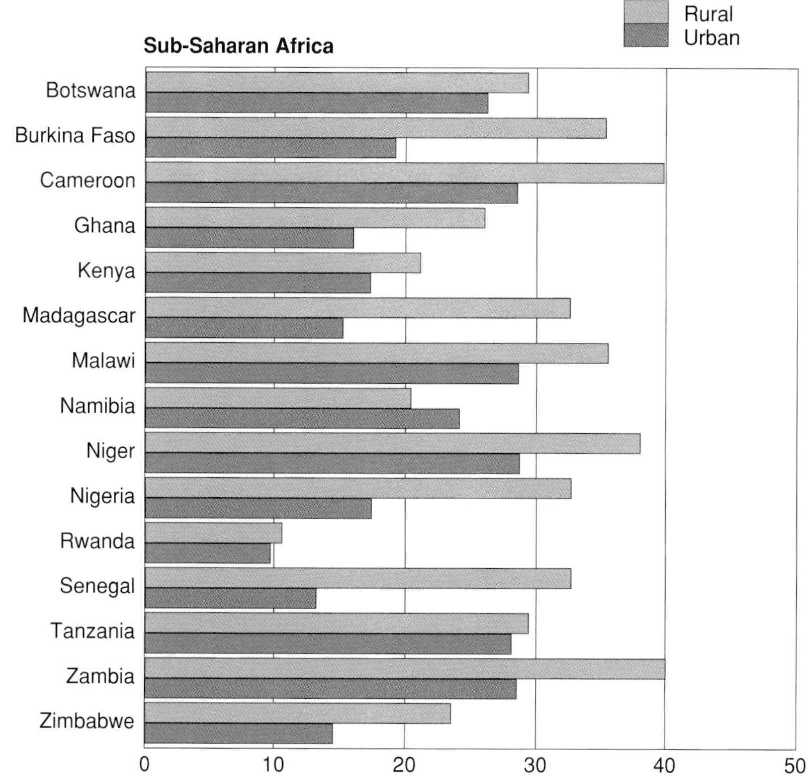

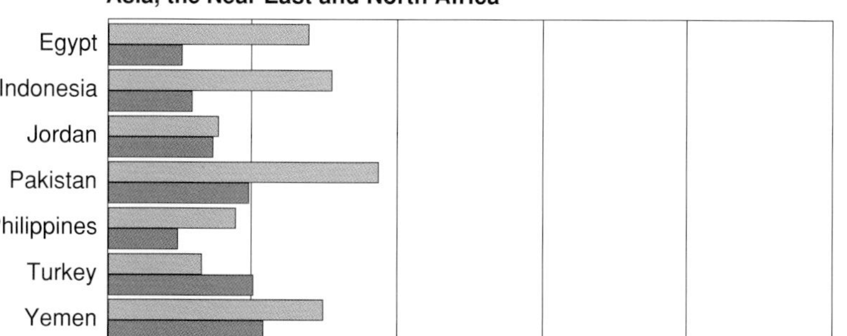

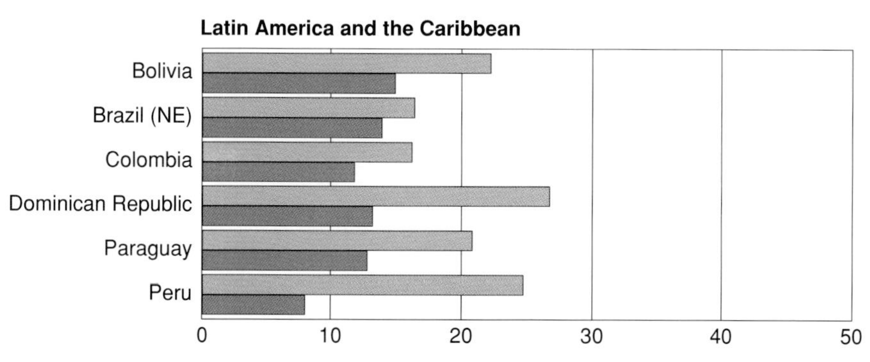

Source: U.S. Bureau of the Census (1996b).

Adolescent Childbearing — Lower in Urban Areas...

Urban women have lower fertility because they desire smaller families, marry later, and are more likely to use family planning. Offsetting these effects to some extent, urban women breast-feed less often and for shorter durations than rural-resident women, leading to earlier return of ovulation following a birth and correspondingly shorter birth intervals (United Nations 1987). While these generalizations refer to all women rather than to adolescent women per se, data from countries where DHS or CDC surveys were conducted in the late 1980's or early 1990's are consistent with the statement. With few exceptions, the percentage of urban adolescent women who have begun childbearing is less than the corresponding percentage of rural women.

About 24 percent of rural women in the developing world begin childbearing in their teenage years, versus 16 percent of urban women (based on countries with survey data, including those countries shown in figure 53). Both shares are higher in Sub-Saharan Africa — 30 percent of rural and 21 percent of urban adolescents — than in other major regions of the world.

...and Among More Educated Women

Women with more education marry later and have lower fertility within marriage. The United Nations' (1987:214) analysis of World Fertility Survey data indicated that in the late 1970's and early 1980's women with seven or more years of schooling married nearly 4 years later, on average, than women with no education — reducing adolescent and, potentially, lifetime fertility. The same women also had about 25 percentage points higher contraceptive use (another fertility reducing effect), although they breast-fed children 8 months less than women with no education (a counterbalancing effect that could increase fertility).

More recent survey data show that, regardless of the absolute level of fertility among adolescents, the proportion of young women who have begun childbearing (i.e., have either given birth or are now pregnant) among those with secondary or higher education is only about 30 percent of that for women with no education among 16 countries for which DHS data are available (figure 54). Even a primary education is associated with significantly later initiation of childbearing — on average, the proportion of young women with primary schooling who begin childbearing as adolescents is about 60 percent of that of women with no schooling (based on data from the 16 countries shown).

Figure 54.
Adolescent Women Who Have Begun Childbearing by Level of Education

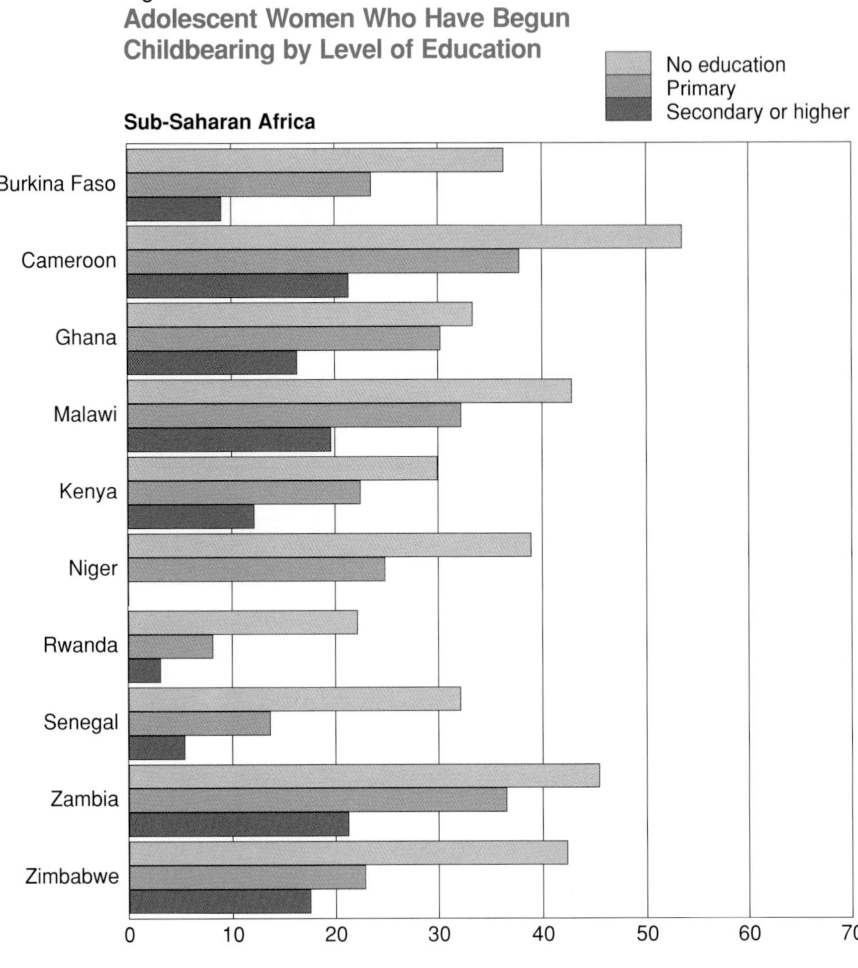

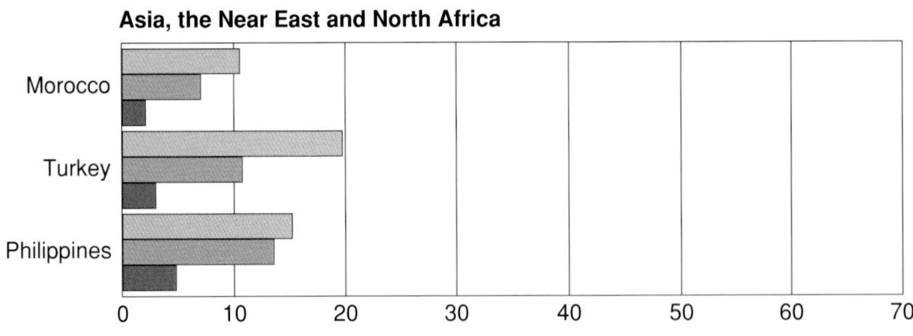

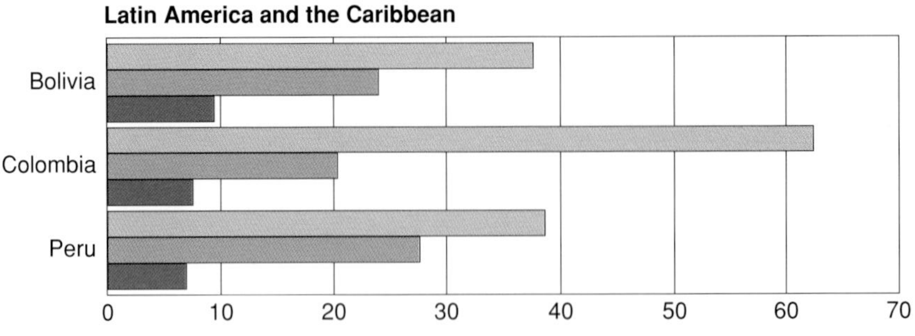

Percent of women ages 15-19

Source: U.S. Bureau of the Census (1996b).

Figure 55.
Early Marriage and Adolescent Fertility

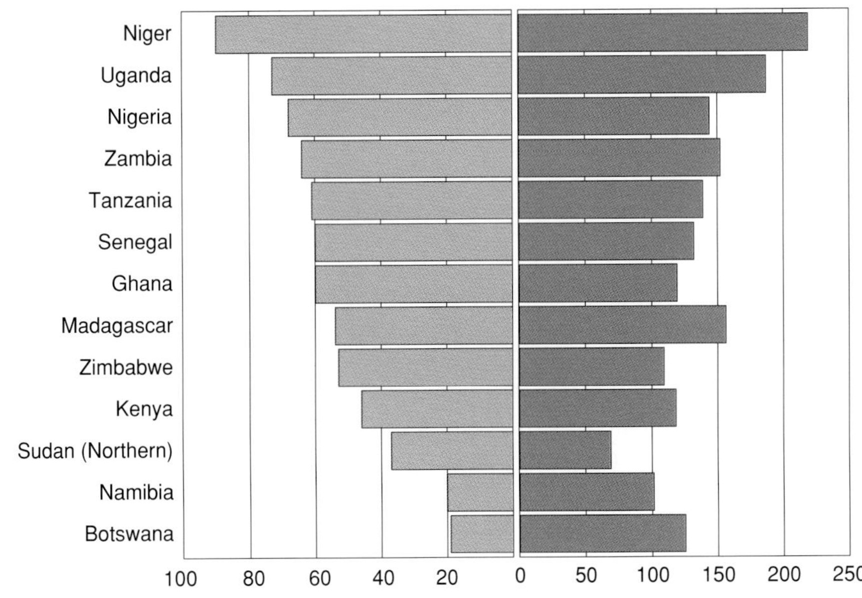

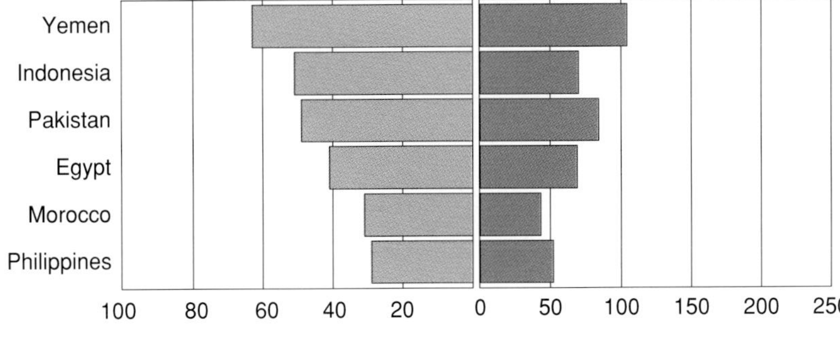

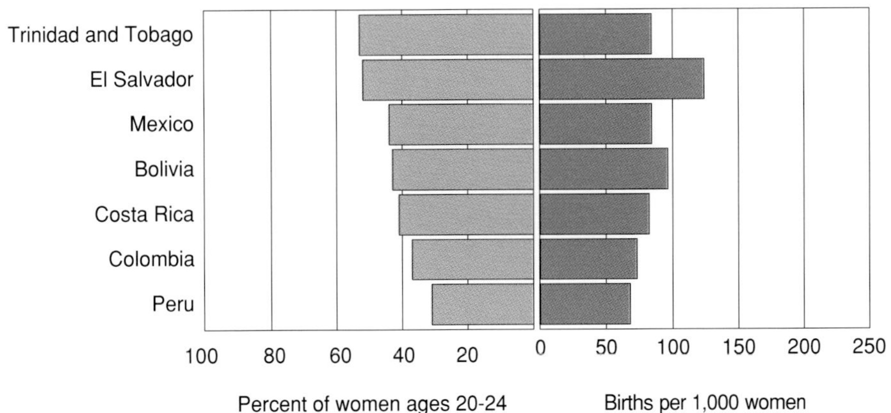

Percent of women ages 20-24 married by age 20

Births per 1,000 women ages 15-19

Source: U.S. Bureau of the Census (1996b).

Age at Marriage Explains Differences in Adolescent Fertility

Marriage marks the transition to adulthood in many societies; the point at which certain options in education, employment, and participation in society are foreclosed; and the beginning of regular exposure to the risks of pregnancy and childbearing.

Variation in age of entry into marriage helps explain differences in fertility across populations and helps explain trends in fertility within individual populations over time. Populations with later mean ages at first marriage also tend to be more urbanized, to have higher levels of educational attainment and, more often, to use family planning within marriage.

The relationship between the pace of marriage by age 20 and adolescent fertility, based on survey data collected in the late 1980's and early 1990's, is illustrated in figure 55.

Proportions of teenage women marrying are declining in most countries, including Sub-Saharan African countries. Figure 56 shows the percentage of women from two age groups — 20 to 24 and 35 to 39 — who reported being married by age 20 (defined to include both formal marriage and simply living in union with a man). A comparison of these percentages provides evidence of the trend in teenage marriages over approximately a 15-year period.

Smaller proportions of the younger cohorts of women report being married when they were adolescents than do older women from the same populations. The differences are somewhat smaller for Latin America and the Caribbean, but the same general trend is evident for Africa, Asia, and Latin America.

Even though there is a general trend towards later marriage throughout the developing world, teenage marriages continue to prevail in many countries, and in Africa in particular. In just over half the Sub-Saharan African countries represented here, at least 1 out of every 4 women ages 15 to 19 is married. And as figure 56 shows, on average, about half of the women in the countries represented here marry by age 20.

Figure 56.
Trends in Early Marriage

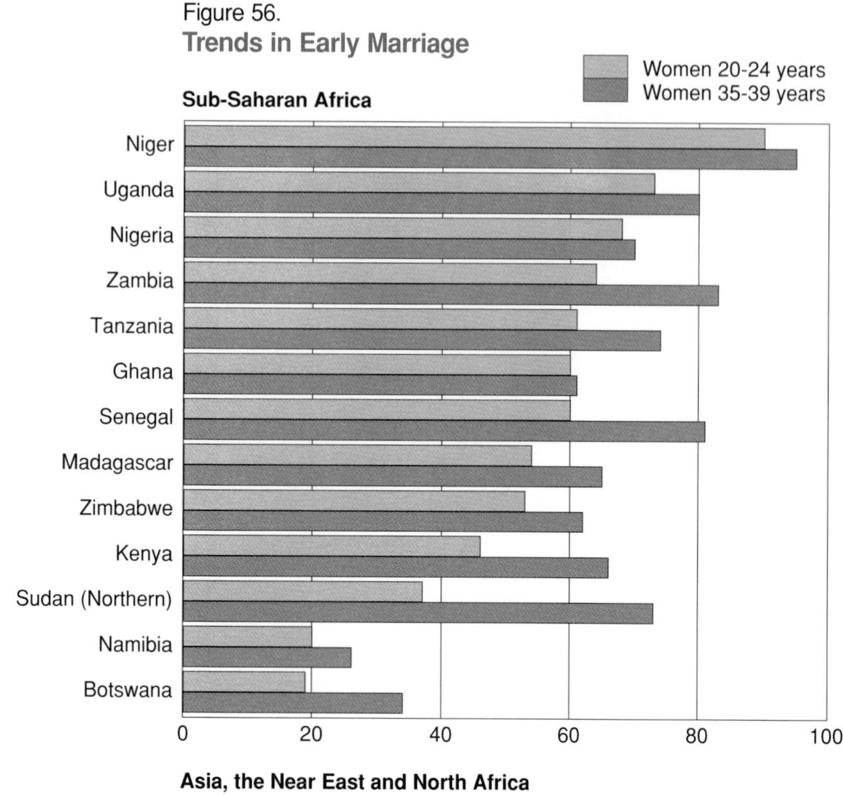

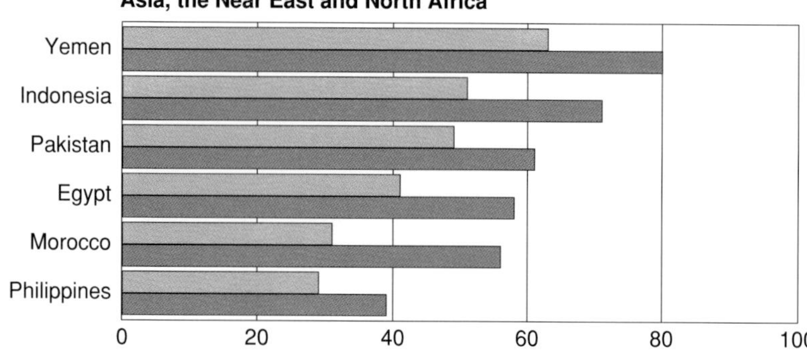

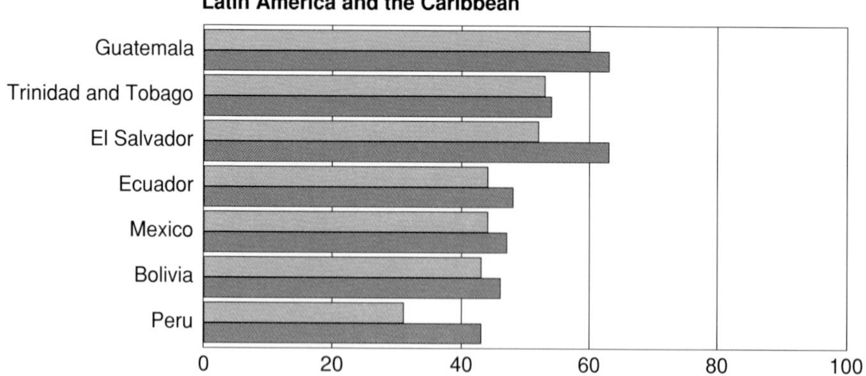

Percent of women who married before age 20

Note: Percents are by age of woman at time of survey.
Source: U.S. Bureau of the Census (1996b).

Figure 57.
Trends in the Use of Contraceptive Methods by Adolescent Women

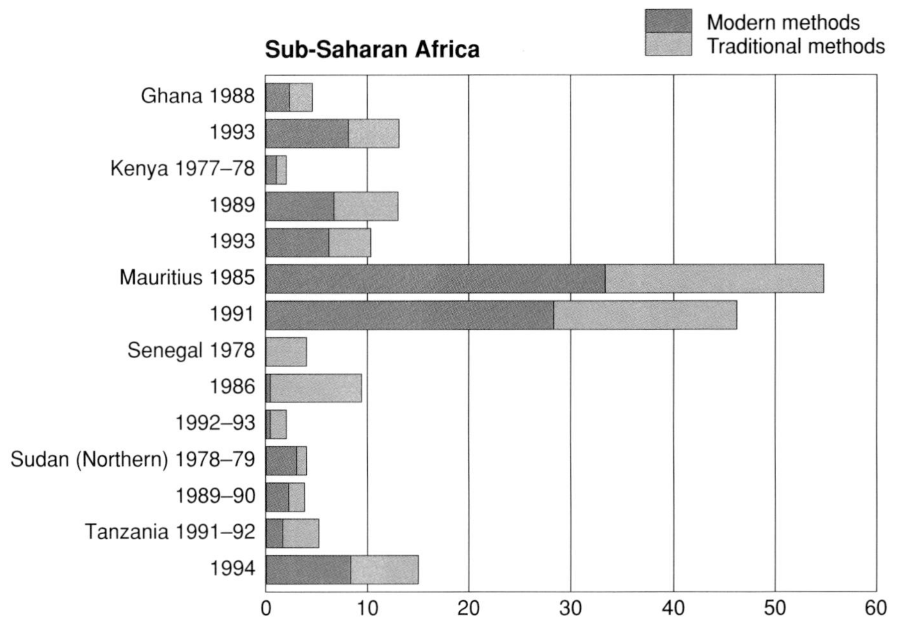

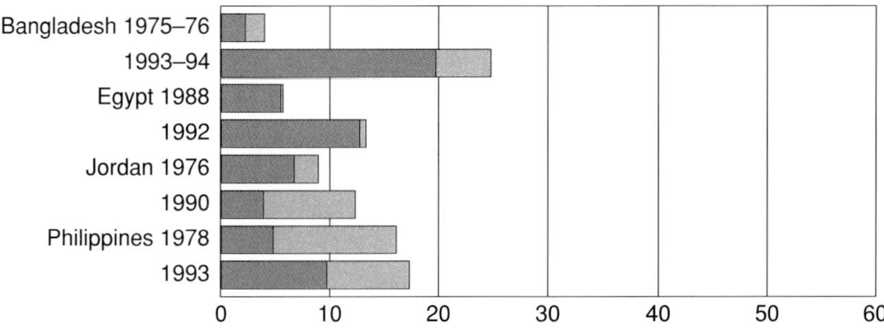

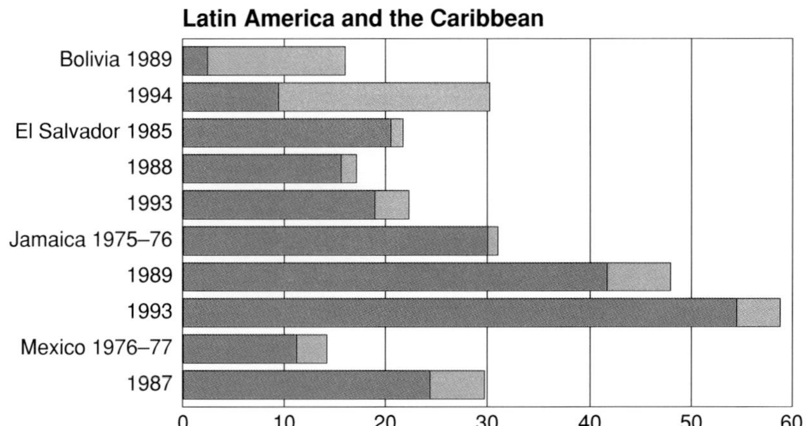

Percent of married women ages 15-19

Source: U.S. Bureau of the Census (1996b).

Contraceptive Use Plays Secondary but Growing Role

Since the late 1960's, general improvements in public acceptance of women's rights in the area of fertility limitation and the expansion of government services to under-served populations have been associated with substantial increases in the use of contraception by women in all age groups. However, the extent to which contraceptive use, rather than rising age at marriage, has been important in determining declines in fertility rates has varied from country to country. In general, the use of family planning by adolescent women has been and remains less important a determinant of their fertility than age at entry into union (United Nations 1987:178).

A comparison of WFS and DHS data documents regional changes that have occurred in modern method prevalence. The data suggest that use of family planning by married adolescents has risen in most, though not in all, countries of the developing world during the past 10 to 20 years (figure 57). Prevalence has risen as adolescent women have become increasingly aware of, and motivated to use, contraceptives for delaying the onset of childbearing or for spacing their pregnancies, and as family planning services have become more readily available in many countries.

Contraceptive Use Less Common Among Adolescent Wives Than Among Older Women

Once married, adolescent women living in much of the developing world begin their reproductive lives with relatively low reliance on contraception. And, at least in some countries, when they ***do*** use contraception to delay or limit their childbearing, they may use less efficient (traditional, rather than modern) methods more often than older women (figure 58).

Age-specific differences in method mix are generally small, but where there do seem to be sizeable within-country differences — as in Senegal and Tanzania in Sub-Saharan Africa, in Yemen in the Near East, and in Guatemala in Latin America — these consistently point to use of less effective methods by ***adolescent*** women.

Figure 58.
Use of Contraceptive Methods by Adolescent and Older Women

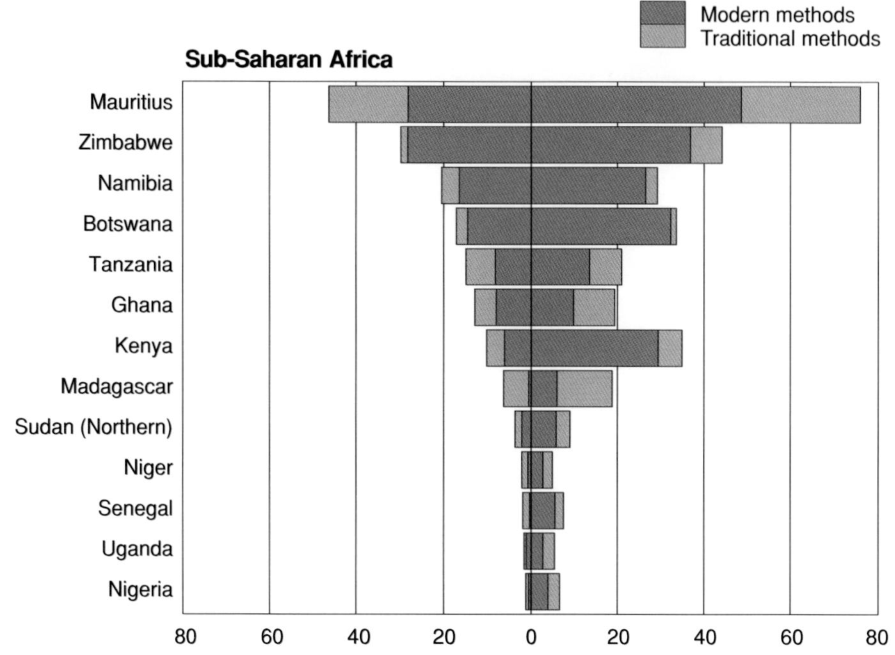

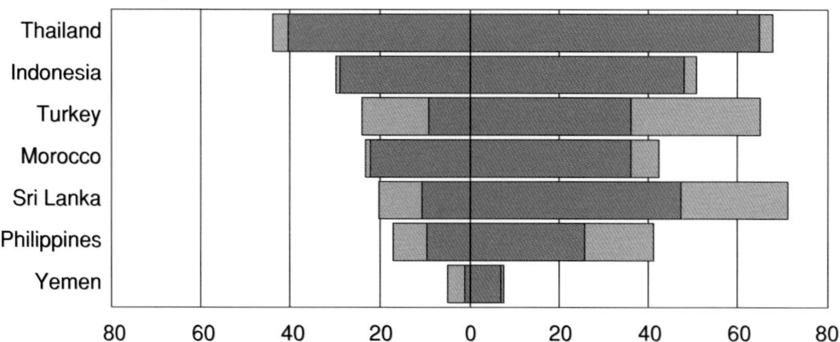

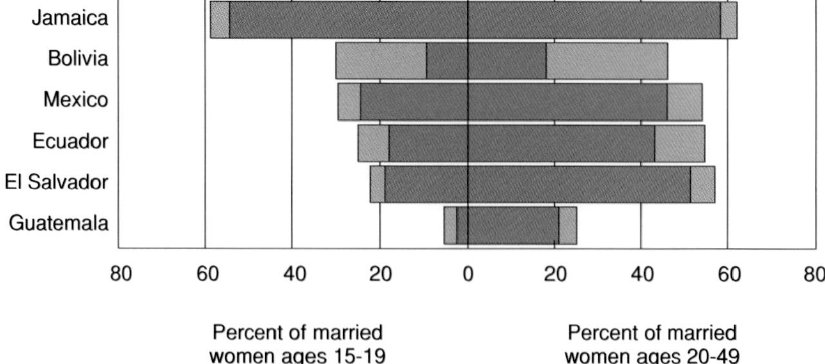

Source: U.S. Bureau of the Census (1996b).

Figure 59.
Extent of Unmet Need for Family Planning Among Married Adolescent Women

Unmet Need for Spacing *and* Limiting	Sub-Saharan Africa	Asia, the Near East and North Africa	Latin America and the Caribbean
Under 20 percent	Cameroon Niger Nigeria Sudan (Northern)	Indonesia Morocco	Colombia Paraguay
20 - 29 percent	Burkina Faso Burundi Madagascar Malawi Rwanda Senegal Tanzania Uganda Zambia	Egypt Jordan Pakistan Sri Lanka Thailand Turkey	Brazil Guatemala
30 - 39 percent	Botswana Mali Namibia	Philippines Tunisia	Bolivia Dominican Republic Ecuador Peru Trinidad and Tobago
40 percent or more	Ghana Kenya Liberia Togo		El Salvador

Source: U.S. Bureau of the Census (1996b).

12 Million Adolescent Women Have Unmet Need for Family Planning

The term "unmet need" refers to women at risk of pregnancy who do not want additional children or want to postpone their next birth, but are not presently using any method of contraception. For whatever reasons, most age groups in most populations include a group of women who may be said to have unmet need.

Demographic and Health Surveys data indicate that between 15 percent and 48 percent of currently married adolescent women in each region of the developing world classify themselves as having unmet need for contraception (figure 59).

The implied number of married adolescents with unmet need is in itself a rather large figure. It represents nearly 3 million women in Sub-Saharan Africa; 8 million women in Asia, the Near East and North Africa; and approximately 1 million women in Latin America and the Caribbean. Most of the unmet need reported is for spacing or postponement rather than fertility limitation, since very few couples in the age range 15 to 19 intend to stop family formation at this age.

However, survey data suggest the existence of some additional unmet need attributable to sexually active, unmarried teenagers who are not using any means of contraception. DHS data from seven African countries (Botswana, Ghana, Liberia, Nigeria, Togo, Uganda, and Zimbabwe, reported in Macro International, Inc. 1993a-1993g) indicate that, on average, only 16 percent of (ever) sexually active unmarried teens in these countries are currently using contraception, and only 8 percent are using a modern method of contraception (figure 60). Comparable data are not yet available for other parts of the world, and the extent to which similar unmet need exists among unmarried adolescent populations elsewhere is unknown.

Figure 60.
Contraceptive Prevalence Among Sexually Active, Unmarried Adolescent Women

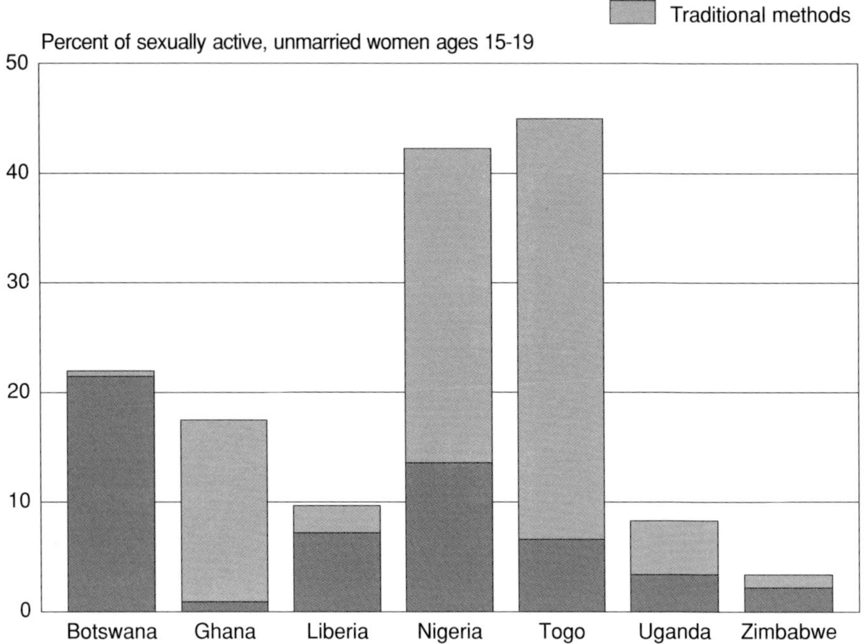

Source: Macro International (1993a-1993g).

The Challenge of Teenage Pregnancy and Childbearing

The Cairo Program of Action calls upon all countries to "assess the extent of national unmet need for good-quality family planning services and its integration in the reproductive health context, paying particular attention to the most vulnerable and underserved groups in the population" (section 7.16). The pregnancies associated with adolescent unmet need are high-risk pregnancies — in terms of both maternal and infant health — as well as being unplanned. For this reason, perhaps even more than for reasons having to do with the various social disadvantages and societal costs of early childbearing, this group of women should be considered for special attention as governments of the developing world formulate their responses to the reproductive health challenges highlighted in Cairo.

Appendix A
Detailed Tables

New estimates and projections of population and vital rates are made for each issue of the *World Population Profile* based on the latest information available. Sometimes the latest information requires making a revision to estimated data for the past as well as new projections for the future. Therefore, the user is cautioned against creating time series of population or the components of population change from different issues of the report.

A data diskette has been prepared to accompany *World Population Profile: 1996.* Available on request, at no charge, the WP96 data diskette is a 3.5" diskette containing all data shown in the Appendix A tables and some additional detail. Data are stored on diskette in Lotus 1-2-3 *.wk1 format.

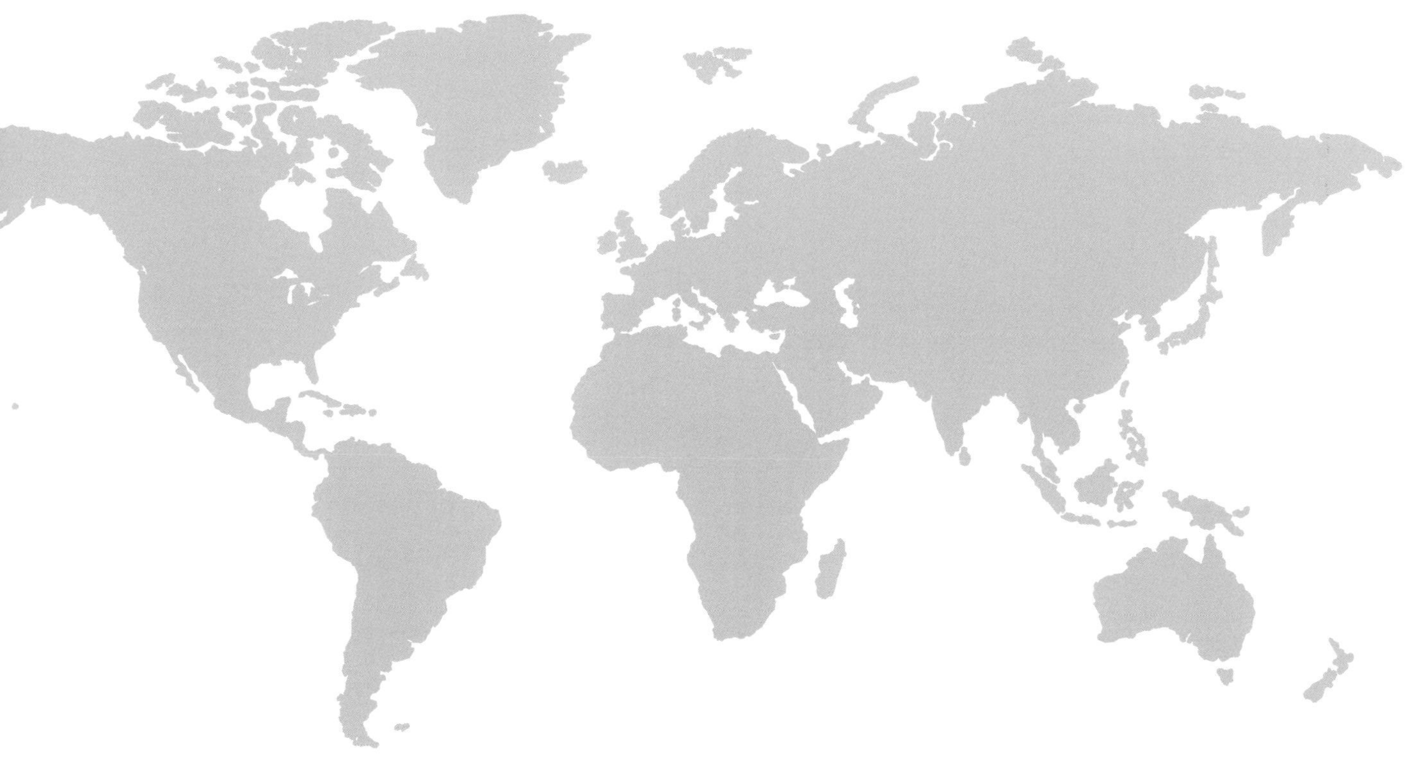

Table A-1.
World Population by Region and Development Category: 1950 to 2020

[Figures may not add to totals because of rounding]

Region	Midyear population (millions)								
	1950	1960	1970	1980	1990	1996	2000	2010	2020
WORLD	2,556	3,039	3,706	4,458	5,282	5,772	6,091	6,862	7,600
Less Developed Countries	1,749	2,129	2,703	3,377	4,139	4,601	4,903	5,634	6,351
More Developed Countries	807	910	1,003	1,081	1,142	1,171	1,189	1,228	1,249
AFRICA	229	283	360	470	624	732	807	1,009	1,230
Sub-Saharan Africa	185	227	289	379	504	594	659	831	1,023
North Africa	44	56	71	91	120	137	149	178	207
NEAR EAST	43	57	74	100	134	157	175	223	276
ASIA	1,368	1,628	2,039	2,501	2,989	3,271	3,448	3,852	4,219
LATIN AMERICA AND THE CARIBBEAN	166	218	285	362	443	489	517	584	643
EUROPE AND THE NEW INDEPENDENT STATES	572	639	703	750	789	800	807	827	834
Western Europe	304	326	352	367	377	387	391	397	394
Eastern Europe	88	100	108	117	122	120	120	123	122
New Independent States	180	214	242	266	289	293	295	307	318
NORTH AMERICA	166	199	226	252	277	295	307	333	361
OCEANIA	12	16	19	23	27	29	30	34	37
EXCLUDING CHINA (MAINLAND AND TAIWAN):									
World	1,985	2,377	2,871	3,455	4,128	4,541	4,816	5,498	6,162
Less Developed Countries	1,179	1,467	1,868	2,374	2,985	3,370	3,627	4,270	4,913
Asia	797	966	1,204	1,498	1,835	2,039	2,172	2,488	2,780
Less Developed Countries	714	872	1,099	1,382	1,711	1,914	2,046	2,361	2,657

Source: U.S. Bureau of the Census, International Data Base.

Table A-2.
Average Annual Rates of Growth by Region and Development Category: 1950 to 2020

Region	Percent						
	1950-60	1960-70	1970-80	1980-90	1990-2000	2000-10	2010-20
WORLD	1.7	2.0	1.8	1.7	1.4	1.2	1.0
Less Developed Countries	2.0	2.4	2.2	2.0	1.7	1.4	1.2
More Developed Countries	1.2	1.0	0.7	0.6	0.4	0.3	0.2
AFRICA	2.1	2.4	2.7	2.8	2.6	2.2	2.0
Sub-Saharan Africa	2.1	2.4	2.7	2.9	2.7	2.3	2.1
North Africa	2.4	2.4	2.6	2.7	2.1	1.8	1.5
NEAR EAST	2.7	2.6	3.0	3.0	2.7	2.4	2.1
ASIA	1.7	2.2	2.0	1.8	1.4	1.1	0.9
LATIN AMERICA AND THE CARIBBEAN	2.7	2.7	2.4	2.0	1.6	1.2	1.0
EUROPE AND THE NEW INDEPENDENT STATES	1.1	0.9	0.7	0.5	0.2	0.2	0.1
Western Europe	0.7	0.8	0.4	0.3	0.4	0.1	–0.1
Eastern Europe	1.3	0.9	0.8	0.4	–0.2	0.2	(Z)
New Independent States	1.7	1.3	0.9	0.8	0.2	0.4	0.3
NORTH AMERICA	1.8	1.3	1.1	0.9	1.0	0.8	0.8
OCEANIA	2.3	2.1	1.6	1.6	1.4	1.1	0.9
EXCLUDING CHINA (MAINLAND AND TAIWAN):							
World	1.8	1.9	1.9	1.8	1.5	1.3	1.1
Less Developed Countries	2.2	2.4	2.4	2.3	1.9	1.6	1.4
Asia	1.9	2.2	2.2	2.0	1.7	1.4	1.1
Less Developed Countries	2.0	2.3	2.3	2.1	1.8	1.4	1.2

(Z) Between –0.05 percent and +0.05 percent.

Source: U.S. Bureau of the Census, International Data Base.

Table A-3.
Population, Vital Events, and Rates, by Region and Development Category: 1996

[Population and events in thousands. Figures may not add to totals because of rounding]

Region	Midyear population	Births	Deaths	Natural increase	Births per 1,000 population	Deaths per 1,000 population	Rate of natural increase (percent)
WORLD	5,772,351	133,350	53,756	79,594	23	9	1.4
Less Developed Countries	4,601,370	119,521	41,403	78,118	26	9	1.7
More Developed Countries	1,170,981	13,829	12,354	1,475	12	11	0.1
AFRICA	731,538	28,875	10,099	18,776	39	14	2.6
Sub-Saharan Africa	594,313	24,966	9,109	15,857	42	15	2.7
North Africa	137,225	3,908	990	2,918	28	7	2.1
NEAR EAST	157,333	4,999	929	4,070	32	6	2.6
ASIA	3,270,944	73,616	27,203	46,414	23	8	1.4
LATIN AMERICA AND THE CARIBBEAN	488,608	11,334	3,444	7,890	23	7	1.6
EUROPE AND THE NEW INDEPENDENT STATES	799,589	9,612	9,420	192	12	12	(Z)
Western Europe	386,600	4,141	3,939	202	11	10	0.1
Eastern Europe	120,190	1,356	1,352	3	11	11	(Z)
New Independent States	292,799	4,115	4,129	-14	14	14	(Z)
NORTH AMERICA	295,424	4,381	2,448	1,933	15	8	0.7
OCEANIA	28,915	533	213	320	18	7	1.1
EXCLUDING CHINA (MAINLAND AND TAIWAN):							
World	4,540,880	112,445	45,265	67,181	25	10	1.5
Less Developed Countries	3,369,899	98,617	32,911	65,706	29	10	1.9
Asia	2,039,473	52,712	18,711	34,001	26	9	1.7
Less Developed Countries	1,914,023	51,434	17,744	33,690	27	9	1.8

(Z) Between -0.05 percent and +0.05 percent.

Source: U.S. Bureau of the Census, International Data Base.

Table A-4.
Population by Country or Area: 1950 to 2020

[Midyear population in thousands. Figures may not add to totals because of rounding]

Region and country or area	1950	1960	1970	1980	1990	1996	2000	2010	2020
WORLD	2,555,898	3,038,930	3,706,003	4,457,645	5,281,545	5,772,351	6,091,477	6,862,111	7,600,071
Less Developed Countries	1,749,380	2,128,647	2,702,711	3,376,731	4,139,079	4,601,370	4,902,940	5,633,946	6,351,222
More Developed Countries	806,519	910,283	1,003,292	1,080,914	1,142,465	1,170,981	1,188,538	1,228,165	1,248,849
AFRICA	228,862	282,953	359,866	470,021	624,425	731,538	807,495	1,009,052	1,230,003
Sub-Saharan Africa	184,942	227,264	289,224	378,573	504,208	594,313	658,832	830,949	1,022,851
Angola	4,118	4,797	5,606	6,794	8,430	10,343	11,513	14,982	19,272
Benin	1,673	2,055	2,620	3,444	4,676	5,710	6,517	8,955	11,920
Botswana	430	497	584	903	1,304	1,478	1,557	1,598	1,553
Burkina Faso	4,376	4,866	5,626	6,939	9,033	10,623	11,684	14,150	16,569
Burundi	2,363	2,812	3,513	4,138	5,633	5,943	6,493	8,229	10,197
Cameroon	4,888	5,609	6,727	8,761	11,905	14,262	15,966	20,630	25,896
Cape Verde	146	197	269	296	375	449	503	646	812
Central African Republic	1,260	1,467	1,827	2,244	2,806	3,274	3,539	4,177	4,780
Chad	2,608	3,042	3,733	4,507	5,889	6,977	7,760	10,055	12,831
Comoros	148	183	236	334	460	569	656	919	1,249
Congo	768	931	1,183	1,620	2,204	2,528	2,750	3,298	3,817
Côte d'Ivoire	2,860	3,565	5,427	8,276	11,926	14,762	16,172	20,261	24,634
Djibouti	60	78	158	279	370	428	454	588	751
Equatorial Guinea	211	244	270	256	369	431	478	615	783
Eritrea	1,403	1,612	2,153	2,555	2,896	3,910	4,537	6,018	7,674
Ethiopia	20,175	24,252	29,673	36,413	48,242	57,172	63,514	81,169	100,813
Gabon	416	446	514	808	1,078	1,173	1,244	1,445	1,675
Gambia, The	305	391	502	644	848	1,020	1,154	1,561	2,073
Ghana	5,297	6,958	8,789	10,880	15,190	17,698	19,272	22,929	26,516
Guinea	2,586	3,019	3,587	4,320	5,936	7,412	7,640	9,450	11,849
Guinea-Bissau	573	617	620	789	998	1,151	1,263	1,579	1,925
Kenya	6,121	8,157	11,272	16,685	23,896	28,177	30,490	33,920	35,236
Lesotho	726	859	1,067	1,346	1,735	1,971	2,114	2,428	2,693
Liberia	824	1,055	1,397	1,900	2,265	2,110	3,048	4,540	5,991
Madagascar	4,620	5,482	6,766	8,678	11,525	13,671	15,295	20,096	25,988
Malawi	2,817	3,450	4,489	6,129	9,136	9,453	10,011	10,662	10,719
Mali	3,688	4,486	5,525	6,728	8,234	9,653	10,911	14,966	20,427
Mauritania	960	1,057	1,227	1,456	1,935	2,336	2,653	3,630	4,859
Mauritius	481	663	830	964	1,074	1,139	1,194	1,322	1,428
Mayotte	22	28	37	52	80	101	117	168	233
Mozambique	6,250	7,472	9,304	12,103	14,056	17,878	19,829	25,116	30,810
Namibia	464	591	765	975	1,409	1,677	1,886	2,513	3,267
Niger	2,482	3,168	4,182	5,629	7,644	9,113	10,260	13,678	17,983
Nigeria	31,797	39,230	49,309	65,699	86,488	103,912	117,328	157,375	205,160
Reunion	244	338	445	507	600	679	730	847	962
Rwanda	2,429	3,083	3,813	5,170	7,145	6,853	8,900	10,080	11,040
Saint Helena	5	5	6	6	7	7	7	7	7
Sao Tome and Principe	60	63	74	94	123	144	159	196	232
Senegal	2,654	3,270	4,318	5,640	7,408	9,093	10,390	14,362	19,497
Seychelles	33	42	54	66	73	78	80	84	89
Sierra Leone	2,087	2,396	2,789	3,333	4,283	4,793	5,580	7,399	9,716
Somalia	3,015	3,655	4,535	6,865	8,334	9,639	10,880	14,524	18,955
South Africa	13,596	17,417	22,740	29,252	37,191	41,743	44,462	49,200	52,264
Sudan	8,051	10,589	13,788	19,064	26,628	31,065	35,454	46,512	58,545
Swaziland	277	352	455	607	853	999	1,137	1,566	2,128
Tanzania	8,909	10,876	14,038	18,689	24,826	29,058	31,045	36,076	40,102
Togo	1,172	1,456	1,964	2,596	3,680	4,571	5,263	7,401	10,146
Uganda	5,522	7,262	9,724	12,252	17,040	20,158	21,891	26,355	30,872
Zaire	13,569	15,860	20,934	27,954	37,831	46,499	51,374	69,293	91,548
Zambia	2,553	3,254	4,247	5,638	8,019	9,159	9,899	11,471	13,022
Zimbabwe	2,853	4,011	5,515	7,298	10,121	11,271	11,777	11,905	11,344

Table A-4.
Population by Country or Area: 1950 to 2020—Continued

[Midyear population in thousands. Figures may not add to totals because of rounding]

Region and country or area	1950	1960	1970	1980	1990	1996	2000	2010	2020
AFRICA—Continued									
North Africa	43,920	55,689	70,642	91,448	120,217	137,225	148,663	178,103	207,152
Algeria	8,893	10,909	13,932	18,862	25,352	29,183	31,788	38,479	44,783
Egypt	21,198	26,847	33,574	42,441	56,106	63,575	68,437	80,689	92,350
Libya	961	1,338	2,056	3,119	4,355	5,445	6,294	8,913	12,391
Morocco	9,343	12,423	15,909	20,457	26,164	29,779	32,229	38,442	44,519
Tunisia	3,517	4,149	5,099	6,443	8,048	9,020	9,671	11,280	12,751
Western Sahara	7	22	72	126	191	223	245	301	357
NEAR EAST	43,098	56,730	73,866	99,583	134,155	157,333	174,888	222,916	276,264
Bahrain	115	157	220	348	502	590	642	759	870
Cyprus	494	573	615	627	681	745	777	858	936
Gaza Strip	245	308	342	454	638	929	1,168	1,741	2,452
Iraq	5,163	6,822	9,414	13,233	18,425	21,422	24,731	34,545	46,260
Israel	1,286	2,141	2,903	3,737	4,303	5,215	5,507	6,242	6,935
Jordan	561	849	1,503	2,168	3,277	4,212	4,704	6,112	7,529
Kuwait	145	292	748	1,370	2,128	1,950	2,420	3,160	3,560
Lebanon	1,364	1,786	2,383	3,137	3,367	3,776	4,115	4,973	5,748
Oman	489	597	774	1,164	1,751	2,187	2,512	3,516	4,731
Qatar	25	45	113	231	452	548	587	660	735
Saudi Arabia	3,860	4,718	6,109	9,949	15,871	19,409	22,246	31,198	43,255
Syria	3,495	4,533	6,258	8,692	12,620	15,609	17,759	23,329	28,926
Turkey	21,122	28,217	35,758	45,121	56,123	62,484	66,618	76,570	85,643
United Arab Emirates	72	103	249	1,000	2,252	3,057	3,582	4,873	6,080
West Bank	771	805	695	916	1,275	1,717	1,973	2,538	3,135
Yemen	3,891	4,783	5,782	7,439	10,489	13,483	15,547	21,841	29,469
ASIA	1,367,916	1,628,004	2,038,533	2,501,054	2,988,568	3,270,944	3,448,007	3,852,380	4,218,889
Afghanistan	8,150	9,829	12,431	14,985	14,767	22,664	26,668	34,098	43,050
Bangladesh	45,646	54,622	67,403	88,077	110,118	123,063	132,081	153,195	172,041
Bhutan	734	867	1,045	1,281	1,585	1,823	1,996	2,474	3,035
Brunei	45	83	128	185	254	300	331	410	490
Burma	19,488	22,836	27,386	33,766	41,078	45,976	49,388	58,236	67,501
Cambodia	4,163	5,364	6,996	6,499	8,731	10,861	12,098	15,679	20,208
China	570,561	661,870	835,002	1,002,585	1,153,989	1,231,471	1,275,652	1,364,323	1,438,406
Mainland	562,580	650,661	820,403	984,736	1,133,710	1,210,005	1,253,438	1,340,357	1,413,251
Taiwan	7,981	11,209	14,598	17,848	20,279	21,466	22,214	23,966	25,155
Hong Kong	2,237	3,075	3,959	5,063	5,688	6,305	6,685	7,401	7,967
India	369,880	445,857	555,043	692,394	855,591	952,108	1,012,909	1,155,830	1,289,473
Indonesia	83,414	100,655	122,889	154,936	187,728	206,612	219,267	249,679	276,017
Iran	16,357	21,577	28,933	39,274	56,946	66,094	71,879	88,231	104,282
Japan	83,805	94,092	104,345	116,807	123,537	125,450	126,582	127,548	123,620
Laos	1,886	2,309	2,845	3,293	4,191	4,976	5,557	7,168	8,923
Macau	188	169	249	318	456	497	516	547	570
Malaysia	6,434	8,428	10,910	13,764	17,507	19,963	21,610	25,691	29,830
Maldives	79	92	115	154	218	271	310	423	554
Mongolia	779	955	1,248	1,662	2,216	2,497	2,655	3,018	3,393
Nepal	8,990	10,035	11,919	15,001	19,104	22,094	24,364	30,783	37,767
North Korea	9,471	10,568	14,388	17,999	21,412	23,904	25,491	28,491	30,969
Pakistan	39,448	50,387	65,706	85,219	113,914	129,276	141,145	170,750	198,722
Philippines	21,131	28,557	38,680	51,092	65,037	74,481	80,961	97,119	112,963
Singapore	1,022	1,646	2,075	2,414	3,039	3,397	3,620	4,026	4,330
South Korea	20,846	24,784	32,241	38,124	42,869	45,482	47,351	51,235	53,451
Sri Lanka	7,533	9,879	12,532	14,900	17,227	18,553	19,377	21,331	22,877
Thailand	20,042	27,513	37,091	47,026	55,052	58,851	61,164	66,092	69,298
Vietnam	25,587	31,955	42,978	54,234	66,314	73,977	78,350	88,602	99,153

Table A-4.
Population by Country or Area: 1950 to 2020—Continued

[Midyear population in thousands. Figures may not add to totals because of rounding]

Region and country or area	1950	1960	1970	1980	1990	1996	2000	2010	2020
LATIN AMERICA AND THE CARIBBEAN	165,794	217,900	285,461	362,189	442,502	488,608	517,166	583,672	643,058
Anguilla	5	6	6	7	7	7	7	8	8
Antigua and Barbuda	46	55	66	69	64	66	68	74	80
Argentina	17,150	20,616	23,962	28,237	32,386	34,673	36,202	39,947	43,190
Aruba	50	57	59	60	64	66	68	72	74
Bahamas, The	70	112	170	210	241	259	269	293	314
Barbados	211	232	239	252	254	257	260	272	284
Belize	66	92	122	144	190	219	242	299	356
Bolivia	2,766	3,404	4,270	5,296	6,388	7,165	7,680	8,941	10,246
Brazil	53,443	71,695	95,684	122,830	150,062	162,661	169,545	183,747	194,246
British Virgin Islands	6	7	10	11	12	13	14	16	18
Cayman Islands	6	8	10	17	27	35	41	60	81
Chile	6,091	7,585	9,369	11,094	13,121	14,333	14,996	16,382	17,535
Colombia	11,592	15,953	21,430	26,580	32,983	36,813	39,172	44,504	49,266
Costa Rica	867	1,248	1,736	2,307	3,022	3,463	3,744	4,416	5,044
Cuba	5,785	7,027	8,543	9,653	10,544	11,007	11,272	11,839	12,266
Dominica	51	60	71	75	81	83	84	89	96
Dominican Republic	2,312	3,159	4,373	5,697	7,213	8,089	8,635	9,928	11,152
Ecuador	3,310	4,447	6,146	8,315	10,116	11,466	12,360	14,534	16,546
El Salvador	1,940	2,574	3,583	4,602	5,219	5,829	6,252	7,332	8,473
French Guiana	26	32	48	68	116	151	173	216	251
Grenada	76	90	95	90	94	95	98	115	141
Guadeloupe	208	269	321	337	378	408	426	463	492
Guatemala	2,969	3,975	5,287	7,232	9,633	11,278	12,408	15,284	18,131
Guyana	428	571	715	759	747	712	693	695	685
Haiti	3,097	3,723	4,605	5,068	6,060	6,732	7,223	8,681	10,252
Honduras	1,431	1,952	2,683	3,625	4,741	5,605	6,192	7,643	9,042
Jamaica	1,385	1,632	1,944	2,229	2,466	2,594	2,664	2,896	3,208
Martinique	217	282	325	339	374	399	416	451	474
Mexico	28,485	38,579	52,236	68,686	85,121	95,772	102,912	120,115	136,096
Montserrat	13	12	12	12	13	13	13	13	13
Netherlands Antilles	110	136	158	173	195	209	217	234	246
Nicaragua	1,098	1,493	2,053	2,776	3,591	4,272	4,729	5,863	6,973
Panama	893	1,148	1,531	1,956	2,387	2,655	2,828	3,238	3,625
Paraguay	1,476	1,910	2,477	3,379	4,651	5,504	6,104	7,730	9,474
Peru	7,633	9,931	13,193	17,295	21,841	24,523	26,198	29,988	33,226
Puerto Rico	2,218	2,358	2,716	3,206	3,605	3,819	3,850	4,017	4,227
Saint Kitts and Nevis	44	51	46	44	40	41	43	50	57
Saint Lucia	79	88	103	122	146	158	165	183	202
Saint Vincent and the Grenadines	66	81	88	98	113	118	121	132	146
Suriname	208	285	373	355	398	436	465	534	598
Trinidad and Tobago	632	841	955	1,091	1,256	1,272	1,273	1,323	1,409
Turks and Caicos Islands	5	6	6	7	12	14	15	17	18
Uruguay	2,194	2,531	2,824	2,920	3,106	3,239	3,333	3,582	3,811
Venezuela	5,009	7,556	10,758	14,768	19,325	21,983	23,596	27,345	30,876
Virgin Islands	27	33	63	98	101	97	99	107	111

Table A-4.
Population by Country or Area: 1950 to 2020—Continued

[Midyear population in thousands. Figures may not add to totals because of rounding]

Region and country or area	1950	1960	1970	1980	1990	1996	2000	2010	2020
EUROPE AND THE NEW INDEPENDENT STATES	571,680	639,043	702,509	750,268	788,688	799,589	806,782	826,727	833,550
Western Europe	304,424	325,740	351,579	366,795	377,228	386,600	391,354	397,045	393,786
Andorra	6	8	20	34	53	68	73	79	78
Austria	6,935	7,047	7,467	7,549	7,718	8,014	8,108	8,259	8,329
Belgium	8,639	9,119	9,638	9,847	9,962	10,098	10,144	10,135	10,015
Denmark	4,271	4,581	4,929	5,123	5,141	5,211	5,255	5,311	5,307
Faroe Islands	32	35	39	43	47	49	51	54	57
Finland	4,009	4,430	4,606	4,780	4,986	5,100	5,153	5,246	5,283
France	41,829	45,670	50,787	53,870	56,739	58,317	59,239	61,047	61,334
Germany	68,375	72,481	77,783	78,298	79,357	83,536	85,684	88,975	88,870
Gibraltar	23	24	26	29	31	32	33	34	36
Greece	7,566	8,327	8,793	9,643	10,123	10,719	10,878	10,920	10,689
Guernsey	45	47	53	53	61	65	67	72	76
Iceland	143	176	204	228	255	268	277	293	306
Ireland	2,963	2,832	2,950	3,401	3,508	3,563	3,627	3,846	4,034
Isle of Man	55	48	53	64	69	73	76	81	87
Italy	47,105	50,198	53,661	56,451	57,661	57,460	57,807	57,660	55,665
Jersey	57	63	69	76	84	87	89	93	95
Liechtenstein	14	16	21	25	29	31	32	34	36
Luxembourg	296	314	339	364	382	407	415	428	436
Malta	312	329	326	364	354	372	382	404	420
Monaco	18	21	24	27	30	32	32	33	34
Netherlands	10,114	11,486	13,032	14,144	14,952	15,532	15,801	16,140	16,222
Norway	3,265	3,581	3,877	4,086	4,242	4,346	4,387	4,424	4,446
Portugal	8,443	9,037	9,044	9,778	9,871	9,865	9,906	10,080	10,005
San Marino	13	15	19	21	23	25	25	26	27
Spain	28,063	30,641	33,876	37,488	38,793	38,853	38,658	37,465	35,444
Sweden	7,014	7,480	8,043	8,310	8,559	8,861	8,994	9,228	9,469
Switzerland	4,694	5,362	6,267	6,385	6,779	7,125	7,268	7,519	7,696
United Kingdom	50,127	52,372	55,632	56,314	57,418	58,490	58,894	59,159	59,289
Eastern Europe	87,685	99,523	108,452	117,500	122,482	120,190	120,364	122,631	122,218
Albania	1,227	1,623	2,157	2,699	3,273	3,249	3,427	3,858	4,257
Bosnia and Herzegovina	2,662	3,240	3,703	4,092	4,360	2,656	2,618	2,892	2,966
Bulgaria	7,251	7,867	8,490	8,844	8,966	8,613	8,769	8,928	8,777
Croatia	3,851	4,140	4,411	4,593	4,754	5,004	5,044	4,986	4,821
Czech Republic	8,925	9,660	9,795	10,289	10,310	10,321	10,358	10,445	10,271
Hungary	9,338	9,984	10,337	10,711	10,352	10,003	9,795	9,456	9,103
Macedonia, The Former Yugoslav Republic of	1,229	1,392	1,629	1,893	2,031	2,104	2,152	2,261	2,296
Montenegro	397	467	525	579	616	635	647	673	679
Poland	24,824	29,590	32,526	35,578	38,109	38,643	39,010	40,342	40,833
Romania	16,311	18,403	20,253	22,109	22,775	21,657	20,996	20,741	20,135
Serbia	6,734	7,583	8,385	9,262	9,705	9,979	10,140	10,389	10,388
Slovakia	3,463	3,994	4,524	4,966	5,263	5,374	5,472	5,735	5,837
Slovenia	1,473	1,580	1,718	1,885	1,969	1,951	1,937	1,926	1,856
New Independent States	179,571	213,780	242,478	265,973	288,978	292,799	295,064	307,051	317,547
Baltics	5,585	6,091	6,862	7,443	7,947	7,574	7,431	7,344	7,228
Estonia	1,096	1,211	1,363	1,482	1,573	1,459	1,422	1,401	1,370
Latvia	1,936	2,115	2,361	2,525	2,672	2,469	2,380	2,293	2,212
Lithuania	2,553	2,765	3,138	3,436	3,702	3,646	3,629	3,650	3,646

Table A-4.
Population by Country or Area: 1950 to 2020—Continued

[Midyear population in thousands. Figures may not add to totals because of rounding]

Region and country or area	1950	1960	1970	1980	1990	1996	2000	2010	2020
EUROPE AND THE NEW INDEPENDENT STATES— Continued									
New Independent States— Continued									
Commonwealth of Independent States	173,986	207,689	235,616	258,529	281,031	285,225	287,633	299,707	310,318
Armenia	1,355	1,869	2,520	3,115	3,366	3,464	3,481	3,577	3,665
Azerbaijan	2,885	3,882	5,169	6,173	7,200	7,677	7,902	8,410	9,007
Belarus	7,722	8,168	9,027	9,644	10,215	10,416	10,545	10,924	11,059
Georgia	3,516	4,147	4,694	5,048	5,457	5,220	5,132	5,188	5,205
Kazakstan	6,693	9,982	13,106	14,994	16,708	16,916	16,943	17,564	18,408
Kyrgyzstan	1,739	2,171	2,964	3,623	4,390	4,530	4,664	5,403	6,257
Moldova	2,336	2,999	3,595	3,996	4,398	4,464	4,543	4,818	5,000
Russia	101,937	119,632	130,245	139,045	148,081	148,190	147,950	149,991	149,652
Tajikistan	1,530	2,081	2,939	3,969	5,332	5,916	6,384	8,019	10,019
Turkmenistan	1,204	1,585	2,181	2,875	3,668	4,149	4,466	5,362	6,380
Ukraine	36,775	42,644	47,236	50,047	51,592	50,864	50,380	49,915	49,038
Uzbekistan	6,293	8,531	11,940	16,000	20,624	23,418	25,245	30,536	36,628
NORTH AMERICA	166,074	198,662	226,481	251,907	276,653	295,424	306,742	333,486	361,226
Bermuda	39	44	53	55	59	62	64	69	74
Canada	13,737	17,909	21,324	24,070	26,620	28,821	29,989	32,534	34,753
Greenland	22	32	46	50	56	58	60	65	69
Saint Pierre and Miquelon	5	5	5	6	6	7	7	8	8
United States	152,271	180,671	205,052	227,726	249,911	266,476	276,621	300,811	326,322
OCEANIA	12,476	15,638	19,287	22,622	26,553	28,915	30,397	33,879	37,080
American Samoa	19	20	27	32	47	60	69	85	86
Australia	8,267	10,361	12,660	14,616	17,033	18,261	18,950	20,434	21,696
Cook Islands	15	18	21	18	18	20	20	22	24
Federated States of Micronesia	31	42	57	77	109	125	133	141	143
Fiji	287	393	521	635	738	782	823	933	1,037
French Polynesia	62	81	114	151	196	225	245	294	343
Guam	60	67	86	107	134	157	171	202	230
Kiribati	33	41	49	58	72	81	87	95	98
Marshall Islands	11	15	22	31	46	58	68	100	144
Nauru	3	4	7	8	9	10	11	11	12
New Caledonia	55	79	112	139	168	188	200	230	255
New Zealand	1,908	2,372	2,811	3,113	3,299	3,548	3,698	4,029	4,326
Northern Mariana Islands	6	9	12	17	44	52	57	71	86
Palau	7	9	12	13	15	17	18	20	21
Papua New Guinea	1,412	1,747	2,288	2,991	3,823	4,395	4,812	5,925	7,044
Solomon Islands	107	126	163	233	336	413	470	620	767
Tonga	46	64	83	93	101	106	110	119	128
Tuvalu	5	5	6	7	9	10	11	12	15
Vanuatu	52	66	85	117	154	178	193	230	266
Wallis and Futuna	7	8	9	11	14	15	15	17	18
Western Samoa	82	110	142	155	186	214	235	288	341

Source: U.S. Bureau of the Census, International Data Base.

Table A-5.
Population, Vital Events, and Rates, by Region and Country: 1996

[Population and events in thousands. Figures may not add to totals because of rounding]

Region and country or area	Midyear population	Births	Deaths	Natural increase	Births per 1,000 population	Deaths per 1,000 population	Rate of natural increase (percent)
WORLD	5,772,351	133,350	53,756	79,594	23	9	1.4
Less Developed Countries	4,601,370	119,521	41,403	78,118	26	9	1.7
More Developed Countries	1,170,981	13,829	12,354	1,475	12	11	0.1
AFRICA	731,538	28,875	10,099	18,776	39	14	2.6
Sub-Saharan Africa	594,313	24,966	9,109	15,857	42	15	2.7
Angola	10,343	461	183	278	45	18	2.7
Benin	5,710	267	77	190	47	14	3.3
Botswana	1,478	49	25	24	33	17	1.6
Burkina Faso	10,623	500	212	287	47	20	2.7
Burundi	5,943	256	90	166	43	15	2.8
Cameroon	14,262	606	193	413	42	14	2.9
Cape Verde	449	20	4	16	44	8	3.6
Central African Republic	3,274	131	58	73	40	18	2.2
Chad	6,977	309	122	187	44	17	2.7
Comoros	569	26	6	20	46	10	3.6
Congo	2,528	99	44	55	39	17	2.2
Côte d'Ivoire	14,762	627	232	395	42	16	2.7
Djibouti	428	18	7	12	43	15	2.7
Equatorial Guinea	431	17	6	11	40	14	2.6
Eritrea	3,910	178	61	117	46	16	3.0
Ethiopia	57,172	2,633	1,002	1,631	46	18	2.9
Gabon	1,173	33	16	17	28	14	1.5
Gambia, The	1,020	46	15	31	46	15	3.1
Ghana	17,698	619	197	422	35	11	2.4
Guinea	7,412	316	139	177	43	19	2.4
Guinea-Bissau	1,151	46	19	27	40	16	2.3
Kenya	28,177	941	290	650	33	10	2.3
Lesotho	1,971	64	27	37	33	14	1.9
Liberia	2,110	90	25	65	43	12	3.1
Madagascar	13,671	583	197	386	43	14	2.8
Malawi	9,453	393	231	161	42	24	1.7
Mali	9,653	496	188	308	51	19	3.2
Mauritania	2,336	110	36	74	47	15	3.2
Mauritius	1,139	21	7	14	19	6	1.2
Mayotte	101	5	1	4	48	10	3.8
Mozambique	17,878	814	339	474	46	19	2.7
Namibia	1,677	63	13	49	37	8	2.9
Niger	9,113	496	224	272	54	25	3.0
Nigeria	103,912	4,457	1,321	3,136	43	13	3.0
Reunion	679	16	3	13	24	5	1.9
Rwanda	6,853	266	139	127	39	20	1.9
Saint Helena	7	(Z)	(Z)	(Z)	9	6	0.3
Sao Tome and Principe	144	5	1	4	34	9	2.6
Senegal	9,093	413	107	306	45	12	3.4
Seychelles	78	2	1	1	21	7	1.4
Sierra Leone	4,793	226	87	138	47	18	2.9
Somalia	9,639	426	127	298	44	13	3.1
South Africa	41,743	1,165	431	734	28	10	1.8
Sudan	31,065	1,268	355	912	41	11	2.9
Swaziland	999	43	11	32	43	11	3.2

Table A-5.
Population, Vital Events, and Rates, by Region and Country: 1996—Continued

[Population and events in thousands. Figures may not add to totals because of rounding]

Region and country or area	Midyear population	Births	Deaths	Natural increase	Births per 1,000 population	Deaths per 1,000 population	Rate of natural increase (percent)
AFRICA—Continued							
Sub-Saharan Africa—Continued							
Tanzania	29,058	1,200	566	635	41	19	2.2
Togo	4,571	211	49	163	46	11	3.6
Uganda	20,158	926	418	508	46	21	2.5
Zaire	46,499	2,237	786	1,451	48	17	3.1
Zambia	9,159	410	217	193	45	24	2.1
Zimbabwe	11,271	365	205	159	32	18	1.4
North Africa	137,225	3,908	990	2,918	28	7	2.1
Algeria	29,183	832	172	660	29	6	2.3
Egypt	63,575	1,792	553	1,238	28	9	1.9
Libya	5,445	242	42	200	44	8	3.7
Morocco	29,779	816	172	644	27	6	2.2
Tunisia	9,020	217	47	170	24	5	1.9
Western Sahara	223	10	4	6	47	18	2.8
NEAR EAST	157,333	4,999	929	4,070	32	6	2.6
Bahrain	590	14	2	12	24	3	2.0
Cyprus	745	11	6	6	15	8	0.8
Gaza Strip	929	47	4	43	51	4	4.6
Iraq	21,422	923	141	782	43	7	3.7
Israel	5,215	106	33	72	20	6	1.4
Jordan	4,212	154	17	138	37	4	3.3
Kuwait	1,950	40	4	35	20	2	1.8
Lebanon	3,776	105	24	81	28	6	2.2
Oman	2,187	83	10	73	38	4	3.3
Qatar	548	12	2	10	21	4	1.7
Saudi Arabia	19,409	744	104	640	38	5	3.3
Syria	15,609	617	91	526	40	6	3.4
Turkey	62,484	1,391	345	1,046	22	6	1.7
United Arab Emirates	3,057	81	9	72	26	3	2.3
West Bank	1,717	62	8	55	36	4	3.2
Yemen	13,483	610	129	480	45	10	3.6
ASIA	3,270,944	73,616	27,203	46,414	23	8	1.4
Afghanistan	22,664	975	412	564	43	18	2.5
Bangladesh	123,063	3,753	1,380	2,374	31	11	1.9
Bhutan	1,823	70	28	42	38	15	2.3
Brunei	300	8	2	6	26	5	2.0
Burma	45,976	1,380	536	844	30	12	1.8
Cambodia	10,861	472	171	301	44	16	2.8
China	1,231,471	20,904	8,492	12,413	17	7	1.0
Mainland	1,210,005	20,582	8,373	12,209	17	7	1.0
Taiwan	21,466	322	118	204	15	6	0.9
Hong Kong	6,305	66	33	33	11	5	0.5
India	952,108	24,698	9,150	15,548	26	10	1.6
Indonesia	206,612	4,890	1,731	3,159	24	8	1.5
Iran	66,094	2,225	437	1,789	34	7	2.7
Japan	125,450	1,278	967	311	10	8	0.2
Laos	4,976	209	69	140	42	14	2.8
Macau	497	7	2	5	14	4	1.0
Malaysia	19,963	523	110	413	26	5	2.1

Table A-5.
Population, Vital Events, and Rates, by Region and Country: 1996—Continued

[Population and events in thousands. Figures may not add to totals because of rounding]

Region and country or area	Midyear population	Births	Deaths	Natural increase	Births per 1,000 population	Deaths per 1,000 population	Rate of natural increase (percent)
ASIA—Continued							
Maldives	271	11	2	10	42	7	3.5
Mongolia	2,497	64	22	42	26	9	1.7
Nepal	22,094	817	278	540	37	13	2.4
North Korea	23,904	546	130	416	23	5	1.7
Pakistan	129,276	4,675	1,450	3,224	36	11	2.5
Philippines	74,481	2,198	496	1,702	30	7	2.3
Singapore	3,397	55	15	40	16	5	1.2
South Korea	45,482	739	257	481	16	6	1.1
Sri Lanka	18,553	332	108	224	18	6	1.2
Thailand	58,851	1,018	412	606	17	7	1.0
Vietnam	73,977	1,701	514	1,187	23	7	1.6
LATIN AMERICA AND THE CARIBBEAN	488,608	11,334	3,444	7,890	23	7	1.6
Anguilla	7	(Z)	(Z)	(Z)	24	8	1.6
Antigua and Barbuda	66	1	(Z)	1	17	5	1.2
Argentina	34,673	673	299	374	19	9	1.1
Aruba	66	1	(Z)	1	14	6	0.8
Bahamas, The	259	5	1	3	19	6	1.3
Barbados	257	4	2	2	15	8	0.7
Belize	219	7	1	6	33	6	2.7
Bolivia	7,165	232	77	155	32	11	2.2
Brazil	162,661	3,383	1,495	1,888	21	9	1.2
British Virgin Islands	13	(Z)	(Z)	(Z)	20	6	1.4
Cayman Islands	35	1	(Z)	1	15	5	1.0
Chile	14,333	259	81	178	18	6	1.2
Colombia	36,813	786	171	614	21	5	1.7
Costa Rica	3,463	83	14	68	24	4	2.0
Cuba	11,007	158	72	86	14	7	0.8
Dominica	83	2	(Z)	2	18	5	1.3
Dominican Republic	8,089	190	46	144	24	6	1.8
Ecuador	11,466	287	63	224	25	6	2.0
El Salvador	5,829	165	34	131	28	6	2.2
French Guiana	151	4	1	3	25	5	2.0
Grenada	95	3	1	2	29	6	2.3
Guadeloupe	408	7	2	5	18	6	1.2
Guatemala	11,278	383	81	302	34	7	2.7
Guyana	712	14	7	7	19	10	0.9
Haiti	6,732	257	107	149	38	16	2.2
Honduras	5,605	187	33	154	33	6	2.8
Jamaica	2,594	56	14	42	22	6	1.6
Martinique	399	7	2	4	17	6	1.1
Mexico	95,772	2,513	439	2,074	26	5	2.2
Montserrat	13	(Z)	(Z)	(Z)	15	10	0.5
Netherlands Antilles	209	3	1	2	16	5	1.1
Nicaragua	4,272	145	26	119	34	6	2.8
Panama	2,655	62	14	47	23	5	1.8
Paraguay	5,504	170	24	147	31	4	2.7
Peru	24,523	597	150	446	24	6	1.8

Table A-5.
Population, Vital Events, and Rates, by Region and Country: 1996—Continued

[Population and events in thousands. Figures may not add to totals because of rounding]

Region and country or area	Midyear population	Births	Deaths	Natural increase	Births per 1,000 population	Deaths per 1,000 population	Rate of natural increase (percent)
LATIN AMERICA AND THE CARIBBEAN—Continued							
Puerto Rico	3,819	59	28	31	16	7	0.8
Saint Kitts and Nevis	41	1	(Z)	1	23	9	1.4
Saint Lucia	158	3	1	3	22	6	1.6
Saint Vincent and the Grenadines	118	2	1	2	19	5	1.4
Suriname	436	11	3	8	24	6	1.8
Trinidad and Tobago	1,272	21	9	12	16	7	0.9
Turks and Caicos Islands	14	(Z)	(Z)	(Z)	13	5	0.8
Uruguay	3,239	55	29	26	17	9	0.8
Venezuela	21,983	536	112	424	24	5	1.9
Virgin Islands	97	2	1	1	18	5	1.2
EUROPE AND THE NEW INDEPENDENT STATES	799,589	9,612	9,420	192	12	12	(Z)
Western Europe	386,600	4,141	3,939	202	11	10	0.1
Andorra	68	1	(Z)	1	13	7	0.5
Austria	8,014	88	82	6	11	10	0.1
Belgium	10,098	113	103	10	11	10	0.1
Denmark	5,211	64	58	6	12	11	0.1
Faroe Islands	49	1	(Z)	1	17	8	1.0
Finland	5,100	61	50	12	12	10	0.2
France	58,317	631	541	90	11	9	0.2
Germany	83,536	807	936	–129	10	11	–0.2
Gibraltar	32	(Z)	(Z)	(Z)	15	9	0.6
Greece	10,719	114	100	14	11	9	0.1
Guernsey	65	1	1	(Z)	13	10	0.3
Iceland	268	4	2	2	15	7	0.9
Ireland	3,563	49	30	19	14	8	0.5
Isle of Man	73	1	1	(Z)	14	12	0.2
Italy	57,460	567	564	3	10	10	(Z)
Jersey	87	1	1	(Z)	13	10	0.3
Liechtenstein	31	(Z)	(Z)	(Z)	13	7	0.6
Luxembourg	407	5	4	1	12	9	0.3
Malta	372	5	3	2	13	7	0.6
Monaco	32	(Z)	(Z)	(Z)	11	12	–0.1
Netherlands	15,532	189	132	57	12	8	0.4
Norway	4,346	54	45	9	12	10	0.2
Portugal	9,865	104	101	3	11	10	(Z)
San Marino	25	(Z)	(Z)	(Z)	11	8	0.3
Spain	38,853	314	368	–54	8	9	–0.1
Sweden	8,861	114	96	18	13	11	0.2
Switzerland	7,125	84	65	19	12	9	0.3
United Kingdom	58,490	767	657	110	13	11	0.2
Eastern Europe	120,190	1,356	1,352	3	11	11	(Z)
Albania	3,249	72	25	47	22	8	1.5
Bosnia and Herzegovina	2,656	17	42	–25	6	16	–1.0
Bulgaria	8,613	72	117	–45	8	14	–0.5
Croatia	5,004	49	57	–8	10	11	–0.2
Czech Republic	10,321	107	112	–5	10	11	–0.1

Table A-5.
Population, Vital Events, and Rates, by Region and Country: 1996—Continued

[Population and events in thousands. Figures may not add to totals because of rounding]

Region and country or area	Midyear population	Births	Deaths	Natural increase	Births per 1,000 population	Deaths per 1,000 population	Rate of natural increase (percent)
EUROPE AND THE NEW INDEPENDENT STATES—Continued							
Eastern Europe—Continued							
Hungary	10,003	107	151	-43	11	15	-0.4
Macedonia, The Former Yugoslav Republic of	2,104	28	18	10	13	8	0.5
Montenegro	635	8	5	3	12	8	0.4
Poland	38,643	461	390	71	12	10	0.2
Romania	21,657	212	266	-54	10	12	-0.3
Serbia	9,979	140	102	37	14	10	0.4
Slovakia	5,374	68	50	18	13	9	0.3
Slovenia	1,951	16	18	-2	8	9	-0.1
New Independent States	292,799	4,115	4,129	-14	14	14	(Z)
Baltics	7,574	90	107	-17	12	14	-0.2
Estonia	1,459	16	21	-5	11	14	-0.3
Latvia	2,469	27	38	-10	11	15	-0.4
Lithuania	3,646	47	49	-1	13	13	(Z)
Commonwealth of Independent States	285,225	4,025	4,022	3	14	14	(Z)
Armenia	3,464	56	27	30	16	8	0.9
Azerbaijan	7,677	171	67	104	22	9	1.4
Belarus	10,416	127	142	-16	12	14	-0.1
Georgia	5,220	67	64	3	13	12	0.1
Kazakstan	16,916	322	163	159	19	10	0.9
Kyrgyzstan	4,530	118	40	78	26	9	1.7
Moldova	4,464	73	52	20	16	12	0.5
Russia	148,190	1,504	2,421	-917	10	16	-0.6
Tajikistan	5,916	200	50	150	34	8	2.5
Turkmenistan	4,149	121	37	84	29	9	2.0
Ukraine	50,864	568	771	-203	11	15	-0.4
Uzbekistan	23,418	699	188	511	30	8	2.2
NORTH AMERICA	295,424	4,381	2,448	1,933	15	8	0.7
Bermuda	62	1	(Z)	1	15	7	0.8
Canada	28,821	384	207	178	13	7	0.6
Greenland	58	1	(Z)	1	17	7	1.0
Saint Pierre and Miquelon	7	(Z)	(Z)	(Z)	13	6	0.7
United States	266,476	3,995	2,241	1,754	15	8	0.7
OCEANIA	28,915	533	213	320	18	7	1.1
American Samoa	60	2	(Z)	2	36	4	3.2
Australia	18,261	255	126	130	14	7	0.7
Cook Islands	20	(Z)	(Z)	(Z)	23	5	1.8
Federated States of Micronesia	125	4	1	3	28	6	2.2
Fiji	782	18	5	13	23	6	1.7
French Polynesia	225	6	1	5	27	5	2.2
Guam	157	4	1	3	24	4	2.0
Kiribati	81	2	1	2	31	12	1.9
Marshall Islands	58	3	(Z)	3	46	7	3.8
Nauru	10	(Z)	(Z)	(Z)	18	5	1.3

Table A-5.
Population, Vital Events, and Rates, by Region and Country: 1996—Continued

[Population and events in thousands. Figures may not add to totals because of rounding]

Region and country or area	Midyear population	Births	Deaths	Natural increase	Births per 1,000 population	Deaths per 1,000 population	Rate of natural increase (percent)
OCEANIA—Continued							
New Caledonia	188	4	1	3	22	5	1.7
New Zealand	3,548	56	27	29	16	8	0.8
Northern Mariana Islands	52	2	(Z)	2	33	5	2.8
Palau	17	(Z)	(Z)	(Z)	22	7	1.5
Papua New Guinea	4,395	145	44	101	33	10	2.3
Solomon Islands	413	16	2	14	38	4	3.4
Tonga	106	3	1	2	24	7	1.7
Tuvalu	10	(Z)	(Z)	(Z)	24	9	1.5
Vanuatu	178	5	2	4	31	9	2.2
Wallis and Futuna	15	(Z)	(Z)	(Z)	24	5	1.9
Western Samoa	214	7	1	5	31	6	2.5

(Z) Between –500 and +500 for events and between –0.05 percent and +0.05 percent for rates.

Source: U.S. Bureau of the Census, International Data Base.

Table A-6.
All Women and Currently Married Women of Reproductive Age (15 to 49 Years), by Region and Country: 1990 to 2010

[Midyear population in thousands. Figures may not add to totals because of rounding]

Region and country or area	Date of marriage data	All women				Currently married women			
		1990*	1996	2000	2010	1990*	1996	2000	2010
WORLD		1,265,371	1,472,548	1,566,686	1,766,099	835,680	1,008,069	1,086,296	1,238,305
Less Developed Countries		1,036,040	1,175,390	1,269,421	1,478,186	697,375	824,111	901,745	1,057,830
More Developed Countries		229,331	297,159	297,265	287,913	138,305	183,958	184,551	180,474
AFRICA		142,562	169,232	189,199	244,732	94,563	112,238	125,316	164,363
Sub-Saharan Africa		114,123	135,165	151,044	197,326	77,461	91,573	102,037	134,154
Angola	1970	1,895	2,302	2,578	3,559	1,396	1,701	1,903	2,617
Benin	1992	1,064	1,291	1,475	2,101	758	918	1,051	1,501
Botswana	1988	310	372	397	409	118	143	152	151
Burkina Faso	1993	2,031	2,357	2,573	3,182	1,676	1,935	2,099	2,555
Burundi	1987	1,291	1,342	1,481	1,925	832	856	923	1,172
Cameroon	1991	2,586	3,108	3,500	4,670	1,940	2,293	2,574	3,426
Cape Verde	1990	86	103	118	165	36	45	52	70
Central African Republic	**	655	755	817	984	491	562	604	722
Chad	1964	1,371	1,613	1,795	2,385	1,126	1,325	1,473	1,958
Comoros	1980	101	125	144	211	67	83	96	141
Congo	**	513	599	666	824	379	445	493	615
Côte d'Ivoire	1988	2,581	3,208	3,573	4,674	1,852	2,282	2,523	3,299
Djibouti	**	81	93	98	132	57	65	68	92
Equatorial Guinea	1983	88	101	113	152	54	63	70	94
Eritrea	**	635	936	1,067	1,372	438	647	753	978
Ethiopia	1990	10,799	12,730	14,108	18,553	7,566	8,880	9,789	12,754
Gabon	1961	259	274	288	351	214	226	238	292
Gambia, The	1983	194	234	266	369	158	189	215	298
Ghana	1993	3,565	4,210	4,751	6,308	2,349	2,848	3,218	4,271
Guinea	1954	1,388	1,729	1,808	2,350	1,286	1,602	1,675	2,178
Guinea-Bissau	**	244	284	312	393	183	212	234	296
Kenya	1993	5,252	6,603	7,479	9,083	2,270	2,852	3,234	4,075
Lesotho	1976	407	477	525	632	285	331	363	442
Liberia	1986	498	463	673	1,040	334	311	451	695
Madagascar	1992	2,593	3,119	3,521	4,762	1,546	1,862	2,101	2,850
Malawi	1992	2,078	2,136	2,303	2,601	1,479	1,508	1,611	1,812
Mali	1987	1,826	2,144	2,420	3,385	1,433	1,666	1,880	2,633
Mauritania	1977	427	518	594	850	268	325	372	533
Mauritius	1983	296	324	337	350	179	197	208	219
Mayotte	1966	17	21	25	38	13	16	19	29
Mozambique	1980	3,320	4,237	4,725	6,214	2,493	3,187	3,544	4,670
Namibia	1992	321	397	456	618	133	167	194	271
Niger	1992	1,751	2,066	2,296	3,079	1,478	1,753	1,951	2,598
Nigeria	1990	18,939	22,866	25,939	36,142	14,375	17,236	19,517	27,263
Reunion	1982	163	180	192	226	75	91	100	115
Rwanda	1992	1,539	1,568	2,113	2,408	881	853	1,122	1,309
Sao Tome and Principe	1991	28	35	39	52	15	19	22	30
Senegal	1992-93	1,686	2,069	2,383	3,409	1,180	1,456	1,672	2,374
Seychelles	1971	19	22	23	25	7	9	10	11
Sierra Leone	**	1,008	1,099	1,265	1,757	749	820	945	1,305
Somalia	**	1,820	2,087	2,385	3,318	1,274	1,467	1,668	2,317
South Africa	1985	9,379	10,638	11,416	12,842	4,559	5,237	5,636	6,298
Sudan	1990	6,083	7,030	8,176	11,281	3,529	4,049	4,687	6,523
Swaziland	1986	204	239	272	376	74	86	99	139
Tanzania	1991-92	5,648	6,759	7,282	8,607	3,677	4,360	4,692	5,512

Table A-6.
All Women and Currently Married Women of Reproductive Age (15 to 49 Years), by Region and Country: 1990 to 2010—Continued

[Midyear population in thousands. Figures may not add to totals because of rounding]

Region and country or area	Date of marriage data	All women 1990*	All women 1996	All women 2000	All women 2010	Currently married women 1990*	Currently married women 1996	Currently married women 2000	Currently married women 2010
AFRICA—Continued									
Sub-Saharan Africa—Continued									
Togo	1988	832	1,019	1,177	1,708	600	731	840	1,218
Uganda	1991	3,738	4,299	4,675	6,041	2,529	2,903	3,116	3,973
Zaire	1955	8,446	10,312	11,364	15,728	6,450	7,851	8,660	11,960
Zambia	1992	1,755	1,983	2,149	2,551	1,160	1,263	1,349	1,575
Zimbabwe	1988	2,313	2,692	2,914	3,138	1,441	1,643	1,770	1,924
North Africa		28,439	34,066	38,156	47,406	17,103	20,666	23,279	30,209
Algeria	1992	5,740	7,158	8,268	10,481	2,910	3,701	4,294	5,952
Egypt	1992	13,552	15,963	17,553	21,471	8,915	10,492	11,593	14,548
Libya	1964	911	1,139	1,330	2,007	733	922	1,077	1,622
Morocco	1992	6,270	7,499	8,444	10,422	3,444	4,210	4,801	6,189
Tunisia	1988	1,966	2,308	2,562	3,025	1,102	1,340	1,515	1,898
NEAR EAST		30,309	36,696	41,554	54,519	20,038	24,497	27,947	37,325
Bahrain	1989	117	141	155	182	67	85	95	108
Cyprus	1982	172	184	192	206	118	127	130	139
Gaza Strip	1967	130	186	234	368	85	120	151	230
Iraq	1977	3,915	4,688	5,496	8,108	2,665	3,203	3,786	5,636
Israel	1987	1,039	1,303	1,366	1,505	696	886	935	1,044
Jordan	1990	717	957	1,093	1,551	399	551	643	947
Kuwait	1985	480	454	582	786	321	302	386	527
Lebanon	1970	817	1,001	1,112	1,356	466	583	676	878
Oman	1977-79	342	446	529	785	287	372	443	663
Qatar	1987	78	97	108	139	54	65	70	88
Saudi Arabia	1987	3,027	3,732	4,372	6,433	1,991	2,433	2,781	4,027
Syria	1992	2,660	3,412	4,014	5,815	1,456	1,903	2,260	3,359
Turkey	1993	13,795	16,190	17,753	20,641	9,322	11,143	12,413	15,036
United Arab Emirates	1966	433	626	760	1,053	336	464	549	740
West Bank	1967	296	405	467	636	195	268	312	417
Yemen	1991-92	2,288	2,876	3,321	4,955	1,582	1,992	2,318	3,488
ASIA		764,126	851,451	907,730	1,022,784	523,519	615,308	667,892	758,229
Afghanistan	1972-73	3,323	5,156	6,102	7,969	2,674	4,161	4,926	6,448
Bangladesh	1989	25,287	30,400	34,185	42,230	19,847	23,918	26,979	34,031
Bhutan	**	371	422	462	584	305	350	382	480
Brunei	1981	63	76	84	99	40	49	54	63
Burma	1992	10,157	11,588	12,648	15,254	5,523	6,418	7,064	8,601
Cambodia	**	2,275	2,611	2,891	3,797	1,379	1,676	1,798	2,269
China	1980/90	311,905	336,496	348,874	367,489	194,490	235,283	253,189	264,099
Mainland	1990	306,441	330,451	342,550	361,354	190,805	231,110	248,758	259,611
Taiwan	1980	5,464	6,045	6,323	6,136	3,685	4,172	4,431	4,488
Hong Kong	1991	1,534	1,723	1,802	1,753	881	1,064	1,116	1,079
India	1992-93	209,231	237,868	258,915	306,810	162,989	187,519	204,237	244,479
Indonesia	1991	48,926	56,670	61,535	68,602	33,387	39,002	43,121	49,509
Iran	1976	12,110	14,651	16,811	23,441	9,171	11,113	12,674	18,046
Japan	1990	31,466	31,038	29,416	27,028	18,684	18,529	17,817	17,467
Laos	**	956	1,142	1,289	1,769	572	683	772	1,056
Macau	1981	129	145	151	143	75	95	101	91
Malaysia	1980	4,518	5,155	5,629	6,724	2,845	3,350	3,637	4,342

Table A-6.
All Women and Currently Married Women of Reproductive Age (15 to 49 Years), by Region and Country: 1990 to 2010—Continued

[Midyear population in thousands. Figures may not add to totals because of rounding]

Region and country or area	Date of marriage data	All women				Currently married women			
		1990*	1996	2000	2010	1990*	1996	2000	2010
ASIA—Continued									
Maldives	1985	47	57	67	100	35	43	50	74
Mongolia	**	524	637	722	907	354	440	505	658
Nepal	1991	4,293	5,112	5,750	7,559	3,332	3,929	4,434	5,921
North Korea	**	6,213	6,763	7,092	7,820	3,754	4,690	5,143	5,459
Pakistan	1991	24,861	28,862	32,653	43,676	17,032	19,814	22,425	30,327
Philippines	1993	16,241	19,068	20,988	25,670	9,514	11,328	12,628	15,692
Singapore	1990	934	1,025	1,049	1,020	525	630	668	622
South Korea	1990	12,115	12,986	13,414	13,040	7,279	8,298	8,867	9,021
Sri Lanka	1987	4,654	5,171	5,490	5,777	4,282	4,745	5,029	5,276
Thailand	1987	15,474	17,170	17,974	18,021	14,456	15,979	16,673	16,606
Vietnam	1989	16,519	19,461	21,739	25,503	10,095	12,204	13,605	16,511
LATIN AMERICA AND THE CARIBBEAN		113,131	129,482	139,281	158,618	66,544	77,603	84,465	98,816
Anguilla	1984	2	2	2	2	1	1	1	1
Antigua and Barbuda	**	19	20	21	21	9	10	11	11
Argentina	1980	7,705	8,539	9,001	9,891	4,793	5,232	5,552	6,280
Aruba	1981	19	19	19	17	9	10	10	9
Bahamas, The	1980	69	75	79	83	30	35	38	41
Barbados	1980	70	72	74	70	33	36	37	36
Belize	1980	42	51	59	81	18	22	26	37
Bolivia	1994	1,516	1,732	1,879	2,335	908	1,049	1,152	1,455
Brazil	1980	39,466	45,027	47,806	51,275	23,660	27,467	29,531	32,808
Chile	1985	3,485	3,786	3,985	4,370	2,027	2,227	2,345	2,575
Colombia	1990	9,022	10,209	10,991	12,467	4,827	5,699	6,197	7,129
Costa Rica	1986	773	895	981	1,162	466	550	602	716
Cuba	1981	2,978	3,013	3,028	3,096	1,941	2,083	2,108	2,137
Dominica	1981	21	22	23	25	10	12	13	14
Dominican Republic	1991	1,841	2,133	2,331	2,747	1,050	1,252	1,381	1,660
Ecuador	1990	2,535	3,044	3,375	4,047	1,537	1,886	2,127	2,650
El Salvador	1993	1,219	1,491	1,637	2,039	660	812	924	1,191
French Guiana	1982	29	37	42	50	9	12	14	16
Grenada	1981	21	21	22	30	9	10	10	14
Guadeloupe	1990	104	113	117	127	31	37	40	46
Guatemala	1990	2,176	2,644	2,986	3,949	1,371	1,666	1,893	2,548
Guyana	1980	195	193	193	193	99	100	101	105
Haiti	1989	1,365	1,492	1,669	2,212	833	890	967	1,290
Honduras	1974	1,077	1,336	1,526	2,027	650	810	931	1,265
Jamaica	1982	634	688	725	805	137	165	184	222
Martinique	1982	104	111	114	119	32	38	42	46
Mexico	1990	21,559	25,173	27,450	32,690	12,857	15,427	17,141	21,002
Netherlands Antilles	1981	56	58	59	60	23	26	27	27
Nicaragua	1992-93	823	1,034	1,197	1,604	503	634	737	1,014
Panama	1990	604	685	735	858	341	396	431	511
Paraguay	1990	1,095	1,318	1,498	1,940	672	813	918	1,204
Peru	1992	5,378	6,313	6,962	8,300	2,968	3,549	3,967	4,951
Puerto Rico	1980	954	1,006	1,003	1,023	551	586	586	608
Saint Kitts and Nevis	1980	9	11	12	15	2	3	3	4
Saint Lucia	1980	37	43	47	54	19	23	26	32

Table A-6.
All Women and Currently Married Women of Reproductive Age (15 to 49 Years), by Region and Country: 1990 to 2010—Continued

[Midyear population in thousands. Figures may not add to totals because of rounding]

Region and country or area	Date of marriage data	All women 1990*	All women 1996	All women 2000	All women 2010	Currently married women 1990*	Currently married women 1996	Currently married women 2000	Currently married women 2010
LATIN AMERICA AND THE CARIBBEAN—Continued									
Saint Vincent and the Grenadines	1980	28	32	35	38	14	16	18	21
Suriname	1980	103	113	123	149	40	48	53	65
Trinidad and Tobago	1987	324	340	353	356	180	190	194	208
Uruguay	1985	740	789	811	860	446	474	494	533
Venezuela	1981	4,935	5,797	6,310	7,433	2,778	3,306	3,634	4,336
EUROPE AND THE NEW INDEPENDENT STATES		135,637	201,858	203,471	197,851	88,360	132,513	134,017	133,011
Western Europe		52,956	95,725	95,018	91,144	32,509	60,528	60,821	58,767
Andorra	**	14	17	18	17	9	12	12	11
Austria	1980	1,966	1,995	1,992	1,931	1,220	1,289	1,292	1,246
Belgium	1981	2,438	2,463	2,418	2,267	1,712	1,769	1,742	1,614
Denmark	1988	1,310	1,279	1,232	1,183	646	652	644	617
Faroe Islands	1977	11	11	12	13	7	8	8	8
Finland	1988	1,258	1,258	1,216	1,145	675	682	649	600
France	1990	14,193	14,691	14,574	13,999	8,908	9,520	9,458	9,120
Germany	1988	19,399	20,070	20,460	20,142	12,364	13,227	13,497	13,157
Gibraltar	1981	7	8	8	8	5	5	5	6
Greece	1981	2,397	2,633	2,660	2,495	1,677	1,862	1,901	1,839
Guernsey	1981	16	17	16	17	10	12	12	12
Iceland	1983	65	69	70	72	35	38	39	40
Ireland	1988	851	911	940	953	471	504	523	575
Isle of Man	1981	16	18	18	20	10	12	12	13
Italy	1981	(NA)	14,357	13,955	12,775	(NA)	9,745	9,725	9,032
Jersey	**	(NA)	23	23	22	(NA)	17	17	15
Liechtenstein	1987	8	9	9	8	5	5	5	5
Luxembourg	1990	97	103	102	97	59	65	64	59
Malta	1985	91	95	94	93	57	58	57	57
Monaco	**	7	7	7	7	5	5	5	5
Netherlands	1990	3,967	3,988	3,882	3,709	2,215	2,365	2,335	2,178
Norway	1990	1,056	1,061	1,044	1,020	530	559	561	543
Portugal	1981	(NA)	2,550	2,533	2,417	(NA)	1,762	1,798	1,776
San Marino	**	6	6	6	6	4	4	4	4
Spain	1988	(NA)	10,143	10,126	9,309	(NA)	5,926	6,175	6,292
Sweden	1990	2,048	2,028	1,985	2,045	911	922	910	905
Switzerland	1988	1,734	1,770	1,754	1,719	976	1,035	1,032	986
United Kingdom	1989	(NA)	14,144	13,864	13,653	(NA)	8,470	8,338	8,052
Eastern Europe		12,752	30,774	30,792	29,273	8,703	21,240	21,369	21,057
Albania	1989	828	871	947	1,083	563	602	658	765
Bosnia and Herzegovina	1981	(NA)	663	671	684	(NA)	460	458	500
Bulgaria	1975	(NA)	2,120	2,155	2,119	(NA)	1,628	1,672	1,690
Croatia	1981	(NA)	1,265	1,267	1,156	(NA)	896	902	840
Czech Republic	1989	(NA)	2,652	2,580	2,432	(NA)	1,770	1,764	1,709
Hungary	1989	2,535	2,531	2,439	2,189	1,656	1,637	1,616	1,476
Macedonia, The Former Yugoslav Republic of	1981	(NA)	539	547	535	(NA)	374	378	377
Montenegro	1981	(NA)	165	169	167	(NA)	114	118	119
Poland	1984	9,388	10,084	10,250	9,626	6,485	6,839	6,878	6,757
Romania	1977	(NA)	5,507	5,352	5,024	(NA)	3,926	3,889	3,818

Table A-6.
All Women and Currently Married Women of Reproductive Age (15 to 49 Years), by Region and Country: 1990 to 2010—Continued

[Midyear population in thousands. Figures may not add to totals because of rounding]

Region and country or area	Date of marriage data	All women				Currently married women			
		1990*	1996	2000	2010	1990*	1996	2000	2010
EUROPE AND THE NEW INDEPENDENT STATES—Continued									
Eastern Europe—Continued									
Serbia	1981	(NA)	2,449	2,468	2,411	(NA)	1,697	1,713	1,705
Slovakia	1989	(NA)	1,417	1,444	1,399	(NA)	939	967	971
Slovenia	1981	(NA)	510	503	447	(NA)	359	357	330
New Independent States		69,929	75,359	77,660	77,435	47,147	50,745	51,827	53,187
Baltics		1,953	1,874	1,853	1,761	1,251	1,204	1,181	1,148
Estonia	1989	381	362	354	331	240	227	219	213
Latvia	1989	648	600	584	539	410	380	364	346
Lithuania	1989	923	912	916	891	600	598	598	589
Commonwealth of Independent States		67,976	73,485	75,807	75,673	45,897	49,541	50,646	52,039
Armenia	1989	851	922	954	929	579	632	646	644
Azerbaijan	1989	1,824	2,023	2,145	2,334	1,122	1,294	1,369	1,479
Belarus	1989	2,462	2,662	2,748	2,710	1,688	1,828	1,870	1,895
Georgia	1989	1,350	1,348	1,343	1,288	880	887	881	867
Kazakstan	1989	4,175	4,464	4,573	4,709	2,724	2,914	2,968	3,133
Kyrgyzstan	1989	1,028	1,120	1,199	1,454	675	740	785	974
Moldova	1989	1,107	1,175	1,211	1,214	775	814	828	856
Russia	1989	36,024	38,917	39,733	37,315	24,366	26,100	26,345	25,654
Tajikistan	1989	1,190	1,378	1,547	2,064	808	950	1,056	1,438
Turkmenistan	1989	873	1,045	1,167	1,457	547	668	746	944
Ukraine	1989	12,301	12,705	12,763	12,072	8,504	8,793	8,777	8,537
Uzbekistan	1989	4,791	5,725	6,426	8,127	3,228	3,921	4,375	5,618
NORTH AMERICA		72,974	76,645	78,022	79,537	38,848	41,652	42,203	41,709
Canada	1991	7,154	7,583	7,657	7,649	4,326	4,679	4,716	4,602
Greenland	1986	15	15	16	17	6	6	7	7
United States	1990	65,806	69,047	70,350	71,871	34,516	36,967	37,480	37,100
OCEANIA		6,632	7,185	7,429	8,059	3,808	4,257	4,455	4,852
Australia	1990	4,474	4,724	4,774	4,853	2,560	2,808	2,860	2,875
Fiji	1986	188	205	221	251	124	134	144	169
French Polynesia	1988	49	56	61	75	19	24	26	33
Marshall Islands	1980	9	12	15	22	6	8	10	15
New Caledonia	1983	44	49	53	60	23	27	29	35
New Zealand	1991	860	918	936	1,007	417	461	480	510
Papua New Guinea	**	856	1,033	1,155	1,495	566	679	770	1,023
Solomon Islands	1976	71	92	107	155	46	59	70	104
Tuvalu	1979	2	3	3	3	1	1	1	2
Vanuatu	1979	35	43	48	62	22	27	31	41
Western Samoa	1981	43	50	57	76	23	29	34	46

* Region and world subtotals are sums of country data and therefore exclude countries for which data are not available.

** Marital status by 5-year age groups not available. For these countries, the data on number of currently married women are estimated using marital status data from another country in the region.

(NA) Data not available. See appendix B.

Note: The category "currently married women" includes women in consensual unions. Estimates are based on component projections of the female population and the percent of women who are married or in consensual unions in each 5-year age group from the most recent source in the International Data Base. Countries without component projections are omitted.

Source: U.S. Bureau of the Census, International Data Base.

Table A-7.
Population by Age Group and Percent Female, by Region and Development Category: 1996 to 2020

[Population in millions. Figures may not add to totals because of rounding]

Region	Total, all ages	0 to 4 years	5 to 14 years	15 to 19 years	20 to 44 years	45 to 64 years	65 to 79 years	80 years and over
				POPULATION 1996				
WORLD	5,771	616	1,178	523	2,192	886	313	64
Less Developed Countries	4,600	546	1,021	443	1,755	621	187	27
More Developed Countries	1,171	70	157	80	437	265	126	36
AFRICA	731	123	198	79	235	75	20	3
Sub-Saharan Africa	594	105	164	64	186	59	15	2
North Africa	137	18	34	15	49	16	5	1
NEAR EAST	157	23	39	16	55	18	6	1
ASIA	3,271	343	673	299	1,295	486	151	23
LATIN AMERICA AND THE CARIBBEAN	488	54	107	51	185	66	21	4
EUROPE AND THE NEW INDEPENDENT STATES	800	48	114	57	297	176	84	23
Western Europe	387	21	46	24	144	91	45	15
Eastern Europe	120	7	18	10	44	27	12	3
New Independent States	293	20	51	23	109	58	26	6
NORTH AMERICA	295	22	43	20	114	59	29	9
OCEANIA	28	3	5	2	11	5	2	1
EXCLUDING CHINA (MAINLAND AND TAIWAN):								
World	4,540	513	956	427	1,660	684	245	54
Less Developed Countries	3,369	444	800	347	1,223	419	120	17
Asia	2,039	241	452	202	763	284	84	13
Less Developed Countries	1,914	235	438	194	720	249	69	9
				PERCENT FEMALE				
WORLD	50	49	49	49	49	50	55	65
Less Developed Countries	49	49	49	49	49	50	53	59
More Developed Countries	51	49	49	49	50	52	59	70
AFRICA	50	50	50	50	50	52	53	55
Sub-Saharan Africa	50	50	50	50	50	52	53	56
North Africa	50	49	49	49	49	51	53	53
NEAR EAST	48	49	49	49	47	48	52	59
ASIA	49	48	48	48	49	49	53	60
LATIN AMERICA AND THE CARIBBEAN	50	49	49	49	50	52	56	61
EUROPE AND THE NEW INDEPENDENT STATES	52	49	49	49	50	52	60	71
Western Europe	51	49	49	49	49	51	57	69
Eastern Europe	51	49	49	49	50	52	59	67
New Independent States	53	49	49	49	50	55	66	78
NORTH AMERICA	51	49	49	49	50	52	56	67
OCEANIA	50	49	49	49	49	50	54	65
EXCLUDING CHINA (MAINLAND AND TAIWAN):								
World	50	49	49	49	49	51	56	65
Less Developed Countries	49	49	49	49	49	51	53	57
Asia	49	49	49	49	49	50	53	57
Less Developed Countries	49	49	49	49	49	50	52	53

Table A-7.
Population by Age Group and Percent Female, by Region and Development Category: 1996 to 2020—Con.

[Population in millions. Figures may not add to totals because of rounding]

Region	Total, all ages	0 to 4 years	5 to 14 years	15 to 19 years	20 to 44 years	45 to 64 years	65 to 79 years	80 years and over
				POPULATION 2000				
WORLD	6,090	619	1,205	557	2,305	989	345	69
Less Developed Countries	4,902	549	1,054	476	1,871	707	212	32
More Developed Countries	1,188	70	151	81	434	282	133	37
AFRICA	807	131	216	89	263	83	22	3
Sub-Saharan Africa	659	113	182	72	208	65	17	2
North Africa	148	18	35	16	55	18	5	1
NEAR EAST	175	24	42	18	62	21	6	1
ASIA	3,448	337	682	317	1,360	553	172	27
LATIN AMERICA AND THE CARIBBEAN	517	54	108	52	200	75	24	5
EUROPE AND THE NEW INDEPENDENT STATES	807	49	107	58	297	184	89	22
Western Europe	391	21	45	23	144	95	49	15
Eastern Europe	120	7	16	9	44	29	13	2
New Independent States	295	21	46	25	109	61	27	5
NORTH AMERICA	307	21	45	22	113	67	29	10
OCEANIA	30	3	5	2	11	6	2	1
EXCLUDING CHINA (MAINLAND AND TAIWAN):								
World	4,815	522	984	457	1,772	753	269	57
Less Developed Countries	3,626	452	833	376	1,338	471	136	20
Asia	2,172	240	461	216	826	317	96	15
Less Developed Countries	2,046	234	449	209	783	281	79	11
				PERCENT FEMALE				
WORLD	50	49	49	49	49	50	55	65
Less Developed Countries	49	49	49	49	49	50	53	59
More Developed Countries	51	49	49	49	50	52	58	69
AFRICA	50	50	50	50	50	52	54	56
Sub-Saharan Africa	50	50	50	50	50	52	54	57
North Africa	50	49	49	49	49	51	54	55
NEAR EAST	48	49	49	49	48	47	52	59
ASIA	49	48	48	49	49	49	52	60
LATIN AMERICA AND THE CARIBBEAN	50	49	49	49	50	52	56	62
EUROPE AND THE NEW INDEPENDENT STATES	52	49	49	49	50	52	60	71
Western Europe	51	49	49	49	49	50	57	69
Eastern Europe	51	49	49	49	50	52	59	68
New Independent States	53	49	49	49	50	55	65	79
NORTH AMERICA	51	49	49	49	50	51	56	67
OCEANIA	50	49	49	49	49	50	54	64
EXCLUDING CHINA (MAINLAND AND TAIWAN):								
World	50	49	49	49	49	51	56	65
Less Developed Countries	49	49	49	49	49	51	54	57
Asia	49	49	49	49	49	50	53	58
Less Developed Countries	49	49	49	49	49	50	53	54

Table A-7.
Population by Age Group and Percent Female, by Region and Development Category: 1996 to 2020—Con.

[Population in millions. Figures may not add to totals because of rounding]

Region	Total, all ages	0 to 4 years	5 to 14 years	15 to 19 years	20 to 44 years	45 to 64 years	65 to 79 years	80 years and over
				POPULATION 2010				
WORLD	6,861	632	1,218	598	2,595	1,299	415	103
Less Developed Countries	5,633	561	1,072	524	2,177	973	275	52
More Developed Countries	1,228	71	146	74	418	326	140	51
AFRICA	1,009	151	260	112	345	107	29	4
Sub-Saharan Africa	831	131	223	95	275	81	22	3
North Africa	178	19	37	17	70	26	7	1
NEAR EAST	223	28	50	22	80	31	9	2
ASIA	3,852	326	651	334	1,527	750	221	44
LATIN AMERICA AND THE CARIBBEAN	583	52	106	53	231	103	32	7
EUROPE AND THE NEW INDEPENDENT STATES	827	51	102	50	290	212	90	31
Western Europe	397	19	42	22	133	109	52	20
Eastern Europe	123	8	15	7	44	31	13	4
New Independent States	307	24	44	20	113	72	26	8
NORTH AMERICA	333	22	44	25	110	88	32	13
OCEANIA	33	3	5	3	12	7	3	1
EXCLUDING CHINA (MAINLAND AND TAIWAN):								
World	5,496	544	1,033	495	2,041	979	321	84
Less Developed Countries	4,268	473	887	421	1,623	652	181	32
Asia	2,488	237	466	231	973	430	127	24
Less Developed Countries	2,361	231	453	225	932	396	107	17
				PERCENT FEMALE				
WORLD	50	49	49	49	49	50	54	63
Less Developed Countries	49	49	49	49	49	50	53	60
More Developed Countries	51	49	49	49	49	51	56	67
AFRICA	50	50	50	50	49	52	56	59
Sub-Saharan Africa	50	50	50	50	50	52	56	59
North Africa	50	49	49	49	49	51	55	59
NEAR EAST	49	49	49	49	49	47	51	59
ASIA	49	49	48	48	49	49	53	60
LATIN AMERICA AND THE CARIBBEAN	51	49	49	49	50	52	56	63
EUROPE AND THE NEW INDEPENDENT STATES	52	49	49	49	49	52	58	69
Western Europe	51	49	49	49	49	50	55	66
Eastern Europe	51	49	49	49	49	52	59	69
New Independent States	53	49	49	49	50	54	64	75
NORTH AMERICA	51	49	49	49	50	51	54	64
OCEANIA	50	49	49	49	49	50	53	62
EXCLUDING CHINA (MAINLAND AND TAIWAN):								
World	50	49	49	49	49	51	55	64
Less Developed Countries	50	49	49	49	49	50	54	59
Asia	49	49	49	49	49	50	54	59
Less Developed Countries	49	49	49	49	49	50	53	56

Table A-7.
Population by Age Group and Percent Female, by Region and Development Category: 1996 to 2020—Con.

[Population in millions. Figures may not add to totals because of rounding]

Region	Total, all ages	0 to 4 years	5 to 14 years	15 to 19 years	20 to 44 years	45 to 64 years	65 to 79 years	80 years and over
				POPULATION 2020				
WORLD	7,599	644	1,256	609	2,769	1,613	567	142
Less Developed Countries	6,350	578	1,114	533	2,373	1,277	395	79
More Developed Countries	1,249	66	142	76	395	335	171	62
AFRICA	1,230	168	299	133	445	140	39	6
Sub-Saharan Africa	1,023	148	261	115	363	103	29	5
North Africa	207	20	38	19	81	37	10	2
NEAR EAST	276	32	59	26	99	44	13	3
ASIA	4,219	322	644	319	1,578	974	316	67
LATIN AMERICA AND THE CARIBBEAN	643	51	103	52	247	135	45	11
EUROPE AND THE NEW INDEPENDENT STATES	834	45	99	53	272	222	105	39
Western Europe	394	18	38	21	118	116	59	24
Eastern Europe	122	6	15	8	42	31	16	5
New Independent States	318	21	47	24	112	75	29	10
NORTH AMERICA	361	24	47	24	116	91	45	15
OCEANIA	36	3	5	3	12	8	4	1
EXCLUDING CHINA (MAINLAND AND TAIWAN):								
World	6,160	559	1,079	521	2,264	1,204	423	111
Less Developed Countries	4,911	492	936	445	1,869	868	252	49
Asia	2,780	236	467	231	1,073	565	172	36
Less Developed Countries	2,657	231	455	224	1,038	531	150	27
				PERCENT FEMALE				
WORLD	50	49	49	49	49	50	54	62
Less Developed Countries	50	49	49	49	49	50	53	60
More Developed Countries	51	49	49	49	49	51	55	65
AFRICA	50	49	50	50	49	51	57	61
Sub-Saharan Africa	50	50	50	50	49	52	57	61
North Africa	50	49	49	49	49	50	55	62
NEAR EAST	49	49	49	49	49	48	49	58
ASIA	49	49	49	49	49	49	53	60
LATIN AMERICA AND THE CARIBBEAN	51	49	49	49	50	52	56	63
EUROPE AND THE NEW INDEPENDENT STATES	51	49	49	49	49	51	56	67
Western Europe	51	49	49	49	49	50	54	64
Eastern Europe	52	49	49	49	49	52	58	69
New Independent States	53	49	49	49	50	54	64	75
NORTH AMERICA	51	49	49	49	50	51	53	63
OCEANIA	50	49	49	49	49	50	53	61
EXCLUDING CHINA (MAINLAND AND TAIWAN):								
World	50	49	49	49	49	50	55	63
Less Developed Countries	50	49	49	49	49	50	54	60
Asia	49	49	49	49	49	50	53	59
Less Developed Countries	49	49	49	49	49	50	53	58

Source: U.S. Bureau of the Census, International Data Base.

Table A-8.
Total Fertility Rates by Region and Country: 1985 to 2020

Region and country or area	1985	1990	1996	2000	2005	2010	2015	2020
WORLD	4.2	3.4	2.9	2.8	2.7	2.5	2.4	2.3
Less Developed Countries	4.7	3.7	3.3	3.1	2.9	2.7	2.6	2.5
More Developed Countries	1.9	1.9	1.6	1.8	1.8	1.8	1.8	1.8
AFRICA	6.3	5.9	5.5	5.2	4.8	4.4	4.1	3.7
Sub-Saharan Africa	6.5	6.3	5.9	5.6	5.2	4.8	4.4	4.0
Angola	6.7	6.7	6.3	6.1	5.6	5.2	4.7	4.2
Benin	7.1	7.1	6.6	6.3	5.9	5.4	4.8	4.3
Botswana	(NA)	4.8	4.3	3.8	3.3	2.9	2.6	2.4
Burkina Faso	7.2	7.2	6.8	6.5	6.0	5.4	4.9	4.3
Burundi	7.0	7.0	6.6	6.3	5.8	5.3	4.8	4.4
Cameroon	6.3	6.3	6.0	5.7	5.4	5.0	4.6	4.2
Cape Verde	6.7	6.7	6.1	5.7	5.1	4.5	3.9	3.5
Central African Republic	(NA)	5.8	5.4	5.2	4.8	4.4	4.1	3.7
Chad	5.9	5.9	5.8	5.6	5.3	5.0	4.6	4.3
Comoros	7.0	7.0	6.7	6.3	5.9	5.4	4.9	4.3
Congo	5.9	5.6	5.1	4.8	4.4	4.0	3.6	3.2
Côte d'Ivoire	(NA)	6.7	6.1	5.8	5.4	4.9	4.4	4.0
Djibouti	6.4	6.4	6.1	5.8	5.4	5.0	4.5	4.1
Equatorial Guinea	5.5	5.5	5.2	4.9	4.7	4.4	4.1	3.8
Eritrea	6.7	6.7	6.5	6.4	6.0	5.5	5.0	4.5
Ethiopia	6.7	7.1	7.0	6.8	6.4	5.9	5.4	4.9
Gabon	4.1	4.1	3.9	3.7	3.5	3.4	3.2	3.0
Gambia, The	6.5	6.5	6.2	5.9	5.5	5.1	4.7	4.4
Ghana	6.4	5.7	4.6	4.0	3.3	2.8	2.5	2.3
Guinea	6.1	6.1	5.7	5.5	5.1	4.7	4.3	3.9
Guinea-Bissau	5.9	5.9	5.3	5.0	4.6	4.2	3.8	3.4
Kenya	6.9	5.7	4.5	3.7	3.0	2.6	2.3	2.2
Lesotho	5.3	4.9	4.3	3.9	3.5	3.1	2.8	2.6
Liberia	6.6	6.6	6.2	6.0	5.6	5.2	4.8	4.4
Madagascar	6.5	6.2	5.9	5.6	5.3	5.0	4.7	4.3
Malawi	7.4	6.9	5.9	5.3	4.6	3.9	3.4	3.0
Mali	(NA)	7.3	7.2	6.9	6.5	6.1	5.6	5.2
Mauritania	7.3	7.3	6.8	6.5	6.1	5.6	5.0	4.5
Mauritius	2.0	2.3	2.2	2.1	2.1	2.0	2.0	1.9
Mayotte	7.0	7.0	6.6	6.3	5.9	5.4	4.9	4.4
Mozambique	6.6	6.2	6.2	5.8	5.1	4.5	3.9	3.4
Namibia	(NA)	5.5	5.1	4.9	4.6	4.3	4.0	3.8
Niger	(NA)	7.5	7.4	7.2	6.8	6.3	5.7	5.2
Nigeria	6.6	6.6	6.2	6.0	5.5	5.1	4.6	4.2
Reunion	2.9	2.9	2.7	2.6	2.5	2.4	2.3	2.2
Rwanda	7.8	6.7	6.0	5.7	5.4	5.0	4.6	4.2
Saint Helena	(NA)	1.3	1.1	1.1	(NA)	(NA)	(NA)	(NA)
Sao Tome and Principe	5.8	4.9	4.3	3.9	3.4	3.0	2.7	2.5
Senegal	6.6	6.6	6.3	6.0	5.7	5.3	4.9	4.5
Seychelles	3.1	2.3	2.1	2.0	1.9	1.8	1.8	1.8
Sierra Leone	6.4	6.5	6.4	6.1	5.7	5.3	4.8	4.4
Somalia	7.3	7.3	7.0	6.5	6.0	5.4	4.8	4.2
South Africa	4.6	3.8	3.4	3.1	2.8	2.6	2.4	2.3
Sudan	6.5	6.5	5.9	5.5	4.9	4.4	3.8	3.4
Swaziland	6.5	6.2	6.1	5.9	5.6	5.4	5.1	4.9
Tanzania	6.5	6.2	5.7	5.3	4.9	4.4	4.0	3.6
Togo	7.2	7.2	6.8	6.5	6.0	5.6	5.1	4.6
Uganda	7.4	7.1	6.6	6.2	5.7	5.2	4.6	4.1
Zaire	6.7	6.7	6.6	6.4	6.0	5.6	5.2	4.7
Zambia	7.1	6.9	6.5	6.3	5.9	5.4	5.0	4.5
Zimbabwe	6.0	5.3	4.1	3.5	2.8	2.4	2.2	2.1

Table A-8.
Total Fertility Rates by Region and Country: 1985 to 2020—Continued

Region and country or area	1985	1990	1996	2000	2005	2010	2015	2020
AFRICA—Continued								
North Africa	5.3	4.3	3.7	3.3	2.9	2.7	2.5	2.4
Algeria	5.6	4.4	3.6	3.2	2.8	2.5	2.3	2.2
Egypt	(NA)	4.2	3.6	3.2	2.9	2.6	2.5	2.3
Libya	6.8	6.6	6.3	6.0	5.7	5.3	5.0	4.6
Morocco	5.1	4.4	3.6	3.1	2.7	2.5	2.3	2.2
Tunisia	4.5	3.3	2.9	2.7	2.5	2.3	2.2	2.1
Western Sahara	(NA)	7.2	6.9	6.6	(NA)	(NA)	(NA)	(NA)
NEAR EAST	5.1	5.0	4.6	4.3	4.0	3.7	3.5	3.2
Bahrain	4.0	3.4	3.1	2.9	2.8	2.7	2.6	2.4
Cyprus	2.4	2.4	2.2	2.1	2.0	2.0	1.9	1.9
Gaza Strip	7.6	8.1	7.8	7.3	6.6	5.9	5.0	4.3
Iraq	(NA)	7.3	6.4	5.8	5.3	4.8	4.3	3.9
Israel	3.1	3.0	2.8	2.7	2.5	2.4	2.3	2.2
Jordan	7.1	6.1	5.1	4.5	3.8	3.3	2.9	2.7
Kuwait	4.5	3.0	2.8	2.4	2.2	2.1	2.0	2.0
Lebanon	4.2	3.7	3.2	3.0	2.7	2.5	2.4	2.3
Oman	(NA)	6.5	6.1	5.8	5.4	5.0	4.6	4.1
Qatar	(NA)	4.6	4.3	2.9	2.6	2.4	2.2	2.1
Saudi Arabia	6.8	6.6	6.4	6.3	6.0	5.7	5.4	5.1
Syria	7.3	6.7	5.9	5.2	4.3	3.6	3.1	2.7
Turkey	3.8	3.1	2.6	2.4	2.2	2.1	2.1	2.0
United Arab Emirates	(NA)	4.9	4.5	4.2	3.9	3.5	3.3	3.0
West Bank	5.2	5.4	4.7	4.2	3.7	3.3	2.9	2.7
Yemen	7.8	7.7	7.3	6.9	6.2	5.6	4.9	4.2
ASIA	4.2	3.1	2.7	2.5	2.4	2.2	2.1	2.1
Afghanistan	6.8	6.5	6.1	5.9	5.5	5.1	4.7	4.3
Bangladesh	5.5	4.5	3.6	3.1	2.7	2.4	2.2	2.1
Bhutan	5.5	5.5	5.3	5.1	4.8	4.5	4.1	3.8
Brunei	3.7	3.5	3.4	3.3	3.2	3.1	3.0	3.0
Burma	4.6	4.2	3.8	3.6	3.3	3.1	2.9	2.7
Cambodia	5.8	5.8	5.8	5.8	5.5	5.2	4.9	4.6
China	(NA)	2.2	1.8	1.8	1.8	1.8	1.8	1.8
Mainland	(NA)	2.2	1.8	1.8	1.8	1.8	1.8	1.8
Taiwan	(NA)	1.8	1.8	1.8	1.7	1.7	1.7	1.7
Hong Kong	1.5	1.3	1.3	1.4	1.4	1.4	1.4	1.4
India	4.3	3.8	3.2	2.9	2.6	2.4	2.3	2.2
Indonesia	3.4	3.0	2.7	2.5	2.4	2.3	2.2	2.1
Iran	(NA)	6.0	4.7	3.9	3.1	2.6	2.3	2.2
Japan	1.7	1.5	1.5	1.5	1.5	1.5	1.6	1.6
Laos	6.4	6.4	5.9	5.4	4.8	4.2	3.7	3.2
Macau	(NA)	1.4	1.5	1.6	1.6	1.6	1.6	1.6
Malaysia	4.0	3.5	3.3	3.1	2.9	2.7	2.6	2.5
Maldives	7.0	6.6	6.1	5.6	5.0	4.4	3.9	3.4
Mongolia	(NA)	4.5	3.0	2.5	2.2	2.1	2.0	2.0
Nepal	6.0	5.6	5.1	4.7	4.2	3.8	3.4	3.1
North Korea	2.6	2.5	2.3	2.2	2.1	2.0	2.0	1.9
Pakistan	6.7	6.2	5.2	4.6	3.8	3.2	2.7	2.4
Philippines	4.3	4.1	3.7	3.4	3.1	2.9	2.7	2.5
Singapore	1.6	1.6	1.7	1.8	1.8	1.8	1.8	1.8
South Korea	(NA)	1.6	1.8	1.8	1.8	1.8	1.8	1.8
Sri Lanka	2.9	2.3	2.1	2.0	1.9	1.8	1.8	1.8
Thailand	(NA)	2.0	1.9	1.8	1.8	1.8	1.8	1.8
Vietnam	(NA)	3.7	2.7	2.3	2.1	2.0	2.0	2.0

Table A-8.
Total Fertility Rates by Region and Country: 1985 to 2020—Continued

Region and country or area	1985	1990	1996	2000	2005	2010	2015	2020
LATIN AMERICA AND THE CARIBBEAN	3.6	3.1	2.7	2.5	2.3	2.2	2.1	2.0
Anguilla	3.9	3.1	3.0	3.0	2.9	2.8	2.7	2.6
Antigua and Barbuda	1.7	1.7	1.7	1.7	1.7	1.7	1.7	1.7
Argentina	3.0	2.8	2.6	2.5	2.4	2.3	2.2	2.1
Aruba	1.9	1.8	1.8	1.8	1.8	1.8	1.8	1.8
Bahamas, The	2.7	2.2	2.0	1.8	1.8	1.8	1.8	1.8
Barbados	2.0	1.8	1.8	1.8	1.8	1.8	1.8	1.8
Belize	5.6	5.0	4.1	3.6	3.1	2.7	2.5	2.3
Bolivia	5.2	4.9	4.3	3.8	3.2	2.8	2.6	2.4
Brazil	3.3	2.6	2.3	2.1	2.0	1.9	1.9	1.8
British Virgin Islands	(NA)	2.3	2.3	2.2	(NA)	(NA)	(NA)	(NA)
Cayman Islands	(NA)	1.6	1.4	1.3	(NA)	(NA)	(NA)	(NA)
Chile	2.5	2.6	2.2	2.0	1.9	1.8	1.7	1.7
Colombia	3.2	2.8	2.4	2.2	2.0	1.9	1.9	1.9
Costa Rica	3.4	3.2	2.9	2.7	2.5	2.4	2.3	2.2
Cuba	1.9	1.8	1.7	1.8	1.8	1.8	1.8	1.8
Dominica	2.8	2.1	1.9	1.9	1.8	1.8	1.8	1.8
Dominican Republic	3.7	3.2	2.7	2.4	2.2	2.1	2.1	2.0
Ecuador	(NA)	3.5	2.9	2.6	2.4	2.2	2.1	2.1
El Salvador	4.6	3.8	3.2	2.9	2.7	2.5	2.4	2.3
French Guiana	3.7	3.7	3.4	3.3	3.1	2.9	2.8	2.7
Grenada	4.2	4.2	3.8	3.5	3.2	2.9	2.7	2.5
Guadeloupe	2.4	2.2	1.9	1.8	1.8	1.7	1.7	1.7
Guatemala	5.7	5.3	4.5	4.0	3.5	3.0	2.7	2.5
Guyana	3.0	2.5	2.2	2.1	1.9	1.9	1.8	1.8
Haiti	6.3	6.4	5.7	5.2	4.5	3.9	3.3	2.9
Honduras	(NA)	5.2	4.4	3.8	3.2	2.8	2.5	2.3
Jamaica	3.1	2.7	2.4	2.2	2.1	2.0	1.9	1.9
Martinique	2.0	2.0	1.8	1.8	1.8	1.8	1.8	1.8
Mexico	3.9	3.5	3.0	2.8	2.6	2.4	2.3	2.2
Montserrat	(NA)	2.3	1.9	1.7	(NA)	(NA)	(NA)	(NA)
Netherlands Antilles	2.3	2.0	1.9	1.8	1.8	1.8	1.8	1.8
Nicaragua	5.7	4.9	4.0	3.5	3.0	2.6	2.4	2.2
Panama	3.4	3.1	2.7	2.6	2.4	2.3	2.2	2.1
Paraguay	5.0	4.6	4.1	3.9	3.5	3.2	3.0	2.8
Peru	4.3	3.8	3.0	2.7	2.3	2.1	1.9	1.9
Puerto Rico	(NA)	2.2	1.9	1.8	1.8	1.8	1.8	1.8
Saint Kitts and Nevis	3.1	2.8	2.5	2.4	2.2	2.1	2.1	2.0
Saint Lucia	3.8	2.7	2.3	2.1	1.9	1.9	1.8	1.8
Saint Vincent and the Grenadines	3.3	2.7	2.0	1.9	1.8	1.8	1.8	1.8
Suriname	3.4	3.0	2.7	2.5	2.3	2.2	2.1	2.0
Trinidad and Tobago	3.2	2.2	2.0	1.9	1.8	1.8	1.8	1.8
Turks and Caicos Islands	(NA)	2.6	1.9	1.6	(NA)	(NA)	(NA)	(NA)
Uruguay	2.5	2.5	2.3	2.3	2.2	2.2	2.1	2.1
Venezuela	(NA)	3.5	2.9	2.5	2.3	2.2	2.1	2.0
Virgin Islands	(NA)	2.9	2.3	2.0	(NA)	(NA)	(NA)	(NA)
EUROPE AND THE NEW INDEPENDENT STATES	2.0	2.0	1.6	1.9	1.8	1.8	1.8	1.7
Western Europe	1.6	1.6	1.5	1.6	1.6	1.6	1.6	1.6
Andorra	(NA)	1.7	1.7	1.7	1.7	1.7	1.7	1.7
Austria	(NA)	1.5	1.5	1.5	1.5	1.5	1.6	1.6
Belgium	(NA)	1.6	1.6	1.6	1.6	1.6	1.6	1.6
Denmark	(NA)	1.7	1.7	1.7	1.7	1.7	1.7	1.7
Faroe Islands	2.2	2.7	2.4	2.2	2.1	2.0	1.9	1.8

Table A-8.
Total Fertility Rates by Region and Country: 1985 to 2020—Continued

Region and country or area	1985	1990	1996	2000	2005	2010	2015	2020
EUROPE AND THE NEW INDEPENDENT STATES— Continued								
Western Europe—Continued								
Finland	(NA)	1.8	1.8	1.8	1.8	1.8	1.8	1.8
France	(NA)	1.8	1.5	1.7	1.7	1.7	1.7	1.6
Germany	(NA)	1.5	1.3	1.6	1.6	1.5	1.5	1.5
Gibraltar	2.4	2.5	2.3	2.1	2.0	1.9	1.9	1.8
Greece	(NA)	1.4	1.5	1.5	1.5	1.5	1.6	1.6
Guernsey	(NA)	1.6	1.7	1.8	1.8	1.8	1.8	1.8
Iceland	(NA)	2.3	2.0	1.8	1.8	1.8	1.8	1.8
Ireland	(NA)	2.1	1.9	1.8	1.8	1.8	1.8	1.8
Isle of Man	(NA)	1.8	1.8	1.8	1.8	1.8	1.8	1.8
Italy	(NA)	(NA)	1.3	1.6	1.5	1.5	1.5	1.5
Jersey	(NA)	(NA)	1.5	1.5	1.5	1.5	1.6	1.6
Liechtenstein	1.5	1.4	1.5	1.5	1.5	1.5	1.6	1.6
Luxembourg	1.4	1.6	1.7	1.7	1.7	1.7	1.7	1.7
Malta	(NA)	2.0	1.9	1.8	1.8	1.8	1.8	1.8
Monaco	1.8	1.7	1.7	1.7	1.7	1.7	1.7	1.7
Netherlands	1.5	1.6	1.6	1.5	1.5	1.5	1.6	1.6
Norway	(NA)	2.0	1.7	1.5	1.5	1.5	1.6	1.6
Portugal	(NA)	(NA)	1.4	1.5	1.5	1.5	1.5	1.5
San Marino	1.3	1.5	1.5	1.5	1.5	1.5	1.6	1.6
Spain	(NA)	(NA)	1.3	1.5	1.5	1.5	1.5	1.5
Sweden	1.7	2.1	1.9	1.8	1.8	1.8	1.8	1.8
Switzerland	1.5	1.6	1.6	1.6	1.6	1.6	1.6	1.6
United Kingdom	(NA)	(NA)	1.8	1.8	1.8	1.7	1.7	1.7
Eastern Europe	2.2	2.1	1.5	1.9	1.8	1.7	1.7	1.6
Albania	(NA)	3.0	2.7	2.4	2.2	2.1	1.9	1.9
Bosnia and Herzegovina	(NA)	(NA)	1.0	1.7	1.6	1.6	1.6	1.5
Bulgaria	(NA)	(NA)	1.2	1.7	1.7	1.6	1.6	1.6
Croatia	(NA)	(NA)	1.4	1.7	1.6	1.6	1.6	1.5
Czech Republic	(NA)	(NA)	1.4	1.7	1.7	1.7	1.6	1.6
Hungary	1.8	1.8	1.5	1.8	1.7	1.7	1.6	1.6
Macedonia, The Former Yugoslav Republic of	(NA)	(NA)	1.8	2.2	2.0	1.8	1.7	1.7
Montenegro	(NA)	(NA)	1.5	1.8	1.7	1.6	1.6	1.6
Poland	2.3	2.0	1.7	1.9	1.8	1.8	1.7	1.7
Romania	2.3	(NA)	1.3	1.8	1.7	1.7	1.6	1.6
Serbia	(NA)	(NA)	2.0	2.1	1.9	1.8	1.7	1.6
Slovakia	(NA)	(NA)	1.7	2.0	1.9	1.8	1.7	1.7
Slovenia	(NA)	(NA)	1.1	1.5	1.6	1.6	1.5	1.5
New Independent States	(NA)	2.3	1.9	2.2	2.1	2.1	2.0	2.0
Baltics	(NA)	2.0	1.7	2.0	1.9	1.8	1.8	1.8
Estonia	(NA)	2.0	1.6	2.0	1.9	1.8	1.8	1.8
Latvia	(NA)	2.0	1.6	2.0	1.9	1.8	1.8	1.8
Lithuania	(NA)	2.0	1.8	2.0	1.9	1.8	1.8	1.8
Commonwealth of Independent States	(NA)	2.3	1.9	2.2	2.1	2.1	2.0	2.0
Armenia	(NA)	2.6	2.1	2.3	2.1	2.0	2.0	1.9
Azerbaijan	(NA)	2.9	2.6	2.6	2.4	2.2	2.1	2.0
Belarus	(NA)	1.9	1.7	1.9	1.8	1.8	1.8	1.7

Table A-8.
Total Fertility Rates by Region and Country: 1985 to 2020—Continued

Region and country or area	1985	1990	1996	2000	2005	2010	2015	2020
EUROPE AND THE NEW INDEPENDENT STATES— Continued								
New Independent States— Continued								
Commonwealth of Independent States—Continued								
Georgia	(NA)	2.2	1.7	2.2	2.1	2.0	1.9	1.9
Kazakstan	(NA)	2.8	2.4	2.3	2.2	2.2	2.1	2.1
Kyrgyzstan	(NA)	3.8	3.2	3.1	2.9	2.8	2.7	2.6
Moldova	(NA)	2.4	2.2	2.4	2.2	2.0	1.9	1.9
Russia	(NA)	1.9	1.4	1.9	1.9	1.8	1.8	1.7
Tajikistan	(NA)	5.4	4.4	4.5	4.2	3.9	3.6	3.4
Turkmenistan	(NA)	4.3	3.6	3.5	3.3	3.1	3.0	2.8
Ukraine	(NA)	1.9	1.6	1.9	1.8	1.8	1.7	1.7
Uzbekistan	(NA)	4.3	3.7	3.6	3.4	3.2	3.0	2.9
NORTH AMERICA	1.8	2.1	2.1	2.1	2.1	2.1	2.1	2.1
Bermuda	(NA)	1.8	1.8	1.8	(NA)	(NA)	(NA)	(NA)
Canada	1.7	1.8	1.8	1.8	1.8	1.8	1.8	1.8
Greenland	2.2	2.4	2.2	2.1	2.0	1.9	1.9	1.8
Saint Pierre and Miquelon	(NA)	1.8	1.6	1.6	(NA)	(NA)	(NA)	(NA)
United States	1.8	2.1	2.1	2.1	2.1	2.1	2.1	2.1
OCEANIA	2.7	2.6	2.4	2.3	2.2	2.1	2.1	2.0
American Samoa	(NA)	(NA)	4.2	3.9	(NA)	(NA)	(NA)	(NA)
Australia	1.9	1.9	1.8	1.8	1.8	1.8	1.8	1.8
Cook Islands	4.0	3.4	3.2	3.1	(NA)	(NA)	(NA)	(NA)
Federated States of Micronesia	(NA)	4.2	4.0	3.8	(NA)	(NA)	(NA)	(NA)
Fiji	(NA)	3.1	2.8	2.7	2.5	2.4	2.3	2.2
French Polynesia	3.9	3.4	3.3	3.1	3.0	2.8	2.7	2.6
Guam	(NA)	2.5	2.2	1.8	(NA)	(NA)	(NA)	(NA)
Kiribati	(NA)	4.0	3.7	(NA)	(NA)	(NA)	(NA)	(NA)
Marshall Islands	(NA)	7.1	6.8	6.6	6.3	6.0	5.6	5.3
Nauru	(NA)	2.8	2.1	(NA)	(NA)	(NA)	(NA)	(NA)
New Caledonia	3.0	2.8	2.5	2.4	2.3	2.2	2.1	2.1
New Zealand	(NA)	2.3	2.0	1.8	1.8	1.8	1.8	1.8
Northern Mariana Islands	(NA)	2.7	2.7	(NA)	(NA)	(NA)	(NA)	(NA)
Palau	(NA)	3.1	2.8	2.4	(NA)	(NA)	(NA)	(NA)
Papua New Guinea	5.6	5.1	4.5	4.1	3.6	3.3	3.0	2.7
Solomon Islands	6.9	6.3	5.4	4.8	4.0	3.4	2.9	2.6
Tonga	(NA)	3.9	3.5	3.3	(NA)	(NA)	(NA)	(NA)
Tuvalu	3.1	3.1	3.1	3.1	3.0	2.9	2.8	2.7
Vanuatu	5.7	5.0	4.0	3.5	3.0	2.6	2.4	2.2
Wallis and Futuna	(NA)	3.7	3.0	(NA)	(NA)	(NA)	(NA)	(NA)
Western Samoa	5.3	4.7	3.9	3.5	3.1	2.7	2.5	2.3

(NA) Data not available.

Note: Regional rates are weighted means of country rates. Countries lacking data for a specific year are excluded from the calculation of a regional rate for that year. For some regions, especially for 1985, regional TFR may not be representative of the region.

Source: U.S. Bureau of the Census, International Data Base.

Table A-9.
Infant and Child Mortality, by Region, Country, and Sex: 1996

Region and country or area	Infant mortality rate[1]			Child mortality rates[2]					
				Ages 1 to 4			Under age 5		
	Both sexes	Males	Females	Both sexes	Males	Females	Both sexes	Males	Females
WORLD	60	62	59	34	35	34	92	94	90
Less Developed Countries	66	68	64	38	39	38	101	103	99
More Developed Countries	11	12	9	2	2	2	13	14	11
AFRICA	90	96	84	64	66	62	148	155	140
Sub-Saharan Africa	95	101	88	71	73	68	158	167	150
Angola	139	151	126	69	72	66	198	212	184
Benin	105	114	96	52	53	50	151	161	141
Botswana	54	57	51	56	55	57	107	109	105
Burkina Faso	118	125	111	91	90	93	198	203	193
Burundi	102	113	92	60	60	59	156	166	145
Cameroon	79	86	72	57	58	56	131	138	124
Cape Verde	54	59	49	20	21	19	73	78	67
Central African Republic	112	120	103	71	69	73	175	181	169
Chad	120	132	109	82	88	77	193	208	177
Comoros	75	83	67	32	34	30	105	115	95
Congo	108	115	101	76	78	75	176	184	168
Côte d'Ivoire	82	85	80	65	66	64	142	145	139
Djibouti	107	116	98	75	78	72	174	185	162
Equatorial Guinea	98	105	90	59	63	55	151	161	140
Eritrea	119	129	108	63	65	62	175	185	164
Ethiopia	123	133	112	73	72	73	187	196	177
Gabon	90	102	78	40	44	36	127	142	111
Gambia, The	118	130	106	58	61	55	170	183	155
Ghana	80	87	74	50	52	47	126	134	117
Guinea	134	146	122	88	93	83	210	225	195
Guinea-Bissau	116	124	108	81	83	80	188	197	179
Kenya	55	58	52	42	40	43	95	96	93
Lesotho	82	92	71	47	49	45	125	136	113
Liberia	108	116	100	40	40	40	144	152	135
Madagascar	94	95	92	73	75	70	159	163	156
Malawi	140	147	132	120	122	118	243	251	235
Mali	103	109	96	134	140	127	223	234	211
Mauritania	82	85	79	68	78	58	144	156	132
Mauritius	17	20	14	3	4	3	21	24	17
Mayotte	75	83	67	32	34	30	105	115	95
Mozambique	126	135	116	68	68	68	185	194	176
Namibia	47	51	43	21	20	22	67	71	63
Niger	118	119	116	188	181	196	284	278	290
Nigeria	72	76	69	75	82	67	142	152	131
Reunion	8	8	7	1	1	1	9	9	8
Rwanda	119	127	111	84	85	84	193	201	185
Saint Helena	35	37	33	(NA)	(NA)	(NA)	(NA)	(NA)	(NA)
Sao Tome and Principe	61	66	57	40	41	38	99	104	93
Senegal	64	71	57	64	73	56	124	139	109
Seychelles	13	15	10	16	19	13	28	34	23
Sierra Leone	136	151	119	79	90	68	204	228	179
Somalia	121	130	112	42	44	40	158	168	147
South Africa	49	51	47	26	25	27	74	75	73
Sudan	76	76	76	51	53	49	123	125	121
Swaziland	88	98	79	36	43	29	121	136	106

Table A-9.
Infant and Child Mortality, by Region, Country, and Sex: 1996—Continued

Region and country or area	Infant mortality rate[1]			Child mortality rates[2]					
				Ages 1 to 4			Under age 5		
	Both sexes	Males	Females	Both sexes	Males	Females	Both sexes	Males	Females
AFRICA—Continued									
Sub-Saharan Africa—Continued									
Tanzania	106	118	94	83	87	79	180	194	166
Togo	84	91	77	48	51	45	128	138	118
Uganda	99	108	90	88	90	86	179	189	169
Zaire	108	118	98	62	64	60	164	175	152
Zambia	96	102	90	102	104	101	189	195	182
Zimbabwe	73	78	68	60	60	60	128	133	123
North Africa	59	62	56	20	20	21	78	80	75
Algeria	49	51	46	9	9	9	57	60	55
Egypt	73	75	71	29	27	31	100	100	100
Libya	60	64	55	25	27	23	83	89	77
Morocco	43	48	38	14	16	11	56	63	49
Tunisia	35	38	32	10	10	9	45	48	42
Western Sahara	146	151	139	(NA)	(NA)	(NA)	(NA)	(NA)	(NA)
NEAR EAST	47	50	44	14	15	13	60	64	56
Bahrain	17	20	14	3	4	3	20	24	17
Cyprus	8	11	6	1	1	-	9	12	7
Gaza Strip	28	28	27	9	8	10	36	36	37
Iraq	60	66	54	16	18	14	75	83	67
Israel	8	9	7	1	2	1	10	11	9
Jordan	32	34	28	9	10	8	40	44	36
Kuwait	11	12	10	2	2	1	13	15	11
Lebanon	37	41	33	9	10	8	45	50	40
Oman	27	31	24	6	7	5	33	37	29
Qatar	20	23	16	4	5	3	23	28	19
Saudi Arabia	46	48	44	14	14	14	60	62	58
Syria	40	41	39	12	12	13	52	52	52
Turkey	43	47	39	10	12	9	53	58	48
United Arab Emirates	20	24	17	4	4	3	24	28	20
West Bank	26	28	25	9	8	9	35	36	33
Yemen	72	75	68	30	29	31	99	102	96
ASIA	61	60	62	33	33	34	91	90	93
Afghanistan	150	155	145	83	83	82	220	225	215
Bangladesh	102	110	94	52	47	57	149	152	146
Bhutan	116	114	119	80	71	90	187	177	198
Brunei	24	26	22	5	5	5	29	31	27
Burma	81	88	73	35	37	34	113	122	104
Cambodia	108	116	100	79	81	78	179	187	170
China	39	31	48	7	7	7	46	38	55
Mainland	40	32	49	7	7	7	46	38	55
Taiwan	7	8	7	2	2	2	9	10	8
Hong Kong	5	5	5	1	1	1	6	6	6
India	71	71	71	53	52	53	120	120	120
Indonesia	63	69	57	27	30	23	88	97	79
Iran	53	53	52	31	29	33	82	81	83
Japan	4	5	4	1	2	1	6	6	5
Laos	97	106	87	53	52	54	145	153	136
Macau	5	6	5	2	2	1	7	8	6
Malaysia	24	29	19	7	7	6	30	36	25

Table A-9.
Infant and Child Mortality, by Region, Country, and Sex: 1996—Continued

Region and country or area	Infant mortality rate[1]			Child mortality rates[2] Ages 1 to 4			Child mortality rates[2] Under age 5		
	Both sexes	Males	Females	Both sexes	Males	Females	Both sexes	Males	Females
ASIA—Continued									
Maldives	47	47	48	19	18	20	65	64	67
Mongolia	70	74	66	39	38	40	106	109	103
Nepal	79	81	77	57	58	55	131	134	128
North Korea	26	29	23	6	6	5	31	35	28
Pakistan	97	98	95	59	53	65	150	146	154
Philippines	36	40	32	15	16	13	50	56	44
Singapore	5	5	4	1	1	1	6	6	5
South Korea	8	9	8	3	3	2	11	11	10
Sri Lanka	21	23	19	8	8	7	28	31	26
Thailand	33	36	30	11	13	8	44	49	38
Vietnam	38	39	38	18	17	20	56	55	57
LATIN AMERICA AND THE CARIBBEAN	40	44	36	15	17	13	54	59	49
Anguilla	17	23	12	3	4	2	20	26	13
Antigua and Barbuda	17	20	14	3	4	3	20	24	17
Argentina	28	31	25	5	5	4	33	36	29
Aruba	8	10	7	2	2	1	10	12	8
Bahamas, The	23	26	20	3	4	3	26	30	23
Barbados	19	21	16	2	3	2	21	24	18
Belize	34	38	30	9	10	8	43	47	38
Bolivia	68	73	62	67	73	61	130	141	119
Brazil	55	59	52	23	26	20	77	84	70
British Virgin Islands	19	22	16	(NA)	(NA)	(NA)	(NA)	(NA)	(NA)
Cayman Islands	8	10	7	(NA)	(NA)	(NA)	(NA)	(NA)	(NA)
Chile	14	15	12	2	3	2	16	17	15
Colombia	26	29	23	7	8	6	33	37	29
Costa Rica	14	14	13	3	3	3	16	17	15
Cuba	8	9	7	2	3	2	10	11	9
Dominica	10	12	7	1	2	1	11	14	8
Dominican Republic	48	52	43	11	12	10	59	64	53
Ecuador	35	40	30	12	13	10	46	52	40
El Salvador	32	34	30	9	10	7	40	44	37
French Guiana	15	15	14	4	4	3	18	20	17
Grenada	12	13	10	5	6	4	17	19	14
Guadeloupe	8	9	7	2	2	2	10	11	9
Guatemala	51	55	47	29	28	29	78	81	75
Guyana	51	56	47	28	30	25	77	84	70
Haiti	104	111	96	69	70	67	166	174	157
Honduras	42	46	38	14	15	12	55	60	49
Jamaica	16	18	14	2	2	1	17	19	15
Martinique	7	8	6	1	2	1	9	10	8
Mexico	25	30	20	5	6	4	30	36	23
Montserrat	12	14	10	(NA)	(NA)	(NA)	(NA)	(NA)	(NA)
Netherlands Antilles	9	10	8	1	1	1	10	11	9
Nicaragua	46	52	39	15	17	13	60	68	52
Panama	30	31	28	7	7	7	37	39	35
Paraguay	23	25	22	6	5	6	29	30	28
Peru	52	54	50	16	16	16	67	69	65

Table A-9.
Infant and Child Mortality, by Region, Country, and Sex: 1996—Continued

Region and country or area	Infant mortality rate[1]			Child mortality rates[2]					
				Ages 1 to 4			Under age 5		
	Both sexes	Males	Females	Both sexes	Males	Females	Both sexes	Males	Females
LATIN AMERICA AND THE CARIBBEAN—Continued									
Puerto Rico	12	14	11	2	2	2	14	15	13
Saint Kitts and Nevis	19	21	17	14	18	9	32	39	25
Saint Lucia	20	21	19	7	8	5	27	29	24
Saint Vincent and the Grenadines	17	18	16	7	7	7	24	24	23
Suriname	29	34	24	7	9	6	36	43	30
Trinidad and Tobago	18	21	16	5	6	3	23	26	19
Turks and Caicos Islands	13	15	10	(NA)	(NA)	(NA)	(NA)	(NA)	(NA)
Uruguay	15	17	14	3	3	3	18	19	16
Venezuela	30	33	26	6	6	5	35	39	31
Virgin Islands	13	15	10	(NA)	(NA)	(NA)	(NA)	(NA)	(NA)
EUROPE AND THE NEW INDEPENDENT STATES	25	28	22	6	6	6	31	34	27
Western Europe	6	7	6	1	2	1	8	9	7
Andorra	8	8	7	1	1	1	9	10	8
Austria	7	8	6	1	2	1	8	9	7
Belgium	7	8	6	1	1	1	8	9	7
Denmark	7	7	6	1	2	1	8	9	7
Faroe Islands	8	9	7	2	2	1	9	11	7
Finland	5	5	5	1	1	1	6	6	6
France	5	6	4	2	3	2	8	9	6
Germany	6	7	5	1	2	1	7	8	7
Gibraltar	8	9	7	1	1	1	9	10	8
Greece	8	9	8	1	1	1	9	10	9
Guernsey	6	8	5	1	1	1	7	9	6
Iceland	4	4	4	1	(Z)	1	5	5	5
Ireland	7	8	6	2	2	1	8	10	7
Isle of Man	8	9	7	1	1	1	9	10	8
Italy	7	8	6	1	1	1	8	9	7
Jersey	5	5	4	1	1	1	6	7	5
Liechtenstein	5	5	4	2	3	1	7	7	5
Luxembourg	7	7	6	1	2	(Z)	7	9	6
Malta	8	8	7	1	1	1	9	10	7
Monaco	7	8	6	1	1	1	8	9	7
Netherlands	6	7	5	1	1	1	7	8	6
Norway	6	7	5	1	2	1	7	8	6
Portugal	8	8	7	2	2	2	10	11	9
San Marino	6	7	5	1	1	1	6	7	5
Spain	7	8	6	1	2	1	8	9	8
Sweden	6	6	5	1	1	1	6	7	6
Switzerland	6	7	6	2	3	1	8	10	7
United Kingdom	6	7	6	1	1	1	8	9	7
Eastern Europe	18	20	16	4	4	3	21	24	19
Albania	49	52	47	14	14	13	62	65	59
Bosnia and Herzegovina	43	46	40	34	34	33	75	78	72
Bulgaria	16	18	13	4	5	3	20	23	16
Croatia	10	12	9	2	2	1	12	13	10
Czech Republic	8	9	7	1	1	1	10	11	9

Table A-9.
Infant and Child Mortality, by Region, Country, and Sex: 1996—Continued

Region and country or area	Infant mortality rate[1]			Child mortality rates[2]					
				Ages 1 to 4			Under age 5		
	Both sexes	Males	Females	Both sexes	Males	Females	Both sexes	Males	Females
EUROPE AND THE NEW INDEPENDENT STATES— Continued									
Eastern Europe—Continued									
Hungary	12	14	11	2	2	2	14	16	13
Macedonia, The Former Yugoslav Republic of	30	31	28	4	5	4	34	36	32
Montenegro	28	33	22	2	2	3	30	34	25
Poland	12	14	11	2	2	2	14	16	13
Romania	23	27	20	6	7	5	29	33	24
Serbia	23	25	20	3	4	3	26	29	23
Slovakia	11	12	9	2	2	2	12	14	11
Slovenia	7	9	6	1	2	1	9	10	7
New Independent States	46	51	41	11	12	11	57	62	51
Baltics	18	20	16	4	4	3	22	24	19
Estonia	17	20	14	4	4	4	22	25	18
Latvia	21	23	19	4	5	3	25	28	22
Lithuania	17	19	15	3	3	3	20	22	18
Commonwealth of Independent States	47	52	42	11	12	11	58	63	52
Armenia	39	44	34	10	15	5	48	58	38
Azerbaijan	75	81	67	14	16	13	88	96	80
Belarus	13	15	12	3	3	2	16	18	14
Georgia	23	24	21	4	5	4	27	29	24
Kazakstan	63	65	62	11	6	16	74	71	77
Kyrgyzstan	78	87	68	25	32	18	101	116	85
Moldova	48	58	37	7	9	4	54	66	41
Russia	25	27	22	5	5	5	30	32	27
Tajikistan	113	135	91	22	23	20	132	154	109
Turkmenistan	82	90	73	19	9	29	99	98	100
Ukraine	23	24	21	4	5	4	27	28	25
Uzbekistan	80	90	69	27	31	23	105	118	90
NORTH AMERICA	7	8	7	2	2	1	9	10	8
Bermuda	13	15	11	(NA)	(NA)	(NA)	(NA)	(NA)	(NA)
Canada	6	7	5	1	1	1	7	8	6
Greenland	24	29	19	5	4	5	28	33	24
Saint Pierre and Miquelon	10	12	8	(NA)	(NA)	(NA)	(NA)	(NA)	(NA)
United States	8	8	7	2	2	1	9	10	8
OCEANIA	24	24	23	9	9	9	32	32	32
American Samoa	19	22	16	(NA)	(NA)	(NA)	(NA)	(NA)	(NA)
Australia	6	6	5	1	1	1	7	7	6
Cook Islands	25	28	21	(NA)	(NA)	(NA)	(NA)	(NA)	(NA)
Federated States of Micronesia	36	41	31	(NA)	(NA)	(NA)	(NA)	(NA)	(NA)
Fiji	17	19	16	15	17	12	32	36	28
French Polynesia	14	17	12	13	16	10	27	32	22
Guam	15	18	13	(NA)	(NA)	(NA)	(NA)	(NA)	(NA)
Kiribati	98	107	90	(NA)	(NA)	(NA)	(NA)	(NA)	(NA)
Marshall Islands	47	48	46	27	29	25	72	76	69
Nauru	41	(NA)	(NA)	(NA)	(NA)	(NA)	(NA)	(NA)	(NA)

Table A-9.
Infant and Child Mortality, by Region, Country, and Sex: 1996—Continued

Region and country or area	Infant mortality rate[1]			Child mortality rates[2]					
				Ages 1 to 4			Under age 5		
	Both sexes	Males	Females	Both sexes	Males	Females	Both sexes	Males	Females
OCEANIA—Continued									
New Caledonia	14	16	11	4	5	2	18	21	14
New Zealand	7	8	6	2	2	1	8	10	7
Northern Mariana Islands	38	43	33	(NA)	(NA)	(NA)	(NA)	(NA)	(NA)
Palau	25	29	21	(NA)	(NA)	(NA)	(NA)	(NA)	(NA)
Papua New Guinea	60	59	61	24	22	26	83	80	86
Solomon Islands	26	29	22	7	8	6	32	37	27
Tonga	20	(NA)	(NA)	(NA)	(NA)	(NA)	(NA)	(NA)	(NA)
Tuvalu	28	31	25	18	20	16	45	50	41
Vanuatu	65	70	60	36	38	35	99	105	92
Wallis and Futuna	24	24	23	(NA)	(NA)	(NA)	(NA)	(NA)	(NA)
Western Samoa	34	39	29	10	11	8	44	50	37

(NA) Data not available.
(Z) Less than 0.5 per 1,000.

[1]Infant mortality rate is the number of deaths of infants under 1 year of age during a calendar year per 1,000 live births occurring in the same year. It is the probability of dying between birth and exact age 1.

[2]Child mortality (ages 1 to 4) is the probability of dying between exact age 1 and exact age 5 (i.e., between the first and fifth birthdays). Under-5 mortality is the probability of dying between birth and exact age 5 (after birth, before the fifth birthday).

Note: Regional rates are weighted means of country rates. Countries lacking data for a specific year are excluded from the calculation of a regional rate for that year.

Source: U.S. Bureau of the Census, International Data Base.

Table A-10.
Life Expectancy at Birth, by Region, Country, and Sex: 1996 and 2020

Region and country or area	Both sexes		Males		Females	
	1996	2020	1996	2020	1996	2020
WORLD	62	69	61	66	64	71
Less Developed Countries	61	67	60	65	63	70
More Developed Countries	74	79	71	75	78	82
AFRICA	52	57	50	55	53	59
Sub-Saharan Africa	50	55	48	53	51	57
Angola	47	60	45	57	49	63
Benin	53	63	51	60	55	67
Botswana	46	38	45	39	47	38
Burkina Faso	43	40	43	40	43	39
Burundi	49	49	48	47	50	50
Cameroon	53	52	52	51	54	54
Cape Verde	63	72	61	69	65	74
Central African Republic	46	44	45	44	47	45
Chad	48	56	45	53	50	59
Comoros	59	68	56	65	61	72
Congo	46	51	44	49	47	52
Côte d'Ivoire	47	49	46	48	47	50
Djibouti	50	61	48	58	52	64
Equatorial Guinea	53	64	51	61	55	67
Eritrea	50	58	49	56	52	60
Ethiopia	47	47	46	46	48	48
Gabon	56	66	53	62	59	70
Gambia, The	51	62	49	59	53	66
Ghana	56	64	54	61	58	66
Guinea	45	57	43	54	47	61
Guinea-Bissau	48	59	47	57	50	61
Kenya	56	47	56	48	56	47
Lesotho	52	53	50	50	54	56
Liberia	59	68	56	65	61	72
Madagascar	52	61	51	58	53	63
Malawi	36	34	36	35	36	33
Mali	47	59	45	56	49	62
Mauritania	49	61	46	57	52	65
Mauritius	71	77	67	72	75	81
Mayotte	59	68	56	65	61	72
Mozambique	44	58	43	56	46	59
Namibia	64	73	63	71	66	76
Niger	41	53	41	51	40	54
Nigeria	54	63	53	60	56	65
Reunion	75	80	72	77	78	83
Rwanda	40	37	40	38	41	36
Saint Helena	75	(NA)	73	(NA)	77	(NA)
Sao Tome and Principe	64	69	62	66	66	71
Senegal	56	67	54	63	59	70
Seychelles	69	76	64	73	74	80
Sierra Leone	47	61	45	57	50	65
Somalia	55	64	55	63	56	65
South Africa	59	55	57	53	62	57
Sudan	55	65	54	63	56	66
Swaziland	57	67	53	63	61	71

Table A-10.
Life Expectancy at Birth, by Region, Country, and Sex: 1996 and 2020—Continued

Region and country or area	Both sexes		Males		Females	
	1996	2020	1996	2020	1996	2020
AFRICA—Continued						
Sub-Sarahan Africa—Continued						
Tanzania	42	41	41	41	44	41
Togo	58	68	56	65	60	71
Uganda	40	40	40	40	41	40
Zaire	47	54	45	52	48	57
Zambia	36	35	36	35	36	35
Zimbabwe	42	38	42	39	42	37
North Africa	65	73	64	70	67	75
Algeria	68	75	67	73	69	76
Egypt	61	68	60	66	63	71
Libya	65	73	62	70	67	75
Morocco	70	79	68	76	72	82
Tunisia	73	78	71	76	74	80
Western Sahara	47	(NA)	46	(NA)	48	(NA)
NEAR EAST	69	77	67	74	70	79
Bahrain	74	80	72	77	77	83
Cyprus	76	81	74	79	79	84
Gaza Strip	72	80	71	78	73	82
Iraq	67	74	66	72	68	76
Israel	78	81	76	78	81	84
Jordan	72	77	71	74	74	79
Kuwait	76	81	74	78	78	84
Lebanon	70	76	67	73	73	79
Oman	71	76	69	74	73	78
Qatar	73	79	71	76	76	82
Saudi Arabia	69	78	67	76	71	81
Syria	67	74	66	71	68	76
Turkey	72	80	70	77	74	83
United Arab Emirates	73	77	71	75	75	80
West Bank	73	79	71	76	74	82
Yemen	60	74	58	72	61	77
ASIA	63	71	62	69	65	74
Afghanistan	46	58	46	58	45	59
Bangladesh	56	65	56	64	56	67
Bhutan	51	62	52	62	51	62
Brunei	71	75	70	74	73	76
Burma	56	67	54	64	58	70
Cambodia	50	62	48	60	51	64
China	70	77	68	74	71	80
Mainland	70	77	68	74	71	80
Taiwan	76	81	73	79	79	84
Hong Kong	82	84	79	81	86	87
India	60	69	59	68	60	71
Indonesia	62	71	60	68	64	74
Iran	67	75	66	73	69	78
Japan	80	82	77	79	83	85
Laos	53	64	51	63	54	66
Macau	80	82	77	79	83	85
Malaysia	70	76	67	72	73	80

Table A-10.
Life Expectancy at Birth, by Region, Country, and Sex: 1996 and 2020—Continued

Region and country or area	Both sexes		Males		Females	
	1996	2020	1996	2020	1996	2020
ASIA—Continued						
Maldives	66	78	65	76	68	81
Mongolia	61	69	59	66	63	72
Nepal	54	66	53	65	54	68
North Korea	70	76	67	72	74	79
Pakistan	58	65	58	63	59	67
Philippines	66	71	63	68	69	74
Singapore	78	82	75	79	81	86
South Korea	73	80	70	76	77	83
Sri Lanka	72	77	70	74	75	80
Thailand	69	74	65	71	72	78
Vietnam	67	74	65	72	69	77
LATIN AMERICA AND THE CARIBBEAN	68	74	65	71	72	78
Anguilla	74	77	71	74	77	80
Antigua and Barbuda	74	78	72	76	76	81
Argentina	72	75	68	72	75	78
Aruba	77	79	73	75	81	83
Bahamas, The	73	78	68	74	77	81
Barbados	74	78	72	75	77	81
Belize	69	73	67	71	71	76
Bolivia	60	71	57	68	63	75
Brazil	62	68	57	64	67	71
British Virgin Islands	73	(NA)	71	(NA)	75	(NA)
Cayman Islands	77	(NA)	75	(NA)	79	(NA)
Chile	74	79	71	76	78	82
Colombia	73	79	70	76	76	82
Costa Rica	76	78	73	75	78	81
Cuba	77	80	75	77	80	83
Dominica	77	81	75	78	80	84
Dominican Republic	69	76	67	73	71	78
Ecuador	71	78	68	75	74	81
El Salvador	69	77	65	74	73	80
French Guiana	76	81	73	78	79	84
Grenada	71	76	68	72	73	79
Guadeloupe	77	81	74	78	81	84
Guatemala	65	73	63	71	68	77
Guyana	60	53	58	50	63	55
Haiti	49	55	47	52	51	58
Honduras	68	76	66	73	71	79
Jamaica	75	79	73	77	77	82
Martinique	79	81	76	79	82	84
Mexico	74	80	70	76	77	83
Montserrat	76	(NA)	74	(NA)	77	(NA)
Netherlands Antilles	77	80	75	77	79	82
Nicaragua	66	75	63	72	68	78
Panama	74	78	71	75	77	81
Paraguay	74	79	72	77	75	80
Peru	69	77	67	75	71	80
Puerto Rico	75	81	71	77	80	84
Saint Kitts and Nevis	67	74	64	71	70	78
Saint Lucia	70	75	67	71	74	79
Saint Vincent and the Grenadines	73	78	71	77	74	80
Suriname	70	76	68	73	73	79

Table A-10.
Life Expectancy at Birth, by Region, Country, and Sex: 1996 and 2020—Continued

Region and country or area	Both sexes		Males		Females	
	1996	2020	1996	2020	1996	2020
LATIN AMERICA AND THE CARIBBEAN—Continued						
Trinidad and Tobago	70	74	68	71	73	76
Turks and Caicos Islands	75	(NA)	73	(NA)	77	(NA)
Uruguay	75	80	72	77	78	83
Venezuela	72	78	69	75	75	81
Virgin Islands	75	(NA)	74	(NA)	77	(NA)
EUROPE AND THE NEW INDEPENDENT STATES	71	76	67	72	75	80
Western Europe	77	81	74	78	80	84
Andorra	79	81	76	78	82	84
Austria	77	81	74	78	80	84
Belgium	77	81	74	78	81	84
Denmark	76	81	73	78	79	84
Faroe Islands	78	81	75	78	82	85
Finland	76	81	73	78	80	84
France	78	81	74	78	82	85
Germany	76	81	73	78	79	84
Gibraltar	77	81	74	78	80	84
Greece	78	81	76	78	81	84
Guernsey	78	81	76	78	81	84
Iceland	79	82	77	79	82	84
Ireland	76	81	73	78	79	84
Isle of Man	77	81	74	78	80	84
Italy	78	81	75	79	81	85
Jersey	77	81	74	78	81	84
Liechtenstein	78	80	74	76	81	84
Luxembourg	77	81	74	78	81	84
Malta	77	81	75	78	80	84
Monaco	78	81	74	78	82	85
Netherlands	78	81	75	78	81	84
Norway	78	81	74	78	81	84
Portugal	75	80	72	77	79	84
San Marino	81	82	77	79	85	86
Spain	77	81	74	78	81	84
Sweden	79	81	76	78	82	84
Switzerland	79	81	75	78	82	85
United Kingdom	76	81	74	78	79	84
Eastern Europe	71	77	67	73	75	80
Albania	68	76	65	73	71	79
Bosnia and Herzegovina	56	78	51	75	61	82
Bulgaria	71	76	67	73	75	80
Croatia	73	77	69	74	77	81
Czech Republic	74	78	70	74	78	81
Hungary	69	75	64	71	74	80
Macedonia, The Former Yugoslav Republic of	72	77	70	74	74	80
Montenegro	75	78	71	75	79	82
Poland	72	77	68	73	76	81
Romania	69	75	66	72	74	79
Serbia	72	77	69	74	75	80
Slovakia	73	77	69	74	77	81
Slovenia	75	78	71	75	79	82

Table A-10.
Life Expectancy at Birth, by Region, Country, and Sex: 1996 and 2020—Continued

Region and country or area	Both sexes		Males		Females	
	1996	2020	1996	2020	1996	2020
EUROPE AND THE NEW INDEPENDENT STATES—Continued						
New Independent States	65	72	59	68	70	76
Baltics	68	74	62	71	74	78
Estonia	68	74	63	70	74	78
Latvia	67	74	61	70	73	78
Lithuania	68	75	62	71	74	79
Commonwealth of Independent States	65	72	59	68	70	76
Armenia	69	74	64	70	74	78
Azerbaijan	65	71	60	67	70	75
Belarus	69	75	63	71	74	79
Georgia	68	73	63	69	73	78
Kazakstan	64	70	59	65	70	75
Kyrgyzstan	64	70	59	65	69	74
Moldova	65	72	61	68	70	76
Russia	63	73	57	69	70	77
Tajikistan	64	70	61	66	68	74
Turkmenistan	61	69	57	65	67	73
Ukraine	67	74	62	70	72	77
Uzbekistan	65	70	60	66	69	75
NORTH AMERICA	77	79	73	76	80	83
Bermuda	75	(NA)	73	(NA)	77	(NA)
Canada	79	83	76	80	83	86
Greenland	68	79	64	76	73	82
Saint Pierre and Miquelon	76	(NA)	75	(NA)	78	(NA)
United States	76	79	73	76	80	82
OCEANIA	71	77	69	74	74	79
American Samoa	73	(NA)	71	(NA)	75	(NA)
Australia	79	83	76	80	83	86
Cook Islands	71	(NA)	69	(NA)	73	(NA)
Federated States of Micronesia	68	(NA)	66	(NA)	70	(NA)
Fiji	66	72	63	69	68	75
French Polynesia	71	75	68	72	74	78
Guam	74	(NA)	72	(NA)	76	(NA)
Kiribati	54	(NA)	53	(NA)	56	(NA)
Marshall Islands	64	71	62	69	65	73
Nauru	67	(NA)	64	(NA)	69	(NA)
New Caledonia	74	80	71	77	78	83
New Zealand	77	81	74	78	80	84
Northern Mariana Islands	67	(NA)	66	(NA)	69	(NA)
Palau	71	(NA)	69	(NA)	73	(NA)
Papua New Guinea	57	66	56	65	58	68
Solomon Islands	71	77	69	74	74	80
Tonga	68	(NA)	66	(NA)	71	(NA)
Tuvalu	63	69	62	68	65	70
Vanuatu	60	70	58	67	62	73
Wallis and Futuna	73	(NA)	72	(NA)	73	(NA)
Western Samoa	69	76	66	73	71	79

(NA) Data not available.

Note: Regional life expectancies are weighted means of country-specific values. Countries lacking data for a specific year are excluded from the calculation of a regional life expectancy for that year.

Source: U.S. Bureau of the Census, International Data Base.

Table A-11.
Percent of Currently Married Women Using Contraception, by Method: All Available Years

[Data refer to ages 15 to 49 years unless specified otherwise]

Region, country or area, and year	No method	All methods	Pill	IUD	Condom	Sterilization		Other modern	Traditional	Source	Remarks
						Male	Female				
AFRICA											
Sub-Saharan Africa											
Benin											
1982	73.2	26.8	0.3	0.2	0.2	(NA)	(NA)	(NA)	26.1	WFS	1
Botswana											
1984	72.2	27.8	10.0	4.8	1.2	(NA)	1.5	1.1	9.2	CPS	
1988	67.0	33.0	14.8	5.6	1.3	0.3	4.3	5.4	1.3	DHS	
Burkina Faso											
1993	92.1	7.9	2.1	0.7	0.8	(NA)	0.3	0.2	3.7	DHS	
Burundi											
1987	91.3	8.7	0.2	0.3	0.1	(NA)	0.1	0.5	7.5	DHS	
Cameroon											
1978	96.9	3.1	0.3	0.2	0.2	(NA)	(NA)	0.2	2.2	WFS	1
1991	83.9	16.1	1.2	0.3	0.9	(NA)	1.2	0.7	11.8	DHS	
Central African Republic											
1994-95	85.2	14.8	1.1	0.1	1.0	(NA)	0.4	0.7	11.5	DHS	
Côte d'Ivoire											
1980-81	96.2	3.8	0.5	0.1	(NA)	(NA)	(NA)	(NA)	3.2	WFS	1
1994	88.6	11.4	2.2	0.3	0.7	(NA)	0.2	0.9	7.1	DHS	
Ethiopia											
1990	95.7	4.3	1.9	0.3	0.1	(Z)	0.2	(Z)	1.7	Survey	
Gambia, The											
1990	88.0	12.0	3.0	1.0	0.4	(Z)	0.4	2.0	5.0	UN	
Ghana											
1976	98.0	2.0	(NA)	(NA)	(NA)	(NA)	(NA)	(NA)	(NA)	PC	2
1978	96.0	4.0	(NA)	(NA)	(NA)	(NA)	(NA)	(NA)	(NA)	SS	2
1979-80	87.6	12.4	3.1	0.4	0.8	(NA)	0.1	(NA)	8.0	WFS	1
1988	87.1	12.9	1.8	0.5	0.3	(NA)	1.0	1.6	7.7	DHS	
1993	79.7	20.3	3.2	0.9	2.2	(NA)	0.9	2.8	10.1	DHS	
Guinea											
1992	98.3	1.7	0.5	(NA)	0.1	(NA)	(NA)	0.4	0.7	DHS	
Kenya											
1977-78	93.3	6.7	2.0	0.7	0.1	(Z)	0.8	0.6	2.5	WFS	3
1979	93.3	6.7	(NA)	(NA)	(NA)	(NA)	(NA)	(NA)	(NA)	SS	2
1984	83.0	17.0	3.1	3.0	0.3	(Z)	2.6	0.6	7.3	CPS	
1989	73.1	26.9	5.2	3.7	0.5	(Z)	4.7	3.7	9.0	DHS	
1993	67.0	33.0	9.6	4.3	0.9	(NA)	5.6	7.2	5.4	DHS	
Lesotho											
1977	92.8	7.2	1.7	0.2	0.2	(NA)	1.1	0.3	3.7	WFS	1
1991-92	77.0	23.0	7.0	3.0	1.0	(Z)	1.0	6.0	4.0	UN	72
Liberia											
1986	93.7	6.3	3.3	0.6	(NA)	(NA)	1.1	0.5	0.9	DHS	
Madagascar											
1992	82.7	17.3	1.5	0.6	0.6	(Z)	1.0	1.7	11.9	DHS	
Malawi											
1984	93.1	6.9	0.7	0.3	(NA)	(NA)	(NA)	0.1	5.8	Survey	4
1992	87.0	13.0	2.2	0.3	1.6	(Z)	1.7	1.6	5.6	DHS	

Table A-11.
Percent of Currently Married Women Using Contraception, by Method: All Available Years—Continued

[Data refer to ages 15 to 49 years unless specified otherwise]

Region, country or area, and year	No method	All methods	Pill	IUD	Condom	Sterilization Male	Sterilization Female	Other modern	Traditional	Source	Remarks
AFRICA—Continued											
Sub-Saharan Africa—Continued											
Mali											
1987	95.3	4.7	0.9	0.1	(Z)	(NA)	0.1	0.2	3.4	DHS	
Mauritania											
1981	99.2	0.8	(Z)	(Z)	(Z)	(Z)	0.2	0.1	0.5	WFS	1,5
1990	96.0	4.0	1.0	(Z)	(NA)	(NA)	(NA)	(NA)	3.0	Survey	
Mauritius											
1975	54.3	45.7	21.0	1.5	5.1	(NA)	(NA)	1.6	16.4	Survey	6,7
1985	24.7	75.3	21.0	2.3	9.5	(NA)	4.7	6.8	31.0	CDC	8
1991	25.0	75.0	21.0	3.0	10.0	(NA)	7.0	7.0	27.0	CDC	2
Namibia											
1989	73.6	26.4	6.6	0.9	(NA)	0.1	6.0	12.5	0.1	Survey	7,9
1992	71.1	28.9	8.3	2.1	0.3	0.2	7.4	7.8	2.9	DHS	
Niger											
1992	95.6	4.4	1.5	0.2	(Z)	(NA)	0.1	0.5	2.2	DHS	
Nigeria											
1981-82	93.8	6.2	0.3	0.1	(NA)	(NA)	0.1	0.2	5.5	WFS	1
1990	94.0	6.0	1.2	0.8	0.4	(NA)	0.3	0.8	2.5	DHS	
Reunion											
1990	27.1	72.9	39.9	18.1	2.6	(Z)	5.1	1.5	5.8	Survey	
Rwanda											
1983	89.9	10.1	0.2	0.3	(NA)	(NA)	(NA)	0.4	9.3	Survey	3,10
1992	78.8	21.2	3.0	0.2	0.2	(NA)	0.7	8.7	8.3	DHS	
Senegal											
1978	96.2	3.8	0.3	0.2	0.1	(Z)	(Z)	(Z)	3.2	WFS	11
1986	88.7	11.3	1.2	0.7	0.1	(NA)	0.2	0.2	9.0	DHS	
1992-93	92.6	7.4	2.2	1.4	0.4	(NA)	0.4	0.3	2.7	DHS	
South Africa											
1975-76	49.8	50.2	14.0	4.6	(NA)	(NA)	7.1	10.8	13.7	Survey	6,12,13
1981-82	52.0	48.0	14.4	5.8	2.9	(NA)	7.7	14.4	2.9	Survey	7
1988	50.3	49.7	13.2	5.3	0.7	1.4	8.0	19.8	1.2	Survey	7
Sudan (Northern)											
1979	95.5	4.5	3.0	0.1	0.1	0.1	0.3	0.2	0.7	WFS	14
1989-90	91.3	8.7	3.9	0.7	0.1	(NA)	0.8	0.1	3.1	DHS	14
Swaziland											
1988	80.2	19.8	5.5	1.8	0.7	0.2	3.2	5.7	2.8	Survey	15
Tanzania											
1988	93.0	7.0	5.6	(NA)	(NA)	(NA)	(NA)	(NA)	1.4	USAID	2
1991-92	89.6	10.4	3.4	0.4	0.7	(Z)	1.6	0.4	3.9	DHS	
1994	79.6	20.4	5.6	1.0	1.7	(NA)	2.0	2.8	7.4	DHS	
Togo											
1988	66.1	33.9	0.4	0.8	0.4	(NA)	0.6	0.8	30.9	DHS	
Uganda											
1988-89	95.1	4.9	1.1	0.2	(NA)	(NA)	0.8	0.4	2.4	DHS	

Table A-11.
Percent of Currently Married Women Using Contraception, by Method: All Available Years—Continued

[Data refer to ages 15 to 49 years unless specified otherwise]

Region, country or area, and year	No method	All methods	Pill	IUD	Condom	Sterilization: Male	Sterilization: Female	Other modern	Tradi-tional	Source	Re-marks
AFRICA—Continued											
Sub-Saharan Africa—Continued											
Zambia											
1992	84.8	15.2	4.3	0.5	1.8	(Z)	2.1	0.2	6.3	DHS	
Zaire											
1991	92.0	7.7	0.4	0.1	0.5	0.1	0.2	1.0	6.0	CDC	12
Zimbabwe											
1979	86.0	14.0	5.0	(NA)	(NA)	(NA)	(NA)	(NA)	9.0	SS	2
1984	61.6	38.4	22.6	0.7	0.7	0.1	1.6	0.9	11.8	CPS	
1988	56.9	43.1	31.1	1.1	1.2	0.2	2.3	0.3	6.9	DHS	
1994	51.9	48.1	33.1	1.0	2.3	0.2	2.3	3.4	6.0	DHS	
North Africa											
Algeria											
1986-87	64.5	35.5	26.5	2.1	0.6	(Z)	1.3	0.8	4.2	Survey	
1992	49.1	50.9	38.9	2.4	0.5	(Z)	1.1	0.3	7.7	PAPCHILD	
Egypt											
1974-75	73.5	26.5	(NA)	(NA)	(NA)	(NA)	(NA)	(NA)	(NA)	Survey	
1980	75.9	24.1	16.5	4.0	1.1	0.1	0.7	0.7	1.1	WFS	
1982	66.5	33.5	(NA)	(NA)	(NA)	(NA)	(NA)	(NA)	(NA)	Survey	
1984	69.7	30.3	16.5	8.4	1.3	(NA)	1.5	1.0	1.6	CPS	
1988	62.2	37.8	15.3	15.8	2.4	(NA)	1.5	0.5	2.4	DHS	
1991	52.4	47.6	15.9	24.1	(NA)	(NA)	(NA)	(NA)	7.6	Survey	16
1992	52.9	47.1	12.9	27.9	2.0	(NA)	1.1	0.9	2.3	DHS	
Morocco											
1970	99.0	1.0	0.7	0.2	(NA)	(NA)	(NA)	(NA)	(Z)	SS	
1971	97.0	3.0	2.4	0.6	(NA)	(NA)	(NA)	(NA)	(Z)	SS	
1972	96.0	4.0	3.2	0.7	(NA)	(NA)	(NA)	(NA)	0.1	SS	
1973	94.0	6.0	4.8	0.8	(NA)	(NA)	(NA)	(NA)	0.4	SS	
1974	93.0	7.0	5.8	0.7	(NA)	(NA)	(NA)	(NA)	0.5	SS	
1979	84.5	15.5	13.0	1.4	(NA)	(NA)	(NA)	(NA)	1.1	SS	
1979-80	81.0	19.0	13.4	1.5	0.3	(NA)	0.8	0.1	2.9	WFS	
1983-84	74.5	25.5	16.5	2.5	0.4	(Z)	1.7	0.3	4.2	CPS	
1987	64.1	35.9	23.0	2.9	0.5	(NA)	2.2	0.4	6.9	DHS	
1992	58.5	41.5	28.1	3.2	0.9	(NA)	3.0	0.3	5.9	DHS	
Tunisia											
1978	68.6	31.4	6.5	8.7	1.2	(NA)	7.5	0.8	6.6	WFS	
1980	73.0	27.0	(NA)	(NA)	(NA)	(NA)	(NA)	(NA)	(NA)	Survey	6
1983	58.9	41.1	5.3	13.2	1.3	(NA)	12.5	1.9	6.9	CPS	
1988	50.2	49.8	8.8	17.0	1.3	(NA)	11.5	1.8	9.4	DHS	
NEAR EAST											
Bahrain											
1989	46.6	53.4	13.1	1.7	8.2	(NA)	7.1	0.2	23.0	Survey	7,31
Iraq											
1974	86.0	14.0	8.4	0.6	1.4	(NA)	0.6	1.5	1.5	Survey	
1989	86.3	13.7	4.7	2.8	1.0	(NA)	1.4	0.5	3.2	Survey	7,31
Jordan											
1972	78.9	21.1	13.4	0.9	1.1	—— 0.9 ——		1.8	3.1	Survey	6,32
1976	74.8	25.2	11.9	2.0	1.4	0.1	1.8	0.5	7.4	WFS	
1983	74.0	26.0	7.8	8.3	0.6	—— 3.8 ——		0.3	5.3	Survey	
1985	73.5	26.5	6.0	10.8	0.4	(Z)	4.9	0.2	4.2	Survey	33
1990	65.1	34.9	4.6	15.3	0.8	(Z)	5.6	0.6	8.0	DHS	

Table A-11.
Percent of Currently Married Women Using Contraception, by Method: All Available Years—Continued

[Data refer to ages 15 to 49 years unless specified otherwise]

Region, country or area, and year	No method	All methods	Pill	IUD	Condom	Sterilization		Other modern	Tradi-tional	Source	Re-marks
						Male	Female				
NEAR EAST—Continued											
Kuwait											
1987	65.4	34.6	24.0	3.7	1.5	(NA)	2.0	0.5	2.9	Survey	7,31
Lebanon											
1971	47.0	53.0	13.8	1.1	6.9	1.1	(NA)	(NA)	35.0	Survey	25
Oman											
1988	91.4	8.6	2.4	1.5	1.1	(NA)	2.2	0.3	1.1	Survey	7,31
Qatar											
1987	67.7	32.3	13.1	8.6	2.2	(NA)	4.5	0.5	3.4	Survey	7
Syria											
1973	77.3	22.7	11.6	(NA)	0.7	(NA)	0.2	(NA)	10.2	Survey	19
1978	80.0	20.0	12.0	1.0	1.0	(NA)	(NA)	1.0	5.0	WFS	2
1993	60.4	39.6	9.9	15.7	0.3	0.	2.2	0.2	11.3	PAPCHILD	
Turkey											
1963	78.1	21.9	0.8	(NA)	3.4	(NA)	(NA)	17.7	(NA)	Survey	2
1968	68.0	32.0	1.8	1.3	3.6	(NA)	(NA)	25.3	(NA)	Survey	2
1973	62.0	38.0	4.0	1.9	3.9	(NA)	(NA)	28.2	(NA)	Survey	2
1978	49.7	50.3	8.1	4.0	4.1	0.2	0.6	33.4	(NA)	WFS	1
1983	48.8	51.2	7.5	7.4	4.1	(NA)	1.1	2.6	28.5	Survey	
1988	36.6	63.4	6.2	14.0	7.2	0.1	1.7	1.9	32.3	Survey	
1993	37.4	62.6	4.9	18.8	6.6	0.	2.9	1.3	28.1	DHS	
Yemen											
1979	98.7	1.3	0.7	0.1	0.1	0.1	0.1	0.1	0.1	WFS	7,34
1991-92	92.9	7.1	3.2	1.2	0.1	0.1	0.8	0.6	1.1	DHS	35
ASIA											
Afghanistan											
1972-73	98.0	2.0	1.1	0.4	0.2	(NA)	(NA)	0.2	(NA)	Survey	2
Bangladesh											
1969	96.4	3.6	(NA)	(NA)	(NA)	(NA)	(NA)	(NA)	(NA)	Survey	17
1975-76	92.1	7.9	2.9	0.4	0.7	0.5	0.3	(Z)	3.1	WFS	7
1977	91.1	8.9	2.3	1.1	(NA)	—— 2.1 ——		(NA)	3.3	PC	2,11
1979	87.4	12.6	3.8	0.3	1.5	0.9	2.5	0.4	3.2	CPS	11
1980	88.0	12.0	4.4	0.7	(NA)	—— 3.0 ——		(NA)	3.8	PC	2,11
1981	80.4	19.6	3.7	0.4	1.7	0.8	4.2	0.7	8.0	CPS	
1983	80.9	19.1	3.3	1.0	1.5	1.2	6.2	0.5	5.4	CPS	7
1985	74.7	25.3	5.1	1.4	1.8	1.5	7.9	0.7	6.9	CPS	7
1989	68.6	31.4	9.4	1.4	1.7	1.2	8.8	0.8	8.1	Survey	7
1991	60.1	39.9	13.9	1.8	2.5	1.2	9.1	2.6	8.7	Survey	7
1993-94	55.4	44.6	17.4	2.2	3.0	1.1	8.1	4.5	8.4	DHS	
Burma											
1991	83.2	16.8	4.0	0.9	0.1	1.8	3.7	3.3	3.1	Survey	
China											
Mainland											
1979	34.9	65.1	(NA)	(NA)	(NA)	(NA)	(NA)	(NA)	(NA)	SS	18
1982	30.5	69.5	5.8	34.9	1.4	7.0	17.7	2.8	(NA)	Survey	
1988	28.9	71.1	3.5	29.5	1.9	7.8	27.2	1.2	(NA)	Survey	
1992	23.1	76.9	2.7	30.3	2.0	8.8	32.1	1.0	(NA)	SS	64

Table A-11.
Percent of Currently Married Women Using Contraception, by Method: All Available Years—Continued

[Data refer to ages 15 to 49 years unless specified otherwise]

Region, country or area, and year	No method	All methods	Pill	IUD	Condom	Sterilization		Other modern	Tradi- tional	Source	Re- marks
						Male	Female				
ASIA—Continued											
China—Continued											
Taiwan											
1971	56.0	44.0	7.9	20.2	(NA)	(NA)	(NA)	(NA)	15.8	PC	2
1977	39.0	61.0	(NA)	(NA)	(NA)	(NA)	(NA)	(NA)	(NA)	PC	2
1981	30.0	70.0	5.6	25.2	(NA)	2.1	18.2	(NA)	18.9	PC	2
1984	25.9	74.1	(NA)	(NA)	(NA)	(NA)	(NA)	(NA)	(NA)	PC	2
1985	22.0	78.0	(NA)	(NA)	(NA)	(NA)	(NA)	(NA)	(NA)	Survey	2
Hong Kong											
1967	58.0	42.0	(NA)	(NA)	(NA)	(NA)	(NA)	(NA)	(NA)	Survey	19
1969	58.0	42.0	16.0	(NA)	(NA)	(NA)	(NA)	(NA)	26.0	PC	2,20
1972	45.8	54.2	19.5	5.4	3.8	— 12.5 —		6.0	7.1	Survey	2
1977	22.6	77.4	27.9	2.5	(NA)	— 17.6 —		20.5	8.7	Survey	2
1982	23.3	76.7	20.6	3.7	15.5	1.2	21.1	5.7	9.0	Survey	2
1984	27.6	72.4	22.2	3.5	(NA)	— 21.0 —		(NA)	25.7	PC	2
1987	19.2	80.8	16.4	4.5	26.0	0.9	22.9	4.3	5.9	Survey	
India											
1970	86.4	13.6	(NA)	0.7	2.5	(NA)	6.1	0.4	4.0	Survey	2,21
1980	67.6	32.4	0.9	0.4	3.8	(NA)	20.6	0.1	6.6	Survey	22
1988	57.1	42.9	1.1	1.7	4.7	(NA)	30.8	0.3	4.3	Survey	2
1990	55.1	44.9	(NA)	(NA)	(NA)	— 31.3 —		8.6	5.0	Survey	2,23
1992-93	59.3	40.7	1.2	1.9	2.4	3.5	27.4	(NA)	4.3	Survey	
Indonesia											
1973	91.4	8.6	3.3	3.4	0.5	(NA)	(NA)	(NA)	1.5	Survey	
1976	73.8	26.2	14.9	5.6	1.8	(Z)	0.3	0.3	3.3	WFS	
1979	78.6	21.4	11.4	4.4	0.7	(Z)	0.3	4.6	(NA)	Survey	
1980	74.0	26.0	14.3	6.2	0.9	(NA)	(NA)	4.6	(NA)	Census	
1981	63.8	36.2	(NA)	(NA)	(NA)	(NA)	(NA)	(NA)	(NA)	PC	2
1985	61.5	38.5	15.4	11.9	0.7	0.4	1.2	9.0	(NA)	Survey	
1987	49.4	50.6	17.5	13.6	1.7	0.2	2.9	10.7	4.0	DHS	
1991	50.3	49.7	14.8	13.3	0.8	0.6	2.7	14.8	2.6	DHS	
1994	45.3	54.7	17.1	10.3	0.9	0.7	3.1	20.1	2.7	DHS	
Iran											
1969	97.0	3.0	(NA)	(NA)	(NA)	(NA)	(NA)	(NA)	(NA)	PC	2
1978	77.0	23.0	19.8	2.1	(NA)	— 0.2 —		(NA)	0.9	PC	2,11
1992	35.0	65.0	23.0	7.0	6.0	1.0	8.0	(Z)	20.0	UN	2
Japan											
1961	57.7	42.3	(NA)	(NA)	(NA)	(NA)	(NA)	(NA)	(NA)	Survey	24
1963	56.0	44.0	(NA)	(NA)	(NA)	(NA)	(NA)	(NA)	(NA)	Survey	
1965	44.5	55.5	(NA)	2.4	36.3	— 3.2 —		3.6	26.8	Survey	25
1967	47.0	53.0	(NA)	3.4	36.1	— 2.0 —		3.3	24.8	Survey	25
1969	47.9	52.1	0.9	3.8	35.5	— 2.8 —		4.1	21.8	Survey	25
1971	47.4	52.6	0.8	4.3	38.9	— 2.1 —		2.9	20.7	Survey	25
1973	40.7	59.3	1.4	5.3	44.5	— 2.1 —		2.5	22.1	Survey	25
1975	39.5	60.5	1.8	5.2	47.1	— 2.8 —		2.3	22.2	Survey	25
1977	39.6	60.4	2.0	5.5	47.7	— 3.2 —		1.8	20.6	Survey	25
1979	37.8	62.2	2.0	5.2	50.4	— 2.5 —		1.4	18.6	Survey	25
1981	44.5	55.5	(NA)	(NA)	(NA)	(NA)	(NA)	(NA)	(NA)	Survey	
1984	42.7	57.3	1.3	3.6	46.1	(NA)	(NA)	(NA)	18.1	Survey	25
1986	35.7	64.3	1.0	3.5	44.6	1.6	8.3	0.7	18.2	Survey	25
1988	43.7	56.3	1.0	3.0	43.2	0.9	3.3	0.3	13.8	Survey	25
1990	42.0	58.0	(NA)	3.3	42.9	— 5.7 —		(NA)	14.1	Survey	25,26
1992	36.0	64.0	(NA)	(NA)	(NA)	(NA)	(NA)	(NA)	(NA)	Survey	

Table A-11.
Percent of Currently Married Women Using Contraception, by Method: All Available Years—Continued

[Data refer to ages 15 to 49 years unless specified otherwise]

Region, country or area, and year	No method	All methods	Pill	IUD	Condom	Sterilization		Other modern	Tradi-tional	Source	Re-marks
						Male	Female				
ASIA—Continued											
Malaysia											
1966-67	91.2	8.8	4.1	0.2	0.8	(NA)	(NA)	0.2	3.6	Survey	2,27,28
1970	84.0	16.0	12.1	(NA)	(NA)	(NA)	(NA)	(NA)	4.0	Survey	2,27
1974	64.5	35.5	18.0	0.8	3.2	— 3.8 —		0.1	9.6	WFS	2,27
1979	64.0	36.0	25.0	1.0	(NA)	— 6.0 —		(Z)	4.0	PC	2,27
1981	57.7	42.3	16.9	0.8	(NA)	— 5.0 —		0.4	19.2	PC	2,27
1984	48.6	51.4	11.6	2.0	7.7	0.2	7.7	1.0	21.3	Survey	27
1988	52.0	48.0	15.0	4.0	6.0	— 7.0 —		1.0	17.0	UN	27
Nepal											
1976	97.1	2.9	0.5	0.1	0.3	0.1	1.9	(NA)	0.1	WFS	1
1981	93.2	6.8	1.1	0.1	0.4	2.9	2.3	0.1	(Z)	CPS	2
1986	84.9	15.1	0.9	0.1	0.6	6.2	6.8	0.5	(NA)	Survey	
1991	74.9	25.1	1.1	0.2	0.6	7.5	12.1	2.6	1.0	Survey	
Pakistan											
1968-69	94.5	5.5	(NA)	(NA)	(NA)	(NA)	(NA)	(NA)	(NA)	Survey	1
1975	96.0	4.0	0.8	0.5	0.8	— 0.7 —		(NA)	1.3	WFS	11
1980	93.6	6.4	0.6	1.1	(NA)	— 0.6 —		(NA)	4.2	PC	2,20
1984-85	90.9	9.1	1.4	0.8	2.1	(Z)	2.6	0.7	1.5	CPS	1
1990-91	88.2	11.8	0.7	1.3	2.7	(Z)	3.5	0.8	2.8	DHS	
Philippines											
1968	85.3	14.7	1.1	0.8	0.5	(Z)	0.2	0.9	11.2	Survey	
1972	91.9	8.1	4.9	2.0	(NA)	(NA)	(NA)	(NA)	1.3	PC	2
1973	82.4	17.6	6.9	2.6	0.8	(Z)	0.5	(NA)	6.8	Survey	2
1976	78.3	21.7	11.1	4.0	3.0	(NA)	(NA)	(NA)	3.6	Survey	
1977	78.0	22.0	11.1	4.0	0.	(NA)	(NA)	(NA)	6.9	PC	2
1978	62.9	37.1	4.8	2.4	3.8	0.6	4.7	(NA)	20.8	WFS	
1979	63.0	37.0	5.5	2.5	4.1	0.5	3.7	(NA)	20.7	PC	2
1980	54.6	45.4	5.0	1.8	1.8	0.4	6.5	(NA)	29.9	Survey	2
1981	52.0	48.0	16.3	4.3	13.9	0.5	2.9	(NA)	10.1	PC	2
1983	66.6	33.4	5.5	2.6	1.5	0.6	8.9	(NA)	14.3	Survey	2
1986	68.2	31.8	(NA)	(NA)	(NA)	(NA)	(NA)	(NA)	(NA)	CPS	6,29
1988	63.8	36.2	6.9	2.4	0.7	0.4	11.0	0.2	14.5	Survey	2
1993	60.0	40.0	8.5	3.0	1.0	0.4	11.9	0.1	15.1	DHS	
Singapore											
1970	55.0	45.0	37.8	(NA)	(NA)	(NA)	(NA)	(NA)	7.2	PC	2
1973	40.6	59.4	21.6	3.0	16.8	— 10.8 —		(NA)	7.2	Survey	2
1977	28.7	71.3	17.0	3.1	20.8	0.9	21.0	(NA)	8.5	Survey	2
1978	29.0	71.0	17.0	2.8	(NA)	0.7	21.3	(NA)	29.1	PC	2
1982	25.8	74.2	11.6	(NA)	24.3	0.6	22.3	14.2	1.2	Survey	2
South Korea											
1964	91.0	9.0	(NA)	(NA)	(NA)	(NA)	(NA)	(NA)	(NA)	Survey	2
1965	84.0	16.0	(NA)	(NA)	(NA)	(NA)	(NA)	(NA)	(NA)	Survey	2
1966	80.0	20.0	0.5	9.2	3.1	— 2.0 —		(NA)	5.1	Survey	2
1967	80.0	20.0	(NA)	(NA)	(NA)	(NA)	(NA)	(NA)	(NA)	Survey	2
1971	75.0	25.0	7.0	7.2	3.3	— 3.4 —		(NA)	4.3	Survey	2
1973	64.0	36.3	8.0	7.9	6.5	(Z)	4.6	(NA)	9.3	Survey	2
1974	63.0	37.0	9.0	8.0	6.0	— 5.0 —		(NA)	9.0	WFS	2
1976	55.8	44.2	7.8	10.5	6.3	4.2	4.1	(NA)	11.4	Survey	2
1978	51.2	48.8	6.6	9.5	5.8	5.6	10.9	(NA)	10.4	Survey	2
1979	45.5	54.5	7.2	9.6	5.2	5.9	14.5	0.7	11.4	Survey	2

Table A-11.
Percent of Currently Married Women Using Contraception, by Method: All Available Years—Continued

[Data refer to ages 15 to 49 years unless specified otherwise]

Region, country or area, and year	No method	All methods	Pill	IUD	Condom	Sterilization		Other modern	Tradi-tional	Source	Re-marks
						Male	Female				
ASIA—Continued											
South Korea—Continued											
1982	42.3	57.7	5.4	6.7	7.2	5.1	23.0	(NA)	10.3	Survey	2
1985	29.6	70.4	4.3	7.4	7.2	8.9	31.6	11.0	(Z)	Survey	2
1988	22.7	77.3	2.8	6.7	10.2	11.0	37.2	2.3	7.1	Survey	2
1991	21.0	79.0	3.0	9.0	10.0	12.0	35.0	(Z)	10.0	UN	2
Sri Lanka											
1975	68.0	32.0	1.5	4.7	2.3	0.7	9.2	(NA)	13.6	WFS	
1977	59.0	41.0	(NA)	(NA)	(NA)	—— 18.0 ——		(NA)	23.0	PC	2
1982	45.1	54.9	2.6	2.5	3.2	3.6	17.0	(NA)	25.9	CPS	
1987	38.3	61.7	4.1	2.1	1.9	4.9	24.9	2.7	21.2	DHS	30
Thailand											
1970	85.6	14.4	3.8	2.1	0.1	2.0	5.1	1.1	(Z)	Survey	2
1973	73.6	26.4	10.8	4.7	0.1	2.8	6.4	1.4	(Z)	Survey	2
1975	66.9	33.1	13.7	5.9	0.4	2.1	6.3	2.3	2.5	WFS	2
1978	46.9	53.1	22.0	4.0	2.2	3.4	12.9	8.6	(Z)	CPS	2
1981	41.0	59.0	20.2	4.2	1.9	4.2	18.7	7.1	2.7	CPS	2
1984	35.4	64.6	19.8	5.0	1.8	4.4	23.6	7.6	2.5	CPS	2
1985	41.0	59.0	20.7	6.3	0.5	3.7	19.5	7.6	0.6	Survey	
1987	34.5	65.5	18.6	6.9	1.1	5.7	22.8	8.5	1.9	DHS	
Vietnam											
1988	46.9	53.2	0.4	33.1	1.2	0.3	2.7	(NA)	15.4	Survey	
1994	35.0	65.0	2.1	33.3	4.0	0.2	3.9	0.3	21.2	Nguyen	
LATIN AMERICA AND THE CARIBBEAN											
Antigua and Barbuda											
1981	61.1	38.9	16.1	4.6	1.9	(NA)	8.7	5.8	1.8	CPS	2,11
1988	47.4	52.6	26.0	1.0	6.0	(NA)	11.0	6.0	2.0	Survey	2
Bahamas, The											
1988	35.1	64.9	33.1	3.9	2.5	(NA)	17.2	6.6	1.7	Survey	2
Barbados											
1980-81	52.6	47.4	17.2	4.2	5.2	—— 13.9 ——		5.0	1.9	CPS	2,11
1988	45.0	55.0	26.2	5.3	7.2	0.3	10.4	3.8	1.8	Survey	
Belize											
1985	57.1	42.9	14.9	1.8	2.0	0.1	11.0	2.3	10.9	Survey	2,36
1991	53.3	46.7	14.9	1.9	1.9	(NA)	18.7	6.7	2.5	CDC	2
Bolivia											
1983	76.4	23.6	2.7	3.4	0.4	(NA)	2.4	1.0	13.7	CPS	37
1989	69.7	30.3	1.9	4.8	0.3	(NA)	4.4	0.8	18.0	DHS	
1994	54.7	45.3	2.8	8.1	1.3	(NA)	4.6	0.9	27.6	DHS	
Brazil											
1980	44.2	55.8	(NA)	(NA)	(NA)	(NA)	(NA)	(NA)	(NA)	PC	2
1986	34.2	65.8	25.1	1.0	1.7	0.8	26.8	1.1	9.3	DHS	2
Chile											
1978	57.0	43.0	(NA)	(NA)	(NA)	(NA)	(NA)	(NA)	(NA)	SS	2
Colombia											
1969	72.0	28.0	4.8	2.5	2.0	(NA)	1.7	1.7	15.4	Survey	
1974	69.0	31.0	(NA)	(NA)	(NA)	(NA)	(NA)	(NA)	(NA)	PC	2
1976	57.0	43.0	13.8	8.6	1.7	(NA)	5.6	2.2	11.2	WFS	
1978	53.9	46.1	17.1	7.4	1.8	(NA)	7.4	3.7	8.8	CPS	
1980	51.5	48.5	17.5	8.7	0.5	(NA)	11.2	3.4	7.3	CPS	

Table A-11.
Percent of Currently Married Women Using Contraception, by Method: All Available Years—Continued

[Data refer to ages 15 to 49 years unless specified otherwise]

Region, country or area, and year	No method	All methods	Pill	IUD	Condom	Sterilization Male	Sterilization Female	Other modern	Tradi-tional	Source	Re-marks
LATIN AMERICA AND THE CARIBBEAN—Continued											
Colombia—Continued											
1984	44.9	55.1	21.0	9.3	(NA)	—— 16.8 ——		(NA)	8.0	PC	2
1986	35.2	64.8	16.4	11.0	1.7	0.4	18.3	4.7	12.3	DHS	
1990	33.9	66.1	14.1	12.4	2.9	0.5	20.9	3.9	11.5	DHS	
Costa Rica											
1976	32.0	68.0	22.5	5.2	8.8	1.0	15.9	3.7	10.9	WFS	38
1978	36.5	63.5	25.2	4.7	(NA)	—— 14.0 ——		19.6	(NA)	CPS	
1981	35.4	64.6	20.7	5.9	8.1	0.4	17.2	3.4	9.1	CPS	
1984	35.0	65.0	22.8	5.7	(NA)	—— 17.8 ——		18.6	(NA)	SS	2
1986	32.0	68.0	18.8	7.3	12.7	0.5	16.4	1.8	10.6	Survey	
1992-93	25.0	75.0	18.0	9.0	16.0	1.0	20.0	1.0	10.0	UN	
Cuba											
1987	30.0	70.0	10.0	33.0	2.0	(NA)	22.0	(Z)	2.0	Survey	39
Dominica											
1981	51.0	49.0	16.5	2.0	3.6	—— 14.7 ——		10.4	1.8	CPS	2,11
1987	50.2	49.8	16.5	1.7	5.6	(NA)	12.6	11.8	1.7	Survey	
Dominican Republic											
1975	68.2	31.8	8.1	2.8	(NA)	0.1	11.9	(NA)	8.9	WFS	
1977	69.0	31.0	8.0	3.0	(NA)	—— 12.0 ——		(NA)	8.0	PC	2
1980	58.0	42.0	9.0	5.0	(NA)	(NA)	21.0	(NA)	6.0	WFS	
1983	72.2	27.8	5.1	2.2	(NA)	—— 17.2 ——		(NA)	3.3	CPS	
1986	50.0	50.0	8.8	3.0	1.4	0.1	32.9	0.5	3.3	DHS	
1991	43.6	56.4	9.8	1.8	1.2	(NA)	38.5	0.5	4.7	DHS	
Ecuador											
1979	64.9	35.1	9.5	4.8	1.0	0.2	9.3	3.2	7.1	WFS	
1982	60.1	39.9	10.3	6.4	1.1	(NA)	12.4	3.4	6.3	DHS	
1987	55.7	44.3	8.5	9.8	0.6	(NA)	15.0	1.9	8.4	DHS	
1989	47.1	52.9	8.6	11.9	1.3	(NA)	18.3	1.4	11.3	Survey	
1994	43.2	56.8	10.2	11.8	2.6	(NA)	19.8	1.6	10.8	CDC	
El Salvador											
1975	78.4	21.6	7.3	2.3	0.6	(NA)	9.6	0.5	1.5	Survey	2,40
1976	80.0	20.0	5.7	2.0	0.3	(NA)	10.5	0.4	1.1	Survey	2,6
1978	65.6	34.4	8.7	3.3	1.5	(NA)	18.0	1.2	1.7	CPS	2
1985	52.7	47.3	6.6	3.3	1.2	0.7	31.8	1.0	2.7	DHS	
1988	52.9	47.1	7.6	2.0	2.4	0.6	29.6	1.3	3.4	Survey	2
1993	46.7	53.3	8.7	2.1	2.1	(NA)	31.5	4.0	5.0	Survey	2
Grenada											
1985	69.0	31.0	8.0	2.7	8.6	(NA)	(NA)	7.8	3.9	CPS	2
1990	46.0	54.0	15.0	3.0	22.0	(NA)	(NA)	9.0	5.0	UN	28
Guadeloupe											
1976	56.0	44.0	9.8	3.4	(NA)	—— 11.6 ——		6.3	13.0	WFS	
Guatemala											
1974	96.0	4.0	(NA)	(NA)	(NA)	(NA)	(NA)	(NA)	(NA)	PC	2
1978	80.6	19.4	5.5	1.7	0.9	—— 6.8 ——		4.4	(NA)	CPS	41
1983	75.0	25.0	4.7	2.6	1.2	0.9	10.2	5.4	(NA)	Survey	2,41
1987	76.8	23.2	3.9	1.8	1.2	0.9	10.4	0.9	4.1	DHS	2
Guyana											
1975	67.9	32.1	9.9	5.8	3.1	—— 7.9 ——		2.3	3.0	WFS	2,11

Table A-11.
Percent of Currently Married Women Using Contraception, by Method: All Available Years—Continued

[Data refer to ages 15 to 49 years unless specified otherwise]

Region, country or area, and year	No method	All methods	Pill	IUD	Condom	Sterilization Male	Sterilization Female	Other modern	Traditional	Source	Remarks
LATIN AMERICA AND THE CARIBBEAN—Continued											
Haiti											
1976	95.0	5.0	(NA)	(NA)	(NA)	(NA)	(NA)	(NA)	(NA)	SS	2
1977	81.2	18.8	3.3	0.4	1.1	0.2	0.2	0.1	13.5	WFS	
1983	93.1	6.9	2.2	0.2	0.5	—— 0.8 ——		(NA)	3.2	CPS	
1987	92.3	7.7	2.5	0.5	0.2	(NA)	1.5	0.9	2.0	Survey	
1989	89.8	10.2	4.1	0.6	0.5	(NA)	2.5	1.7	0.8	CPS	
1994	82.0	18.0	3.1	(NA)	2.6	(NA)	3.1	4.3	4.4	DHS	
Honduras											
1981	73.1	26.9	11.7	2.4	0.3	0.2	8.0	1.0	3.3	CPS	
1984	65.1	34.9	12.7	3.8	0.9	0.2	12.1	0.7	4.6	Survey	2
1987	59.4	40.6	13.4	4.3	1.8	(NA)	12.6	4.9	3.5	Survey	2
1991-92	53.0	47.0	10.0	5.0	3.0	(NA)	16.0	1.0	12.0	UN	2,65
Jamaica											
1975-76	59.5	40.5	13.0	2.0	7.1	—— 7.8 ——		8.4	2.2	WFS	2,11
1979	45.1	54.9	23.8	2.0	6.5	(Z)	9.8	12.1	0.7	CPS	
1983	48.6	51.4	26.8	2.2	(NA)	—— 10.9 ——		(NA)	11.5	CPS	
1989	45.4	54.6	19.5	1.5	8.6	0.1	13.6	8.0	3.4	CPS	
1993	38.0	62.0	21.5	1.0	16.9	(NA)	12.5	6.5	3.6	CDC	2
Martinique											
1976	49.0	51.3	17.3	2.6	4.6	(Z)	11.7	1.7	13.5	WFS	2
Mexico											
1973	87.0	13.0	11.4	1.2	(NA)	(NA)	(NA)	(NA)	0.4	SS	2
1976	71.0	29.0	11.9	5.5	(NA)	—— 2.8 ——		(NA)	8.9	WFS	
1978	73.8	26.2	9.3	4.3	0.7	0.1	4.7	7.1	(NA)	CPS	
1979	62.0	38.0	15.2	6.1	(NA)	0.4	8.7	(NA)	7.6	CPS	
1982	50.1	49.9	14.3	6.7	1.0	0.4	14.4	6.3	6.8	Survey	
1987	47.3	52.7	9.7	10.2	1.9	0.8	18.6	3.4	8.1	DHS	
Montserrat											
1984	47.6	52.4	30.5	11.0	3.4	(NA)	1.6	5.6	0.3	CPS	2
Nicaragua											
1981	73.0	27.0	10.5	2.3	0.8	0.1	7.1	2.0	4.3	CPS	2,42
1992-93	51.3	48.7	12.9	9.3	2.6	0.3	18.5	1.3	3.7	CDC	
Panama											
1976	43.0	57.0	18.7	4.0	1.3	—— 23.9 ——		3.7	5.4	WFS	43
1979	39.4	60.6	19.0	3.7	1.7	—— 29.7 ——		2.2	4.3	CPS	2
1984	41.8	58.2	11.8	6.0	1.6	0.4	32.4	2.0	4.0	Survey	2
Paraguay											
1977	71.4	28.6	11.8	4.0	2.6	(Z)	3.2	1.7	5.2	CPS	2
1979	67.9	32.1	10.5	4.8	1.4	0.1	1.8	7.8	5.8	WFS	2,11
1987	55.2	44.8	13.5	5.1	2.3	—— 4.0 ——		4.1	15.8	CDC	2
1990	51.6	48.4	13.6	5.7	2.6	(NA)	7.4	6.0	13.2	DHS	
Peru											
1969-70	74.0	26.0	3.0	1.0	3.0	(NA)	2.0	1.0	16.0	Survey	
1977-78	58.7	41.3	5.5	1.8	1.4	(NA)	3.6	7.6	21.4	WFS	1
1981	59.0	41.0	5.0	4.0	1.0	(NA)	4.0	6.0	21.0	CPS	
1986	54.2	45.8	6.5	7.4	0.7	(NA)	6.1	2.3	22.8	DHS	
1991-92	41.0	59.0	5.7	13.4	2.8	0.1	7.9	2.9	26.2	DHS	
Puerto Rico											
1968	40.0	60.0	11.3	1.6	2.1	1.4	34.1	0.3	9.3	Survey	6
1974	38.0	62.0	20.3	3.7	(NA)	—— 28.9 ——		2.9	6.2	Survey	2
1976	35.4	64.6	12.7	3.4	(NA)	2.8	35.4	(NA)	10.3	Survey	6
1982	29.6	70.4	9.3	4.1	4.6	4.4	39.7	(NA)	8.3	Survey	2

Table A-11.
Percent of Currently Married Women Using Contraception, by Method: All Available Years—Continued

[Data refer to ages 15 to 49 years unless specified otherwise]

Region, country or area, and year	No method	All methods	Pill	IUD	Condom	Sterilization: Male	Sterilization: Female	Other modern	Traditional	Source	Remarks
LATIN AMERICA AND THE CARIBBEAN—Continued											
Saint Kitts and Nevis											
1984	59.4	40.6	19.7	3.8	5.6	(NA)	2.6	5.3	3.6	CPS	2
Saint Lucia											
1981	57.3	42.7	21.1	1.0	3.9	—— 10.8 ——		3.5	2.4	CPS	2,11
1988	52.3	47.3	18.4	4.3	5.8	(Z)	8.6	9.0	1.3	Survey	2
Saint Vincent and the Grenadines											
1981	58.5	41.5	13.0	2.3	8.3	—— 11.7 ——		4.2	2.0	CPS	2,11
1988	41.7	58.3	24.3	2.7	7.4	(Z)	13.1	10.8	(Z)	Survey	2
Trinidad and Tobago											
1970-71	56.4	43.6	17.1	3.0	9.8	0.1	2.0	4.5	9.2	Survey	2
1977	46.1	53.9	18.8	2.4	15.6	—— 4.5 ——		(NA)	12.6	WFS	2
1987	47.3	52.7	14.0	4.4	11.8	0.2	8.2	6.1	7.9	DHS	
Venezuela											
1977	39.7	60.3	18.8	10.5	5.9	0.1	9.4	5.0	10.7	WFS	1,2
EUROPE AND THE NEW INDEPENDENT STATES											
Western Europe											
Austria											
1981-82	28.6	71.4	40.0	8.4	4.0	0.3	1.0	2.6	15.2	Survey	18,45
Belgium											
1966	28.0	72.0	5.0	(NA)	3.0	(NA)	2.0	1.0	62.0	Survey	46
1975-76	13.0	87.0	30.0	3.0	8.0	(NA)	6.0	(Z)	39.0	WFS	2,47
1982-83	19.0	81.0	32.0	8.0	6.0	(NA)	17.0	(Z)	17.0	Survey	43,47
1991	21.0	79.0	46.0	5.0	5.0	8.0	11.0	(Z)	4.0	UN	46,47
Denmark											
1970	33.0	67.0	25.0	3.0	20.0	(NA)	(NA)	6.0	13.0	Survey	49
1975	37.0	63.0	22.0	9.0	25.0	(NA)	(NA)	4.0	2.0	WFS	48
1988	22.0	78.0	26.0	11.0	22.0	5.0	5.0	3.0	7.0	UN	2
Finland											
1971	23.0	77.0	20.0	3.0	31.0	(Z)	(Z)	(Z)	23.0	Survey	49,50
1977	20.0	80.0	11.0	29.0	32.0	1.0	4.0	1.0	3.0	WFS	49,50
France											
1972	36.0	64.0	11.0	1.0	8.0	(Z)	(Z)	1.0	43.0	Survey	49,50
1978	21.3	78.7	26.6	10.3	6.1	(NA)	4.6	(NA)	31.1	WFS	43
1988	20.1	79.9	27.0	24.4	4.2	(NA)	8.7	(NA)	15.6	Survey	44
1994	24.9	75.1	36.9	19.6	5.2	0.3	4.6	1.1	7.5	Survey	
Germany											
1985	22.1	77.9	33.7	14.6	5.7	2.1	10.3	1.2	10.1	Survey	51
1992	25.0	75.0	59.0	6.0	4.0	—— 1.0 ——		2.0	3.0	UN	67
Ireland											
1973	40.1	59.9	(NA)	(NA)	(NA)	(NA)	(NA)	(NA)	(NA)	Survey	
Italy											
1979	22.0	78.0	14.0	2.0	13.0	(Z)	1.0	2.0	46.0	WFS	55

Table A-11.
Percent of Currently Married Women Using Contraception, by Method: All Available Years—Continued

[Data refer to ages 15 to 49 years unless specified otherwise]

Region, country or area, and year	No method	All methods	Pill	IUD	Condom	Sterilization Male	Sterilization Female	Other modern	Traditional	Source	Remarks
EUROPE AND THE NEW INDEPENDENT STATES—Continued											
Western Europe—Continued											
Netherlands											
1969	41.0	59.0	27.0	1.0	14.0	(NA)	(NA)	2.0	16.0	Survey	18
1975	25.0	75.0	50.0	4.0	10.0	2.0	2.0	1.0	5.0	WFS	18
1977	27.0	73.0	40.0	4.3	8.0	(NA)	12.9	(NA)	7.8	Survey	50,56
1982	23.0	77.0	38.0	10.0	7.0	11.0	8.0	(NA)	3.0	Survey	57
1985	24.0	76.0	30.0	9.0	8.0	(NA)	25.0	(NA)	4.0	Survey	58
1988	24.0	76.0	41.0	7.0	8.0	11.0	4.0	(NA)	4.0	Survey	57
1993	26.0	74.0	47.0	3.0	8.0	9.0	4.0	— 3.0 —		Survey	68
Norway											
1977	29.0	71.0	13.0	28.0	16.0	2.0	4.0	2.0	7.0	Survey	25,48,50
1988	24.5	75.5	17.8	24.1	14.0	4.3	10.4	1.1	10.7	Survey	25,43
Portugal											
1979-80	33.7	66.3	19.1	3.6	5.6	0.1	0.9	3.5	33.6	WFS	
Spain											
1977	49.7	50.3	11.7	0.5	4.9	(NA)	0.3	0.1	32.9	WFS	1
1985	40.6	59.4	15.5	5.7	12.2	0.3	4.3	(NA)	21.5	Survey	44
Sweden											
1981	22.0	78.0	23.0	20.0	25.0	(NA)	2.0	(NA)	7.0	WFS	43
Switzerland											
1980	28.8	71.2	28.0	10.6	8.4	(NA)	15.8	2.1	6.4	Survey	18,24
United Kingdom											
1970	25.0	75.0	19.0	4.0	28.0	— 4.0 —		4.0	22.0	Survey	6,25,60
1975	24.0	76.0	30.0	6.0	18.0	— 13.0 —		2.0	10.0	Survey	6,25,60
1976	23.0	77.0	32.0	8.0	16.0	8.0	8.0	2.0	7.0	Survey	6,25,61
1983	17.0	83.0	24.0	7.0	17.0	14.0	14.0	3.0	8.0	Survey	25,48,75
1986	19.0	81.0	19.0	8.0	16.0	16.0	15.0	4.0	8.0	Survey	25,56
1989	28.0	72.0	25.0	6.0	16.0	12.0	11.0	1.0	7.0	Survey	25,39,55
Eastern Europe											
Bulgaria											
1976	24.0	76.0	2.0	2.0	2.0	1.0	1.0	(NA)	68.0	WFS	48
Czechoslovakia											
1970	34.0	66.0	3.0	9.0	13.0	(Z)	(Z)	(NA)	41.0	Survey	49
1977	5.0	95.0	14.0	18.0	13.0	(Z)	3.0	1.0	46.0	WFS	49
Czech Republic											
1993	31.1	68.9	8.1	15.3	16.7	(NA)	2.7	2.2	24.1	CDC	70
Hungary											
1958	42.0	58.0	(NA)	(NA)	12.0	(NA)	(NA)	6.0	40.0	Survey	52
1966	33.4	66.6	0.1	0.1	11.6	(NA)	(NA)	6.4	48.4	Survey	53
1974	26.0	74.0	27.0	6.0	7.0	(NA)	1.0	3.0	30.0	Survey	52
1977	26.9	73.1	36.1	9.6	4.3	(NA)	(NA)	1.8	21.3	WFS	53
1986	26.9	73.1	39.3	18.6	3.5	(NA)	(NA)	0.9	10.7	Survey	39,54
Poland											
1972	40.0	60.0	2.0	1.0	10.0	(NA)	(NA)	(NA)	48.0	Survey	49
1977	25.0	75.0	7.0	2.0	14.0	(NA)	(NA)	3.0	49.0	WFS	49

Table A-11.
Percent of Currently Married Women Using Contraception, by Method: All Available Years—Continued

[Data refer to ages 15 to 49 years unless specified otherwise]

Region, country or area, and year	No method	All methods	Pill	IUD	Condom	Sterilization Male	Sterilization Female	Other modern	Traditional	Source	Remarks
EUROPE AND THE NEW INDEPENDENT STATES— Continued											
Eastern Europe— Continued											
Romania											
1978	42.0	58.0	1.0	(Z)	3.0	(NA)	(NA)	1.0	53.0	WFS	2
1993	42.7	57.3	3.2	4.3	4.0	(NA)	1.4	1.0	43.4	CDC	2
Slovenia											
1989	8.4	91.6	25.0	24.4	4.7	—— 0.2 ——		2.5	34.8	Survey	2,71
Slovakia											
1991	26.0	74.0	5.0	11.0	21.0	(Z)	4.0	(Z)	32.0	UN	2,66,70
Yugoslavia SFR											
1976	45.0	55.0	5.0	2.0	2.0	(NA)	(NA)	3.0	43.0	UN	49,50
New Independent States											
Baltics											
Estonia											
1990	64.5	35.5	(NA)	(NA)	(NA)	(NA)	(NA)	(NA)	(NA)	Survey	62
Latvia											
1990	68.5	31.5	(NA)	(NA)	(NA)	(NA)	(NA)	(NA)	(NA)	Survey	62
Lithuania											
1990	80.5	19.5	(NA)	(NA)	(NA)	(NA)	(NA)	(NA)	(NA)	Survey	62
Commonwealth of Independent States											
Armenia											
1990	78.4	21.6	(NA)	(NA)	(NA)	(NA)	(NA)	(NA)	(NA)	Survey	62
Azerbaijan											
1990	82.8	17.2	(NA)	(NA)	(NA)	(NA)	(NA)	(NA)	(NA)	Survey	62
Belarus											
1990	77.2	22.8	(NA)	(NA)	(NA)	(NA)	(NA)	(NA)	(NA)	Survey	62
1995	49.6	50.4	6.7	29.0	4.8	—— 0.8 ——		0.8	8.3	Survey	69
Georgia											
1990	82.9	17.1	(NA)	(NA)	(NA)	(NA)	(NA)	(NA)	(NA)	Survey	62
Kazakstan											
1990	70.0	30.0	(NA)	(NA)	(NA)	(NA)	(NA)	(NA)	(NA)	Survey	62
Kyrgyzstan											
1990	69.5	30.5	(NA)	(NA)	(NA)	(NA)	(NA)	(NA)	(NA)	Survey	62
Moldova											
1990	78.2	21.8	(NA)	(NA)	(NA)	(NA)	(NA)	(NA)	(NA)	Survey	62
Russia											
1990	68.5	31.5	(NA)	(NA)	(NA)	(NA)	(NA)	(NA)	(NA)	Survey	62
1994	33.2	66.8	4.0	33.1	(NA)	(NA)	(NA)	11.5	18.2	Survey	
Tajikistan											
1990	79.2	20.8	(NA)	(NA)	(NA)	(NA)	(NA)	(NA)	(NA)	Survey	62

Table A-11.
Percent of Currently Married Women Using Contraception, by Method: All Available Years—Continued

[Data refer to ages 15 to 49 years unless specified otherwise]

Region, country or area, and year	No method	All methods	Pill	IUD	Condom	Sterilization Male	Sterilization Female	Other modern	Traditional	Source	Remarks
EUROPE AND THE NEW INDEPENDENT STATES—Continued											
New Independent States—Continued											
Commonwealth of Independent States—Continued											
Turkmenistan											
1990	80.2	19.8	(NA)	(NA)	(NA)	(NA)	(NA)	(NA)	(NA)	Survey	62
Ukraine											
1990	76.6	23.4	(NA)	(NA)	(NA)	(NA)	(NA)	(NA)	(NA)	Survey	62
Uzbekistan											
1990	71.9	28.1	(NA)	(NA)	(NA)	(NA)	(NA)	(NA)	(NA)	Survey	62
NORTH AMERICA											
Canada											
1984	26.9	73.1	11.0	5.8	7.9	12.9	30.6	1.5	3.6	Survey	44
United States											
1965	36.8	63.2	15.1	0.8	13.9	3.3	4.6	8.3	17.3	Survey	2
1973	30.4	69.6	25.1	6.7	9.4	7.8	8.6	5.9	6.2	Survey	2
1976	32.2	67.8	22.5	6.3	7.3	9.0	9.5	5.9	7.1	Survey	2
1982	32.0	69.6	13.4	4.8	9.8	10.8	18.7	6.5	5.5	Survey	2
1988	25.7	74.3	15.1	1.5	10.6	12.9	23.4	5.6	5.3	Survey	2,39
1990	29.3	70.7	14.5	1.0	9.9	13.6	23.7	5.1	2.9	Survey	2
OCEANIA											
American Samoa											
1979	78.0	22.0	(NA)	(NA)	(NA)	(NA)	(NA)	(NA)	(NA)	Lucas	2,63
Australia											
1986	23.9	76.1	24.0	4.9	4.4	10.4	27.7	0.8	3.9	Survey	38,39
Cook Islands											
1983	60.0	40.0	(NA)	(NA)	(NA)	(NA)	(NA)	(NA)	(NA)	UNESCAP	18
Fiji											
1973	66.6	33.4	10.6	9.7	(NA)	(NA)	8.2	4.8	(NA)	SS	
1974	59.1	40.9	8.2	4.7	6.0	0.1	15.8	6.1	(NA)	WFS	
1977	64.8	35.2	6.2	5.5	5.6	(NA)	15.7	2.2	(NA)	SS	
1978	62.0	38.0	8.0	5.0	6.0	(NA)	17.0	2.0	(NA)	SS	
Guam											
1979	93.0	7.0	(NA)	(NA)	(NA)	(NA)	(NA)	(NA)	(NA)	Lucas	2,63
Kiribati											
1977	78.0	22.0	(NA)	(NA)	(NA)	(NA)	(NA)	(NA)	(NA)	SPC	2
1978	78.0	22.0	(NA)	(NA)	(NA)	(NA)	(NA)	(NA)	(NA)	SPC	2
1982	80.6	19.4	(NA)	(NA)	(NA)	(NA)	(NA)	(NA)	(NA)	SPC	2
New Zealand											
1976	30.5	69.5	28.6	4.4	8.0	9.1	11.4	(NA)	9.8	Survey	18,25
Papua New Guinea											
1980	95.5	4.5	(NA)	(NA)	(NA)	(NA)	(NA)	(NA)	(NA)	UNESCAP	

Table A-11.
Percent of Currently Married Women Using Contraception, by Method: All Available Years—Continued

[Data refer to ages 15 to 49 years unless specified otherwise]

Region, country or area, and year	No method	All methods	Pill	IUD	Condom	Sterilization		Other modern	Tradi-tional	Source	Re-marks
						Male	Female				
OCEANIA—Continued											
Solomon Islands											
1979	77.0	23.0	(NA)	(NA)	(NA)	(NA)	(NA)	(NA)	(NA)	Lucas	2,63
Tonga											
1976	54.3	45.7	3.1	9.6	10.5	0.1	5.0	(NA)	17.4	Survey	2
Tuvalu											
1983	70.0	30.0	(NA)	(NA)	(NA)	(NA)	(NA)	(NA)	(NA)	UNESCAP	18
Vanuatu											
1979	87.0	13.0	(NA)	(NA)	(NA)	(NA)	(NA)	(NA)	(NA)	Lucas	2,63
Western Samoa											
1982	81.5	18.5	(NA)	(NA)	(NA)	(NA)	(NA)	(NA)	(NA)	SS	2

(NA) Data not available.
(Z) Less than 0.05 percent.

Note: Data refer to currently married women (and women in consensual and visiting unions) ages 15 to 49 years unless coverage is unknown or is otherwise specified in the remarks. Figures shown for traditional methods may include modern methods not reported separately. Countries with no data available are omitted from the table.

Remarks:
1. Data refer to women exposed to the risk of pregnancy (currently married nonpregnant women who consider themselves to be fecund).
2. Data refer to ages 15-44.
3. Data refer to ages 15 to 50 years.
4. Data refer to all women ages 15 to 49 years, regardless of marital status, who have used a contraceptive method.
5. Data refer to sedentary population.
6. Data refer to ever-married women.
7. Data refer to ages under 50 years.
8. Data refer to island of Mauritius. Total prevalence rate for Rodrigues is 51.0 percent.
9. "Other modern" refers to injection and traditional refers only to rhythm.
10. Total prevalence rate refers to all women in union, while data by method are based on fecund women in union.
11. Total prevalence rate refers to currently married women, while data by method are based on exposed women.
12. Data refer to ages 12 to 49 years.
13. "Other modern" methods include douche, which is not reported separately.
14. Data refer to Northern Sudan only.
15. Data refer to ever-married women and unmarried women who have had a child.
16. Traditional includes all methods other than pill and IUD.
17. Data refer to ages under 56 years.
18. Age range is not specified.
19. Data refer to ages 15 to 45 years.
20. Figure shown for pill refers to pill and injectables.
21. Data exclude Jammu and Kashmir, North-East Frontier Agency, and offshore islands.
22. Data exclude North-East Frontier Agency, offshore islands, and Assam.
23. "Other modern" refers to all modern methods.
24. Data refer to sample of husbands and wives.
25. Sum of data by method exceeds total prevalence rate because some women reported using more than one method.
26. Pill is included with IUD.
27. Data refer to Peninsular Malaysia only.
28. Traditional methods include sterilization, which is not reported separately.
29. Data refer to program methods only (pill, IUD, injection, sterilization, condom, rhythm, and vaginal methods).
30. Data exclude the northern and eastern provinces.
31. Data refer to nationals only.
32. Data by method were recalculated because some women reported using more than one method.
33. Data refer to ages 17 to 51 years.
34. Data refer to the former Yemen Arab Republic (Sana'a).
35. Excludes breastfeeding.
36. Data refer to all women ages 15 to 47 years.
37. Data refer to women who have ever been either married or in a consensual union.
38. Data refer to ages 20 to 49 years.

Table A-11.
Percent of Currently Married Women Using Contraception, by Method: All Available Years—Continued

Remarks—Continued

39. "Other modern" methods refer to female barrier methods.
40. Total prevalence rate refers to currently married women, while data by method are based on ever-married women.
41. "Other modern" methods include withdrawal, which is not reported separately.
42. Total prevalence rate refers to women in union, while data by method are based on all respondents, regardless of marital status.
43. Data refer to ages 20 to 44 years.
44. Data refer to ages 18 to 49 years.
45. Data refer to women who married in 1974 and 1978.
46. Data refer to ages 20 to 40 years.
47. Data refer to the Flemish population only.
48. Data refer to ages 18 to 44 years.
49. Data refer to ages under 45 years.
50. Data refer to women in their first marriage.
51. Data refer to Federal Republic of Germany.
52. Data refer to ages under 35 years.
53. Data refer to ages under 40 years.
54. Data refer to ages 15 to 39 years.
55. Data refer to all women ages 18 to 44 years.
56. Data refer to ages 16 to 49 years.
57. Data refer to ages 18 to 37 years.
58. Data refer to ages 21 to 39 years.
59. Data refer to ages 20 to 42 years.
60. Data refer to ages 16 to 40 years.
61. Data refer to ages 18 to 39 years.
62. May include women over age 50 years.
63. Estimate.
64. Contraceptive prevalence figures are based on adjusted service statistics data reported in Banister (1995) rather than from the 1992 Fertility Survey by the State Family Planning Commission.
65. Traditional includes male sterilization.
66. Data refer to all sexually active women.
67. Data refer to ages 20 to 39.
68. Data refer to ages 18 to 42.
69. Data refer to ages 18 to 34.
70. Data for 1970 and 1977 are available for Czechoslovakia.
71. Data for 1976 are available for Yugoslavia SFR.
72. Data refer to all women ages 15 to 49.
73. From Haub (1995).
74. From National Center for Health Statistics (1990).
75. Abstinence is not included here as a method of contraception.

Source: U.S. Bureau of the Census, International Data Base. Original sources are as follows:

Census Census data.
CDC Centers for Disease Control family health, contraceptive prevalence, or other health survey data.
CPS Contraceptive Prevalence Survey progam data (Westinghouse Health Systems or the Centers for Disease Control).
DHS Demographic and Health Survey data.
Lucas Lucas and Ware (1981).
Nguyen Nguyen, Knodel, Mai, and Hoang (1996).
PAPCHILD League of Arab States, Pan Arab Project for Child Development data.
PC Population Council. Data from this source usually refer to program service statistics, sometimes with an estimate for private sector contraceptive use. Such data are often unreliable unless confirmed by an independent source such as a nationwide contraceptive prevalence or fertility survey.
SPC South Pacific Commission.
SS Service statistics based on number of family planning acceptors or amount of supplies distributed and assumptions about discontinuation rates. See also PC.
Survey A nationwide survey conducted by a national government or independent organization, but not related to CPS, DHS, or WFS.
UNESCAP United Nations Economic and Social Commission for Asia and the Pacific.
USAID U.S. Agency for International Development, mission reports.
UN United Nations (1994).
WFS World Fertility Survey data.

Table A-12.
Percent of Currently Married Women Using Contraception, by Age: All Available Years

Region, country or area, and year	15 to 19 years	20 to 24 years	25 to 29 years	30 to 34 years	35 to 39 years	40 to 44 years	45 to 49 years	Source	Remarks
AFRICA									
Sub-Saharan Africa									
Benin									
1982	17.8	25.0	27.6	29.0	26.3	27.7	34.4	WFS	
Botswana									
1984	19.7	33.1	34.4	33.8	26.3	14.5	11.9	CPS	
1988	17.2	25.8	37.1	35.6	38.3	36.1	16.7	DHS	
Burkina Faso									
1993	5.9	8.1	9.5	9.9	6.0	7.6	5.3	DHS	
Burundi									
1987	4.3	9.1	9.6	10.2	7.1	8.0	6.1	DHS	
Cameroon									
1978	2.0	3.7	3.9	2.7	2.7	3.1	2.0	WFS	
1991	18.4	17.0	17.2	13.6	17.1	17.0	8.6	DHS	
Central African Republic									
1994-95	12.5	19.1	17.9	16.9	11.7	10.1	4.5	DHS	
Côte d'Ivoire									
1980-81	2.6	4.4	3.4	6.2	2.2	3.5	3.4	WFS	
1994	8.7	13.7	11.8	13.6	11.6	9.1	5.3	DHS	
Ghana									
1979-80	9.2	9.2	14.8	14.8	12.9	12.9	10.1	WFS	
1988	4.6	11.1	13.2	14.4	15.2	18.4	7.7	DHS	
1993	13.0	16.9	21.1	20.5	26.0	23.2	14.3	DHS	
Guinea									
1992	0.7	0.8	1.5	2.3	3.3	1.8	1.0	DHS	
Kenya									
1977-78	4.0	7.0	8.0	13.0	9.0	14.0	12.0	WFS	1
1984	5.6	12.2	17.6	21.2	21.3	20.1	20.0	CPS	
1989	13.0	20.1	26.1	31.5	34.2	30.6	23.7	DHS	
1993	10.2	23.7	37.6	39.9	36.4	37.3	30.6	DHS	
Lesotho									
1977	2.4	3.9	9.9	10.8	11.7	5.5	6.1	WFS	
Liberia									
1986	2.1	5.4	7.7	8.1	5.2	8.3	8.0	DHS	
Madagascar									
1992	6.5	13.8	18.0	22.3	21.7	18.5	11.3	DHS	
Malawi									
1984	10.5	6.4	10.3	7.6	9.2	8.4	4.1	Survey	
1992	7.3	12.0	14.8	16.2	16.4	13.2	6.4	DHS	
Mali									
1987	8.2	5.5	4.8	5.6	3.4	2.0	(NA)	DHS	
Mauritius									
1985	54.7	71.7	78.4	84.2	85.1	76.7	45.0	CDC	
1991	46.3	65.5	71.5	79.9	81.3	73.2	(NA)	CDC	
Namibia									
1992	20.5	30.6	32.3	29.3	32.6	23.7	24.6	DHS	
Niger									
1992	2.2	5.4	5.4	5.4	4.7	3.4	2.0	DHS	

Table A-12.
Percent of Currently Married Women Using Contraception, by Age: All Available Years—Continued

Region, country or area, and year	15 to 19 years	20 to 24 years	25 to 29 years	30 to 34 years	35 to 39 years	40 to 44 years	45 to 49 years	Source	Remarks
AFRICA—Continued									
Sub-Saharan Africa—Continued									
Nigeria									
1981-82	6.5	6.5	6.0	6.0	5.0	5.0	12.8	WFS	
1990	1.3	5.1	6.0	6.5	8.7	8.4	4.6	DHS	
Rwanda									
1983	6.1	7.2	9.2	10.0	8.4	4.5	3.2	Survey	2
1992	10.8	14.4	17.4	25.3	22.1	31.0	20.1	DHS	
Senegal									
1978	5.7	4.2	7.5	5.4	4.9	3.6	(Z)	WFS	1
1986	9.4	10.9	13.2	13.2	13.3	12.4	4.4	DHS	
1992-93	2.0	4.8	8.3	9.0	9.5	9.9	5.8	DHS	
Sudan (Northern)									
1979	5.8	4.7	8.8	7.1	5.5	6.1	2.6	WFS	
1989-90	6.8	6.8	6.8	10.3	10.3	10.3	10.3	DHS	
Swaziland									
1988	5.9	18.9	20.9	23.3	21.2	16.3	16.8	Survey	3
Tanzania									
1991-92	5.2	10.1	10.1	13.2	12.7	11.0	7.2	DHS	
1994	15.0	17.7	21.1	24.0	22.2	21.8	17.6	DHS	
Togo									
1988	16.7	33.9	34.9	39.0	37.4	37.3	26.2	DHS	
Uganda									
1988-89	1.7	2.8	4.3	5.9	8.1	8.2	7.9	DHS	
Zaire									
1991	2.8	6.4	12.6	9.1	7.5	4.3	2.1	CDC	12
Zambia									
1992	8.7	13.1	15.3	18.3	22.5	17.4	9.0	DHS	
Zimbabwe									
1984	24.9	43.6	42.3	42.8	37.1	37.6	21.2	CPS	
1988	30.0	45.8	50.3	50.5	41.7	37.2	22.8	DHS	
1994	31.4	49.9	58.0	51.8	50.0	45.0	27.7	DHS	
North Africa									
Algeria									
1992	25.3	39.3	53.4	55.7	56.6	52.9	38.8	PAPCHILD	
Egypt									
1980	5.3	17.5	31.6	39.9	41.1	43.5	39.8	WFS	1
1984	5.6	16.9	30.4	42.9	43.2	38.5	21.0	CPS	
1988	5.5	24.3	37.1	46.8	52.8	47.5	23.4	DHS	
1992	13.3	29.7	46.0	58.8	59.6	55.5	34.5	DHS	
Morocco									
1979-80	20.1	20.1	31.6	31.6	36.3	36.3	31.1	WFS	1
1983-84	18.1	18.1	29.9	29.9	28.3	28.3	17.3	CPS	
1987	17.0	25.6	36.1	42.9	42.6	41.7	30.4	DHS	
1992	23.3	35.2	39.5	45.4	47.8	47.0	35.1	DHS	
Tunisia									
1978	16.0	16.0	31.2	31.2	37.0	37.0	42.8	WFS	
1983	28.4	28.4	38.8	38.8	50.8	50.8	34.3	CPS	
1988	11.1	34.9	44.0	55.0	59.2	61.2	43.2	DHS	

Table A-12.
Percent of Currently Married Women Using Contraception, by Age: All Available Years—Continued

Region, country or area, and year	15 to 19 years	20 to 24 years	25 to 29 years	30 to 34 years	35 to 39 years	40 to 44 years	45 to 49 years	Source	Remarks
NEAR EAST									
Bahrain									
1989	29.6	44.9	59.9	60.7	57.0	51.5	40.3	Survey	
Jordan									
1976	9.0	17.0	26.0	32.0	33.0	33.0	19.0	WFS	
1983	4.0	16.8	25.1	32.9	30.4	31.7	25.5	Survey	
1990	7.7	22.3	30.0	41.9	47.3	49.3	32.8	DHS	
Kuwait									
1987	8.2	28.6	33.3	42.2	39.1	36.7	28.4	Survey	
Oman									
1987-89	2.7	4.5	10.3	11.0	13.4	7.1	6.0	Survey	
Qatar									
1987	11.0	19.3	32.2	40.2	40.3	37.8	19.3	Survey	
Syria									
1978	9.0	15.0	19.0	24.0	31.0	24.0	(NA)	WFS	
1993	11.9	33.6	35.4	47.4	52.4	47.8	31.9	PAPCHILD	
Turkey									
1963	8.9	15.3	25.9	27.9	24.1	17.5	(NA)	Survey	
1968	16.0	24.7	30.3	41.6	36.9	32.0	(NA)	Survey	
1973	16.0	28.1	43.5	45.8	44.2	31.4	(NA)	Survey	
1978	21.6	42.2	51.2	61.5	54.6	56.0	51.5	WFS	
1983	49.0	49.0	68.0	68.0	66.0	66.0	49.0	Survey	1
1988	58.4	58.4	82.2	82.2	83.9	83.9	71.8	Survey	1
1993	24.1	51.1	68.0	76.5	76.8	61.0	41.7	DHS	
Yemen									
1979	—— 1.0 ——		2.0	1.0	2.0	—— 1.0 ——		WFS	
1991-92	1.4	5.0	8.5	7.9	9.8	7.7	5.0	DHS	
ASIA									
Bangladesh									
1975-76	4.0	8.0	9.0	12.0	12.0	9.0	5.1	WFS	1
1979	5.2	11.1	13.8	17.0	17.1	15.9	9.2	CPS	
1981	9.5	17.6	23.8	25.3	23.2	23.4	12.5	CPS	
1989	15.3	25.8	36.5	41.6	42.8	39.0	22.1	Survey	
1991	18.7	32.6	45.6	52.5	57.0	46.4	29.9	Survey	
1993-94	24.7	37.6	50.6	57.2	58.5	51.9	29.3	DHS	
China									
Mainland									
1988	11.2	38.1	70.6	87.6	91.4	84.1	51.7	Survey	
Hong Kong									
1972	35.8	35.8	48.6	61.5	63.6	54.2	(NA)	Survey	
1977	56.6	56.6	72.9	83.7	87.9	80.2	(NA)	Survey	
1982	62.0	62.0	73.2	82.0	86.2	74.2	(NA)	Survey	
India									
1970	3.1	6.9	13.5	17.3	17.8	16.5	(NA)	Survey	
1980	5.7	16.0	32.0	44.7	52.1	47.0	47.0	Survey	
1988	9.0	23.0	44.0	58.0	66.0	61.0	(NA)	Survey	
1990	(NA)	19.2	43.3	57.6	65.2	59.5	(NA)	Survey	
1992-93	7.1	21.0	42.4	55.8	61.0	56.3	45.8	Survey	

Table A-12.
Percent of Currently Married Women Using Contraception, by Age: All Available Years—Continued

Region, country or area, and year	15 to 19 years	20 to 24 years	25 to 29 years	30 to 34 years	35 to 39 years	40 to 44 years	45 to 49 years	Source	Remarks
ASIA—Continued									
Indonesia									
1976	12.0	27.0	33.0	33.0	30.0	24.0	12.0	WFS	
1979	4.0	19.5	34.4	35.7	31.4	20.2	11.8	Survey	
1980	10.3	22.7	32.3	34.8	31.6	23.5	15.3	Census	
1985	15.4	34.6	45.6	48.2	45.4	33.9	21.0	Survey	
1987	25.5	47.2	54.0	58.7	55.9	42.7	24.4	DHS	
1991	30.0	51.0	53.6	56.8	57.5	48.3	27.4	DHS	
1994	36.4	55.5	59.6	61.0	59.7	53.4	32.9	DHS	
Japan									
1986	100.0	55.1	56.7	71.0	73.1	70.7	46.9	Survey	7
Malaysia									
1966-67	5.0	5.0	11.0	11.0	9.0	9.0	(NA)	Survey	
1970	11.7	11.7	19.8	19.8	14.4	14.4	(NA)	Survey	
1974	21.2	38.2	48.0	44.7	41.8	36.5	16.2	WFS	1
Nepal									
1976	0.3	1.3	2.5	5.3	5.7	3.8	5.3	WFS	
1981	(Z)	3.0	6.0	11.0	10.0	11.0	(NA)	CPS	
1986	1.3	7.2	15.5	24.6	22.3	18.3	11.5	Survey	1
1991	2.5	10.2	24.0	35.2	38.7	36.9	23.1	Survey	
Pakistan									
1975	(Z)	2.0	5.0	6.0	8.0	5.0	4.0	WFS	
1984-85	1.4	4.4	7.8	11.9	12.4	12.2	13.1	CPS	
1990-91	2.6	6.3	9.6	13.4	20.4	15.8	11.8	DHS	
Philippines									
1986	9.1	21.0	33.1	40.0	40.0	35.5	20.0	CPS	
1993	17.2	31.9	39.1	45.8	48.2	43.1	27.2	DHS	
Singapore									
1982	60.0	60.0	72.4	72.4	79.0	79.0	(NA)	Survey	
South Korea									
1971	7.0		15.0	28.0	38.0	27.0	(NA)	Survey	
1974	13.0		29.0	45.0	54.0	38.0	(NA)	WFS	
1976	15.4		31.9	55.8	61.5	45.1	(NA)	Survey	
1978	16.1		38.0	62.0	66.3	46.9	(NA)	Survey	
1979	18.3		40.9	68.5	71.9	53.3	(NA)	CPS	
1988	45.0		65.0	87.0	90.0	82.0	(NA)	Survey	
Sri Lanka									
1975	14.0	19.0	30.0	43.0	41.0	35.0	20.0	WFS	
1982	27.7	41.3	51.6	63.8	70.8	64.7	35.8	CPS	
1987	20.2	42.3	57.3	66.8	73.8	71.5	56.1	DHS	
Thailand									
1970	3.8	11.0	14.4	22.0	18.0	13.1	(NA)	Survey	
1973	6.0	20.1	28.6	31.4	35.6	19.4	(NA)	Survey	
1975	18.1	30.9	41.0	44.0	42.3	30.5	(NA)	WFS	
1978	31.3	44.2	54.4	61.1	62.8	49.5	(NA)	CPS	
1981	29.0	47.5	60.4	67.7	68.6	56.4	(NA)	CPS	
1984	39.5	54.4	63.4	71.9	73.8	64.2	(NA)	CPS	
1985	32.0	48.5	59.7	73.5	69.4	64.5	37.7	Survey	
1987	43.0	56.8	69.1	75.0	73.3	69.4	48.4	DHS	
Vietnam									
1988	5.3	31.7	52.2	59.8	68.8	65.4	47.1	Survey	

For South Korea, the 15 to 19 and 20 to 24 years columns share one printed value, which is placed in the 15 to 19 years column.

Table A-12.
Percent of Currently Married Women Using Contraception, by Age: All Available Years—Continued

Region, country or area, and year	15 to 19 years	20 to 24 years	25 to 29 years	30 to 34 years	35 to 39 years	40 to 44 years	45 to 49 years	Source	Remarks
LATIN AMERICA AND THE CARIBBEAN									
Antigua and Barbuda									
1981	12.2	38.1	46.9	45.9	58.9	57.9	(NA)	CPS	
Bahamas, The									
1988	40.7	63.4	68.8	64.4	—— 78.1 ——		(NA)	Survey	
Barbados									
1980-81	27.7	45.3	53.6	58.6	65.1	33.6	(NA)	CPS	
Belize									
1991	26.2	36.9	45.6	53.6	54.8	56.3	(NA)	CDC	
Bolivia									
1983	11.5	22.4	27.0	23.6	25.7	20.5	12.2	CPS	
1989	16.0	22.6	34.3	39.2	36.2	28.1	14.8	DHS	
1994	30.2	39.2	51.0	53.8	50.0	46.3	24.8	DHS	
Brazil									
1986	47.6	54.1	67.9	73.8	68.9	66.5	(NA)	DHS	
Colombia									
1978	21.4	41.9	50.6	54.9	54.6	49.3	28.4	CPS	
1980	24.7	44.2	53.7	60.9	60.6	44.5	28.5	CPS	
1986	29.4	56.8	68.9	73.7	75.8	70.4	47.6	DHS	
1990	36.9	54.6	66.5	74.7	76.9	74.3	54.0	DHS	
Costa Rica									
1976	(NA)	63.6	69.6	72.5	75.4	70.3	51.1	WFS	
1981	45.6	58.2	64.8	71.6	74.9	69.9	56.2	CPS	
1986	51.0	60.0	65.0	67.0	84.0	78.0	68.0	Survey	
1993	53.0	66.0	76.0	79.0	82.0	80.0	65.0	Survey	
Dominica									
1981	32.6	42.1	54.1	54.5	69.0	69.8	(NA)	CPS	
Dominican Republic									
1986	25.2	37.8	51.3	60.7	64.9	54.8	42.1	DHS	
1991	17.4	42.5	55.0	66.2	71.3	69.0	55.0	DHS	
Ecuador									
1979	14.0	37.0	37.0	37.0	37.0	37.0	37.0	WFS	
1982	20.1	42.2	42.2	42.2	40.1	40.1	40.1	DHS	
1987	15.3	34.3	46.4	53.4	54.5	51.1	29.7	DHS	
1989	25.0	39.1	55.2	63.0	61.3	58.6	44.8	Survey	
1994	27.1	49.3	60.6	65.4	66.1	59.3	49.1	CDC	
El Salvador									
1975	10.9	15.0	26.9	36.9	21.7	9.4	(NA)	Survey	
1978	8.3	33.3	43.7	38.3	40.6	29.0	(NA)	CPS	
1985	21.7	35.3	53.7	63.0	56.8	51.6	35.7	DHS	
1988	17.1	36.6	51.1	57.3	59.4	53.2	(NA)	Survey	
1993	22.5	40.0	57.8	66.4	66.6	55.5	(NA)	Survey	
Grenada									
1985	17.2	34.9	40.6	49.1	51.8	51.8	(NA)	CPS	4
Guatemala									
1978	4.8	12.7	20.9	23.5	27.7	14.5	13.4	CPS	
1983	9.3	15.8	29.6	32.3	31.3	28.4	(NA)	Survey	
1987	5.4	15.5	21.3	30.2	31.1	28.0	(NA)	DHS	
Guyana									
1975	17.5	24.5	33.2	43.3	39.6	32.6	(NA)	WFS	

Table A-12.
Percent of Currently Married Women Using Contraception, by Age: All Available Years—Continued

Region, country or area, and year	15 to 19 years	20 to 24 years	25 to 29 years	30 to 34 years	35 to 39 years	40 to 44 years	45 to 49 years	Source	Remarks
LATIN AMERICA AND THE CARIBBEAN—Continued									
Haiti									
1977	——15.3——		——20.1——		——20.2——		17.5	WFS	
1987	1.6	5.0	——7.5——		——8.3——			Survey	2
1989	5.1	5.1	7.1	16.0	13.8	10.6	6.5	CPS	
1994	10.7	15.5	19.8	22.4	19.7	17.6	11.9	DHS	
Honduras									
1981	8.4	22.7	30.7	33.1	31.7	29.4	23.0	CPS	
1984	13.1	30.3	33.8	44.3	45.2	33.2	(NA)	Survey	
Jamaica									
1975-76	30.6	39.2	43.2	50.6	43.4	32.5	(NA)	WFS	
1989	47.9	52.5	56.8	58.3	59.0	57.3	42.8	CPS	
1993	58.8	61.1	60.3	64.8	63.1	64.0	(NA)	CDC	
Mexico									
1976	14.0	27.0	39.0	38.0	38.0	25.0	11.0	WFS	
1978	5.2	27.7	36.9	46.4	38.2	29.3	12.4	CPS	
1979	19.0	37.0	45.0	50.0	43.0	33.0	16.0	CPS	
1982	24.2	50.0	56.5	63.1	58.7	43.4	21.4	Survey	
1987	30.2	46.9	54.0	62.3	61.3	60.2	34.2	DHS	
Montserrat									
1984	49.8	47.0	66.0	54.9	——46.7——		(NA)	CPS	
Nicaragua									
1992-93	23.2	41.6	53.2	58.2	60.5	55.5	38.9	CDC	
Panama									
1984	22.6	42.8	57.2	65.2	73.8	72.1	(NA)	Survey	
Paraguay									
1979	26.9	49.9	54.4	50.4	50.6	45.8	31.4	WFS	1
1987	31.1	45.6	49.0	46.3	45.4	39.7	(NA)	CDC	
1990	35.4	41.5	52.4	53.8	54.9	50.1	34.5	DHS	
Peru									
1977-78	23.7	38.4	45.6	49.7	41.6	39.1	30.9	WFS	
1981	34.0	51.0	51.0	59.0	59.0	55.0	55.0	CPS	1
1986	22.9	39.4	50.4	55.3	53.5	47.4	24.9	DHS	
1991-92	29.1	49.1	59.5	67.3	69.9	63.8	42.7	DHS	
Saint Kitts and Nevis									
1984	30.4	41.0	43.8	42.2	42.2	50.9	(NA)	CPS	3
Saint Lucia									
1981	26.5	37.1	55.4	46.4	57.8	55.0	(NA)	CPS	
Saint Vincent and the Grenadines									
1981	21.4	36.1	46.8	68.5	51.8	65.5	(NA)	CPS	
Trinidad and Tobago									
1977	42.9	52.1	58.7	60.7	55.0	44.0	(NA)	WFS	
1987	42.4	55.3	53.8	57.1	55.8	52.9	36.3	DHS	
Venezuela									
1977	54.4	54.4	65.0	65.0	59.4	59.4	(NA)	WFS	

Table A-12.
Percent of Currently Married Women Using Contraception, by Age: All Available Years—Continued

Region, country or area, and year	15 to 19 years	20 to 24 years	25 to 29 years	30 to 34 years	35 to 39 years	40 to 44 years	45 to 49 years	Source	Remarks
EUROPE AND THE NEW INDEPENDENT STATES									
Western Europe									
France									
1978	(NA)	66.8	79.5	82.5	83.8	77.4	(NA)	WFS	
1988	50.0	63.9	72.3	84.3	87.1	84.4	73.4	Survey	6
1994	(NA)	83.8	71.2	73.6	82.4	78.9	63.1	Survey	
Italy									
1979	81.0	81.0	78.0	78.0	78.0	78.0	(NA)	WFS	
Netherlands									
1993	(NA)	81.0	75.0	71.0	(NA)	(NA)	(NA)	Survey	
Norway									
1977	87.0	84.0	83.0	88.0	85.0	78.0	(NA)	WFS	
Portugal									
1979-80	76.8	72.6	77.2	81.2	77.5	76.0	69.4	WFS	
Spain									
1977	—— 58.8 ——		62.0	61.2	55.1	43.5	27.9	WFS	
1985	44.8	63.9	64.8	68.0	62.5	53.1	34.2	Survey	6
Sweden									
1981	(NA)	77.2	73.0	78.0	80.5	80.5	(NA)	WFS	
United Kingdom									
1983	66.0	72.0	82.0	85.0	88.0	85.0	(NA)	Survey	6
Eastern Europe									
Czech Republic									
1993	51.0	59.6	72.8	78.3	71.2	65.4	(NA)	Survey	
Hungary									
1977	68.1	75.8	83.4	81.2	75.6	(NA)	(NA)	WFS	
1986	58.6	57.7	74.7	76.7	76.7	(NA)	(NA)	Survey	
Romania									
1993	39.9	52.8	65.9	69.3	57.3	44.4	(NA)	CDC	
New Independent States									
Russia									
1994	(NA)	60.8	73.3	75.3	74.2	61.6	44.8	Survey	
NORTH AMERICA									
Canada									
1984	(NA)	61.3	68.2	75.4	81.4	78.0	68.1	Survey	5
United States									
1965	63.1	63.1	63.1	63.3	63.3	63.3	(NA)	Survey	
1973	70.2	70.2	70.2	69.1	69.1	69.1	(NA)	Survey	
1976	69.4	68.1	69.4	72.5	66.5	59.5	(NA)	Survey	
1982	53.1	66.6	68.9	70.3	66.9	67.8	(NA)	Survey	
1988	58.9	72.2	70.9	74.1	79.8	74.1	(NA)	Survey	
1990	55.6	60.5	64.4	70.2	77.9	75.5	(NA)	Survey	
OCEANIA									
Fiji									
1974	21.0	32.3	40.7	49.5	50.0	44.9	27.8	WFS	

Table A-12.
Percent of Currently Married Women Using Contraception, by Age: All Available Years—Continued

(NA) Data not available.
(Z) Less than 0.05 percent.

Note: Data usually refer to currently married women (and women in consensual and visiting unions). Exceptions are noted in table A-11 or in the remarks below for situations that differ from table A-11. Countries with no data available by age are omitted from table A-12.

Remarks:

1. Data refer to women exposed to the risk of pregnancy (currently married nonpregnant women who consider themselves to be fecund).
2. Rates by age refer to nonsingle women.
3. Rates by age refer to all women regardless of marital status.
4. Base for rates by age excludes pregnant women.
5. Rate shown for ages 20 to 24 years refers to ages 18 to 24 years.
6. Rate shown for ages 15 to 19 years refers to ages 18 to 19 years.
7. Estimate for 15 to 19 years based on one case.

Source: U.S. Bureau of the Census, International Data Base. See table A-11 for notes on primary data sources.

Table A-13.
Fertility of Women Ages 15 to 19 Years by Region and Country: 1996 and 2020

[Population in thousands. Figures may not add to totals because of rounding]

Region and country or area	Women ages 15 to 19 (in thousands)		Births per 1,000 women		Births (in thousands)	
	1996	2020	1996	2020	1996	2020
WORLD	255,511	297,802	59	46	15,013	13,664
Less Developed Countries	216,403	260,617	63	47	13,652	12,153
More Developed Countries	39,107	37,185	35	41	1,362	1,510
AFRICA	39,148	66,126	122	79	4,787	5,213
Sub-Saharan Africa	31,837	57,055	138	85	4,401	4,843
Angola	514	1,037	118	75	60	78
Benin	310	663	142	92	44	61
Botswana	89	96	80	43	7	4
Burkina Faso	578	1,045	143	84	83	88
Burundi	307	580	58	76	18	44
Cameroon	767	1,482	193	113	148	168
Cape Verde	23	45	61	44	1	2
Central African Republic	175	280	155	90	27	25
Chad	356	689	213	129	76	89
Comoros	30	69	134	82	4	6
Congo	141	216	114	64	16	14
Côte d'Ivoire	797	1,451	161	90	128	131
Djibouti	22	40	199	112	4	5
Equatorial Guinea	22	41	159	95	3	4
Eritrea	226	436	107	74	24	32
Ethiopia	2,981	5,811	116	80	346	465
Gabon	55	79	152	87	8	7
Gambia, The	55	113	190	113	10	13
Ghana	886	1,259	97	41	86	51
Guinea	383	622	154	66	59	41
Guinea-Bissau	62	99	95	56	6	6
Kenya	1,691	1,909	89	38	150	72
Lesotho	109	142	64	42	7	6
Liberia	105	313	170	102	18	32
Madagascar	712	1,365	149	96	106	131
Malawi	536	690	139	59	74	41
Mali	523	1,128	240	152	125	172
Mauritania	126	273	163	96	21	26
Mauritius	57	51	47	41	3	2
Mayotte	5	13	256	139	1	2
Mozambique	961	1,710	124	56	119	95
Namibia	91	169	103	70	9	12
Niger	465	974	209	129	97	126
Nigeria	5,408	11,301	173	100	936	1,133
Reunion	28	37	50	41	1	2
Rwanda	423	682	59	50	25	34
Sao Tome and Principe	8	11	85	45	1	1
Senegal	474	1,062	151	96	72	102
Seychelles	4	3	38	30	(Z)	(Z)
Sierra Leone	245	540	170	102	42	55
Somalia	476	1,005	58	74	28	75
South Africa	2,122	2,523	97	47	207	119
Sudan	1,627	3,088	101	57	164	177
Swaziland	56	114	67	63	4	7
Tanzania	1,700	2,501	129	72	218	180

Table A-13.
Fertility of Women Ages 15 to 19 Years by Region and Country: 1996 and 2020—Continued

[Population in thousands. Figures may not add to totals because of rounding]

Region and country or area	Women ages 15 to 19 (in thousands)		Births per 1,000 women		Births (in thousands)	
	1996	2020	1996	2020	1996	2020
AFRICA—Continued						
Sub-Saharan Africa—Continued						
Togo	241	551	149	94	36	52
Uganda	1,071	1,924	168	92	179	176
Zaire	2,536	5,296	171	108	434	574
Zambia	540	844	158	98	85	82
Zimbabwe	717	681	108	38	77	26
North Africa	7,311	9,071	53	41	386	370
Algeria	1,658	1,983	45	35	74	70
Egypt	3,313	4,015	58	39	191	155
Libya	271	655	141	94	38	62
Morocco	1,606	1,910	42	35	67	67
Tunisia	463	508	33	34	15	17
NEAR EAST	7,941	12,827	70	55	553	701
Bahrain	22	33	24	31	1	1
Cyprus	27	29	25	29	1	1
Gaza Strip	46	138	183	91	8	13
Iraq	1,168	2,475	98	68	115	168
Israel	230	265	19	17	4	5
Jordan	224	375	50	38	11	14
Kuwait	85	120	35	34	3	4
Lebanon	227	266	44	36	10	10
Oman	114	246	107	70	12	17
Qatar	19	24	50	35	1	1
Saudi Arabia	822	2,107	105	86	86	181
Syria	836	1,513	54	38	45	57
Turkey	3,209	3,221	52	35	168	112
United Arab Emirates	104	247	79	49	8	12
West Bank	87	152	106	50	9	8
Yemen	717	1,617	98	61	70	99
ASIA	144,719	154,845	46	33	6,681	5,131
Afghanistan	1,163	2,225	99	67	115	150
Bangladesh	6,880	7,484	145	87	999	649
Bhutan	83	146	86	62	7	9
Brunei	14	20	38	37	1	1
Burma	2,297	3,070	52	41	120	126
Cambodia	450	1,032	71	55	32	57
China	46,576	41,770	17	17	805	702
Mainland	45,603	41,004	17	17	789	689
Taiwan	973	766	17	17	17	13
Hong Kong	221	211	6	7	1	1
India	45,027	51,625	57	36	2,567	1,879
Indonesia	11,157	11,200	56	38	625	421
Iran	3,388	4,732	90	37	306	174
Japan	4,016	3,263	4	4	14	12
Laos	261	476	103	54	27	26
Macau	17	15	7	8	(Z)	(Z)
Malaysia	903	1,237	23	17	20	21
Maldives	12	29	119	56	1	2

Table A-13.
Fertility of Women Ages 15 to 19 Years by Region and Country: 1996 and 2020—Continued

[Population in thousands. Figures may not add to totals because of rounding]

Region and country or area	Women ages 15 to 19 (in thousands)		Births per 1,000 women		Births (in thousands)	
	1996	2020	1996	2020	1996	2020
ASIA—Continued						
Mongolia	136	126	27	18	4	2
Nepal	1,188	1,934	99	58	117	111
North Korea	958	1,124	9	7	8	8
Pakistan	6,492	9,449	66	38	430	363
Philippines	3,973	5,180	47	38	187	197
Singapore	105	130	9	9	1	1
South Korea	1,886	1,679	3	3	6	5
Sri Lanka	894	779	31	30	28	23
Thailand	2,867	2,310	44	41	126	94
Vietnam	3,754	3,599	36	27	134	95
LATIN AMERICA AND THE CARIBBEAN	24,925	25,532	59	37	1,474	957
Anguilla	(Z)	(Z)	14	23	(Z)	(Z)
Antigua and Barbuda	3	2	65	66	(Z)	(Z)
Argentina	1,603	1,658	55	39	89	64
Aruba	2	2	41	40	(Z)	(Z)
Bahamas, The	12	11	51	46	1	(Z)
Barbados	10	9	60	59	1	1
Belize	12	17	102	43	1	1
Bolivia	383	480	83	42	32	20
Brazil	8,462	7,345	44	31	369	224
Chile	621	577	60	46	37	27
Colombia	1,723	1,765	51	32	88	56
Costa Rica	160	200	78	59	12	12
Cuba	338	358	82	87	28	31
Dominica	4	3	50	46	(Z)	(Z)
Dominican Republic	406	423	71	35	29	15
Ecuador	629	672	60	36	38	24
El Salvador	370	381	103	75	38	28
French Guiana	6	10	99	77	1	1
Grenada	5	6	102	53	1	(Z)
Guadeloupe	17	16	31	27	1	(Z)
Guatemala	617	879	99	46	61	40
Guyana	42	27	40	30	2	1
Haiti	343	531	79	45	27	24
Honduras	316	434	92	41	29	18
Jamaica	125	118	63	31	8	4
Martinique	15	16	14	13	(Z)	(Z)
Mexico	5,211	5,848	67	40	347	232
Netherlands Antilles	8	7	41	38	(Z)	(Z)
Nicaragua	249	336	149	47	37	16
Panama	130	143	74	41	10	6
Paraguay	278	437	80	45	22	20
Peru	1,297	1,291	47	28	61	37
Puerto Rico	167	131	51	33	9	4
Saint Kitts and Nevis	2	2	70	40	(Z)	(Z)
Saint Lucia	9	7	56	30	(Z)	(Z)
Saint Vincent and the Grenadines	6	5	49	30	(Z)	(Z)
Suriname	20	23	47	34	1	1
Trinidad and Tobago	63	46	37	30	2	1
Uruguay	136	134	50	39	7	5
Venezuela	1,126	1,181	77	36	87	42

Table A-13.
Fertility of Women Ages 15 to 19 Years by Region and Country: 1996 and 2020—Continued

[Population in thousands. Figures may not add to totals because of rounding]

Region and country or area	Women ages 15 to 19 (in thousands)		Births per 1,000 women		Births (in thousands)	
	1996	2020	1996	2020	1996	2020
EUROPE AND THE NEW INDEPENDENT STATES	27,859	25,744	32	35	905	907
Western Europe	11,703	10,189	16	17	189	168
Andorra	2	2	19	18	(Z)	(Z)
Austria	224	204	22	24	5	5
Belgium	301	249	12	12	4	3
Denmark	150	145	10	10	1	1
Faroe Islands	2	2	24	18	(Z)	(Z)
Finland	159	142	12	12	2	2
France	1,880	1,704	13	14	24	25
Germany	2,164	2,225	12	15	26	33
Gibraltar	1	1	13	10	(Z)	(Z)
Greece	371	275	24	26	9	7
Guernsey	2	2	21	21	(Z)	(Z)
Iceland	10	9	26	23	(Z)	(Z)
Ireland	165	121	14	13	2	2
Isle of Man	2	3	32	31	(Z)	(Z)
Italy	1,659	1,504	9	10	14	15
Jersey	2	2	12	13	(Z)	(Z)
Liechtenstein	1	1	4	4	(Z)	(Z)
Luxembourg	11	11	12	12	(Z)	(Z)
Malta	14	12	11	10	(Z)	(Z)
Monaco	1	1	9	9	(Z)	(Z)
Netherlands	445	409	6	6	3	2
Norway	128	109	16	15	2	2
Portugal	373	282	20	22	7	6
San Marino	1	1	10	10	(Z)	(Z)
Spain	1,487	680	29	34	44	23
Sweden	244	257	13	12	3	3
Switzerland	192	196	7	7	1	1
United Kingdom	1,711	1,641	24	23	41	38
Eastern Europe	4,800	3,959	32	36	156	141
Albania	159	157	14	10	2	1
Bosnia and Herzegovina	108	89	22	34	2	3
Bulgaria	302	267	54	72	16	19
Croatia	171	137	24	27	4	4
Czech Republic	405	317	36	42	15	13
Hungary	380	294	31	33	12	10
Macedonia, The Former Yugoslav Republic of	82	77	37	34	3	3
Montenegro	25	20	22	23	1	(Z)
Poland	1,586	1,338	25	25	40	33
Romania	909	672	41	51	37	34
Serbia	369	339	40	33	15	11
Slovakia	231	201	36	37	8	7
Slovenia	72	52	17	23	1	1

Table A-13.
Fertility of Women Ages 15 to 19 Years by Region and Country: 1996 and 2020—Continued

[Population in thousands. Figures may not add to totals because of rounding]

Region and country or area	Women ages 15 to 19 (in thousands)		Births per 1,000 women		Births (in thousands)	
	1996	2020	1996	2020	1996	2020
EUROPE AND THE NEW INDEPENDENT STATES—Continued						
New Independent States	11,356	11,595	49	52	560	598
Baltics	259	239	45	47	12	11
Estonia	51	47	46	53	2	2
Latvia	80	72	45	49	4	4
Lithuania	127	120	45	45	6	5
Commonwealth of Independent States	11,097	11,356	49	52	549	587
Armenia	146	137	81	75	12	10
Azerbaijan	334	341	29	22	10	7
Belarus	374	366	46	47	17	17
Georgia	199	192	47	52	9	10
Kazakstan	765	685	48	42	37	29
Kyrgyzstan	221	274	59	47	13	13
Moldova	184	197	62	53	11	10
Russia	5,436	5,149	50	61	272	316
Tajikistan	296	489	44	34	13	17
Turkmenistan	209	283	23	18	5	5
Ukraine	1,772	1,586	59	63	104	101
Uzbekistan	1,163	1,658	40	31	46	51
NORTH AMERICA	9,827	11,476	58	62	570	714
Canada	936	969	25	25	24	24
Greenland	2	2	62	51	(Z)	(Z)
United States	8,889	10,505	61	66	546	690
OCEANIA	1,092	1,251	40	33	44	41
Australia	612	630	23	26	14	16
Fiji	42	44	60	49	3	2
French Polynesia	11	15	75	50	1	1
Marshall Islands	3	8	151	109	(Z)	1
New Caledonia	9	10	42	35	(Z)	(Z)
New Zealand	124	129	30	26	4	3
Papua New Guinea	247	348	77	43	19	15
Solomon Islands	23	40	92	43	2	2
Tuvalu	(Z)	1	28	24	(Z)	(Z)
Vanuatu	10	12	63	37	1	(Z)
Western Samoa	10	16	56	39	1	1

(Z) Less than 500.

Note: Regional rates are weighted means of country rates. Countries lacking data for a specific year are excluded from the calculation of a regional rate for that year.

Source: U.S. Bureau of the Census, International Data Base.

Table A-14.
Percent Change in Fertility for Women Ages 15 to 19 Years and 20 to 34 Years for Selected Countries

Country	Year of survey	Annual births per 1,000 women ages 15 to 19 years: Mid-80's to early 90's	Annual births per 1,000 women ages 15 to 19 years: Mid-70's to early 80's	Average number of births by age 20: Mid-80's to early 90's	Average number of births by age 20: Mid-70's to early 80's	Percent change for women 15 to 19 adjusted to 10 years	Additional births by age 35: Mid-80's to early 90's	Additional births by age 35: Mid-70's to early 80's	Percent change for women 20 to 34 adjusted to 10 years
SUB-SAHARAN AFRICA									
Botswana	1988	125	167	0.6	0.8	–25	3.0	4.0	–24
Burkina Faso	1993	154	184	0.8	0.9	–16	4.2	4.8	–12
Burundi	1987	52	90	0.3	0.5	–42	4.4	4.6	–3
Cameroon	1991	174	207	0.9	1.0	–20	3.9	4.1	–7
Ghana	1993 and 1988	119	141	0.6	0.7	–12	3.5	4.2	–13
Kenya	1993	118	166	0.6	0.8	–36	3.6	4.7	–29
Liberia	1986	184	173	0.9	0.9	6	3.9	3.9	1
Madagascar	1992	156	169	0.8	0.8	–10	3.8	4.3	–13
Malawi	1992	159	193	0.8	1.0	–22	4.0	4.6	–17
Mali	1987	201	199	1.0	1.0	1	4.2	4.6	–8
Mauritius	1991 and 1985	36	25	0.2	0.1	88	1.9	1.5	49
Namibia	1992	101	107	0.5	0.5	–6	3.2	3.7	–14
Niger	1992	219	253	1.1	1.3	–13	4.5	5.1	–12
Nigeria	1990	144	166	0.7	0.8	–17	3.8	4.7	–22
Rwanda	1992	56	76	0.3	0.4	–33	4.0	5.1	–26
Senegal	1992-93	132	174	0.7	0.9	–30	3.8	4.5	–17
Sudan (Northern)	1989-90	69	134	0.3	0.7	–49	3.3	4.7	–30
Tanzania	1991-92	139	158	0.7	0.8	–15	3.9	4.3	–12
Togo	1988	127	170	0.6	0.9	–25	4.0	4.5	–12
Uganda	1988-89	187	222	0.9	1.1	–16	4.6	4.8	–5
Zambia	1992	152	200	0.8	1.0	–24	3.9	4.6	–14
Zimbabwe	1988	109	165	0.5	0.8	–34	3.7	4.4	–15
ASIA, THE NEAR EAST AND NORTH AFRICA									
Bangladesh	1993-94 and 1975	140	219	0.7	1.1	–18	2.3	3.9	–21
Egypt	1992	69	124	0.3	0.6	–44	3.1	4.1	–24
India (Uttar Pradesh)	1992-93	65	133	0.3	0.7	–51	2.9	3.8	–25
Indonesia	1991	70	129	0.4	0.6	–57	2.2	3.2	–39
Jordan	1990	52	131	0.3	0.7	–60	4.1	5.5	–26
Morocco	1992	43	74	0.2	0.4	–52	2.6	3.8	–40
Pakistan	1990-91	84	139	0.4	0.7	–33	3.6	4.7	–18
Philippines	1993	52	70	0.3	0.4	–26	2.9	3.6	–19
Sri Lanka	1987	38	44	0.2	0.2	–14	2.2	2.8	–24
Thailand	1987	52	72	0.3	0.4	–28	1.7	2.9	–42
Tunisia	1988	30	46	0.2	0.2	–35	3.2	4.0	–19
Turkey	1993	57	121	0.3	0.6	–53	2.0	3.3	–39
Yemen	1991-92	104	198	0.5	1.0	–59	4.4	5.9	–31
LATIN AMERICA AND THE CARIBBEAN									
Belize	1991	137	(NA)	0.7	(NA)	(NA)	3.0	(NA)	(NA)
Bolivia	1994	96	122	0.5	0.6	–21	3.4	3.9	–15
Brazil	1986	81	86	0.4	0.4	–7	2.7	4.4	–47
Colombia	1990	73	91	0.4	0.5	–20	2.0	2.9	–28
Costa Rica	1993	82	95	0.4	0.5	–34	2.1	2.3	–19

Table A-14.
Percent Change in Fertility for Women Ages 15 to 19 Years and 20 to 34 Years for Selected Countries—Continued

Country	Year of survey	Annual births per 1,000 women ages 15 to 19 years: Mid-80's to early 90's	Annual births per 1,000 women ages 15 to 19 years: Mid-70's to early 80's	Average number of births by age 20: Mid-80's to early 90's	Average number of births by age 20: Mid-70's to early 80's	Percent change for women 15 to 19 adjusted to 10 years	Additional births by age 35: Mid-80's to early 90's	Additional births by age 35: Mid-70's to early 80's	Percent change for women 20 to 34 adjusted to 10 years
LATIN AMERICA AND THE CARIBBEAN— Continued									
Dominican Republic . . .	1991	91	126	0.5	0.6	–28	2.4	3.0	–20
Ecuador.	1987	88	101	0.4	0.5	–26	2.9	3.1	–16
El Salvador	1993	124	124	0.6	0.6	0	2.6	2.7	–7
Guatemala	1987	139	167	0.7	0.8	–17	3.8	4.3	–13
Haiti	1989 and 1977	103	57	0.5	0.3	58	3.5	3.9	–8
Jamaica.	1993 and 1975-76	100	147	0.5	0.7	–18	1.9	3.3	–24
Mexico	1987	84	132	0.4	0.7	–45	2.7	3.3	–21
Nicaragua	1992-93	158	175	0.8	0.9	–10	2.7	3.3	–17
Paraguay.	1990	98	93	0.5	0.5	5	3.1	3.4	–7
Peru	1991-92	68	96	0.3	0.5	–29	2.6	3.5	–25
Trinidad and Tobago. . .	1987	84	94	0.4	0.5	–11	2.3	2.6	–10

(NA) Data not available.

Note: Columns for average number of births by age 20 and additional births by age 35 are based on the reported age-specific fertility rates for ages 15 to 19 and 20 to 34, respectively, taken from birth history data from the most recent available survey, or from surveys conducted in two time periods. Percentage change columns are changes in implied births standardized to a common 10-year inter-survey interval.

Source: U.S. Bureau of the Census (1996b). Data are from World Fertility Surveys, Demographic and Health Surveys, and surveys conducted by the U.S. Centers for Disease Control.

Appendix B
Population Projections and Availability of Data

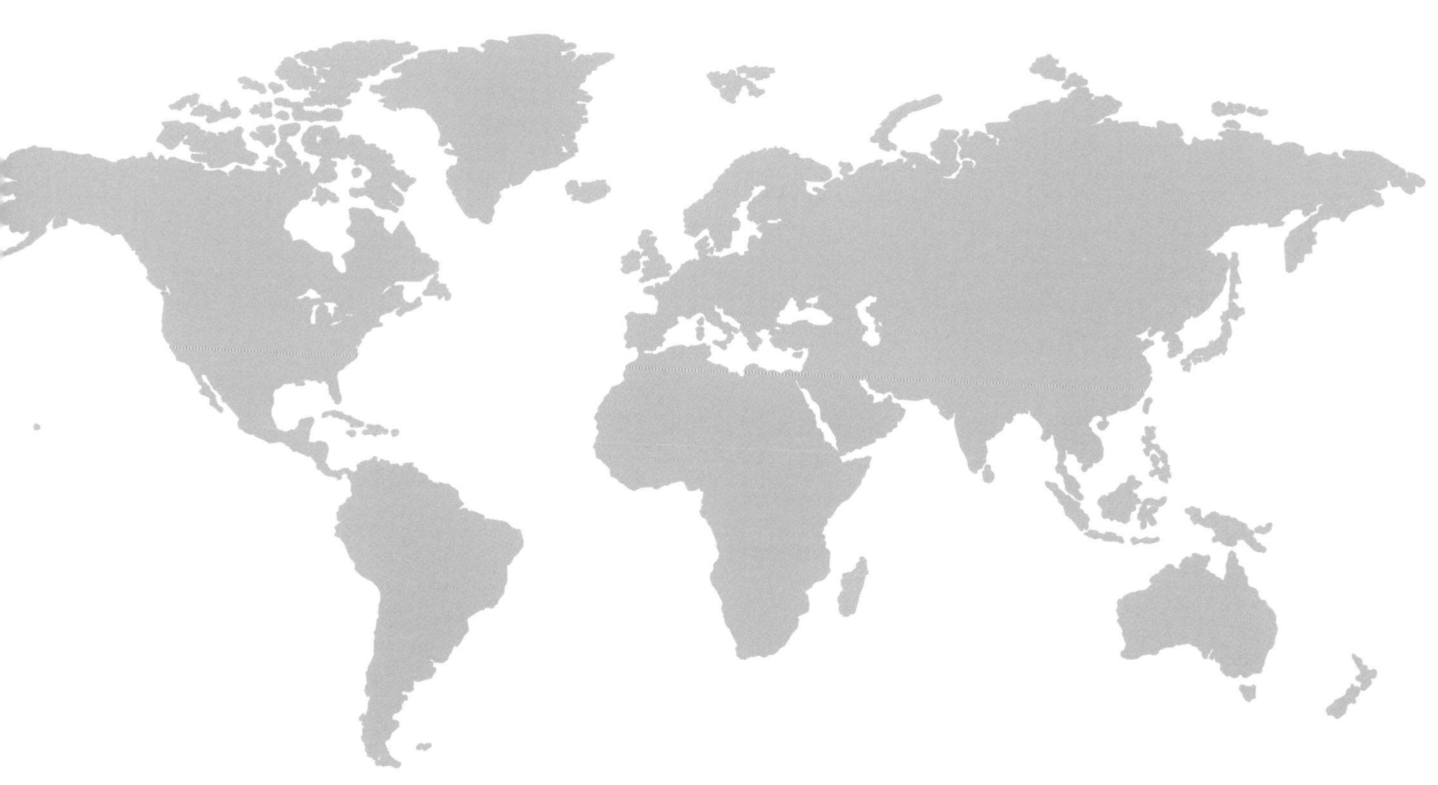

Appendix B
Population Projections and Availability of Data

Making Population Projections

While actually making a population projection is a routine application of a computer program, the complexity of the undertaking lies in the derivation of the input data. Gathering the base data, ensuring that they are of adequate quality, adjusting them as necessary using demographic techniques, and assessing their comparability among countries are all activities that ensure the success of the projection process. Once the base estimates are derived, the researcher also must make reasonable and consistent assumptions about the future course of fertility, mortality, and international migration. Regional and world populations are obtained by first projecting each country population separately and then combining the results to derive aggregated totals. This section (adapted from Arriaga and Associates 1995) briefly summarizes the process of preparing population projections by the cohort component method.

The Cohort Component Method

The cohort component population projection method follows each cohort of people of the same age throughout its lifetime according to its exposure to mortality, fertility, and migration. Starting with a base population by sex and age, the population at each specific age is exposed to the chances of dying as determined by projected mortality levels and patterns by sex and age. Once deaths are estimated, they are subtracted from the population, and those surviving become older. Fertility rates are projected and applied to the female population in childbearing ages to estimate the number of births every year. Each cohort of children born is also followed through time by exposing it to mortality. Finally, the component method takes into account any in-migrants who are incorporated into the population and out-migrants who leave the population. Migrants are added to or subtracted from the population at each specific age. The whole procedure is repeated for each year of the projection period, resulting in the projected population by age and sex, as well as birth and death rates, rates of natural increase, rates of population growth, and other summary measures of fertility, mortality, and migration for each year.

Base Data on Population

For many developed countries, base data on population are taken from population registers or are current official estimates prepared by national statistical offices based on a census for an earlier year. For developing countries, the base population for a projection is taken from the latest census, generally since 1980. However, census enumerations are not perfect, and reported data on a population age and sex structure may be affected by age misreporting and by underenumeration of persons in certain ages. If the projection starts with errors in the base year, such errors will be carried throughout the projection period and will have an impact on the projected number of births as well.

Consequently, before being accepted to serve as a base for the projections, a population must be evaluated to detect errors and adjusted as necessary to correct them. Various methods have been developed to detect age misreporting, including analysis of digit preference, age ratios, and sex ratios. Techniques have been developed for making any needed corrections. Depending on the country-specific data problems, slight smoothing or strong smoothing techniques may be recommended. The base population age and sex structures for most developing countries in this report are at least slightly smoothed for the population ages 10 years and over.

Special attention is given to possible underenumeration of the youngest age groups, 0 to 4 years and 5 to 9 years, because errors in these ages may have a significant impact on the total projection. Suppose, for example, that children ages 0 to 4 years were undercounted in the base population. In the projection, not only would the surviving cohorts of these children be smaller than they should be, but when the female cohorts reached reproductive ages, the number of births they had would also be underestimated. The completeness of enumeration of these youngest age groups is evaluated by checking for consistency between the number counted and the estimated levels of fertility and mortality during the 10-year period prior to the census date, as children of these ages represent the survivors of births during that period.

Base Data on Mortality

When vital registration data are available and complete (which is usually the case only in developed countries), it is easy to construct life tables using microcomputer programs, and to thereby derive both a level and an age pattern of mortality suitable for the projection process. For most developing countries, however, it is necessary to estimate mortality some other way. Various techniques have been developed to evaluate and correct information on deaths by sex and age in relation to information on population. Data on deaths may be provided not only in vital statistics registers, but also in surveys or censuses that include questions concerning deaths during a specific period of time; for example, deaths of any household members during the past year. If registered deaths can be evaluated and adjusted for errors, they can be used to obtain valuable information about the level and pattern of mortality.

There are several techniques[7] for estimating underregistration of deaths. Some of them are based on the assumption that the population is "stable." A stable population is one in which there has been no migration, and neither fertility nor mortality has changed in the past. Other techniques, developed more recently, do not require the assumption of stability. Some methods[8] may be applied to estimate mortality during the first years of life. They are based on data on children ever born and children surviving, by age of mother.

Like mortality in infancy and childhood, mortality in adult ages can be estimated indirectly when reliable data are not available to measure it directly. Two principal techniques have been developed to estimate adult mortality based on information collected in censuses or surveys. They are the orphanhood technique, based on the number of persons whose mother or father has died, and the widowhood technique, based on the number of persons whose first spouse has died. Both provide an estimate of survivorship levels between two adult ages for a period of time prior to the year of data collection. However, these techniques are seldom used for the base mortality patterns of the projections in this report because the reference period to which the estimated mortality pertains is not well defined.

[7]For example, the Coale-Preston technique, the growth balance technique developed by Brass, and the Bennett-Horiuchi technique.

[8]For example, the Brass technique and modifications developed by Trussell, Sullivan, and Feeney; the Palloni-Heligman technique, and the Johnson technique.

Base Data on Fertility

As in the case of mortality, procedures for estimating fertility depend on the availability of data and on the detail of the information. For cases where vital registration is complete, fertility can be measured directly using classical procedures. Most developing countries, however, do not have reliable vital statistics, and so techniques have been developed to measure fertility indirectly based on census or survey information.

Using the age structure of the population, the crude birth rate is sometimes estimated by the rejuvenation technique, in which the population at the youngest ages is "reverse survived" to determine the number of births from which they are survivors. This technique is attractive because it does not require the collection of any data related specifically to fertility. However, the reliability of the estimate depends on the quality of both the census data on age and the survival ratios used for the rejuvenation.

Under certain circumstances, census data by age can be used to obtain not only a crude birth rate but age-specific fertility rates as well. This is done by using the own-children technique based on information on children and women by single years of age. This technique requires data linking individual children to their natural mothers.

Other techniques, such as the Rele technique, use census data by age to calculate the net reproduction rate or total fertility rate based on the relationship of children of specified ages to the number of women in childbearing ages.

Finally, and most importantly for many developing countries, many censuses and surveys include questions related specifically to fertility; for example, the number of children women have had and whether they had a birth in the year preceding the inquiry. Responses to such questions can be used to estimate fertility indirectly. Some techniques to do this include the P/F (Parity/Fertility) ratio developed by Brass, based on the average number of children ever born to women in 5-year age groups and women's age pattern of fertility derived from births in the year preceding the census or survey; the P1/F1 ratio technique, also developed by Brass, based on first births only; and the Arriaga technique, which is similar to the P/F ratio technique but links data for more than one date. All of these methods can be used to estimate the age-specific fertility rates required for making component population projections.

Base Data on International Migration

Although migration is sometimes an important component of population change, it is not generally well recorded except in some European countries, such as Sweden and the Netherlands, that maintain complete and detailed population registers. Some countries collect information on arrivals and departures of passengers at the official borders of the national territory, but such data are seldom processed in such a way as to render them useful for statistical purposes. Even in countries with otherwise excellent statistical systems, information on international migration is often unreliable.

The primary source of information on immigration for purposes of population projections is census data on place of birth of the foreign-born population. To detect emigration as well, in order to calculate the net movement in or out of a country, it is necessary to find data for the countries in which the emigrants have settled (since they are the foreign immigrants of that country). In addition, special migration flows, such as refugee movements, are incorporated by considering reported numbers of refugees from the United Nations High Commissioner on Refugees, country sources, and media reports. Thus, most data on international migration are educated guesses at best, especially since not only total numbers but also age and sex distributions of the migrants are required for the projection process.

Assumptions About the Future

Once levels of mortality, fertility, and migration have been determined for the base year of the projection, each component must be projected into the future. Although the procedure for doing this is mechanical, careful attention must be paid in determining projected levels, trends, and patterns by age. Not only must the assumptions be appropriate for the particular country in question, but consistent assumptions must be made when projections are being carried out for more than one country.

An expected increase in contraceptive prevalence is implicit in the assumptions about future fertility declines for most developing country projections. For many developed countries, future fertility levels are projected to experience only minor change, either slight decreases, or in some cases, slight increases.

In general, mortality is expected to continue to decline in most countries, as development and health advances continue. A particular exception relates to the impact that acquired immune deficiency syndrome (AIDS) will have on the mortality of some countries, where mortality levels in the next decades are expected to increase. (For a description of the method used to incorporate the impact of AIDS mortality on selected populations, see the next section of this appendix.) While there is no single "right" way to make assumptions about the future, the following procedures are those recommended and generally used by the Bureau of the Census for the projections presented in this report.

Projecting Mortality and Fertility

The first step is usually to assign a target level of life expectancy at birth and total fertility rate for some intermediate year in the future or the last year of the projection period. Next, a trend of these measures is determined for the period between the base year and the last year. Then, an age and sex pattern of mortality and a female age pattern of fertility are determined for each projected level of life expectancy and total fertility rate, respectively.

In setting target levels for both mortality and fertility, available data on past trends are taken into consideration. If estimates are available for more than one date in the past, a logistic function can be fitted to these data, since this function approximates expected changes in life expectancy at birth and total fertility rate. The results of the logistic function must be carefully scrutinized, however, to ensure that they yield an acceptable future target for the individual country circumstances.

Recent population and socioeconomic trends and policies of each country are taken into account to determine if the projected trends are plausible. For example, for mortality, information concerning programs of public health are considered in judging the results. For fertility, factors such as trends in age at marriage, the proportion of women using contraception, the strength of family planning programs, and any foreseen changes in women's educational attainment or in their labor force participation in the modern economic sector are considered.

In some instances, no data on past trends are available to which a logistic curve can be fitted. In such circumstances, life expectancies can be projected based on increases related to the general level of mortality. The United Nations has recommended such increases based on countries with available data. For fertility, when trend data are not available for estimating future changes using a logistic function, the past experience of other countries serves as a guideline to determine the pace of future change.

Once levels of life expectancy at birth and total fertility rate have been set for the base year and some future year or the last year of the projection, a logistic function is often used to determine the trend. For developed countries with little expected change in fertility, intermediate levels are often determined linearly rather than logistically.

The next task is to determine an age pattern of mortality and fertility for each of the projected values, since these patterns tend to vary as overall levels change. For each level of projected life expectancy at birth, a set of central death rates is estimated using an iterative interpolation process. The interpolation is logarithmic and uses a set of central death rates for the base year and a "limit" set of rates with very low mortality. Life tables constructed with the interpolated rates correspond to the life expectancies at birth projected previously. Age-specific fertility rates for each projected level of total fertility rate are interpolated between the set for the base year and "model" sets derived from empirical data for populations at various levels of total fertility.

Once mortality and fertility have been tentatively projected for each country according to its particular circumstances, the estimates are compared with projected values for other countries in the same region and with those for other regions. Differences are evaluated to make sure they exist for valid reasons that can be explained by known peculiarities of the particular countries.

Finally, in recent years the Bureau of the Census has concluded that distinctive mortality assumptions must be made for selected countries in this report because of the death risk due to AIDS. Using methodology that takes into account the effect of AIDS, country projections have been prepared that assess its impact on future populations in countries where the infection is significant.

Projecting International Migration

Assumptions about future migration are generally much more speculative than assumptions about fertility and mortality. International migration may occur as a result of changing economic conditions, or as a result of political unrest, persecutions, famines, and other extreme conditions in the countries of origin. Thus, individuals may feel rejected by stagnated economies and attracted by industrialized societies, or refugees may flee in large numbers looking for better or more stable lives elsewhere. Due to the unpredictability of conditions such as crop failure, emerging violence, and bellicose activities, migration forecasts are subject to large errors. If migration is known to have a negligible impact on a country's current growth rate, future migration is often assumed to be nil. If a country's migration is known to be significant, the estimated number of migrants during the past is frequently held constant in projecting to the near future. Projected migration is usually assumed to diminish, reaching zero at some year in the medium- to long-term future. The age and sex composition of international migrants depends on the situation in each country. If information is not available, model patterns by age and sex are sometimes used.

Regional and World Aggregations

As new data are obtained, population projections are updated and published biennially in the *World Population Profile* series.[9] The national projections presented in this report were updated for any country for which significant new information was received since the preparation of the previous profile. For most countries, the cutoff for receipt of new information was September 1995.

Due to the differing nature of the base data for each country, there is no standard starting date for each country's projection. The projection period for a few countries started as recently as 1990 when the base information was current to that date. In contrast, the projection period for many African countries (and a few countries in other regions as well) started as long ago as the 1970's, or even before, although information for a later date on one or more of the variables may have been taken into account for the early years of the projection. "New" information for such a country may pertain to 1980 as opposed to a 1970 figure available for the previous round. Thus, total populations in the revised projections may change for any year in the past.

When the projected population for any individual country changes, so does the aggregated total for the corresponding region and for the world. New aggregations are made for world regions and world totals, combining the latest projected data for all countries, and superseding previously projected world and regional totals given in previous reports.

The differing starting dates complicate aggregations not only of total population but of vital rates and other measures as well. For this reason, regional and global aggregations of crude birth and death rates, life expectancy at birth, infant mortality rates, and age-sex distributions of the population generally can be presented only for the latest year for which all countries have a projected estimate for each variable. In this report, such measures are usually shown for 1996.

Population Projections Incorporating AIDS

Background

Although it has been clear for a number of years that mortality estimates and projections for many countries would have to be revised due to AIDS mortality, the lack of accurate empirical data on AIDS deaths, the paucity of data on HIV infection among the general population, and the absence of tools to project the impact of AIDS epidemics into the future have all

[9]Projections are made by the cohort component method for all but 19 small countries or territories with a combined population in 1996 of 1.1 million, or 0.02 percent of the world total. For these small countries, total populations and vital rates are projected, but not age and sex distributions.

hampered these efforts. Although the accuracy of data on AIDS deaths has not substantially improved, knowledge of HIV infection has expanded and modeling tools have become available to project current epidemics into the future.

The methodology used to project AIDS mortality for this report generally follows the method adopted for *World Population Profile: 1994*, with several modifications. The method consists of the following steps:

1. Establish criteria for selecting countries for which AIDS mortality will be incorporated into the projections.

2. For each selected country, determine the empirical epidemic trend and a point estimate of national HIV prevalence.

3. Model the spread of HIV infection and the development of AIDS in the population, generating alternative epidemic scenarios, and produce the seroprevalence rates and AIDS-related age-specific mortality rates which correspond to each epidemic scenario.

4. Use the empirical levels and trends (from step 2) to establish a factor representing each country's position on a continuum between high and low epidemics (from step 3). Use the derived factor to generate a unique interpolated epidemic.

5. Use weighted country total adult seroprevalence to determine an appropriate location on the total country epidemic curve implied by the interpolation factor. This projects adult HIV seroprevalence for the total country.

6. Interpolate AIDS-related mortality rates, by age and sex, associated with the estimated speed and level of HIV from epidemic results for the period 1990 to 2010.

In the sections that follow, each of these steps is described, and the method is illustrated.

Country Selection Criteria

The International Programs Center (Population Division, Bureau of the Census) maintains an HIV/AIDS Surveillance Data Base. This data base is a compilation of aggregate data from HIV seroprevalence studies in developing countries. Currently, it contains over 25,000 data items drawn from nearly 3,200 publications and presentations. As a part of the updating of the data base, new data are reviewed for inclusion into a summary table which, for each country, lists the most recent and best study of seroprevalence levels for high- and low-risk populations in urban and rural areas.[10]

A review of the data in the summary table suggests that a reasonable cutoff point for selection would be countries that have reached 5 percent HIV prevalence among their low-risk urban populations or, based on recent trends, appear to be likely to reach this level in the near future.

[10]High risk includes samples of prostitutes and their clients, sexually-transmitted disease patients, or other persons with known risk factors. Low risk includes samples of pregnant women, volunteer blood donors, or others with no known risk factors. For a more complete description of the selection criteria, see U.S. Bureau of the Census (1995).

A total of 21 countries now meet these criteria for the incorporation of AIDS mortality in the projections. All but two of these countries are in Africa. The countries are:

Botswana	Ethiopia	South Africa
Burkina Faso	Guyana	Tanzania
Burundi	Haiti	Uganda
Cameroon	Kenya	Zaire
Central African Republic	Lesotho	Zambia
	Malawi	Zimbabwe
Congo	Nigeria	
Côte d'Ivoire	Rwanda	

AIDS mortality was incorporated into projections for two other countries, Brazil and Thailand, because some country-specific modeling work had already been completed. The description of the simplified approach taken in these special cases follows that of the more general procedure.

Empirical Epidemic Trends

For each of the 21 countries meeting the selection criteria, we reviewed the HIV seroprevalence information available in the HIV/AIDS Surveillance Data Base to establish urban seroprevalence trends over time (table B-1, cols.1-4) and to identify available rural data points (table B-1, cols. 5-6). The two data points judged to be most representative for the urban low-risk population were identified and used to calculate the annual change between the dates of the two studies. Rural data were used in conjunction with the urban data to establish a total-country seroprevalence estimate (table B-1, col. 7).

Table B-1.
Empirical Seroprevalence Data for Urban and Rural Areas of Selected Countries

Country	Urban pregnant women				Rural adults		Estimated total country (percent)
	Earlier		Later				
	Year	Percent	Year	Percent	Year	Percent	
Botswana	1990	6.0	1993	19.2	1992	7.5	9.5
Burkina Faso	1987	3.1	1991	8.8	1989	4.1	4.5
Burundi	1986	16.3	1992	20.0	1992	1.8	3.1
Cameroon	1990	1.1	1994	5.7	1992	2.6	2.8
Central African Republic	1986	4.7	1993	16.0	1992	1.7	6.4
Congo	1990	7.7	1991	9.0	1990	5.3	6.7
Côte d'Ivoire	1987	8.0	1992	14.8	1989	3.3	6.1
Ethiopia	1988	3.7	1991	6.2	1993	1.8	2.6
Guyana	1990	1.2	1992	2.0	1992	(NA)	2.0
Haiti	1989	8.0	1993	8.5	1990	4.0	5.2
Kenya	1991	13.0	1992	15.0	1993	(NA)	[a]5.7
Lesotho	1992	5.1	1993	6.1	1993	(NA)	5.8
Malawi	1989	18.6	1994	33.0	1993	12.3	14.9
Nigeria	(NA)	(NA)	(NA)	(NA)	1992	(NA)	[b]1.1
Rwanda	1989	23.2	1991	26.7	1991	8.9	9.9
South Africa	1992	3.1	1993	4.7	1993	4.4	4.2
Tanzania	1988	10.6	1992	17.7	1993	7.1	9.7
Uganda	1987	24.0	1992	29.5	1992	7.8	10.4
Zaire	1985	6.9	1991	9.2	1991	2.9	4.7
Zambia	1987	11.6	1993	24.7	1993	13.5	18.3
Zimbabwe	1990	18.0	1993	25.9	1990	(NA)	12.8

(NA) Not available.

[a]Kenya National AIDS Control Program 1994.
[b]Average of Nigerian states' HIV sentinel surveillance program estimates for pregnant women.

Source: Urban and rural data are from the HIV/AIDS Surveillance Database, International Programs Center, U.S. Bureau of the Census, December 1994.

Alternative Scenarios

To project the impact in the selected countries, three alternative epidemic scenarios were developed, corresponding to low, medium, and high-impact AIDS epidemics. These scenarios were developed using iwgAIDS, which is a complex deterministic model of the spread of HIV infection and the development of AIDS in a population. It was developed under the sponsorship of the Interagency Working Group (iwg) on AIDS Models and Methods of the U.S. Department of State (Stanley et al. 1991).

All three of these epidemic scenarios incorporate increasing levels of behavior change in the form of increased condom use. This assumption corresponds to actual changes in behavior that are now beginning to occur in some countries.

Interpolation of a Unique Epidemic

The empirical urban trend from each country was used to interpolate among the three epidemic scenarios to derive an epidemic trend line matching the observed HIV seroprevalence increase between two data points. Thus, both the level and the rate of increase of the urban epidemic were matched through this procedure, resulting in an interpolation factor used in subsequent steps.

Projected Total Seroprevalence

At this point in the estimation procedure, no direct linkage has been made to the total-country prevalence or to a particular calendar year in this country's epidemic. The next step accomplishes these tasks. The total-country adult prevalence estimate (table B-1, col. 7) was matched with the one implied using the interpolation factor. From this comparison, an "offset" figure was calculated, corresponding to the number of years of difference between the start of the epidemics in the three scenarios and the empirical epidemic at the reference date.

AIDS-Related Mortality Rates

Based on the "interpolation factor" and the "offset" described above, AIDS-related age-sex-specific mortality rates (${}_nm_x$ values) at 5-year intervals from 1990 to 2010 were interpolated and added to non-AIDS ${}_nm_x$ values for the same period. Population projections were prepared with the combined ${}_nm_x$ values as input, using the Rural-Urban Projection Program (RUP) of the Bureau of the Census.

The future course of the AIDS pandemic is uncertain, but making projections for affected countries requires that some assumptions be made about AIDS mortality as well as about non-AIDS mortality. For the projections underlying this report, it was assumed that the epidemics in each of the 23 affected countries would peak in 2010, with no further growth in HIV infection after that year. AIDS mortality was assumed to decline from the level reached in 2010 to nil by 2050, thus implying a return to "normal" mortality levels in the latter year. To implement the projection process, life tables for 2050 that assume no AIDS mortality were used.

The Special Cases of Brazil and Thailand

Modeling activities were also undertaken for Brazil and Thailand with the support of the Interagency Working Group. AIDS epidemics in these two countries have substantial homosexual and intravenous drug use components, while those in Africa do not (WHO/GPA 1993). For Brazil, AIDS-related age-sex-specific mortality rates were estimated from the iwgAIDS model and added directly to the non-AIDS mortality rates previously prepared for the projection program. For Thailand, AIDS-related mortality rates from recent epidemiological and demographic projections (TNESDB 1994) were added to the non-AIDS ${}_nm_x$ values for the 1990 to 2010 period.

Caveats and Limitations

In developing the methodology for these projections, the International Programs Center has attempted to maximize the use of both the empirical data and the modeling tools available. However, there is much that is unknown about the dynamics of AIDS epidemics in countries around the world, and the methodology is necessarily imprecise. As the AIDS pandemic grows, future behavior changes and interventions being implemented in countries around the world may alter the projected course.

Non-AIDS ${}_nm_x$ values were derived by making standard assumptions concerning the improvement in mortality conditions as described earlier in this appendix.

What if AIDS epidemics do not peak early in the next century as projected? Will entire populations become infected with HIV and eventually die from AIDS? The simulations used for this report suggest that this will not happen in any population, although population declines are possible with a sustained widespread epidemic. Variations in sexual behavior help to ensure that the majority of the population in countries around the world are not at high risk of HIV infection. With substantial proportions of the population at lower risk of infection, each of the epidemic scenarios displays a definite plateau in HIV seroprevalence after the initial rapid rise.

Recency of Base Data for the Projections

The first two sections of this appendix described methods for evaluating base data and making projections, without reference to the data situations actually encountered in the various countries. This section reviews the availability of data for the current round of projections as presented in this report.

Demographic Data Are More Recent Than in Past Years

This report presents population estimates and projections for 227 countries or areas of the world. Of these 227 countries, 179 have information on fertility pertaining to some date since 1985, 167 countries have recent data on population size and 172 on mortality (tables B-2, B-3 and B-4). In previous publications, it was reported that fertility data were obtained on a more frequent basis than mortality or population data. Currently, however, more recent data have been available on mortality and population size.

Large Discrepancies Found in Recency of Data by Region

Not surprisingly, the more developed countries have the most recent data on population size, fertility, and mortality. All developed countries have data on population size and mortality since 1985, and all except Monaco have fertility data pertaining to 1985 or later that were considered for the projections in this report. Sub-Saharan Africa has the smallest proportion of countries with data for 1985 or later on all topics.

Current Fertility Level Is Known for Over 91 Percent of World's Population

Perhaps more important than the number of countries with recent information on population size, fertility, and mortality is the proportion of the world's population covered by such information.

As seen in table B-3, 91 percent of the world's people live in countries with data on fertility that pertain to 1985 or later. The proportion is higher in North Africa (96 percent), Asia (96 percent), and the regions of North America, Europe and the New Independent States, and Latin America and the Caribbean (100 percent).

With many countries taking censuses during the 1990 round and the rapid processing of results by computer, information on population size is also available for a large portion of the world's population. Eighty-nine percent of the world's people live in countries with at least population totals available for 1985 or later.

For mortality, about 69 percent of the world's population is covered by information since 1985 (table B-4). However, the available mortality data often pertain only to infants and children and not to the adult population. Nearly one-third of the population of the Near East and 21 percent of that of Sub-Saharan Africa live in countries for which we lack reliable mortality data since 1980.

Information on Contraceptive Prevalence

In the population projections presented in this report, information on the prevalence of family planning is not used directly as input in the computer model. Nevertheless, a knowledge of the extent of contraceptive use and the strength of national family planning programs is an important consideration when setting future target levels and age patterns of fertility for the projections.

Recent data on the current use of family planning methods are gathered primarily by surveys such as the DHS program of Macro International, Inc. and the various family health and contraceptive prevalence surveys of the U.S. Centers for Disease Control. In addition, some countries conduct other national surveys, either for the specific purpose of gathering information on family planning or for other purposes, such as collecting data on maternal and child health. These surveys often include questions about contraceptive use.

In contrast to the practice of collecting information on population size, fertility, and mortality, the gathering of data on contraceptive use is a fairly recent phenomenon. Nonetheless, the practice is becoming more widespread, and many of the larger countries in developing regions now provide such data. Of the 171 countries in developing regions, 92 (54 percent) have gathered information on family planning for some date since 1985, and another 13 (8 percent) during the early 1980's (table B-5).

Differences among the regions have narrowed. The proportion of countries with information available for 1985 or later ranges from 59 percent in Sub-Saharan Africa to 66 percent in North Africa. In the developing regions of the Near East, Asia, and Latin America and the Caribbean, just around 60 percent of countries have contraceptive data available for 1985 or later.

It is primarily the larger countries in each region that gather information on contraceptive use, as shown by the larger proportions of populations than of countries covered by available data. Thus, 94 percent of the population in less developed regions is covered by such data since 1985, with the proportions in North Africa and Asia, excluding the Near East, over 95 percent. Even in Sub-Saharan Africa, information on contraceptive use for 1985 or later is available for 84 percent of the population.

Table B-2.
Distribution of Countries and of Population, by Region and Recency of Reliable Data on Population Size

Region	Year of latest data									
	Total	1990-95	1985-89	1980-84	Before 1980 or none	Total	1990-95	1985-89	1980-84	Before 1980 or none
	Number of countries					Midyear population: 1996 (millions)				
WORLD	227	110	57	40	20	5,772	2,909	2,256	480	128
Less Developed Countries	171	63	48	40	20	4,601	2,226	1,768	480	128
More Developed Countries	56	47	9	–	–	1,171	683	488	–	–
AFRICA	57	13	20	16	8	732	225	257	220	30
Sub-Saharan Africa	51	13	17	14	7	594	225	155	190	25
North Africa	6	–	3	2	1	137	–	102	30	5
NEAR EAST	16	4	4	4	4	157	66	27	23	41
ASIA	27	13	7	4	3	3,271	1,660	1,382	194	35
LATIN AMERICA AND THE CARIBBEAN	45	25	4	14	2	489	396	46	42	4
EUROPE AND THE NEW INDEPENDENT STATES	56	41	14	–	1	800	507	276	–	17
Western	28	28	–	–	–	387	387	–	–	–
Eastern	13	13	–	–	–	120	120	–	–	–
New Independent States	15	–	14	–	1	293	–	276	–	17
Baltics	3	–	3	–	–	266	–	266	–	–
Commonwealth of Independent States	12	–	11	–	1	285	–	268	–	17
NORTH AMERICA	5	3	2	–	–	295	29	267	–	–
OCEANIA	21	11	6	2	2	29	27	2	–	(Z)
	Percent distribution of:									
	Number of countries					Population				
WORLD	100	48	25	18	9	100	50	39	8	2
Less Developed Countries	100	37	28	23	12	100	48	38	10	3
More Developed Countries	100	84	16	–	–	100	58	42	–	–
AFRICA	100	23	35	28	14	100	31	35	30	4
Sub-Saharan Africa	100	25	33	27	14	100	38	26	32	4
North Africa	100	–	50	33	17	100	–	74	22	4
NEAR EAST	100	25	25	25	25	100	42	17	15	26
ASIA	100	48	26	15	11	100	51	42	6	1
LATIN AMERICA AND THE CARIBBEAN	100	56	9	31	4	100	81	9	9	1
EUROPE AND THE NEW INDEPENDENT STATES	100	73	25	–	2	100	63	34	–	2
Western	100	100	–	–	–	100	100	–	–	–
Eastern	100	100	–	–	–	100	100	–	–	–
New Independent States	100	–	93	–	7	100	–	94	–	6
Baltics	100	–	100	–	–	100	–	100	–	–
Commonwealth of Independent States	100	–	92	–	8	100	–	94	–	6
NORTH AMERICA	100	60	40	–	–	100	10	90	–	–
OCEANIA	100	52	29	10	10	100	92	6	2	(Z)

– Represents zero.
(Z) Less than 500,000 or less than 0.5 percent.

Table B-3.
Distribution of Countries and of Population, by Region and Recency of Reliable Data on Fertility

Region	Year of latest data									
	Total	1990-95	1985-89	1980-84	Before 1980 or none	Total	1990-95	1985-89	1980-84	Before 1980 or none
	Number of countries					Midyear population: 1996 (millions)				
WORLD	227	137	42	19	29	5,772	4,970	294	282	226
Less Developed Countries	171	84	40	18	29	4,601	3,799	294	282	226
More Developed Countries	56	53	2	1	–	1,171	1,171	(Z)	–	–
AFRICA	57	23	10	12	12	732	308	113	265	45
Sub-Saharan Africa	51	20	9	12	10	594	240	50	265	39
North Africa	6	3	1	–	2	137	68	64	–	6
NEAR EAST	16	11	1	1	3	157	95	2	16	45
ASIA	27	14	5	–	8	3,271	2,995	145	–	131
LATIN AMERICA AND THE CARIBBEAN	45	28	14	2	1	489	454	33	1	1
EUROPE AND THE NEW INDEPENDENT STATES	56	55	–	1	–	800	800	–	–	–
Western	28	27	–	1	–	387	387	–	–	–
Eastern	13	13	–	–	–	120	120	–	–	–
New Independent States	15	15	–	–	–	293	293	–	–	–
Baltics	3	3	–	–	–	266	266	–	–	–
Commonwealth of Independent States	12	12	–	–	–	285	285	–	–	–
NORTH AMERICA	5	3	2	–	–	295	295	(Z)	–	–
OCEANIA	21	3	10	3	5	29	23	1	(Z)	5
	Percent distribution of:									
	Number of countries					Population				
WORLD	100	60	19	8	13	100	86	5	5	4
Less Developed Countries	100	49	23	11	17	100	83	6	6	5
More Developed Countries	100	95	4	2	–	100	100	(Z)	–	–
AFRICA	100	40	18	21	21	100	42	15	36	6
Sub-Saharan Africa	100	39	18	24	20	100	40	8	45	7
North Africa	100	50	17	–	33	100	50	46	–	4
NEAR EAST	100	69	6	6	19	100	60	1	10	28
ASIA	100	52	19	–	30	100	92	4	–	4
LATIN AMERICA AND THE CARIBBEAN	100	62	31	4	2	100	93	7	–	–
EUROPE AND THE NEW INDEPENDENT STATES	100	98	–	2	–	100	100	–	–	–
Western	100	96	–	4	–	100	100	–	–	–
Eastern	100	100	–	–	–	100	100	–	–	–
New Independent States	100	100	–	–	–	100	100	–	–	–
Baltics	100	100	–	–	–	100	100	–	–	–
Commonwealth of Independent States	100	100	–	–	–	100	100	–	–	–
NORTH AMERICA	100	60	40	–	–	100	100	(Z)	–	–
OCEANIA	100	14	48	14	24	100	78	4	1	17

– Represents zero.
(Z) Less than 500,000 or less than 0.5 percent.

Table B-4.
Distribution of Countries and of Population, by Region and Recency of Reliable Data on Mortality

Region	Total	1990-95	1985-89	1980-84	Before 1980 or none	Total	1990-95	1985-89	1980-84	Before 1980 or none
	Year of latest data									
	Number of countries					Midyear population: 1996 (millions)				
WORLD	227	125	47	15	40	5,772	3,665	356	1,361	391
Less Developed Countries	171	71	45	15	40	4,601	2,494	356	1,361	391
More Developed Countries	56	54	2	–	–	1,171	1,171	(Z)	–	–
AFRICA	57	21	10	6	20	732	293	206	100	132
Sub-Saharan Africa	51	19	8	6	18	594	234	134	100	126
North Africa	6	2	2	–	2	137	59	73	–	6
NEAR EAST	16	7	3	2	4	157	85	6	20	47
ASIA	27	11	5	3	8	3,271	1,745	86	1,232	207
LATIN AMERICA AND THE CARIBBEAN	45	24	19	1	1	489	423	57	8	(Z)
EUROPE AND THE NEW INDEPENDENT STATES	56	56	–	–	–	800	800	–	–	–
Western	28	28	–	–	–	387	387	–	–	–
Eastern	13	13	–	–	–	120	120	–	–	–
New Independent States	15	15	–	–	–	293	293	–	–	–
Baltics	3	3	–	–	–	266	266	–	–	–
Commonwealth of Independent States	12	12	–	–	–	285	285	–	–	–
NORTH AMERICA	5	3	2	–	–	295	295	(Z)	–	–
OCEANIA	21	3	8	3	7	29	23	1	1	5
	Percent distribution of:									
	Number of countries					Population				
WORLD	100	55	21	7	18	100	63	6	24	7
Less Developed Countries	100	42	26	9	23	100	54	8	30	8
More Developed Countries	100	96	4	–	–	100	100	(Z)	–	–
AFRICA	100	37	18	11	35	100	40	28	14	18
Sub-Saharan Africa	100	37	16	12	35	100	39	23	17	21
North Africa	100	33	33	–	33	100	43	53	–	4
NEAR EAST	100	44	19	13	25	100	54	4	13	30
ASIA	100	41	19	11	30	100	53	3	38	6
LATIN AMERICA AND THE CARIBBEAN	100	53	42	2	2	100	87	12	2	(Z)
EUROPE AND THE NEW INDEPENDENT STATES	100	100	–	–	–	100	100	–	–	–
Western	100	100	–	–	–	100	100	–	–	–
Eastern	100	100	–	–	–	100	100	–	–	–
New Independent States	100	100	–	–	–	100	100	–	–	–
Baltics	100	100	–	–	–	100	100	–	–	–
Commonwealth of Independent States	100	100	–	–	–	100	100	–	–	–
NORTH AMERICA	100	60	40	–	–	100	100	(Z)	–	–
OCEANIA	100	14	38	14	33	100	78	3	2	17

– Represents zero.
(Z) Less than 500,000 or less than 0.5 percent.

Table B-5.
Distribution of Countries and of Population, by Region and Recency of Reliable Data on Contraceptive Prevalence

Region	Total	1990-95	1985-89	1980-84	Before 1980 or none	Total	1990-95	1985-89	1980-84	Before 1980 or none
	Year of latest data									
	Number of countries					Midyear population: 1996 (millions)				
WORLD	227	74	41	18	94	5,772	4,190	1,071	99	412
Less Developed Countries	171	59	33	13	66	4,601	3,638	668	37	259
More Developed Countries	56	15	8	5	28	1,171	552	404	63	153
AFRICA	57	23	11	3	20	732	445	187	22	77
Sub-Saharan Africa	51	21	9	3	18	594	386	115	22	71
North Africa	6	2	2	–	2	137	59	73	–	6
NEAR EAST	16	4	5	–	7	157	96	27	–	35
ASIA	27	11	6	1	9	3,271	3,029	171	3	68
LATIN AMERICA AND THE CARIBBEAN	45	14	11	4	16	489	122	283	7	77
EUROPE AND THE NEW INDEPENDENT STATES	56	22	6	4	24	800	498	119	34	149
Western	28	4	4	4	16	387	167	107	34	78
Eastern	13	3	2	–	8	120	37	12	–	71
New Independent States	15	15	–	–	–	293	293	–	–	–
Baltics	3	3	–	–	–	266	–	266	–	–
Commonwealth of Independent States	12	12	–	–	–	285	285	–	–	–
NORTH AMERICA	5	–	1	1	3	295	–	266	29	(Z)
OCEANIA	21	–	1	5	15	29	–	18	5	6
	Percent distribution of:									
	Number of countries					Population				
WORLD	100	33	18	8	41	100	73	19	2	7
Less Developed Countries	100	35	19	8	39	100	79	15	1	6
More Developed Countries	100	27	14	9	50	100	47	34	5	13
AFRICA	100	40	19	5	35	100	61	26	3	11
Sub-Saharan Africa	100	41	18	6	35	100	65	19	4	12
North Africa	100	33	33	–	33	100	43	53	–	4
NEAR EAST	100	25	31	–	44	100	61	17	–	22
ASIA	100	41	22	4	33	100	93	5	(Z)	2
LATIN AMERICA AND THE CARIBBEAN	100	31	24	9	36	100	25	58	1	16
EUROPE AND THE NEW INDEPENDENT STATES	100	39	11	7	43	100	62	15	4	19
Western	100	14	14	14	57	100	43	28	9	20
Eastern	100	23	15	–	62	100	31	10	–	59
New Independent States	100	100	–	–	–	100	100	–	–	–
Baltics	100	100	–	–	–	100	–	100	–	–
Commonwealth of Independent States	100	100	–	–	–	100	100	–	–	–
NORTH AMERICA	100	–	20	20	60	100	–	90	10	(Z)
OCEANIA	100	–	5	24	71	100	–	63	16	21

– Represents zero.
(Z) Less than 500,000 or less than 0.5 percent.

Appendix C
References

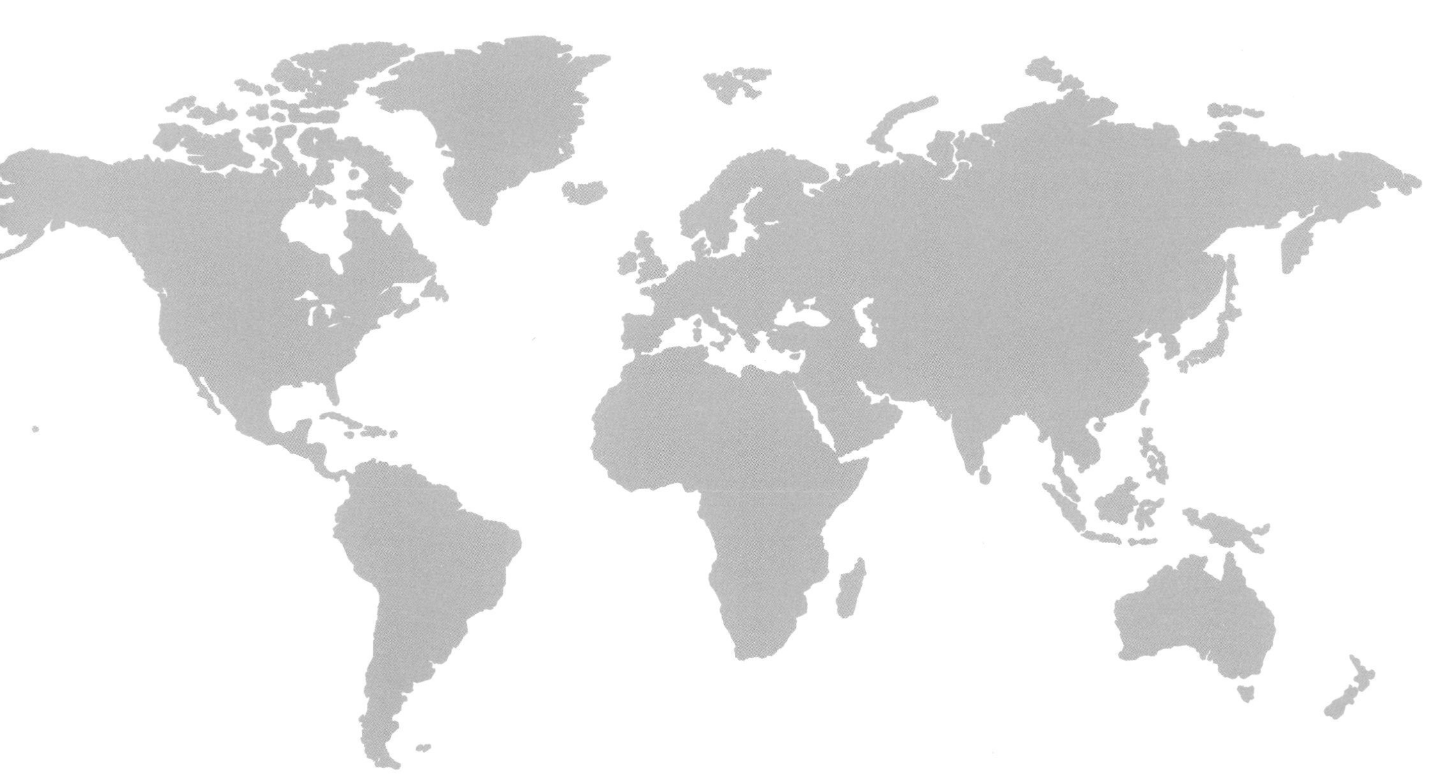

Appendix C
References

Arriaga, Eduardo E. and Associates. 1995. *Population Analysis with Microcomputers*. Washington, DC: U.S. Bureau of the Census, U.S. Agency for International Development and United Nations Population Fund.

Ashford, Lori S. 1995. "New Perspectives on Population: Lessons from Cairo," *Population Bulletin*, 50(1).

Banister, Judith. 1995. "China Contraceptive Use Rate, Pattern Estimates for 1992." Unpublished paper, U.S. Bureau of the Census, International Programs Center.

Bledsoe, Caroline H. and Barney Cohen, eds. 1993. *Social Dynamics of Adolescent Fertility in Sub-Saharan Africa*. Washington, DC: National Academy Press.

Haub, Carl. 1995. World Bank mission survey of married women ages 18-34, conducted by the Ministry of Statistics and Analysis, Belarus. Unpublished summary findings made available by Carl Haub, Population Reference Bureau.

Fourth Asian and Pacific Population Conference. 1992. "The Bali Declaration on Population and Sustainable Development," *Population and Development Review*, 18(4):769-778. The text of the Bali Declaration on Population and Sustainable Development, from the Fourth Asian and Pacific Population Conference, Bali, 19-27 August.

ICPD Program of Action. See United Nations, 1995a.

Indonesia, Central Bureau of Statistics; State Ministry of Population/ National Family Planning Coordinating Board; Ministry of Health; and Macro International, Inc. 1995. *Indonesia Demographic and Health Survey 1994*. Calverton, MD: Central Bureau of Statistics and Macro International, Inc.

Kenya, National AIDS Control Program (KNACP). 1994. "AIDS in Kenya: Background, Projections, Impact, Interventions." Nairobi.

Lucas, David and Helen Ware. 1981. "Fertility and Family Planning in the South Pacific," *Studies in Family Planning*, 12:309.

Macro International, Inc. 1993a. *A Profile of Teenage and Young Adult Women in Botswana*. Calverton, MD.

_____. 1993b. *A Profile of Teenage and Young Adult Women in Ghana*. Calverton, MD.

_____. 1993c. *A Profile of Teenage and Young Adult Women in Liberia*. Calverton, MD.

_____. 1993d. *A Profile of Teenage and Young Adult Women in Nigeria*. Calverton, MD.

_____. 1993e. *A Profile of Teenage and Young Adult Women in Togo*. Calverton, MD.

_____. 1993f. *A Profile of Teenage and Young Adult Women in Uganda*. Calverton, MD.

_____. 1993g. *A Profile of Teenage and Young Adult Women in Zimbabwe*. Calverton, MD.

Maine, Deborah. 1981. *Family Planning: Its Impact on the Health of Women and Children*. New York: Center for Population and Family Health, Columbia University.

National Center for Health Statistics. 1990. 1990 National Survey of Family Growth, unpublished tables.

Nguyen Van Phai, John Knodel, Mai Van Cam, and Hoang Xuyen. 1996. "Fertility and Family Planning in Vietnam: Evidence from the 1994 Inter-censal Demographic Survey," *Studies in Family Planning*, 27(1):1-17.

Omran, Abdel R., ed. 1984. *Family Planning for Health in Africa*. With Alan G. Johnston. Chapel Hill, NC: Carolina Population Center, University of North Carolina at Chapel Hill.

Senderowitz, Judith. 1995. "Adolescent Health. Reassessing the Passage to Adulthood." World Bank Discussion Papers, No. 272.

Stanley, E.A., S. T. Seitz, P. O. Way, P. D. Johnson, and T. F. Curry. 1991. "The iwgAIDS Model for the Heterosexual Spread of HIV and the Demographic Impacts of the AIDS Epidemic," in *The AIDS Epidemic and Its Demographic Consequences*. ST/ESA/SER.A/119. New York: United Nations and World Health Organization, pp. 119-136.

Thailand, National Economic and Social Development Board (TNESDB). 1994. "Projections for HIV/AIDS in Thailand: 1987-2020." Bangkok: Thai Red Cross Society Program on AIDS.

Third African Population Conference. 1993. "The Dakar Declaration on

Population," *Population and Development Review,* 19(1):209-215. The text of the Dakar/Ngor Declaration on Population, Family and Sustainable Development, from the Third African Population Conference, Dara, 7-12 December 1992.

United Nations. 1987. *Fertility Behavior in the Context of Development: Evidence from the World Fertility Survey.* Department for Economic and Social Information and Policy Analysis, Population Division, Population Studies No. 100. ST/ESA/SER.A/100. New York.

_____. 1994. "World Contraceptive Use 1994." Wall chart. ST/ESA/SER.A/143. New York.

_____. 1995a. *Population and Development.* Volume 1. Program of Action adopted at the International Conference on Population and Development, Cairo, 5-13 September 1994. ST/ESA/SER.A/149. New York.

_____. 1995b. *World Population Prospects: The 1994 Revision.* Department for Economic and Social Information and Policy Analysis, Population Division, Population Studies No. 145. ST/ESA/SER.A/145. New York.

_____. 1995c. *World Urbanization Prospects: The 1994 Revision.* Department for Economic and Social Information and Policy Analysis, Population Division, Population Studies No. 150. ST/ESA/SER.A/150. New York.

_____. 1995d. *The Health Rationale for Family Planning: Timing of Births and Child Survival.* ST/ESA/SER.A/141. New York.

United Nations Children's Fund (UNICEF). 1990. *First Call for Children: World Declaration and Plan of Action from the World Summit for Children, and Convention on the Rights of the Child.* New York.

_____. 1994. *The State of the World's Children 1994.* New York: Oxford University Press for UNICEF.

U.S. Bureau of the Census. 1994. *World Population Profile: 1994.* By Ellen Jamison, Frank Hobbs, Peter O. Way and Karen A. Stanecki. Report WP/94. Washington, DC.

_____. 1996a. "Population Trends: Russia." By Ward Kingkade. International Brief series. Washington, DC. [Forthcoming]

_____. 1996b. *Trends in Adolescent Fertility and Contraceptive Use in the Developing World.* By Thomas M. McDevitt, with Arjun Adlakha, Timothy B. Fowler and Vera Harris-Bourne. Report IPC/95-1. Washington, DC.

U.S. Bureau of the Census. International Programs Center, Health Studies Branch. 1995. "Recent HIV Seroprevalence Levels by Country: July 1995," Research Note No. 17. Washington, DC.

Westoff, Charles F. 1991. "Reproductive Preferences: A Comparative View." Demographic and Health Surveys, Comparative Studies No. 3. Columbia, MD: Macro International, Inc.

Westoff, Charles F. and Luis Hernando Ochoa. 1991. "Unmet Need and the Demand for Family Planning." Demographic and Health Surveys, Comparative Studies No. 5. Columbia, MD: Macro International, Inc.

World Commission on Environment and Development. 1987. *Our Common Future.* Oxford and New York: Oxford University Press.

World Health Organization. 1989. *The Health of Youth. Facts for Action: Youth and Reproductive Health.* A42/Technical Discussions/5. Geneva.

World Health Organization/Global Programme on AIDS (WHO/GPA). 1993. "The Current Global Situation of the HIV/AIDS Pandemic." WHO/GPA/CNP/EVA/93.1. January 4.

Zimbabwe, Central Statistical Office, Ministry of Finance, Economic Planning, and Devleopment; and Macro International, Inc. 1989. *Zimbabwe Demographic and Health Survey 1988.* Columbia, MD: Macro International, Inc.

Appendix D
Glossary

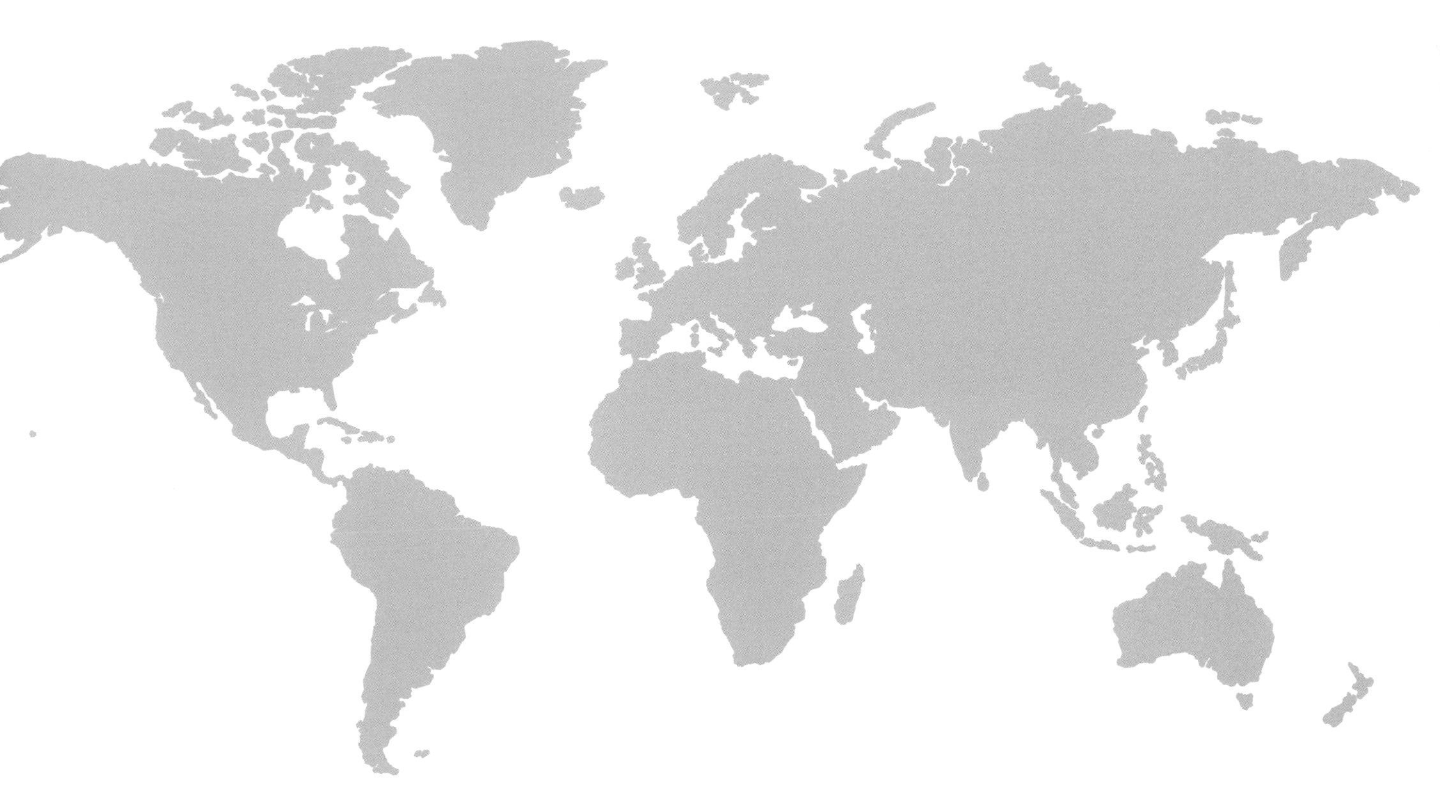

Appendix D
Glossary

Age structure. The distribution of a population according to age, usually by 5-year age groups.

Age-specific fertility rate. The number of births during a year to women in a particular age group, usually per 1,000 women in a 5-year age group at midyear.

Aging. An increase in the proportion of the population in the older ages. May also be measured as an increase in the median age of the population.

AIDS. Acquired immune deficiency syndrome.

Base population. The population, usually by age and sex, for the initial year of a projection.

Birth rate. The average annual number of births during a year per 1,000 population at midyear. Also known as the crude birth rate.

Children ever born. The total number of births a woman has had, regardless of whether the children are living or dead at the time of the inquiry.

Children surviving. The number of children a woman has had that are still living at the time of the inquiry.

Cohort. A group of individuals born in the same calendar year or group of years.

Cohort component method. See component method.

Component method. A method of estimating or projecting a population in which separate components of population change (fertility, mortality, and migration) are used to derive the total population. When such projections are made also by age and sex, the procedure is known as the cohort component method.

Components of change. Fertility, mortality, and migration.

Contraception. The conscious effort of couples to regulate the number and spacing of births. Also known as family planning.

Contraceptive prevalence rate. The percent of currently married women of reproductive age (normally defined as the range 15 to 49 years) who use contraception.

Crude birth rate. See birth rate.

Crude death rate. See death rate.

Currently married women. Women ages 15 to 49 either formally married or living in union with a man (consensual unions). Same as "married women of reproductive age."

Death rate. The average annual number of deaths during a year per 1,000 population at midyear. Also known as the crude death rate.

Development category. The classification of regions into "less developed" and "more developed" according to their general level of economic development. In this report, countries are classified according to the grouping used by the United Nations. See references to these terms in the Glossary for details.

DHS. Demographic and Health Surveys, an ongoing program of household surveys implemented by Macro International, Inc. and collaborating organizations.

Family planning. See contraception.

Growth rate. The average annual percent change in the population, resulting from a surplus (or deficit) of births over deaths and the balance of migrants entering and leaving a country. The rate may be positive or negative. Also known as population growth rate or average annual rate of growth.

HIV. Human immunodeficiency virus. The virus that causes AIDS.

Indirect estimation. The use of special techniques to estimate demographic measures (such as fertility and mortality) when information is not adequate for measuring them directly.

Infant mortality rate. The number of deaths of infants under 1 year of age from a cohort of 1,000 live births. Denoted ${}_1q_0$ or IMR, it is the probability of dying between birth and exact age 1.

IUD. Intrauterine device, a method of contraception.

iwgAIDS. Interagency Working Group on AIDS.

Less developed countries. The "less developed" countries include all of Africa, all of Asia except Japan, the Transcaucasian and Central Asian republics of the NIS, all of Latin America and the Caribbean, and all of Oceania except Australia and New Zealand. This category matches the "less developed country" classification employed by the United Nations. "Less developed" countries are also referred to in the report as "developing" countries.

Life expectancy at birth. The average number of years a group of people born in the same year can be expected to live if mortality at each age remains constant in the future.

Life table. A statistical table that follows a hypothetical cohort of 100,000 persons born at the same time as they progress through successive ages, with the cohort reduced from one age to the next according to a set of death rates by age until all persons eventually die.

Married women of reproductive age (MWRA). Women ages 15 to 49 either formally married or living in union with a man (consensual unions). Same as "currently married women."

Median age. The midpoint age that separates the younger half of a population from the older half.

Modern methods of contraception. Condoms, injectables, IUD's, pills, vaginal methods (spermicides, diaphragms, or caps), and voluntary sterilization of a woman or her partner.

More developed countries. The "more developed" countries and areas include all of North America and Europe (including the Baltics and the four European republics of the NIS) plus Japan, Australia, and New Zealand. This category matches the "more developed" classification employed by the United Nations.

Natural increase. The difference between the number of births and the number of deaths.

Net migration rate. The difference between the number of migrants entering and those leaving a country in a year, per 1,000 midyear population. May also be expressed in percent. A positive figure is known as a net immigration rate and a negative figure as a net emigration rate.

New Independent States (NIS). Fifteen nations formed from the former Soviet Union. The Commonwealth of Independent States (CIS) refers to these countries excluding the three Baltic nations of Latvia, Estonia, and Lithuania.

Pandemic. A global epidemic.

Projections. Data on population and vital rates derived for future years based on statistics from population censuses, vital registration systems, or sample surveys pertaining to the recent past, and on assumptions about future trends.

Rate of natural increase. The difference between the crude birth rate and the crude death rate.

Replacement level fertility. The average number of children each woman would have to bear for a population to remain the same size over the long term. Conventionally taken to be an average of 2.1 children per woman.

Seroprevalence. The percent of a population testing positive for infection in a blood test. In the context of this report, the percent testing positive for antibodies to HIV.

Sustainable development. The term refers to achieving economic and social development in ways that do not exhaust a country's natural resources. See, also, Ashford (1995) and The World Commission on Environment and Development (1987). In the Commission's words: "... sustainable development is ... a process of change in which the exploitation of resources, the direction of investments, the orientation of technological development, and institutional change are made consistent with the future as well as present needs" (Ibid: 9).

Total fertility rate. The average number of children that would be born per woman if all women lived to the end of their childbearing years and bore children according to a given set of age-specific fertility rates.

Traditional methods of contraception. Periodic abstinence, rhythm, withdrawal, douche, and folk methods. Also known as natural methods.

Under-5 mortality. Number of deaths of children under 5 years of age from a cohort of 1,000 live births. Denoted $_5q_0$, it is the probability of dying between birth and exact age 5.

Underenumeration. In a census, the erroneous counting of fewer persons in a population than actually belong to it.

Underregistration. In a vital registration system, the failure to register all vital events that occur in a population.

Unmet need for family planning. Nonuse of contraception among women who would like to regulate their fertility, measured as the proportion of currently married women of reproductive age not using contraception but wishing either to postpone the next wanted birth or to prevent unwanted childbearing after having achieved their desired number of children.

Vital events. Births and deaths.

Vital rates. Birth rates and death rates.

Vital registration. The recording of vital events for legal, administrative, and statistical purposes.

WHO. World Health Organization.

WHO/GPA. World Health Organization/Global Programme on AIDS.